ECONOMICS: A READER

ECONOMICS: A READER
THIRD EDITION

KENNETH G. ELZINGA
University of Virginia

EDITOR

Harper & Row, Publishers
New York   Hagerstown   San Francisco   London

ECONOMICS: A READER, THIRD EDITION

Special Projects Editor: Mary Lou Mosher
Project Editor: Richard T. Viggiano
Designer: Ben Kann
Production Supervisor: Kewal K. Sharma
Compositor: Telecki Publishing Services
Printer and Binder: Fairfield Graphics
Art Studio: Danmark & Michaels Inc.

Library of Congress Cataloging in Publication Data

Elzinga, Kenneth G   comp.
    Economics, a reader.

    1.   Economics — Addresses, essays, lectures.
I. Title.
HB171.5.E58   1978   330'.08   77-15121
ISBN 0-06-041912-1

CONTENTS

CONTENTS BY AUTHOR

(Corresponding chapters in Lipsey and Steiner, *Economics*, Fifth Edition, are listed in the right-hand column.)

PREFACE

Michigan State's Stanley Hollander observed that only a first-rate library could provide a good set of readings; the virtue of a reader, he added, was its greater portability. Without gainsaying the advantages of portability, this reader serves still another purpose: to promote economic education, particularly by focusing on contemporary issues not fully developed in a textbook. A good reader should stimulate interest in economics and provoke discussion about the subject.

But why another economics reader? True, this one does include some rather standard fare. However, there are notable differences. This volume does not, for example, contain the usual selections on methodology. Economists generally enjoy methodology. Most students new to the subject do not. In this reader the introduction is Leonard Silk's explanation of why economics is hard. And that is all. As Sir Dennis Robertson asserted, "the nature of pudding is best discovered by eating it."

Students will find articles here that are interesting and vexing. Wage and price controls, the nonprofit firm, stagflation, the multinational firm, pollution, and urban renewal are considered. There are humorous views also — in the Harvard *Lampoon* farce on international trade and in Terry Southern's satire on whether people can be bought. Thomas Sowell's "Race and Economics" might raise some hackles and so might Ralph K. Winter's critique of Naderism. A selection on Marxist thought is included:

M. Dobb's excellent but largely ignored essay on Marx and his economics.

Students should be acquainted with some of the great debates in economics. Among those included here are Stigler versus Samuelson on the optimal size of government and Kaminow versus Samuelson on how much money matters. A whole class period could easily be spent grappling with and comparing the points raised on opposite sides. Students should also be able to observe, through some in-depth material, how economic theory is applied and tested. Gary S. Becker's article, for example, uses price theory to explain union behavior.

This reader is designed to complement Richard G. Lipsey and Peter O. Steiner's *Economics*, Fifth Edition. A guide to selections in conjunction with chapters of that text can be found on the Contents by Author pages.

Of course, these readings are also adaptable for use with other textbooks on economic principles. Generally, this collection does not duplicate what is covered in such texts. This rule is violated only when a selection — like Boulding's on the theory of a black market — reviews material in a particularly revealing way. Headnotes introduce each author and selection. Probing questions accompany the selections to facilitate discussion and debate.

I have taken the editor's liberty of abridging articles where appropriate. Some readers may want to turn to the original sources for possible elaboration, as well as for the missing footnotes.

Not surprisingly, others have aided me in my editing chores. I would particularly like to thank Peter Steiner and Richard Lipsey, my colleague William Breit, Mary Lou Mosher and Richard T. Viggiano of Harper & Row, my wife Barbara, and the students and teachers who have helped me improve this volume from one edition to the next.

Kenneth G. Elzinga

PART ONE

THE NATURE OF ECONOMICS

ECONOMICS: WHY IT'S HARD
Leonard Silk

Leonard Silk, economist and journalist, has interpreted economic events and phenomena for readers of Business Week *and the* New York Times. *In this article, he chides economists for failing to communicate and offers insight into why economics is hard. Skim the article for now — then reread it after a few weeks of study. Doing so will give you a clearer perspective on both economics and economists.*

ECONOMIC CONFUSION

What explains the economic bewilderment and ignorance of the public? I think the first explanation is simply that economics is a difficult subject, deceptively difficult. Men who have taken doctorates in economics and worked in the field for many years often forget how difficult it is — and forget what a hard time they had in grasping its apparently simple concepts. At the same time, many businessmen and educators apparently believe that economics would not be so difficult if economists would just stop being obscurantist, pedantic, and nitpicky. Those noneconomists who would like to increase economic literacy are constantly asking economists to state some simple, basic economic truths that everyone should be taught. This is not so easy as it sounds.

THE WAYS OF THE ECONOMIST

Honest economists, including both those who have and who have not committed themselves to teaching economics to children and the general public, know that economics is an unusually tricky subject; so do unusually intelligent noneconomists. As Keynes recalled:

Professor Planck, of Berlin, the famous originator of the Quantum Theory, once remarked to me that in

Abridged from Leonard Silk, "The Problem of Communication," in "Efficiency in the Teaching of Economics: The Product," *American Economic Review Proceedings*, 54, no. 3 (May 1964), 596–606. Reprinted by permission.

early life he had thought of studying economics, but had found it too difficult! Professor Planck could easily master the whole corpus of mathematical economics in a few days. He did not mean that! But the amalgam of logic and intuition and the wide knowledge of facts, most of which are not precise, which is required for economic interpretation in its highest form is, quite truly, overwhelmingly difficult for those whose gift mainly consists in the power to imagine and pursue to their furthest points the implications and prior conditions of comparatively simple facts which are known with a high degree of precision.

The economist, on the contrary, is used to dealing with a great deal of information that comes to him in imprecise form. Even if he gets numbers that look clean, he knows that they are only shadows of a world that is anything but neat, precise, orderly, systematic. He knows that he must try to impose order on a disorderly mass of information as his normal job. Other scientists may have to do this in the beginning of their sciences or may have to do it at crucial turning points in its development, but thereafter they are filling in parts of an empirically solid structure, or in the case of mathematics, of a logically consistent structure. The economist must do essentially what an artist or writer does (though he is not so impressionistic or subjective as these): he must apprehend reality freshly every time he confronts it; he is constantly working from life, in all its buzzing, blooming confusion.

Yet the economist has a secret weapon that other people do not have. What he has that other people do not have is: economic theory. This gives him certain habits of thought that enable him to conceptualize problems that he has not seen before or problems that seem always to confront him in a new way. This is what keeps economics exciting for those who like it and what makes the economist — when he is good — such a handyman. He is able to apply his concepts to problems that, to the noneconomist, may seem totally unrelated to one another — the strategy of conflict, the farm problem, the growth of the electronics industry, the decay of a region. All such problems are challenges to the economist's ability to cope with interdependence — and poor data.

The basic bits of economic theory seem simple, obvious, even trivial. Every child realizes without being taught that if a good is cheaper, he is likely to buy more of it. But what is missing for the child is the overall system, the mode of analysis, the analogies among all types of economic activities and problems. And this is what is so hard to teach others. One gets it by doing, not by listening.

I have observed that many political, military, and business leaders like to recruit and use economists, because they are good at coping with fresh problems that are not necessarily economic at all. It is hard for these admirers to understand just what's so good that economists bring to their problems. I submit that it is not merely that some economists have high I.Q.'s, but rather that they have a mode of thought that is rare among scientists or administrators or even other social scientists.

This mode of thought develops out of what I would call the economist's quasi-Talmudic training — which is long on discussion and debate, with continuous passage from the specific to the general and back again — savagely close in its textual criticism — skeptical about its own or anyone else's results — complicated and wide-ranging in its style of inquiry. My teachers Professors Calvin Bryce Hoover and Joseph Spengler impressed upon me that economics could never be a monologue art, that the economist always needed to try his reasoning on some other economist. I think this is generally true. It probably explains why the economics profession is so strong and close a fraternity; the economic monologist is not only out of touch, but always in danger of becoming a crackpot or, less seriously, a layman, if he cannot talk, talk, talk with his brethren — or, at least, read, read, read from them and to them. Preferably both.

But the fraternal way that economists learn and practice their art has much to do with the failure of economists to do an effective job in educating the public.

Many economists are careless in their public utterance; they will invest endless hours of meticulous work in a journal article on some fine point of theory, and then turn around and — off the top of their heads — dictate into a machine or scribble out an argument designed to move the Congress or the general public on some vital matter of state. I have heard it said that their work in the classroom (or in preparation for the classroom) is not well or carefully done, and that the atrocious teacher who is a good researcher has no reason to doubt that he will become a full professor, but the good teacher who is not a creative researcher is wise if he leaves teaching. The really high-prestige economist may disdain to educate students at all, particularly high school students. This is perhaps understandable, both because it offers little or no professional reward and because it is painful to do — since no one has yet discovered how to do it or even whether it is capable of being done at all. Indeed, I think that some economists question whether teaching the public a smattering of economics is worth doing; many economists apparently prefer to stand on what Professor Hughes calls the common professional doctrine of *credat emptor:* let the buyer believe, let the public trust the professional to be right, since the client is not a true judge of the value of the professional's instruction or advice.

But, in economic matters, this is particularly hard for the clients to do. For one thing, the clients have strong economic convictions — and interests — of their own. For another, it is not easy for the clients to know which professional economic tutelage automatically to trust, since there is so much conflicting professional instruction and advice. Some professions — such as medicine or law — have open or tacit rules against casting aspersions upon the professional competence or recommendations of colleagues; not the economists. They frequently appear to be trying to defame one another in public. They are disputatious, within and without the cloisters, and they carry their disagreements to the public for settlement, even exaggerating them for the sake of winning personal acclaim, while failing to get across to the public their areas of substantial agreement on important matters. Perhaps it will be said that no substantial agreement actually exists among economists on important economic topics. If that is so, it is a sorry confession about the state of economics at this juncture, and it will imply that economists have no right to try to invoke the doctrine of *credat emptor* but will have to struggle all the harder to meet the public on its own terms and to convince it of the wisdom of particular policy views. It would also imply that a greater effort should be put forth within the profession to consolidate areas of agreement, unless that would seem a premature and anti-individualist thing to do.

ECONOMIC POLICY AND INDIVIDUAL SELF-INTEREST

Thus far I have given two reasons for the public's economic "illiteracy": (1) economics is a difficult subject, in which simple, basic, and comprehensible truths are hard to come by; and (2) economists generally have been ineffectual or confusing teachers. But there is a third reason that I must mention, however briefly: the inadequacies of the public as students and its resistance to economic reasoning.

Much of the public, I am afraid, resists not only economic but any kind of reasoning. This lesson first struck me as a sometime lecturer to Army troops (can anyone who experienced it ever forget the horrors of "Orientation"?). The realization that most people are not very susceptible to reasoned arguments has been confirmed by my later experiences as an editor, civil servant, and local politician.

Why is this? In part, the public's resistance to reason is (to be as tautological as Wicksteed) irrational — lazy, dull, or nasty. It may reflect a deep streak of anti-intellectualism, simple inertia, or fear and hostility toward any social or economic innovation. (Alabama voter's complete letter to his congressman: "Don't want no changes." His congressman's complete reply: "Ain't gonna be none.")

But not everyone who resists "standard" economic reasoning is irrational or stupid. The high-cost U.S. clothespin or carpet or glass manufacturer who resists free-trade arguments probably knows what he is doing. So does the farmer who wants to keep price supports, the trade unionist who wants to push wages up faster than productivity and re-

strict access to his part of the labor market, or the professor who refuses to give up tenure.

People with vested interests, or vested morals, or just plain moral principles of their own may close the door to economists' conventional logic and produce logic of their own. One man will oppose antitrust laws because they "interfere with the rights of the individual"; another will favor antitrust because it "protects the rights of the individual." Some will favor tax cuts, not because they understand modern fiscal policy, but because they want to pay lower taxes, or because they see lower taxes as a means of arresting the rise in government expenditures, and thereby of "preventing socialism"; while others will oppose tax cuts because they fear that they will overstimulate the economy, breed inflation, lead to government price and wage controls, and ultimately hurt profits and "bring on socialism."

It does no good to hoot and feel superior; one must be self-critical and aware that one's own reasoning or values may sometimes be ritualistic rationalizations of one's own special interests. One must try to understand what's on other people's minds and respond fairly and patiently. Those who resist the economists' reasoning are not necessarily scoundrels or fools. Many are sincere idealists (though idealism may sometimes be the foe of reason).

QUESTIONS

1. What accounts for most of the disagreements among economists?

2. Why does a citizen who would never dispute the findings or claims of a professional physicist disbelieve or suspect the claims or proposals of a professional economist?

3. In what sense is economics more difficult than a pure science such as mathematics or a natural science such as chemistry?

4. What is the basis for the claim that economists are clannish? In this sense, is it your observation that they differ from members of other academic disciplines?

PART TWO

ELEMENTARY DEMAND AND SUPPLY IN ACTION

2 CONGESTED PARKS —
A PRICING DILEMMA
Dan M. Bechter

Demand-and-supply analysis, one of the most important items in the economist's toolkit, has been applied to the study of many sorts of social phenomena. In this article Dan M. Bechter, research officer with the Federal Reserve Bank of Kansas City, examines the economic implications of the record crowds attempting to visit national parkgrounds. Dr. Bechter, who studied at Iowa State and Yale, is a former member of the faculty at Middlebury College.

In the last year or two, newspapers and magazines have been calling attention to the problems caused by record numbers of people crowding into some of our national parks. Yellowstone and Yosemite are receiving most of the publicity, but other national recreation areas are suffering similar popularity troubles. Many state and local parks, too, are being strained to accommodate rapidly increasing attendance. It is easy to conclude that these congestion difficulties justify creating new public parks and expanding outdoor recreation facilities in existing ones. Additions to supply would seem appropriate, considering the rising demand. Yet, the apparently inadequate recreational capacities of various public parks may reflect something other than a lag in adjustment of supply to demand. Governments may be distorting the recreation market by charging too little for the recreational use of public parks. Such an improper pricing practice would be misallocating resources. Some groups would be benefiting — perhaps those that are not intended to — at the expense of others. Economic analysis helps show the nature and probable consequences of the park crowding problem. It also helps reveal the complex and indirect influences on public park fees, the choices of consumers, and the markets for all recreational goods and services.

Abridged from Dan M. Bechter, "Congested Parks — A Pricing Dilemma," Federal Reserve Bank of Kansas City *Monthly Review* (June 1971), pp. 3—7. Reprinted by permission.

WHEN DEMAND CROWDS SUPPLY

Overflowing visitation at a public park provides a textbook display of a shortage. Park crowding means insufficient park space — or types of park space, such as camping space, driving space, fishing space, etc. — to satisfy outdoor recreationists. They want more. Their wants, however, depend directly on what they must pay. The existence of a shortage says only that the quantity demanded exceeds the quantity supplied at the going price. Excessive park crowding, therefore, reflects a park entry or a park privilege fee that is below the one that equates the amount of park space consumers want to the amount available. Chart 1 clarifies the explanation.

Chart 1 shows a set of demand and supply relationships for camping spaces in a hypothetical public park. Demand curve D_1D_1 shows that the lower the price, the larger the number of park camping spaces desired on an average summer day. Vertical line S_1S_1 indicates the number of camping spaces in the park — assumed to be an invariable quantity in the very short run. Now, suppose park officials set the camping fee at $2. Clearly, quantity demanded (60 spaces) exceeds quantity supplied (20 spaces), or a shortage of 40 spaces prevails at that price.

What happens to the 40 camping families whom the park cannot accommodate? Those who can return home may disappointedly do so. Others may not show up, having heard about or previously experienced the shortage. Still others may try to

Chart 1

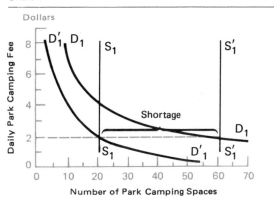

squeeze and shoehorn into the camping area, or pitch their tents in unauthorized areas of the park. Some may find other public or private places to camp nearby. The remainder may stay in motels, sleep along the road, or drive all night.

As can be seen, selling a good or service below the market-clearing price — where demand equals supply, or $4, in the example — simply requires other forms of rationing or adjustment, such as first come, first served, which places a premium on arrival time. Some of these adaptations, in effect, increase the cost of the outdoor recreation experience. They make the consumer spend extra time and money guaranteeing himself participation in the leisure activity. Other adjustments, such as crowding into available space, make outdoor recreation less fun.

The shortage shown in Chart 1 — or any market shortage, for that matter — can be reduced by (a) increasing price, (b) increasing supply, (c) decreasing demand, or (d) a combination of the preceding. Before considering these solutions, consider a part of what is going on outside the park.

Chart 2 shows another set of supply and demand curves — those for camping spaces on private land near the hypothetical public park. Currently, entrepreneurs are making 18 such spaces available, charging the going-market price of $2.50. Note that quantity demanded equals quantity supplied at this price — no shortage here. On a day of normal demand, everyone who wants to camp in a private area

can do so. Some of this demand for private camping space depends, of course, on overflow from the public park. Assuming that campers prefer locations within the park to those outside, it might seem strange that some are willing to pay the extra half dollar charged by private campgrounds. It must be remembered, however, that the park cannot satisfy demand at $2. Also, note that a sizable portion of the left tail of demand curve $D_1 D_1$ (Chart 1) lies above $4, indicating that several campers are willing to pay more than this amount for places inside the park. Some of these people certainly would be willing to locate outside for less when the park is full.

Now, consider each of the solutions to the shortage of public park camping spaces. Suppose first that the park authorities raise their camping fee to $4 (Chart 1). The shortage immediately disappears. Everyone wanting a space at this price within the park finds one, because quantity demanded declines from 60 to 20 spaces. In addition, because of the increase in the park's camping fee, more people will decide in favor of the less expensive private facilities. Demand curve $D_2 D_2$ for private camping spaces (Chart 2) will shift over to $D_2' D_2'$. For a while, there will be a shortage of private camping spaces, and campground owners may raise their prices. Eventually they will expand, or new private campgrounds will open. This is what curve $S_2' S_2'$ shows — the number of camping spaces private landowners will supply, given the opportunity to adjust to various prices. As can be seen, the market price settles at $3 a space, where quantity demanded = quantity supplied = 29 spaces. ($S_2' S_2'$ slopes upward to the right, showing that costs per space increase as space is increased.) Furthermore, the market for motel rooms, and other markets, will be affected. This example only looks at the market for the most obvious substitute for public camping spaces.

Suppose that instead of increasing price, the park officials increase the number of camping spaces from 20 to 60 in Chart 1, shifting supply out to $S_1' S_1'$. Again, the shortage disappears. As a result, however, the private campgrounds may be driven out of business. (In Chart 2, $D_2 D_2$ shifts left — not shown.) Other markets, too, are affected.

Chart 2

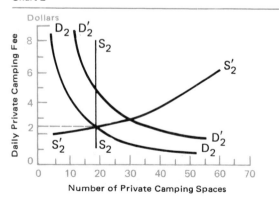

Dollars

Daily Private Camping Fee

Number of Private Camping Spaces

A PRICING DILEMMA

This section focuses on an obstacle that keeps park officials from charging the economically appropriate price for park use even when that price is known — public opinion.

The conditions reported at some popular public parks do not suggest an equilibrium in quantity demanded and quantity supplied.

When people are turned away, and when overuse threatens the park's survival, something must be out of kilter. Park authorities seem to be both encouraging visitation with low fees, and discouraging visitation by not adequately expanding recreation facilities and by otherwise limiting — in nonprice fashions — the activities of the visitors.

Public opinion forces this strange behavior. In theory, at least, economists can usually fit public opinion into the pricing system fairly easily by translating it into dollar values that society places on the activities in question. In this case, however, public opinion is against the pricing system. People strongly resist public park fees and the use of these fees to allocate park use. Americans apparently feel that public parks are theirs to use free of charge (or at nominal cost) as a right of part ownership. Strangely, they do not seem to feel this way about the Nation's highways (we have gasoline taxes as well as turnpike tolls).

Related to the ownership argument is the redistributive argument that entry fees would have to be raised substantially to adequately limit visitation, and that this would discriminate against the poor. It might seem unreasonable or unlikely that the demand for a one-day park visit, for sightseeing only, would be inelastic between carload entry fees of just a few dollars up to $100 or more. But this may well be the case for parks like Yellowstone, because such large increases in entry fees may amount to relatively small percentage increases in the total cost of the park visit. Pointing this out, however, also implies that very few poor people presently can afford to visit such parks anyway. Park-type outdoor recreation is perhaps best thought of as a luxury. Most people would agree that those who want a luxury

should pay for it. Yet, the under-pricing of park-type recreation subsidizes the leisure activities of the affluent — they own the boats, the trailers, the camping equipment, and so on.

Until attitudes change, government officials face great resistance to increases in public park entry and use fees. Perhaps much of this resistance would decrease if proper pricing methods were used. Accelerating park deterioration and other costs of excessive crowding certainly call for changes in the pricing of park recreation. Paradoxically, governments appear to be working in the wrong direction. New highways to parks, for example, lower the time and money cost of a visit. The Golden Eagle Passport — a $10 annual permit that admits the purchaser and his passengers or his family to more than 3,000 designated Federal outdoor recreation areas — encourages more visitation.

Some groups, besides visitors, obviously benefit from park subsidies. Vested interests point to the regional activity generated by park use. Owners and employees of lodging places, restaurants, bait and tackle stores, and many other kinds of businesses and concessions, do not want to give up what is actually a subsidy to them. They logically reason that, if parks increase fees, the demand for the complementary goods and services they sell will decline. Manufacturers of boats, automobiles, and other outdoor recreation equipment also benefit from the subsidization of park use.

FURTHER IDEAS

The cost of park-type outdoor recreation must be borne by someone. This includes not only the direct operating costs, but the opportunity costs of the resources as well. In instances where it is practical and where external costs and benefits are not significant, charging the user enough to cover these costs seems warranted. Privately owned recreation areas do this. For this reason, Professor Milton Friedman would have governments get out of the noncity park business:

If the public wants this kind of activity enough to

pay for it, private enterprises will have every incentive to provide such parks. And, of course, there are many private enterprises of this nature now in existence. I cannot myself conjure up any neighborhood effects [externalities] or important monopoly effects that would justify governmental activity in this area.

But most people, it seems safe to say, simply do not trust private enterprise to preserve the natural beauty of some national and state parks. Many park resource development decisions are irreversible, and the long-run consequences of a misguided short-run profit motive could be severe. On the other hand, public ownership does not guarantee development of resources in the long-run best interest of society either.

QUESTIONS

1. What is the relationship between the supply of national parks and the demand for private campgrounds?
2. Evaluate the argument that higher camping prices for national parks will hurt the poor. What pricing methods, if any, could eliminate the shortage at the national parks without harming low-income campers?
3. What reasons exist for the provision of parks by the federal government, as opposed to their provision by private enterprise?

THE BLACK MARKET
Kenneth Boulding

Boycotts, shortages, and controls are raising the specter of black markets. Kenneth Boulding illustrates the usefulness of the simple demand-and-supply model in explaining the black market and the implications of policing these markets. Professor Boulding, a former president of the American Economic Association, teaches at the University of Colorado and is director of research at the Institute of Behavioral Science there. A prominent economic theorist, Boulding's writings also led to the Distinguished Scholarship in Humanities prize from the American Council of Learned Societies.

THE ANALYSIS OF BLACK MARKETS

The term "black market" usually refers to those transactions which take place illegally at prices higher than a legal maximum. Essentially the same phenomenon is observed when the illegal transactions take place at prices below a legal minimum (e.g., in the case of contraventions of a minimum wage law). However, as it is the former case that . . . is most in the public eye, we may begin the analysis by supposing that there is a legal maximum price for some commodity which is fixed below the "normal" price, i.e., the price that would exist in a free market. A black market can only develop, of course, if the legal maximum is below the hypothetical free market price, so that at the legal price more is demanded than will be supplied. The situation is illustrated in Figure 1. $S'S$, $D'D$ are the normal (free market) supply and demand curves for the commodity in question. PN is the price that would obtain in a perfectly unregulated market. Now suppose that the price control authority sets a legal maximum price equal to OR. At this price only RH will be supplied, but RK will be demanded. If there is no further regulation a "shortage" will develop as stocks are being taken off the market faster than

From Kenneth Boulding, "A Note on the Theory of the Black Market," *Canadian Journal of Economics and Political Science*, 13, no. 1 (February 1947), 115—118. Reprinted by permission.

they are being replaced. Once the cushion of stocks has gone, the quantity bought will be forced into equality with the quantity forthcoming (*RH*) not by the restrictive action of higher prices but by some form of rationing, formal or informal. A black market will develop if some buyers and sellers can be found who are willing to buy or sell at prices higher than the legal maximum in spite of the penalties involved. We can therefore draw black market supply and demand curves, HS_b and GD_b. If we take *H* as the origin, *HG, HK* as the price and quantity axes, any point on the black market supply curve HS_b represents the excess of the black market over the legal price at which the corresponding quantity will be supplied in the black market. Similarly any point on the black market demand curve GD_b represents the quantity demanded in the black market at the corresponding excess of black market over the legal price. If we refer to *0* as the origin, the curve $S'HS_b$ shows the total quantity supplied in both legal and black markets at each legal price below *OR* and at each black market price above *OR*. A similar interpretation can be given of the total legal-and-black market demand curve GD_bKD. The black market supply curve HS_b has been drawn rising from *H* more steeply than the free market supply curve *HS*. This is because there are certain costs and risks of operating in the black market in excess of what would be found in a free market: These costs must be expressed by a higher supply price for each quantity, or, what is the same thing, by having a smaller quantity supplied at each price in the black market (plus the legal market) than would be supplied at that price if the market were entirely free. The more severe the penalties, the greater the moral obloquy, the more effective the law enforcement in regard to the black market sellers, the steeper will be the black market supply curve, and the further will it diverge from the free market supply curve. In the limiting case where the penalties are so great and so well enforced that nobody will venture into the black market at all the black market supply curve becomes perfectly inelastic (*HG*). Similarly the black market demand curve GD_b will lie to the left of the free market demand curve because of the penalties and moral obloquy involved in purchasing

Figure 1

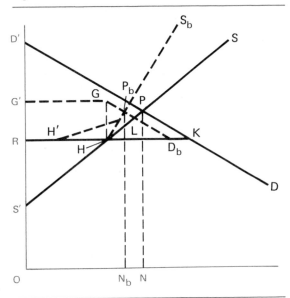

in the black market: At each price there will be a smaller quantity demanded in the legal and black markets together than would be demanded at that price if the market were perfectly free. The black market price will then be P_bN_b, where P_b is the point of intersection of the black market demand and supply curves; the quantity bought and sold in the black market will be *HL*, the total quantity bought and sold in both legal and black markets together will be *RL*.

IMPLICATIONS OF THE ANALYSIS

Some interesting conclusions follow from this analysis. The first is that the black market price may easily be lower than the price which would have obtained in the absence of all regulation. Even if the black market price is higher than the "free" price *PN*, it is very unlikely that the average price in the legal and black markets together would be higher than the free price. Only if the black market demand and supply curves are extremely inelastic will the black market price rise so high as to make the average legal-plus black market price greater than the free price. Another interesting conclusion is that the greater the penalties laid upon black market buyers the further to the left will the black market demand curve lie and the lower will be both the price and the quantity in the black market. The greater the penalties laid on sellers in the black market the further to the left and the more inelastic will the black market supply curve be, hence the *higher* the black market price. It follows that if our main concern is with the *price* in the black market, the less we penalize sellers and the more we penalize buyers the better: It is the housewife, not the grocer, that the law should frown upon. Penalizing either buyers or sellers, of course, diminishes the quantity sold in the black market, but penalizing the buyers has the added advantage that it lowers the price, whereas penalizing the sellers has the added disadvantage that it raises the price. In practice, of course, the political and legal difficulties of penalizing the buyers may make it necessary to concentrate the punitive effort on sellers, but other things being equal it is clearly better to penalize buyers.

In the above analysis it has been assumed that the existence of the black market has not affected the willingness to sell of those sellers who would sell in the free market at the price OR: We have assumed that these sellers constitute the "legal" sellers, selling an amount RH, and that the black market sellers are those who would not have been willing to sell except at prices above OR even in a free market. In fact, however, the existence of the black market may affect the willingness to sell of the "legal market" sellers. When this happens there is a tendency for the black market to encroach on the legal market: Less and less comes forward for sale in the legal market, more and more is diverted to the black market. The result of this encroachment is that the black market supply curve begins to rise at a point further to the left — say at H'. Unless the "encroachers" — those sellers attracted into the black market out of the legal market — are only willing to transfer their supplies at prices above the existing black market price, encroachment will not raise the black market price: The new supply curve is $H'S_b$, which still intersects the black market demand curve at P_b. If however some of the encroachers are only willing to go into the black market at prices above the prevailing black market price the result may be a rise in the black market price. If on the other hand the result of the encroachment is to increase the output of the producers, under the stimulus of the higher black market price, the result may be a decline in the black market price. But, however much the black market price declines under the stimulus of encroachment, it will never fall to the legal price: Hence there will always be a further stimulus to encroachment.

The above analysis throws some light on a problem which besets the economy of any communist or near-communist country where there is a "legal" black market, i.e., where there are two sections to the economy, an "official" section where prices are kept low by authority, and a "free" section where prices are allowed to find their own level. In such a case it is evident that the temptation to "encroachment," i.e., the transfer of supplies from the low-price official market to the high-price free market — is likely to be very great, and unless it is checked by some form of producer-rationing or taxation in kind, encroachment will go on until the official economy disintegrates into a completely free market.

QUESTIONS

1. Using Boulding's definition, have you ever bought or sold in a black market or observed the operation of such a market? Elaborate.

2. Why does a black market supply curve rise more steeply than a free market supply curve?

3. If you were directed to police a black market, and could use your police powers only against either the sellers or the buyers, which would you choose? Why?

4. Develop the graphical analysis explaining the operation of a black market where the illegal transactions occur at prices below a legal minimum.

5. Who benefits from the policing of black markets?

4 THE MARKET FOR AIRPORTS
William D. Grampp

William Grampp examines the problem of airport congestion and takes issue with the conventional solutions. His own analysis and proposals indicate the utility of simple demand-and-supply tools. Professor Grampp teaches at the University of Illinois at Chicago, where he also does research and is known for his writings on the history of economic ideas.

The Federal Aviation Administration has recommended that $6 billion be spent by 1975 to expand existing airport facilities. The aircraft manufacturers are developing planes that use less space for takeoff and landing in relation to their capacity; if they become feasible, they will require entirely new kinds of airports. Each of these kinds of solutions to the problem of airport congestion calls for additional expenditures for related facilities, such as surface transportation from the center of cities to the airports. Before these outlays are made, those who are going to devise the changes and those who will pay for them will want to be sure that they are necessary.

Congestion is said to be the result of the unexpectedly high demand for air transportation, which has grown at a rate of about 18 percent annually over the past five years for the commercial airlines. The airports that were built for them have become crowded sooner than anticipated, and so have the terminals, parking lots, and roads leading to them. The solution appears to be to build more of all of these things, to build planes that use less land space per passenger and to make equipment that enables present aircraft to take off and land more quickly. This is a technical view of congestion. Significantly, it emphasizes resources that are priced outside the market, rather than those priced on the market, such as aircraft, fuel, or labor (even though one does hear grumbles about wages).

In an economic view, the problem goes beyond

Abridged from William D. Grampp, "The Case for Flexible Pricing," *Business Horizons*, 11, no. 5 (October 1968), 21–30. Reprinted by permission.

the technical features. Airports, although they are congested at certain hours, are not congested all of the time. When they are busy, they are busy with the traffic of small and private aircraft, as well as with that of the commercial airliners. The airliners themselves usually fly with unused capacity — and at some times with a large amount of it.

The problem of congestion, in an economic view, is how to use the present capital in aviation more extensively by reducing the demands on it at peak times and increasing them at others. The way to do this is to raise prices at peak times and lower them at others. That, in brief, is what this article proposes. The proposal is based on nothing more than the principles of demand and supply; these principles lead, as we shall see, to some rather surprising conclusions.

CURRENT SITUATION

Commercial planes are not the only planes that use the airports and are not alone in causing congestion. General aviation — operation of aircraft by individuals, business firms, and other organizations, and by the air taxi companies — compounds the problem. At the four busiest airports in the country in 1965, general aviation produced 9–28 percent of all traffic. These planes are slower and less well equipped than commercial airliners, and they use more time in taking off and landing. They pay a fee for the use of airports that is proportional to their weight, just as all aircraft do; this fee is not, however, determined by the economic value of the use. Consequently, a few passengers in a private aircraft may delay many more in an airliner. Under the present system, however, it cannot be determined whether the few are willing to pay a higher price than the many for a place at the head of a takeoff or landing queue. Space presently is not allocated to those who find it most valuable and are willing to pay the most for it.

From an economic viewpoint, civil aviation operates in two markets. In one it sells its final product —space for passengers and cargo — and in the other it buys the means of providing the space — the aircraft, the crew, and so on. In the past, the demand for space was small relative to the supply, and the price was low. Even now, space in the air itself has a zero price, which — from an economic viewpoint — most of it should have because it is abundant. But space on the ground has become scarce at certain times because the demand is large relative to the supply, and the price has not risen enough to make them equal. What users want is at times considerably more than what is available; the result is waiting, which can be a wasteful form of rationing.

At present, queues of aircraft are on the ground waiting to take off, and queues are in the air waiting to land. As the lines get longer, the average speed of the aircraft declines — both the average speed of the traveler from the center of one city to another and the average speed of the plane itself from the times it closes its doors at one terminal until it opens them at another.[1] In addition, there are "invisible" queues, the planes that would take off but do not because there is no space, and the passengers who would travel but do not because there are no seats.

COMPETITIVE BIDDING

Wasteful queueing would be eliminated if the price of the using space were to be set by competitive bidding. At what are now peak hours, less space would be wanted, and it would be used by those who find it most valuable and are willing to pay the highest price for it. At other hours, when there is unused space, the price would be lower and more would be used.

Suppose the best use of an airport at a particular time (of the day, week, or year) is n landings and m takeoffs per hour and that n and m are fixed numbers (although in reality they could be increased at a cost). The operators of the aircraft — the airlines and general aviation — would bid for the landing and takeoff rights, and the bidding would take place some time before the time the rights were to be exercised. If the airlines schedule flights for a six-month period, the rights would be purchased before

the six-month period began. The rights for general aviation could be acquired by brokers who would resell them as the rights were wanted.

In competitive bidding, the price of a landing would rise to that amount at which users wanted to buy no more than n rights, and the price of a takeoff would be that at which users wanted to buy no more than m rights. At the same airport at other times, the prices would be different if there was a different demand and supply of the final product (passenger and cargo space). For any given time, the prices of landings and takeoffs would probably differ among airports. If at a given price, x, the ratio of the amount of space wanted to the amount of space available was equal to 1 at some airports but not at all, the price of x would be charged only where the ratio was 1. Where the ratio was more than 1, the price would be higher than x. Where the ratio was less than 1, which it would be at off-peak times, the amount of space wanted would be less than the amount available. The price would fall below x, and the amount wanted would increase. At certain off-peak times, however, the amount of space might never equal the amount available, even if no charge was levied. In such a circumstance, unused capacity (for reasons explained later) does not indicate a wasteful use of capital. What is wasteful is *excessive* unused capacity, and that is what is avoided by competitive pricing.

The free pricing of airport space would allow users to alter the length of the queues and the amount of unused space in a way that would give each of them the greatest possible return. The rights to take off and land could be stated in units of time and so could be offered as a rental contract that would give the buyer the right to occupy runway and other space for a certain amount of time, for example, one minute for a takeoff between 5:00 and 5:01 P.M. An airline that wanted to put a number of flights into the air at about 5:00 P.M. could buy the desired number of rights and assign them to its own flights in a way that would bring it the greatest revenue. It could schedule "express flights" and put those planes at the head of its own queue. Some travelers would prefer the saving of 10 or 15 minutes to the inducements the airlines now offer,

---

[1] One airline reports that the scheduled flight time from Boston to New York increased about 25 percent between 1965, when turboprops were flown, and 1967, when jets were used.

such as the meals and drinks. The cost might be no more.

The bidding for space would set some rather smart prices at peak times, and, of course, not everyone would be able to afford it. Many in general aviation would be crowded out, for they could not afford to pay as much for rights as the commercial airlines. This seems harsh until one recognizes that the purpose of a price system is to distribute goods to those who value them the most. If an individual who wants to fly his own plane cannot pay as much for a takeoff right as a firm that owns an airliner, the reason is that the takeoff is not worth as much to him as it is to the passengers on the airliner. The individual may very well have less income and assets than the airline and may feel he is powerless against such inequality. But his relative poverty, if it is a problem, is not one that ought to be relieved by airport policy, for there are more direct and effective means of redistribution.[2]

This reasoning, of course, will not persuade the people in general aviation because it does not solve the immediate problem of imposing a loss on people who had previously received assistance from the government. That problem could be managed in either of two ways. Operators in general aviation could be paid to use the less busy airports, and the payments could come out of the higher fees charged at the busy airports. The other way is to give present users, for a specified time into the future, the same rights they have already had for a certain time in the past. The commercial airlines and the operators in general aviation would continue for a stated time to have the same access to all airports, busy and less busy, that they have had. However, the owners of the rights could buy and sell them to each other without any interference or restriction from the airport authorities. In addition, within each group there could be buying and selling: the operators from each other and the airlines from each other. The space at all airports would be used by those

who value it the most, and the value it has would be shown by the price paid for it.

Both the airlines and general aviation would be better off than they are now. The airport authorities would be no worse off because they would continue to be paid landing fees for rights of use. In time, as general aviation had accommodated itself to the new distribution of traffic among airports, the plan would be discontinued. It would be replaced by the simple auctioning of rights of use, and the airports would receive the revenue.

Another fear will be that competitive bidding for space will put the small airlines at a disadvantage. Actually a claim to subsidize space is no stronger for the small airlines than for general aviation or the large airlines. A more substantial fear, however, is that because of the power of the large airlines to bid higher prices, they could obtain control of space and exclude rivals. To examine this possibility in a proper way would take us beyond the limits of this article; what can be said here is that both the market and the government have ways of managing this problem of monopoly.

IMPLICATIONS

Flexible pricing is to an economist the obvious way to reduce shortages and surpluses. It is not obvious to others and especially not to those in an industry such as aviation that has long operated under the eye of the government. In the hearings held last year by the Senate subcommittee on aviation, the proposals for relieving "the airport crisis" were mainly for new construction and new methods of financing construction. Nevertheless, Alan S. Boyd, [former] Secretary of Transportation, suggested that "perhaps we could move some of the peak-time flights to other times" by means of "cheaper fares for off-hour travel." He went on to say that airports "might try offering incentives to both air carriers and general aviation to use airports less at peak hours by raising airport charges for services provided during peak hours, and lowering them during the off-hours." Later, the Port of New York Authority did increase the takeoff and landing fees for general aviation users at peak hours at the major airports around

---

[2]Nevertheless, the airlines are reported to be arguing that general aviation operators should contribute to the support of airports not because the operators use them but because their average income is $35,000 (*The Chicago Sun-Times*, June 30, 1968).

New York City. These incidents do not mean aviation is being converted to flexible pricing, but they do indicate that the idea is being considered. What I propose is an extensive application of it, as the following example will illustrate.

The price of a right to take off from a busy airport at a busy time (say at O'Hare Field at 5 P.M. on Sunday in mid-July) would be higher than the price 24 hours later, and at the latter time it would be higher than at 5 A.M. on the following morning. The price of a landing right for the flight from O'Hare would depend on its destination and arrival time; a flight to Boston would have a lower takeoff cost if, instead of departing from O'Hare, it departed from a less-used airport such as Midway or even Milwaukee. The cost to passengers and shippers of using the aircraft would vary according to the same factors that govern the variation in the prices of takeoffs and landings. If I wanted to travel at peak hours between busy airports, I would pay more than at other times or between other places. I should not be surprised by these price differences any more than I should be surprised by having to pay more to go to the theater on Saturday night than on Monday.

Indeed, variations are now found in airline fares. A more desirable location in the plane costs more, and excursion fares are not in force at peak periods. Why should a more desirable travel time not cost more? Why should there not be a higher fare for departure and arrival at more convenient airports?

These questions may seem odd. If I am going to San Francisco, where can I land except at the San Francisco airport? Actually, I may be going to Berkeley and would be just as willing to arrive at Oakland. Why not use the present flights to Oakland? Because they are infrequent — and they are infrequent because the fare is the same as to San Francisco.

My proposal implies that airports be used through the night. Who would arrive or depart at 3:00 A.M.? Very few, at present fares. However, at lower fares some passengers will undoubtedly use these times as the experience of youth fares has shown. In addition, there are uses for airports other than commercial passenger travel. There is cargo and general aviation, and some of these operators might prefer to use airports at night when rights are cheap, rather than to bid against the airlines for daytime rights.

One of the preconditions of efficiency is a set of prices that measures cost and value accurately and makes possible the kinds of comparisons that lead to sensible decisions. What this article has proposed is a set of prices that is determined by the competitive bidding for space on the aircraft, for space on the ground at the airports, in the air above them, and along the flight paths between them. Behind the proposal is some economic theory. The explanation of the proposal has rested specifically on the idea that prices that are determined by demand and supply will prevent a shortage of space at peak times and, at other times, cause space to be utilized that now is not.

QUESTIONS

1. What is the distinction between a technical view of congestion and queueing and an economic view?
2. What is peak-load pricing? Where have you observed examples of its use?
3. "If a pricing system allocated airport landing space, many general aviation flyers would be unable to afford landings or takeoffs at early morning and late afternoon periods." Comment.
4. Is all queueing and congestion curable with a price increase?

PART THREE

DEMAND: CONSUMER BEHAVIOR

5 DOES EVERY PERSON HAVE A PRICE?
Terry Southern

*Novelist and scriptwriter Terry Southern, with this
portrayal of August Guy Grand in* The Magic Chris-
tian, *promotes the view that everyone has a price.
Do you? Although this is not one of Mr. Southern's
racier writing efforts, its economic implications are
nevertheless provocative.*

Out of the gray granite morass of Wall Street rises
one building like a heron of fire, soaring up in blue-
white astonishment — *Number 18 Wall* — a rocket
of glass and blinding copper. It is the *Grand Investment Building,* perhaps the most contemporary
business structure in our country, known in circles
of high finance simply as *Grand's.*

Offices of *Grand's* are occupied by companies
which deal in *mutual funds* — giant and fantastic
corporations whose policies define the shape of nations.

August Guy Grand himself was a billionaire. He
had 180 millions cash deposit in New York banks,
and this ready capital was of course but a part of his
gross holdings.

In the beginning, Grand's associates, wealthy
men themselves, saw nothing extraordinary about
him; a reticent man of simple tastes, they thought,
a man who had inherited most of his money and
had preserved it through large safe investments in
steel, rubber, and oil. What his associates managed
to see in Grand was usually a reflection of their own
dullness: a club member, a dinner guest, a possibility, a threat — a man whose holdings represented a
prospect and a danger. But this was to do injustice
to Grand's private life, because his private life was
atypical. For one thing, he was the last of the big
spenders; and for another, he had a very unusual attitude towards *people* — he spent about ten million
a year in, as he expressed it himself, *"making it hot
for them."*

At fifty-three, Grand had a thick trunk and a
large balding bullet-head; his face was quite pink, so
that in certain half-lights he looked like a fat radish-
man — though not displeasingly so, for he always
sported well-cut clothes and, near the throat, a diamond the size of a nickel . . . a diamond now that
caught the late afternoon sun in a soft spangle of
burning color when Guy stepped through the sound-
less doors of *Grand's* and into the blue haze of the
almost empty street, past the huge doorman appearing larger than life in gigantic livery, he who touched
his cap with quick but easy reverence.

"Cab, Mr. Grand?"

"Thank you no, Jason," said Guy, "I have the
car today." And with a pleasant smile for the man,
he turned adroitly on his heel, north towards Worth
Street.

Guy Grand's gait was brisk indeed — small sharp
steps, rising on the toes. It was the gait of a man
who appears to be snapping his fingers as he walks.

Half a block on he reached the car, though he
seemed to have a momentary difficulty in recognizing it; beneath the windshield wiper lay a big parking ticket, which Grand slowly withdrew, regarding
it curiously.

"Looks like you've got a *ticket,* bub!" said a
voice somewhere behind him.

Out of the corner of his eye Grand perceived the
man, in a dark summer suit, leaning idly against the
side of the building nearest the car. There was something terse and smug in the tone of his remark, a
sort of nasal piousness.

"Yes, so it seems," mused Grand, without looking up, continuing to study the ticket in his hand.
"How much will you eat it for?" he asked then,
raising a piercing smile at the man.

"How's that, mister?" demanded the latter with
a nasty frown, pushing himself forward a bit from
the building.

Grand cleared his throat and slowly took out his
wallet — a long slender wallet of such fine leather it
would have been limp as silk, had it not been so
chock-full of thousands.

"I asked what would you take to *eat* it? You
know . . ." Wide-eyed, he made a great chewing
motion with his mouth, holding the ticket up near it.

The man, glaring, took a tentative step forward.

"Say, I don't *get* you, mister!"

"Well," drawled Grand, chuckling down at his fat wallet, browsing about in it, "simple enough really . . ." And he took out a few thousand. "*I have this ticket*, as you know, and I was just wondering if you would care to *eat* it, for, say" — a quick glance to ascertain — "six thousand dollars?"

"What do you mean, *'eat it'?*" demanded the dark-suited man in a kind of a snarl. "Say, what're you anyway, bub, a *wise*-guy?"

"*'Wise*-guy' or '*grand*-guy' — call me anything you like . . . as long as you don't call me *'late-for-chow!'* Eh? Ho-ho." Grand rounded it off with a jolly chortle, but was quick to add, unsmiling, "How 'bout it, pal — got a taste for the easy green?"

The man, who now appeared to be openly angry, took another step forward.

"*Listen,* mister . . ." he began in a threatening tone, half clenching his fists.

"I think I should warn you," said Grand quietly, raising one hand to his breast, "that I am armed."

"*Huh?*" The man seemed momentarily dumfounded, staring down in dull rage at the six bills in Grand's hand; then he partially recovered, and cocking his head to one side, regarded Grand narrowly, in an attempt at shrewd skepticism, still heavily flavored with indignation.

"Just who do you think you *are* Mister! Just what is your *game?*"

"Grand's the name, easy-green's the game," said Guy with a twinkle. "Play along?" He brusquely flicked the corners of the six crisp bills, and they crackled with a brittle, compelling sound.

"*Listen* . . ." muttered the man, tight-lipped, flexing his fingers and exhaling several times in angry exasperation, ". . . are *you* trying . . . are you trying to tell ME that you'll give *six thousand dollars* . . . to EAT that" — he pointed stiffly at the ticket in Guy's hand — "to *eat* that TICKET?!?"

"That's about the size of it," said Grand; he glanced at his watch. "It's what you might call a 'limited offer' — expiring in, let's say, *one minute.*"

"Listen, mister," said the man between clenched teeth, "if this is a gag, *so help me* . . ." He shook his head to show how serious he was.

"No threats," Guy cautioned, "or I'll shoot you in the temple — well, what say? Forty-eight seconds remaining."

"Let's *see* that money!" exclaimed the man, quite beside himself now, grabbing at the bills.

Grand allowed him to examine them as he continued to regard his watch. "Thirty-nine seconds remaining," he announced solemnly. "Shall I start the *big count down?*"

Without waiting for the latter's reply, he stepped back and, cupping his hands like a megaphone, began dramatically intoning, "*Twenty-eight . . . twenty-seven . . . twenty-six . . .*" while the man made several wildly gesticulated and incoherent remarks before seizing the ticket, ripping off a quarter of it with his teeth and beginning to chew, eyes blazing.

"*Stout fellow!*" cried Grand warmly, breaking off the count down to step forward and give the chap a hearty clap on the shoulder and hand him the six thousand.

"You needn't actually eat the ticket," he explained. "I was just curious to see if you had your price." He gave a wink and a tolerant chuckle. "Most of us have, I suppose. Eh? Ho-ho."

And with a grand wave of his hand, he stepped inside his car and sped away, leaving the man in the dark summer suit standing on the sidewalk staring after him, fairly agog.

QUESTIONS

1. Is morality — that is, a refusal to do something because it is "wrong and immoral" — simply another way of saying that one's price has not yet been met?

2. Is there anything your best friend would not do at some price?

ARE STUDENTS RATIONAL AT CHOOSING BEER?
J. Douglas McConnell

J. Douglas McConnell, a marketing economist with the Stanford Research Institute, developed this article from his Ph.D. dissertation. The statistical tests may puzzle some readers, but a careful perusal of his research will show the peculiar demand for beer among Stanford graduate students.

This study examines the relationship between price and perceived quality for a frequently purchased consumer product — beer — in an experimental setting, yet one that permitted a considerable degree of realism.

THE METHODOLOGY

A random probability sample of sixty beer drinkers was obtained from Stanford University married-student housing (Escondido Village). The sample consisted of forty-four males and sixteen females. The age spread was from twenty-one years to fifty-two years with a median of twenty-eight years, and income ranged from $2,500 to $15,000 per year with a median level of $5,000. The majority of subjects were graduate students. A cover story concerning a brewer's product test was used to disguise the true purpose of the study.

The beer used in the study was identical for the three "brands" that the sample was told were being used. A brewer supplied sixty cases of lager-type beer from the same batch in unmarked, nonreturnable bottles of one pattern. All bottles were sealed with a plain seal.

The three "brands" were identified by labeling bottles with white self-adhesive labels lettered L, M, and P in red. The brands were further identified by price cards indicating the price per six-pack. Brand P was $0.99 a six-pack, Brand L was $1.20 a six-

Abridged from J. Douglas McConnell, "An Experimental Examination of the Price—Quality Relationship," *Journal of Business,* 41, no. 3 (July 1968), 439—444. Reprinted by permission.

pack, and Brand M was $1.30 a six-pack. Subjects were to make selections from among the three brands, and it was desirable that each selection should approximate the normal purchase situation; that is, selection of less expensive merchandise should leave the consumer with more change in his pocket than the purchase of more expensive brands. Accordingly, it was decided to tape a nickel on each bottle of the least expensive brand (P) and two cents to each bottle of the medium-priced brand (L).

Subjects were visited three days a week for eight consecutive weeks at prearranged times in their apartments. On each visit, the three brands with their respective price cards were set on a tray, and subjects selected any one bottle of beer. They were required to drink each bottle selected at any time convenient to them before making their next selection.

To eliminate any possible position effect, the positions on the first trial were determined at random. Subsequent positions were changed before each trial to insure that all brands occupied each position an equal number of trials. No brand occupied the same position on the tray for two consecutive trials.

Since one of the hypotheses to be investigated related to the question of brand loyalty, half the subjects from Trial 12 onward and the remainder for Trial 18 onward were offered inducements of 1 cent per trial cumulative bonuses to switch to the brand of beer they had chosen least. These inducements resulted in some brand switching but little change in subjects' perception of the three brands. Thus, it is considered that the inducements did not interfere unduly with the price-quality aspect of the study. If anything, they provided subjects with a reason for making additional comparisons among brands.

After their final selection in Trial 24, subjects were given a questionnaire on which they were asked to select from a list of words commonly used to describe beer the three words that best described each brand. The words in the list, shown in Table 1, have generally favorable and unfavorable connotations with respect to beer.

Also, the questionnaire asked subjects to rate the three brands of beer for quality on a five-point

Table 1. *Panel of Words Describing the Three Brands of Beer*

Favorable (implied high quality)	Unfavorable (implied low quality)
Tangy	Flat
Rich flavored	Biting
Smooth	Acidy
Malty	Watery
Full bodied	Bitter
Light	Sour
Dry	

scale ranging from "undrinkable," through "poor," "fair," and "good," to "very pleasant." It was assumed that these points on the scale were monotonically increasing, and values of 0, 1, 2, 3, and 4 were assigned to each point, respectively.

As a third check on subjects' perception of quality, each was asked to indicate which brand he would prefer to receive should he win a lottery with a case of beer as the prize. The bottles of beer in the lottery had no money attached irrespective of brand.

ANALYSIS OF THE RESULTS

Subjects' selections of words describing the brands of beer formed the basis for a one-way analysis of variance. The over-all direction of subjects' selections is readily apparent in Table 2. The differences were significant at the $P < .05$ level.

Using subjects' ratings of the three brands of beer, a simple contingency table (see Table 3) was constructed to test the relationships between per-

ceived quality and the three price levels. The contingency-table analysis produced significant findings, the χ^2 distribution value being significant at the $P < .005$ level.

Differences among the mean rating values were tested using the Student t-distribution and method for correlated observations.

The t-tests of the differences among mean rating values of the three brands indicated that the high- and low-priced brands were perceived as being of significantly different quality at the $P < .01$ level. The high- and medium-priced brands were perceived as being of different quality at the $P < .06$ level. However, the medium-priced brand was not regarded as being of significantly higher quality than the low-priced brand. The "perceptual space" between the high- and the medium-priced brands was greater than between the medium- and low-priced brands, although the actual price differential would have led one to suspect that the reverse should have been the case.

As one would expect, there was a high degree of correlation between ratings and brands preferred. Only nine of the sixty rated all three brands as being of the same quality, and six of the nine were regular consumers of the low-priced beer in the tests.

The lottery results supported the general direction of the findings, since thirty of the sixty subjects selected the high-priced brand, eleven the medium-priced brand, and nineteen the low-priced brand. These selections correlated highly with preferences developed during the study. It is interesting to note that subjects selected the high-priced brand for over 41 percent of all trials and the middle-priced brand for 25 percent of all trials.

Price clearly was used by subjects as an indication of product quality. With a physically homogeneous product and unknown brand names (which had so little meaning that many subjects never used them), subjects perceived the highest-priced brand as being a better-quality product than the other two brands. The medium-priced brand was perceived as being marginally better than the low-priced brand. In fact, if "knowledge" had been complete, the true "economic" subject would have tried each brand

Table 2. *Relationship Between Price of Beer and Descriptive Words (Totals shown are number of words)*

Type of words chosen	Brand of beer and price per six-pack		
	M ($1.30)	L ($1.20)	P ($0.99)
Favorable	93	73	57
Unfavorable	71	82	101

once and then chosen the low-priced brand for the remaining trials. In this way, informed subjects would have maximized their utility, receiving the same beer and five cents on each trial instead of something less. Subjects, however, selected the high-priced brand for over 41 percent of all trials and appeared to be using it as the benchmark against which they compared the other two brands. Price, in the absence of other cues, was a powerful factor in determining how the brands were perceived.

By the end of Trial 3, fifty-one of the sixty subjects had tried all three brands. Fifty-nine had tried all brands by the close of Trial 6. The one remaining subject finally switched and tried the third brand at Trial 13.

As mentioned earlier, all three brands were physically identical. In this respect, the study was similar to Tucker's, in which identical loaves of bread under different brand names were used.[1] Both studies indicated that consumers will differentiate between homogeneous products on the basis of cues supplied by the marketer. For Tucker's consumers, the variable was the brand name. In this study, it was price. The statistical data are supported by comments similar to that made at Trial 20 by a male subject, number 51: "I've just realized that I've been behaving as the marketing people say I would. I tried them all, then settled on the one I liked best (Brand M), and occasionally try the cheap one to check my judgment."

A female subject, number 37, observed at Trial 20 that "L and M are very similar, and I can't see the difference worth the price, but we didn't like P at all."

A possible explanation for this price-quality phenomenon can be drawn from dissonance theory. The consumer seeks to maintain consonance between his cognitive structure and his perception of the real world. In this experiment, the subjects' cognitive set was that "you pay for what you get," and the "quality" beer was therefore high priced and the "poor" beer was low priced, with the medium-

[1]William T. Tucker, "The Development of Brand Loyalty," *Journal of Marketing Research* (August 1964).

Table 3. *Data for Contingency-Table Analysis (Ratings from Likert-type scale)*

	Price levels of beer		
	High	Medium	Low
Undrinkable 0	4	1	4
Poor 1	8	21	20
Fair 2	26	22	23
Good 3	15	12	9
Very pleasant 4	7	4	4
Total	133	117	109
Mean	2.23	1.93	1.80

priced brand somewhere in between. Actual tasting of all three brands revealed no real difference for many subjects. This was dissonant with their set that quality costs more. As there was no way of altering prices to reduce the cognitive dissonance, these subjects had to alter their perception of the products, and this they did by imputing different qualities to the three brands. This varied with individual subjects, some stating that certain brands were undrinkable from their first experience with them.

The question of external validity is of primary importance in any study, particularly a small artificial experiment employing atypical consumers as subjects. It is believed that the results obtained do have some external validity, for the following reasons. Subjects were able to drink their beer in a normal setting at times suiting their usual habits. By continuing the experiment for two months, the "beer man" was accepted as a caller in the same way as the milkman. Subjects' comments relating to brands were spontaneous and indicated that they were involved in the project as consumers and were not simply trying to help a fellow student through his research. At the close of the study, a number of subjects were very reluctant to accept the fact that the three brands of beer were in fact identical.

It could be argued that subjects were reluctant to take the brands with the money attached for reasons of pride. This was not so. For many subjects, the nickel on the lowest-priced brand was the principal reason for selecting it, and when the money (at

Trial 8) was moved from the label to the opposite side of the bottle, a number of subjects had to reassure themselves that the money was still there and available. . . . Finally, one would expect the more intelligent sector of the community to be more aware of product differences and values than those less intelligent and less well educated. The subscribers to *Consumer Reports,* for instance, are heavily skewed toward the college-graduate end of the educational distribution. Yet in this study the subjects were well educated and supposedly more capable of making objective evaluations and comparisons than the purchasing public at large. It is believed, therefore, that the experimental findings have some relevance to the real world and that they have important implications for both business and public policy.

QUESTIONS

1. What are the implications of this test on the nature of the demand for beer? Do the results surprise you? Why or why not? Would you expect similar results from a similar test of other products? If so, which ones?
2. Does this test, in any way, invalidate the "law of demand"?
3. If consumers judge quality on the basis of price, what are the implications, if any, for consumer demand theory?
4. Were those students in the test sample who preferred brand M irrational? Or simply indiscriminate? What is the difference, if any?

7 THE PRICE ELASTICITY OF DEMAND FOR MARIJUANA
Charles T. Nisbet and Firouz Vakil

The concept of elasticity is one of the most useful in economic analysis, and many economists have engaged in trying to measure the elasticities of widely varying products. Charles T. Nisbet and Firouz Vakil have derived estimates of the price elasticity of demand for marijuana at UCLA. Professor Nisbet is on the economics faculty at Evergreen State College; Dr. Vakil is director of the Bureau of Planometrics for the government of Iran.

It is the purpose of this note to add some economic considerations to the growing literature on drug use by offering some estimates of the price and expenditure elasticities of demand for marijuana.

THE SAMPLE AND THE DATA

The data were gathered through the use of an anonymous mail questionnaire. Out of the 926 respondents, 52.8 percent claimed to have never tried marijuana and were classified as "non-smokers," while 47.2 percent said they have tried marijuana and were classified as "smokers." Out of the 437 "smokers," 184 were "purchasers" and 253 were "non-purchasers," obtaining marijuana only from friends.

The intent of the questionnaires was to obtain data with respect to how much marijuana in "lids" (ounces) a consumer, at a given income, is purchasing and would be willing to purchase when facing a number of alternative prices.[1]

Each individual purchaser was thus asked to trace out his particular demand function. The objections to the derivation of this type of hypotheti-

[1]Students were asked to indicate how much their *use* of marijuana changes with variations in prices per unit of time so the increased quantity demanded at lower prices would not represent stocking up or hoarding.

Abridged from Charles T. Nisbet and Firouz Vakil, "Some Estimates of Price and Expenditure Elasticities of Demand for Marijuana among U.C.L.A. Students," *Review of Economics and Statistics* (November 1972), 473—475.

cal demand function are well known: people have not thought out in advance what they will do when confronted with such a hypothetical situation, snap judgments cannot inspire great confidence, expectation of a particular action may diverge from actual action when confronted with the concrete situation. Additional data on actual prices and the corresponding quantities demanded were also collected.[2]

CONCLUSIONS

1. The individual college student's demand curve for marijuana exhibits the standard characteristics prescribed by conventional economic theory.

2. Estimates of price elasticities around the going market price ranged from −0.40 to −1.51 depending on the type of data used and on the functional form. Given that these figures are downwardly biased, it is quite likely that a price elasticity slightly greater than one would give a reasonable estimate.

3. The price elasticity data suggest that policies designed to restrict supply, such as "operation intercept," may be effective in reducing the quantity consumed of marijuana. However, rising prices of marijuana may also encourage substitutes for other more harmful drugs.

QUESTIONS

1. Define price elasticity. What does it measure? Why have economists not chosen simply to use the slope of the demand curve as a substitute for elasticity?
2. Describe the methodology of the Nisbet-Vakil study. What problems, if any, arise with this approach, i.e., what biases might be introduced? How else could price elasticity estimates be made?
3. Could their study be duplicated at your campus (if you are not at UCLA)? What elasticity estimates do you think would be found?

[2] Stigler suggests that when quizzed, individuals tend to see fewer substitution possibilities than when confronted with a higher price. Consequently demand curves based on market surveys tend to be less elastic than empirically estimated demand curves using marking data.

8 DOES ADVERTISING RAISE OR LOWER PRICES?
Robert L. Steiner

Does advertising raise prices? Most people would quickly answer yes. But Robert L. Steiner of the University of Cincinnati offers evidence to the contrary. Professor Steiner is an economist who cannot be chided by the old saw, "yes, but did you ever meet a payroll?" He is a former general manager and president of Kenner Products Company (now a toy division of General Mills) and is at home in both business and academe. In an earlier article Professor Steiner showed the remarkable downward impact that television advertising had on the retail price of toys.

BACKGROUND

With certain classes of merchandise, of which eyeglasses and prescription drugs are examples, retailers' advertising is prohibited or restricted in varying degree by professional codes of conduct and by state and local statutes. On the other hand, in some states there are few if any restrictions. Thus, in effect, an almost laboratory situation would seem to be presented for the measurement of the effects of retailer advertising, for the weights of such advertising should vary substantially in different geographic areas according to the severity of the restictions.

Because the principal, although not the only, restrictions are those embodied in state law, the pioneering research of Professors Lee Benham in eyeglasses and John Cady in prescription drugs has examined whether the mean price is higher or lower in those states where advertising is more or less freely permitted. Although the effects of advertising on price dispersion are mixed, in both eyeglasses and prescription drugs mean retail prices were found to be lower where the dealer's ability to advertise is not inhibited by state statute. On the basis of these findings and research from the FTC, consumer or-

Abridged from Robert L. Steiner, *New Insights into the Effects of Brand Advertising on Price* (Washington, D.C.: American Enterprise Institute, 1977), chap. 13. Reprinted by permission.

ganizations, and other groups which have yielded the same conclusions, a series of successful legal challenges against state boards of pharmacy has been mounted in Virginia, California and elsewhere.

These court decisions favorable to advertising have turned mainly on First Amendment grounds. However, in May, 1976, the U.S. Supreme Court also noted the crucial economic role played by advertising in the American enterprise system in its landmark decision sustaining the lower court's verdict that the Virginia statutes banning retail price advertising of prescription drugs were unconstitutional. While these actions have justifiably been hailed as a victory for commercial speech, at this writing the extent to which they presage a major increase in the volume of retail advertising in prescription drugs and in eyeglasses remains unclear.

PRESCRIPTION DRUGS

The Effects of Advertising Restrictions on Price
Cady's findings are based on a 1970 national survey in 1,930 pharmacies of the retail prices of ten representative prescription drugs conducted by the National Association of Retail Druggists and the Nattional Association of Chain Drug Stores. In that year, 29 states restricted retail price advertising by state statute or pharmacy board regulation.

Using bivariate analysis Cady concludes "the price of each drug is significantly higher ($P < .01$) in states restricting price advertising than in states with no advertising restrictions."

Previously, Cady had probed the possibility that differences in services, such as credit and delivery, between restrictive and non-restrictive states might account for the lower retail prices in the latter group. However, he discovered no relationship between the level of services and restrictions on advertising. Instead, his regression coefficients indicated that 4.3% of the variance in drug prices between the 2 groups of states is associated with advertising. Thus, if the ten items are representative of the universe of all prescription drugs, prices should fall by around 4.3% through the removal of anti-advertising restrictions.

Cady also found that a still larger coefficient is associated with the size of the retail outlet. Over a period of time, then, it might be anticipated that as the market became more competitive following the legalization of retail price advertising, the smaller and less efficient pharmacies would lose market share to the larger retailers. This would result in a reduction in the long-run average cost curve in the [retail] market and in a further fall in retail prices.

There is reason for caution in assuming that freedom from state imposed advertising restrictions has in the past been, or now will be, equivalent to the presence of a meaningful volume of retail price advertising. One must reckon with the practices of "under the table arm twisting by independent pharmacists and their agencies", and "informal harassment of prescription advertisers by local pharmacy boards which permit pharmacist groups to enforce "ethical" sanctions against pharmacies which chose to disclose prices."

EYEGLASSES

Professor Lee Benham has published two studies of eyeglasses in the *Journal of Law and Economics*. The earlier article focuses on the effects of advertising on price and the second is of broader scope in that the various influences of professional control, of which advertising restrictions are but one, are explored. Let us relate the more pertinent findings of these two important articles, in turn.

The Effects of Advertising Restrictions on Price
Benham's data base for the earlier article is a 1963 national survey of 634 individuals who purchased eyeglasses. In that year, around ¾ of the states had some restrictions concerning advertising, which ranged from a virtual ban on the dissemination of any information to statutes which permitted eyeglass advertising so long as price was not disclosed.

The mean cost of a pair of eyeglasses in the 12 states with no advertising restrictions was $26.34, compared to $33.04, in the six states with complete prohibitions — a difference of $6.70 (using regression equations the difference is $7.482). To point up the maximum effect of advertising restrictions, Benham performed the same calculations for Texas and the District of Columbia which are "the extreme laissez-faire states," and for North Carolina which was judged to have had the most extensive restrictions in force over a long period of time. Here, the mean price difference was $19.50 and the regression difference $18.99.

In still another computation, it was found that where advertising was permitted, prices were slightly lower in states that allowed the price of the eyeglasses to appear in the ad. However, a survey of newspapers in Illinois, a state without restrictions, revealed "few advertisements which contained any reference to price, and fewer still quoted specific prices."

As with prescription drugs, no numerical data are furnished of the actual retail advertising expenditures for eyeglasses across the different states. Therefore, the difference in advertising intensity between the restrictive and non-restrictive states and the extent to which prices are disclosed in ads, where permitted, is somewhat uncertain. However, it appears that "commercial firms" (e.g., opticians, rather than optometrists or opthomologists who are classified as professionals) are aggressive merchandisers in the unrestricted states. From interviews with several commercial firms, Benham learned that the larger optical chains were loathe to enter markets where they were unable to advertise. Furthermore, one major chain operator divulged that in the unrestricted states his concern spent around 2 dollars per pair of eyeglasses sold — an advertising to sales ratio of almost 8% (compared to the approximately 1.5% of sales that all retailers spend on advertising).

The Effects of Professional Control Benham's thesis is that through professional control, mainly exercised by the American Optometric Association (AOA), a series of restrictions have become lodged in professional codes of conduct and in state law. The result, and probably the purpose of these efforts, is to restrict competition and raise the price of eyecare to the benefit of the professionals. Yet, the self-serving nature of the restrictions is shrouded in a mass of statements which equate the restrictions with ethical behavior and competition with unseemly conduct.

Three indexes of professional control are formulated for each state. These are, the proportion of optometrists licensed by the AOA, the extent to which advertising is restricted, and the percentage of eyeglasses purchased from commercial firms, rather than from professionals. The data on the price of eyeglasses and where they were purchased are taken from a 1970 study of 1,625 individuals who purchased eyeglasses. All three indexes of professional control are found to be positively and "strongly associated with prices paid for eyeglasses." And all three coefficients are significant at the .001 level.

Among the major conclusions are:

Eyeglass prices are $8.46 lower in states which do not restrict advertising.

There is a price increase of around $12.18 per pair of glasses as membership in the AOA increases across the range found in the survey.

There is a price increase of around $11.71 as the percentage of eyeglasses purchased from commercial [firms] declines over the range found in the survey.

The mean price of eyeglasses in all states purchased from commercial firms was $29.22, from optometrists $30.30, and from physicians (opthomologists) $34.53.

Significantly, commercial firms accounted for 45% of eyeglass sales in states where advertising was not restricted and only 22% in the restricted states.

Of particular public policy importance was the finding that in the states dominated by professional control, a lesser percentage of the population purchased eyeglasses — assumedly because of their higher price.

QUESTIONS

1. Prior to studying economics, what prediction would you have made as to the effect of advertising on a product's price? According to the author what effect does advertising have on the price of ethical drugs and eyeglasses? Do you agree with the method of the studies?

2. What products, if any, have their prices enhanced by advertising? How would you document your answer?

3. "Advertising is simply a type of speech and should be free from any regulation to the same extent as any other type of speech or writing." Comment. Under what conditions, if any, should advertising be regulated?

9 THE FTC'S ATTACK ON RESTRAINTS OF ADVERTISING
Art Buchwald

The Chicago Tribune *dubbed the author of this selection "the greatest satirist in English since Pope and Swift." There is no question that Art Buchwald has entertained millions with his witty columns and commentary. Here he contemplates the end result of the government's policy, one supported by many economists, to eliminate all constraints on advertising — as could be suggested by the preceding article.*

The Federal Trade Commission has attacked the American Medical Association for illegal price fixing. It also says doctors keep patients from getting medical information by forbidding AMA members to advertise.

The big question raised by this attack is what kind of advertising will the public be exposed to if the FTC wins its case?

My friend Beezlebub who owns an advertising agency has already been working on some campaigns and hopes to garner a lot of accounts as soon as medical advertising becomes legal. He gave me a preview of what he had worked up.

First he showed me a large full page ad for a newspaper with a black headline on the top. "SPECIAL GEORGE WASHINGTON $2.00 BIRTHDAY SALE ON ALL MAJOR OPERATIONS.

"Madman Dr. Kelly announces the greatest surgery bargain in history. The first 100 people who show up at the Wesley Heights Clinic on George Washington's Birthday will be given a complete

From Art Buchwald, "You're All Heart, John Cameron Swayze," The Los Angeles Times Syndicate, January 4, 1976. Reprinted by permission.

operation including anesthesia and post operative care for $2.00.

"Yes for only $2.00 you could be lucky enough to have any organ in your body removed at once-in-a-lifetime prices.

"Other Bicentennial bargains Madman Dr. Kelly is giving away include a brain operation for $14.95, a kidney transplant for $29.50 and a complete blood transfusion for $3.95.

"If you can find a doctor in town who will charge less, Madman Dr. Kelly will give you a FREE, yes we said FREE, Plastic Surgery Nose Job. Don't forget for one day only the greatest surgical sale in history at Madman Dr. Kelly's! No phone orders please."

"How do you like it?" Beezlebub asked me.

"It's a heckuva ad," I admitted.

"Come on in the screening room. I want to show you some commercials my TV people worked out." Beezlebub pushed a button and John Cameron Swayze came on the screen.

He was standing on the top of a cliff. "Ladies and gentlemen I am standing on the highest cliff overlooking Acapulco. With me are two gentlemen, both of whom have pacemakers implanted in their hearts. One was implanted by Dr. Wallace Welby. The other by a heart surgeon who charges three times what a Welby implant costs. We're going to do a little experiment now. Are you ready gentlemen?"

The men nod.

John Cameron Swayze pushes both men off the cliff and they plunge 300 feet to the rocks below.

The commercial picks up Swayze at the bottom standing over two bodies. A doctor with a stethoscope is listening to their hearts.

"Well, doctor."

"This man's pacemaker is still working. This other man's heart has stopped." Swayze pulls off a band-aid on the body of the man whose pacemaker is still working. The camera zooms in on a tattoo which reads "Welby M.D."

Swayze looks out at the audience.

"This proves you don't need an expensive doctor to insert a pacemaker. Dr. Welby is cheap in price but not in work. Call this toll-free number today.

Dr. Welby's pacemakers start at $39.50 including installation and three-month guarantee."

"I like it," I told Beezlebub.

"Here's one which I call the 'average woman' type commercial." He pushed a button.

A man with a microphone is standing in a large doctor's office. In the background are three women on couches.

He goes over to the ladies. "Now ladies we're going to have some fun today. We're going to blindfold you and have you analyzed by three psychiatrists. After they're finished I want you to tell me which one you like the best."

A sign flashes on the screen that says "AFTER FIFTY MINUTES."

"All right, ladies, which doctor did you prefer?"

The first lady after her blindfold is taken off says, "I liked number two, he had a nice soft voice."

"Number two," the second lady says. "He seemed to understand my problem."

The third lady, "I don't know who he is but I'm switching to number two."

The announcer, "And now let's see who number two is. It's Dr. Adolph Fremluck, America's favorite psychiatrist. Yes, folks, everyone is switching to Dr. Fremluck, not only for the quality of his work, but his low fees. If you are depressed, paranoid, schizoid or just plain neurotic Dr. Fremluck has a cure for you. He's open every night until 10 and if you take advantage of his special 'January blues rates' he will give you absolutely free a set of Walt Disney coffee mugs with Mickey and Minnie, Donald Duck and all the other characters that made your childhood so miserable. Don't delay. If you're sick in the head Fremluck wants to hear from you today."

QUESTIONS

1. What benefits, if any, does the FTC expect customers to secure in its campaign to end the advertising prohibition of doctors' services?

2. Why has the American Medical Association enforced restrictions on the advertising of doctors' services?

3. What costs to society does Buchwald envision

from medical advertising? Will the expected benefits exceed these costs? How could such an estimate of costs and benefits be made?

 **CONSUMER SOVEREIGNTY: THE LIBERTARIAN VIEW**
Ludwig von Mises

Ludwig von Mises, former Professor of Economics at New York University and now deceased, was recognized as a Distinguished Fellow by the American Economic Association for his theoretical work on the problems of a planned economy. He is best known for his long-standing defense of an unfettered market mechanism. In this selection, he defends the relevancy of consumer sovereignty under capitalism. Discussion questions for this selection and the next one follow the next selection.

CONTROL BY THE CONSUMER

The direction of all economic affairs is in the market society a task of the entrepreneurs. Theirs is the control of production. They are at the helm and steer the ship. A superficial observer would believe that they are supreme. But they are not. They are bound to obey unconditionally the captain's orders. The captain is the consumer. Neither the entrepreneurs nor the farmers nor the capitalists determine what has to be produced. The consumers do that. If a businessman does not strictly obey the orders of the public as they are conveyed to him by the structure of market prices, he suffers losses, he goes bankrupt, and is thus removed from his eminent position at the helm. Other men who did better in satisfying the demand of the consumers replace him.

The consumers patronize those shops in which they can buy what they want at the cheapest price. Their buying and their abstention from buying decides who should own and run the plants and the

From Ludwig von Mises, *Human Action* (New Haven: Yale University Press, 1949), pp. 270–273. Reprinted by permission.

land. They make poor people rich and rich people poor. They determine precisely what should be produced, in what quality, and in what quantities. They are merciless egoistic bosses, full of whims and fancies, changeable and unpredictable. For them nothing counts other than their own satisfaction. They do not care a whit for past merit and vested interests. If something is offered to them that they like better or that is cheaper, they desert their old purveyors. In their capacity as buyers and consumers they are hard-hearted and callous, without consideration for other people.

Only the sellers of goods and services of the first order are in direct contact with the consumers and directly depend on their orders. But they transmit the orders received from the public to all those producing goods and services of the higher orders. For the manufacturers of consumers' goods, the retailers, the service trades, and the professions are forced to acquire what they need for the conduct of their own business from those purveyors who offer them at the cheapest price. If they were not intent upon buying in the cheapest market and arranging their processing of the factors of production so as to fill the demands of the consumers in the best and cheapest way, they would be forced to go out of business. More efficient men who succeeded better in buying and processing the factors of production would supplant them. The consumer is in a position to give free rein to his caprices and fancies. The entrepreneurs, capitalists, and farmers have their hands tied; they are bound to comply in their operations with the orders of the buying public. Every deviation from the lines prescribed by the demand of the consumers debits their account. The slightest deviation, whether willfully brought about or caused by error, bad judgment, or inefficiency, restricts their profits or makes them disappear. A more serious deviation results in losses and thus impairs or entirely absorbs their wealth. Capitalists, entrepreneurs, and landowners can only preserve and increase their wealth by filling best the orders of the consumers. They are not free to spend money which the consumers are not prepared to refund to them in paying more for the products. In the conduct of their business affairs they must be unfeeling and stony-hearted because the consumers, their bosses, are themselves unfeeling and stony-hearted.

The consumers determine ultimately not only the prices of the consumers' goods, but no less the prices of all factors of production. They determine the income of every member of the market economy. The consumers, not the entrepreneurs, pay ultimately the wages earned by every worker, the glamorous movie star as well as the charwoman. With every penny spent the consumers determine the direction of all production processes and the minutest details of the organization of all business activities. This state of affairs has been described by calling the market a democracy in which every penny gives a right to cast a ballot. It would be more correct to say that a democratic constitution is a scheme to assign to the citizens in the conduct of government the same supremacy the market economy gives them in their capacity as consumers. However, the comparison is imperfect. In the political democracy only the votes cast for the majority candidate or the majority plan are effective in shaping the course of affairs. The votes polled by the minority do not directly influence policies. But on the market no vote is cast in vain. Every penny spent has the power to work upon the production processes. The publishers cater not only to the majority by publishing detective stories, but also to the minority reading lyrical poetry and philosophical tracts. The bakeries bake bread not only for healthy people, but also for the sick on special diets. The decision of a consumer is carried into effect with the full momentum he gives it through his readiness to spend a definite amount of money.

It is true, in the market the various consumers have not the same voting right. The rich cast more votes than the poorer citizens. But this inequality is itself the outcome of a previous voting process. To be rich, in a pure market economy, is the outcome of success in filling best the demands of the consumers. A wealthy man can preserve his wealth only by continuing to serve the consumers in the most efficient way.

Thus the owners of the material factors of production and the entrepreneurs are virtually mandataries or trustees of the consumers, revocably appointed by an election daily repeated.

There is in the operation of a market economy only one instance in which the proprietary class is not completely subject to the supremacy of the consumers. Monopoly prices are an infringement of the sway of the consumers.

THE ILLUSION OF BUSINESS CONTROL

The orders given by businessmen in the conduct of their affairs can be heard and seen. Nobody can fail to become aware of them. Even messenger boys know that the boss runs things around the shop. But it requires a little more brains to notice the entrepreneur's dependence on the market. The orders given by the consumers are not tangible, they cannot be perceived by the senses. Many people lack the discernment to take cognizance of them. They fall victim to the delusion that entrepreneurs and capitalists are irresponsible autocrats whom nobody calls to account for their actions.

The outgrowth of this mentality is the practice of applying to business the terminology of political rule and military action. Successful businessmen are called kings or dukes, their enterprises an empire, a kingdom, or a dukedom. If this idiom were only a harmless metaphor, there would be no need to criticize it. But it is the source of serious errors which play a sinister role in contemporary doctrines.

Government is an apparatus of compulsion and coercion. It has the power to obtain obedience by force. The political sovereign, be it an autocrat or the people as represented by its mandataries, has power to crush rebellions as long as his ideological might subsists.

The position which entrepreneurs and capitalists occupy in the market economy is of a different character. A "chocolate king" has no power over the consumers, his patrons. He provides them with chocolate of the best possible quality and at the cheapest price. He does not rule the consumers, he serves them. The consumers are not tied to him. They are free to stop patronizing his shops. He

loses his "kingdom" if the consumers prefer to spend their pennies elsewhere. Nor does he "rule" his workers. He hires their services by paying them precisely that amount which the consumers are ready to restore to him in buying the product. Still less do the capitalists and entrepreneurs exercise political control. The civilized nations of Europe and America were long controlled by governments which did not considerably hinder the operation of the market economy. Today many of these countries too are dominated by parties which are hostile to capitalism and believe that every harm inflicted upon capitalists and entrepreneurs is extremely beneficial to the people.

In an unhampered market economy the capitalists and entrepreneurs cannot expect an advantage from bribing officeholders and politicians. On the other hand, the officeholders and politicians are not in a position to blackmail businessmen and to extort graft from them. In an interventionist country powerful pressure groups are intent upon securing for their members privileges at the expense of weaker groups and individuals. Then the businessmen may deem it expedient to protect themselves against discriminatory acts on the part of the executive officers and the legislature by bribery; once used to such methods, they may even try to employ them in order to secure privileges for themselves. At any rate the fact that businessmen corrupt politicians and officeholders and are blackmailed by such people does not indicate that they are supreme and rule the countries. It is those ruled — and not the rulers — who bribe and are paying tribute.

The majority of businessmen are prevented from resorting to bribery either by their moral convictions or by fear. They venture to preserve the free enterprise system and to defend themselves against discrimination by legitimate democratic methods. They form trade associations and try to influence public opinion. The results of these endeavors have been rather poor, as is evidenced by the triumphant advance of anticapitalist policies. The best that they have been able to achieve is to delay for a while some especially obnoxious measures.

Demagogues misrepresent this state of affairs in

the crassest way. They tell us that these associations of bankers and manufacturers are the true rulers of their countries and that the whole apparatus of what they call "plutodemocratic" government is dominated by them. A simple enumeration of the laws passed in the last decades by any country's legislature is enough to explode such legends.

◖◗ THE MYTH OF CONSUMER SOVEREIGNTY
Paul A. Baran

Until his death in 1964, Paul Baran was perhaps the most noted economist of Marxist persuasion teaching at a major American university — Stanford. His interests in political economy were wide-ranging, including problems of economic growth, monopoly, and police surveillance. In this essay he argues that the idea of consumer sovereignty under capitalism is an illusion.

Like the man condemned to death who was granted "freedom of choice" between being hanged and being shot, bourgeois economics is eternally plagued by the problem whether the irrationality of monopoly is better than the anarchy of competition; whether the cumulation of means of destruction is better than unemployment; whether inequality of income and wealth leading to saving and investment on the part of the rich is better than fair shares and greatly reduced saving and investment. In the same way the problem of consumers' sovereignty is viewed as the question whether the consumer — however much exposed to the barrage of advertising and high-pressure salesmanship — should be left free to spend his income in any way he pleases or be forced to ac-

cept a basket of goods which a "commissar" would judge to be best for him. It can be readily seen that placed before *this* dilemma, the economist is indeed confronted by a Hobson's choice. Kneeling awestricken before the absolute truth of the consumer's "revealed preferences" places him in the disturbing position of having to refuse to make any judgments on the resulting composition of output and hence on all the waste and cultural degradation which so obviously characterize our society. On the other hand, rejecting the consumer's revealed preferences as the *ultima ratio* in favor of a set of decisions imposed by government would be equally distressing, implying as it would the repudiation of all the teachings of welfare economics and — more importantly — of all the principles of individual freedom which the economist rightly strives to uphold.

THE CONSERVATIVE VIEW

The conservative reaction to this perplexity appears in two variants. One school of thought deals with the problem by denying its existence. This school holds that the molding of consumers' tastes and preferences by the advertising and high-pressure sales efforts of corporate business is nothing but a bogey, because in the long run no amount of persuasion and no ingenuity of salesmanship can change "human nature," can force upon the consumer what he does not want. Furthermore — so the argument runs — the revealed preferences of consumers yield results which are quite adequate and call for no particular improvements.

Another conservative current of thought takes a different tack. It freely acknowledges that the consumer's revealed preferences have nothing in common with the traditional notion of consumer *sovereignty*, that the power of the giant corporations is such as to mold consumers' tastes and preferences for the benefit of corporate interests, and that all of this has a deleterious effect on both our economy and our society.

Yet skeptical and realistic as the writers of this orientation are, they place the utmost emphasis on the fact that these irrationalities and calamities are *inherent* in the order of things, which they identify with the economic and social system of monopoly capitalism. "To touch the corporation deeply," remarks Professor Mason, "is to touch much else." And in our day touching "much else" is definitely not on the economist's agenda.

THE LIBERAL VIEW

This is not the stance of the so-called liberal. Considering the consumer's revealed preferences to be the source of our society's irrational allocation of resources, of its distressing moral and cultural condition, the liberal is exercised about the pernicious impact of advertising, about fraudulent product differentiation and artificial product obsolescence; he inveighs against the quality of culture purveyed by the educational system, Hollywood, the newspapers, the radio and TV networks; and, driven by this indignation, he arrives at the conclusion that "the choice is not whether consumers or a central planner should exercise sovereignty but whether and how the producer's power to ignore some consumers and influence the preferences of others should be curbed, modified, or shared in some ways." To accomplish this curbing, modifying, and sharing, he recommends a list of "remedies and policies" ranging from regulatory measures such as those taken by the Food and Drug Administration, through government support for opera houses and theaters, to the formation of Distinguished Citizens Committees the task of which would be to influence public opinion in the direction of rational choices and better taste.

Disappointing as it may be to many, there can be little doubt that at the present stage of capitalist development the conservative "realist" often comes nearer the truth than the liberal meliorist. Just as it makes no sense to deplore war casualties without attacking their cause, war, so it is meaningless to sound the alarm about advertising and all that accompanies it without clearly identifying the *locus* from which the pestilence emanates: the monopolistic and oligopolistic corporation and the non-price-competitive business practices which constitute an integral component of its *modus operandi*. Since this *locus* itself is never approached, is indeed treated as strictly out of bounds by Galbraith, Scitovsky,

and other liberal critics, since nothing is further from their minds (or at least their public utterances) than "touching deeply" the giant corporation, what can be expected from their recommending various regulatory boards and even their possible appointment to Distinguished Citizens Committees? One would think that the record of already existing regulatory agencies is sufficiently eloquent in showing that it is Big Business that does the regulating rather than *vice versa*. And is more evidence needed on the ineffectuality of the Food and Drug Administration, the Federal Trade Commission, and the Federal Communications Commission than has already been assembled thus far? Nor is there any need to elaborate on the profound impact on society exercised by the recent activities and reports of the President's most distinguished Commission on National Goals. But the liberal meliorists ignore all this. Treating the state as an entity which presides over society but does not form a part of it, which sets society's goals and reshuffles its output and income but remains unaffected by the prevailing relations of production and impervious to the dominant interests, they fall prey to a naive rationalism which, by nurturing illusions, merely contributes to the maintenance of the *status quo*.

AN ALTERNATIVE

The "realistic" conservative scores also over the liberal "do-gooder" in his general comprehension of the problem of consumer sovereignty. For in warning against exaggerating the impact of advertising, high-pressure salesmanship, and the like, on the preferences and choices of consumers, they occupy a position of formidable strength. Their statements that consumers like only what they care for and buy only what they wish to spend money on are obviously tautologies, but, being tautologies, they are equally obviously correct. From this, to be sure, it does not follow, as some business economists like to assert, that the barrage of advertising and salesmanship to which the consumer is continually exposed has *no* influence on the formation of his wants. But neither is it true that these business practices constitute *the* decisive factor in making the consumer want what he wants. Professor Henry C. Wallich comes closest to the spot where the dog is buried in his shrewd observation that "to argue that wants created by advertising are synthetic, are not genuine consumer wants is beside the point — it could be argued of all aspects of civilized existence." This, to be sure, is overstating the case. Human wants are not *all* wholly "synthetic," created by an almighty Madison Avenue (or "purified" and "ennobled" by a Madison Avenue "in reverse": government regulatory boards and/or Distinguished Citizens Committees for the Promotion of Good Taste): that view reflects the spirit of limitless manipulability of man which is so characteristic of the "men in gray flannel suits" who dominate the executive offices of corporations and the important bureaus of the government. . . . There is a nearly unanimous consensus among serious students of the problem. The issue is rather *the kind of social and economic order* that does the molding, the kind of "values," volitions, and preferences which it instills into the people under its sway. What renders the social and economic order of monopoly capitalism so irrational and destructive, so crippling to the individual's growth and happiness, is *not* that it influences, shapes, "synthesizes" the individual — as Professor Wallich suggests, every social and economic order does this — but rather *the kind* of influencing, shaping, and "synthesizing" which it perpetrates on its victims.

A clear understanding of this permits a further insight. The cancerous malaise of monopoly capitalism is not that it "happens" to squander a large part of its resources on the production of means of destruction, that it "happens" to allow corporations to engage in liminal and subliminal advertising, in peddling adulterated products, and in inundating human life with moronizing entertainment, commercialized religion, and debased "culture." The cancerous malaise of the system which renders it a formidable obstacle to human advancement, is that all this is not an assortment of fortuitously appearing attributes of the capitalist order, but the very basis of its existence and viability. And such being the case, bigger and better Food and Drug Administrations, a comprehensive network of Distinguished Citizens

Committees, and the like can merely spread a veil over the existing mess rather than clean up the mess itself. To use an earlier comparison once more: building sumptuous cemeteries and expensive monuments for the victims of war does not reduce their number. The best — and the worst — that such seemingly humanitarian efforts can accomplish is to dull people's sensitivity to brutality and cruelty, to reduce their horror of war.

But to return to the starting point of this argument. Neither I nor any other Marxist writers with whose works I am familiar, have ever advocated the abolition of consumer sovereignty and its replacement by the orders of a commissar. The attribution of such an advocacy to socialists is simply one aspect of the ignorance and misrepresentation of Marxian thought that are studiously cultivated by the powers that be. The real problem is an entirely different one, namely, whether an economic and social order should be tolerated in which the individual, from the very cradle on, is so shaped, molded, and "adjusted" as to become an easy prey of profit-greedy capitalist enterprise and a smoothly functioning object of capitalist exploitation and degradation. The Marxian socialist is in no doubt about the answer. Holding that mankind has now reached a level of productivity and knowledge which make it possible to transcend this system and replace it by a better one, he believes that a society can be developed in which the individual would be formed, influenced, and educated not by a profit- and market-determined economy, not by the "values" of corporate presidents and the outpourings of their hired scribes, but by a system of rationally planned production for use, by a universe of human relations determined by and oriented toward solidarity, cooperation, and freedom. Indeed, only in such a society can there be sovereignty of the individual *human being* — not of the "consumer" or the "producer," terms which in themselves reflect the lethal fragmentation of the human personality under capitalism. Only in such a society can the individual freely co-determine the amount of work done, the composition of output consumed, the nature of leisure activities engaged in — free from all the open and hidden persuaders whose motives are preservation of their privileges and maximization of their profits.

QUESTIONS

1. Von Mises compares the entrepreneur to a helmsman who steers the ship (the economy) but is subject to orders and control by the captain (the consumer). Evaluate this analogy. What is the value of an analogy?

2. What is the similarity between the market system and democracy? What does von Mises see as a crucial difference between "voting" in the marketplace versus voting in the election booth?

3. "A 'chocolate king' has no power over the consumers, his patrons." Under what conditions is this statement true? False? From your observation, do "chocolate kings" and other businessmen truly "venture to preserve the free enterprise system" as von Mises claims?

4. What are the two "conservative" views of consumer sovereignty delineated by Baran? How would you test the validity of these views — that is, how would you test or analyze the hypothesis that skillful advertising and promotion can or cannot entice someone to buy that which he or she does not "really want"?

5. What does it mean to advocate a "system of rationally planned production for use, by a universe of human relations determined by and oriented toward solidarity, cooperation, and freedom"?

6. Put yourself in the role of the great synthesizer. Is there a way you can reconcile von Mises and Baran?

PART FOUR

SUPPLY: FIRM BEHAVIOR

12 THE NONPROFIT FIRM: WHY IS IT ALWAYS BROKE?

William Baumol and
William G. Bowen

William Baumol is professor of economics at both New York University and Princeton University; William G. Bowen is both professor of economics and president of Princeton University. Their analysis of the nonprofit firm is based on a study of the economics of the performing arts done for the Twentieth Century Fund. Critics of profit-making enterprises should find this article particularly illuminating.

THE SETTING

Romanticism long ago fixed in our minds the idea that there is something inevitable about the association between artistic achievement and poverty. The starving artist has become a stereotype among whose overtones is the notion that squalor and misery are noble and inspiring. It is one of the happier attributes of our time that we have generally been disabused of this type of absurdity. We readily recognize that poverty is demeaning rather than inspiring — that instead of stimulating the artist it deprives him of the energy, time, or even the equipment with which to create or perform.

While we have come to accept the idea that artists are often impecunious, even a cursory encounter with the facts of the matter usually proves surprising.

A detailed and specific investigation of economic conditions in the performing arts was conducted by Senate and House Committees in 1961 and 1962, and the volumes of *Hearings* which resulted are very revealing. At that time the minimum weekly salary for Off-Broadway actors was $45 per week (it is currently $60); and what makes this figure significant is that most Off-Broadway actors are at the minimum. In such circumstances it is not difficult to see

Abridged from W. J. Baumol and W. G. Bowen, "On the Performing Arts: The Anatomy of Their Economic Problems," *American Economic Review Proceedings,* 55, no. 2 (May 1965), 495–502. Reprinted by permission.

why Joseph Papp, producer of the New York Shakespeare Festival, was able to report that "banks and landlords consider him [the actor] a credit risk without visible means of support."

Dancers are in even worse financial circumstances, as illustrated by the case of a leading modern dance company whose members normally receive $25 after a trip which frequently includes four days of travel, a day of rehearsals, and a public performance.

In the main, performing artists are employed by organizations — by orchestras, opera and dance companies, producers and impresarios, resident theater companies — and the underlying economic pressures which manifest themselves in low performer salaries are transmitted through these organizations. Inadequate financial flows to these groups can threaten not only the welfare of individual performers but also the very existence of the institutions serving the entrepreneurial and managerial functions in the field of the performing arts. And, notwithstanding the publicity that has been given to the alleged "cultural boom" in America, we continue to hear frequently of theatrical groups which collapse, of opera houses whose seasons are in danger, and performing arts organizations of all kinds for whom financial emergency seems to have become a way of life. It is this situation and the threat that it poses for the cultural prospects of our society which constitutes the setting for the study we have undertaken.

The first objective of our study is to explain the strained economic circumstances which beset performing companies, to determine whether they are attributable mainly to fortuitous historical circumstances, to mismanagement or poor institutional arrangements, or whether there is something fundamental in the economic order which accounts for these difficulties. On the basis of our analysis we hope to produce some conditional forecasts of the financial future of the performing arts, the prospective costs, the operating revenues likely to be associated with various levels of activity, and the proportion of the resultant financial gaps which one can expect to be met from current sources of contributed income.

BASIC ECONOMIC CHARACTERISTICS OF NONPROFIT ORGANIZATIONS

Before we turn to the special economic properties of the performing arts, it is useful to devote some discussion to the economics of non-profitmaking organizations in general, for only in this way can the difficulties which beset the performing arts be seen in perspective.

Nonprofit organizations as a group share at least two characteristics: (1) They earn no pecuniary return on invested capital and (2) they claim to fulfill some social purpose. These two features are not wholly independent. Any group which sought to fulfill no social purpose and earned no financial return would presumably disappear from the landscape. Moreover, its goals themselves often help explain why no money is earned by such an organization. While an automobile producer may take pride in the quality of his cars, he is much less likely to regard product quality per se as an ultimate objective of the enterprise than is the head of a nonprofit organization. Nor is the auto producer likely to be nearly as concerned about the social composition of his clientele.

The significant point is that the objectives of the typical nonprofit organization are by their very nature designed to keep it constantly on the brink of financial catastrophe, for to such a group the quality of the services which it provides becomes an end in itself. Better research, more adequate hospital facilities, more generous rehearsal time, better training for those engaged in these activities — all these are not merely incidental desiderata. They are fundamental goals in themselves, and with objectives such as these, the likelihood of surplus funds is slim indeed. These goals constitute bottomless receptacles into which limitless funds can be poured. As soon as more money becomes available to a nonprofit organization, corresponding new uses can easily be found, and still other uses for which no financing has been provided will inevitably arise to take their place. Any lively nonprofit organization always has a group of projects which it cannot afford to undertake and for whose realization it looks hopefully to the future. Once this fundamental fact is grasped, it is hardly surprising that such groups feel themselves constantly strapped. It becomes clear that they are simply built that way.[1]

Nor is it just through its quality aspirations that the social goals of the nonprofit enterprise contribute to its financial difficulties. The concern of the typical nonprofit organization for the size and composition of its clientele often causes operating revenue to be lower than would be the case if services were priced to satisfy a simple profit-maximization goal. Since such a group normally considers itself to be a supplier of virtue, it is natural that it should seek to distribute its bounty as widely and as equitably as possible. The group is usually determined to prevent income and wealth alone from deciding who is to have priority in the consumption of its services. It wishes to offer its products to the needy and the deserving — to students, to the impecunious, to those initially not interested in consuming them, and to a variety of others to whom high prices would serve as an effective deterrent to consumption. In short, a low price for the product of a nonprofit group is normally an inevitable consequence of its objectives, and indeed sometimes becomes an article of faith. The ancient doctrine of "just price" is imbedded in the operations of these groups and carries with it all the difficulties which inevitably accompany an attempt to put it into practice.

The desire to provide a product of as high a quality as possible and to distribute the product in a manner other than that which maximizes revenue combine to produce a situation which is unusual in yet another respect. For such an enterprise a substantial increase in the demand for its product may well worsen the organization's financial health! An

---

[1] The fact that any nonprofit organization can always find uses for a temporary excess of funds — and indeed may be embarrassed to report to its contributors that it has some money left at the end of the year — makes it very difficult to determine its cost functions. If an auto producer finds that a sudden increase in demand has swollen his receipts, he is only too happy to report higher profits; a nonprofit enterprise, however, may well use the extra revenue in a way which, in effect, deliberately raises its costs.

increased number of student applications, an increased number of hospital patients, an increased number of orchestral performances may well increase the size of the contributions required for solvency. More generally, it follows that, contrary to widespread impressions, the much publicized cultural and educational "booms," whatever their composition, may in many cases prove a very mixed financial blessing.

Yet even in such circumstances the organizations cannot simply refuse to expand their activities in response to an increase in demand. By such a refusal the organization would renege on its fundamental objectives, and, incidentally, it might even produce a loss in private and community support.

THE PERFORMING ARTS IN PARTICULAR

It is apparent that all of the standard problems of nonprofit organizations which have just been discussed beset the performing arts. It is not surprising, therefore, that the survival of the great majority of its organizations requires a constant flow of contributions. We can then easily understand why the arts find themselves in their present unhappy financial circumstances. But, up to this point, our discussion has offered no portents for the future. Here we don the inherited mantle of the dismal scientist and argue that one can read the prospects of the arts tomorrow in the economic structure which characterizes them today. The evidence will suggest that the prospects offer no grounds for complacency — that there are fundamental reasons to expect the financial strains which beset the performing arts organizations to increase, chronically, with the passage of time.

To understand the prospective developments on the cost side, it is necessary to digress briefly and consider in general terms the implications of differential rates of growth in productivity within the economy for the relative costs of its various outputs. Let us think of an economy divided into two sectors: one in which productivity is rising and another where productivity is stable. As an illustration, let us suppose that where technological improvements are possible they lead to an increase in

output per man-hour of 4 percent per annum, but that output per man-hour remains absolutely constant in the stable productivity sector. If these sectors are assigned equal weights in the construction of an economy-wide productivity index, the aggregate rate of increase in output per man-hour will be 2 percent per annum. For the moment let us assume that there is only one grade of labor, that labor is free to move back and forth between sectors, and that the real wage rate rises *pari passu* with the aggregate rate of change of productivity, at 2 percent per annum. Finally, let us suppose that the money supply and the level of aggregate demand are controlled in such a way that the price level is kept stable. Assuming that there are no changes in the shares of capital and labor, this means that money wages will also increase at the rate of 2 percent a year.

The implications of this simple model for costs in the two sectors are straightforward. In the rising productivity sector, output per man-hour increases more rapidly than the money wage rate and labor costs per unit must therefore decline. However, in the sector where productivity is stable, there is no offsetting improvement in output per man-hour, and so every increase in money wages is translated automatically into an equivalent increase in unit labor costs — 2 percent per annum in our example. It should be noted that the extent of the increase in costs in the stable productivity sector varies directly with the economy-wide rate of increase in output per man-hour. The faster the general pace of technological advance, the greater will be the increase in the overall wage level and the greater the upward pressure on costs in those industries which do not enjoy increased productivity. Faster technological progress is no blessing for the laggards, at least as far as their costs are concerned.

It is apparent that the live performing arts belong to the stable productivity sector of our economy. The legitimate theater, the symphony orchestra, the chamber group, the opera, the dance — all can serve as textbook illustrations of activities offering little opportunity for major technological change. The output per man-hour of the violinist playing a

Schubert quartet in a standard concert hall is relatively fixed, and it is fairly difficult to reduce the number of actors necessary for a performance of *Henry IV*, Part II.

Moreover, from the standpoint of long-term developments, the essence of the matter is not absolute or relative levels of productivity at a given date but the rates of change in productivity over time. This means that even if the arts could somehow manage to effect technological economies, they would not solve their long-term cost problem if such savings were once-and-for-all in nature. In order to join the ranks of the rising productivity industries, the arts would somehow have to learn not only to increase output per man-hour but to continue to do so into the indefinite future. Otherwise, they must at some juncture fall behind the technologically progressive industries and experience increases in costs which stem not from their own decisions but from the inexorable march of technological change in other parts of the economy.

True, some inefficiences of operation are to be found in the field, and their elimination can help matters somewhat. Moreover, performing arts organizations can reduce the rate of increase in their unit costs by permitting some deterioration in the quality of their product — by fewer rehearsals, the use of more poorly trained performers, shoddy costumes and scenery. But such a course is never popular with organizations dedicated to quality, and, furthermore, it may lead to loss of audience and community support. Nevertheless, it is not an uncommon "temporary" expedient, imposed by the realization that the cutting of corners may be the only alternative to abandonment of the enterprise.

There is one other important avenue for cost saving open to the performing arts which has so far not been considered. We refer to wages paid performers. In the simple model sketched above, we postulated a situation in which a single, market-clearing wage was paid to all persons regardless of the industry in which they were employed. In actual fact, the live performing arts constitute a rather special labor market — a market in which the need for great native ability and extensive training limits the supply, but in which the psychic returns to those who meet these tests often offers a very substantial inducement to remain in the field. For these reasons, the performing arts are relatively insensitive to general wage trends, especially in the short run. It is largely for this reason that performing arts organizations in financial difficulty have often managed to shift part of their financial burden back to the performers — and to the managements, who also are generally very poorly paid by commercial standards. The level of the incomes in this general field must be considered remarkably low by any standards, and particularly so in light of the heavy investment that has often been made by the artists in their education, training, and equipment. And it is surely explained at least in part by the willingness of those who work in these fields to sacrifice money income for the less material pleasures of their participation in the arts.

In sum, the cost structure of the performing arts organizations promises them no easier future. One might anticipate, therefore, that this structural problem would produce discernible effects on pricing policy. Certainly, in most of the industries in which productivity is stable, we would expect the price of the product or service to rise relative to the general price level. And there is a widespread impression that the arts have indeed behaved in accord with this anticipation — that ticket prices have been soaring. Yet our preliminary evidence suggests strongly that this view is incorrect and is largely a product of money illusion. Indeed, our preliminary data indicate that the rate of increase of ticket prices has barely managed to keep up with the price level and has lagged substantially behind increases in costs.

One might undertake to account for the surprisingly modest rate of increase in ticket prices in terms of a revenue maximization model — on the hypothesis that arts organizations believe the demand for their product to be highly elastic. We suspect, however, that a more valid explanation is the role of a doctrine of just price in the objectives of these organizations.

The tendency for increases in prices to lag behind increases in costs means simply that arts organizations have had to raise larger and larger sums from their contributors — and our analysis leads us to expect this trend to continue. Thus our analysis has offered us not only an explanation for the current state of affairs; it has also provided us with a basis for speculation about the future. What it has shown will not, we are afraid, be reassuring to those to whom ready availability of arts constitutes an important objective of society. If our model is valid, and if, as may be suspected, there are limits to the amounts that can be obtained from private contributors, increased support from other sources will have to be found if the performing arts are to continue their present role in the cultural life of this country and especially if it is intended that they will expand their role and flourish.

QUESTIONS

1. Many colleges and universities, including some of the nation's most prestigious, claim that they either face or are likely soon to face a financial crisis. Does this surprise you, or would you be more surprised to learn the contrary? Why?

2. Such divergent nonprofit institutions as government agencies and repertory societies seldom show a surplus at the end of their fiscal year. Why would a nonprofit organization be reluctant to show a temporary surplus of funds?

3. The authors argue that nonprofit entertainment organizations frequently price their product on the basis of a "just price" — that is, a price that is below that which would earn the most revenues so that the impecunious and the uninterested will have greater incentive to attend. How would you test the validity of this argument? What evidence have you observed consistent with their argument?

4. Restate the argument that rising productivity in other sectors of the economy may hamper the development of the performing arts. What, then, would be the implications of productivity gains in the performing arts outstripping those of other sectors?

THE UNIVERSITY AS A FIRM, THE NCAA AS A CARTEL
James V. Koch

This article provides insight into the behavior of both a "firm" and a "cartel," the latter being a group of firms that conspire together to avoid competition. James V. Koch provocatively applies the economic theory of the firm and the cartel to the "business" of college athletics. Professor Koch has many research interests besides the economics of sports. These include education, affirmative action, drug control, and household wealth. He chairs the economics department at Illinois State University.

Despite the claims of the National Collegiate Athletic Association (NCAA) that it is a champion of amateur athletics and physical fitness in colleges and universities, the NCAA is in fact a business cartel composed of university-firms which have varying desires to restrict competition and maximize profits in the area of intercollegiate athletics. The aims and activities of the university-firms in the NCAA are extremely diverse, and therein lies the most important cause of both the long-term and the contemporary problems which have confronted the NCAA. This diversity also explains the recent move of the Association to establish a three-division structure in which the schools operating major intercollegiate athletic programs are grouped in Division I and the remaining schools — perhaps two-thirds of the NCAA members — are organized in Divisions II and III. Economic theory in the area of cartelization has proven to be a remarkably accurate predictor of the stresses and strains which have beset the NCAA. That same theory also offers some insights into the recent move to a three-division structure.

THE NCAA AS A CARTEL

The NCAA is easily the most powerful and the most prestigious organization regulating intercollegiate

Abridged from James V. Koch, "A Troubled Cartel: The NCAA," in *Law and Contemporary Problems*, 38, no. 1, (Winter-Spring, 1973), 135—150. Reprinted by permission.

athletic competition in the United States today. Over 660 colleges and universities are members of the NCAA, and the NCAA will soon be conducting over forty national championships in over twenty sports in addition to the rule-making, record-keeping, and enforcement functions which characterize any cartel.

It is not apparent to some (and particularly to the NCAA itself) that the Association is a cartel which restricts competition in order to further the ends of its members. The NCAA states officially that it is interested only in the "amateur student-athlete" who engages in intercollegiate athletics "for the physical, mental, social and educational benefits he derives therefrom and to whom athletics is an avocation." The NCAA proclaims that its goals are the promotion of "educational leadership, physical fitness, sports participation." Nowhere are goals of profit maximization, cost minimization, or restriction of competition mentioned. However, as we shall see, the actions of the NCAA clearly stamp it as a moderately successful business cartel whose success has been limited primarily by the heterogeneity of its membership.

A cartel has been defined as an organization of firms which makes agreements concerning such matters as prices, outputs, market areas, the use and construction of productive capacity, and advertising expenditures. The NCAA does all of these in the area of intercollegiate athletics in that it: (a) sets the maximum price that can be paid for intercollegiate athletes; (b) regulates the quantity of athletes that can be purchased in a given time period; (c) regulates the duration and intensity of usage of those athletes; (d) occasionally fixes the price at which sports outputs can be sold (for example, the setting of ticket prices at NCAA championship events which are held on the campuses of cartel members); (e) periodically informs cartel members about transactions, costs, market conditions, and sales techniques; (f) occasionally pools and distributes portions of the cartel's profits, particularly those which result from intercollegiate football and basketball; and (g) polices the behavior of the members of the cartel and levies penalties against those members who are deemed to be in violation of cartel rules and regulations.

If the university-firms which are members of the NCAA can be viewed as firms buying inputs and producing outputs, then it is apparent that by far the most detailed restrictions are imposed upon the activities of the firms on the input side of the market. While many different inputs are utilized to produce the output known as intercollegiate sports, the two inputs which are of most interest are the other teams, that is, the competition, and the "student-athletes" purchased by the university-firms.

Competition is an indispensable input to the success of intercollegiate athletics and, when such ingredient is absent, spectators lose interest in the game in question. Only a masochist would have substantial interest in football games between the University of Nebraska and the club team of the University of Chicago. However, a game between the Universities of Nebraska and Oklahoma is a contest and is therefore of great interest to paying spectators. The relevant point here is, of course, that it is in the best interests of the NCAA and its component members to strive by rule, fiat, and enforcement to make competition reasonably equal among members that choose to compete with each other. Cartel limitations upon the number of athletic scholarships that can be granted by a university-firm, the establishment of Division I composed predominantly of universities supporting big-time programs and Divisions II and III composed of universities which maintain more modest goals and expectations, and the division of profits from NCAA activities among members are examples of the NCAA's continual attempt to make the athletic competition among its members strenuous and competitively equal in the sense of the outcome not being predetermined. Tight athletic contests and conference races fill stadiums.

The most detailed and interesting rules imposed by the cartel occur in the area of student-athletes. NCAA rules limit the number of student-athletes that a given university-firm can purchase, how long these student-athletes may be used, and the prices that may be paid for them. Furthermore, the

NCAA has imposed stringent rules limiting the manner in which competing university-firms may bid for the newest crop of prospective student-athletes. Such rules limit the number of visits which a student-athlete may make to a given campus, the amount of his expenses that may be covered by the university-firm, and so forth. The intent, and sometimes also the effect, of such rules is to reduce recruiting and operating costs by restraining competition.

THE CARTEL'S STRUCTURE
AS A SOURCE OF TROUBLE

The most successful business cartels pool and divide profits among the cartel members. Less successful cartels are often limited to dividing prospective sales among members, designating market territories, and reducing costs of competition in whatever manner possible. The curse which ends the existence of most cartels is the practice of chiseling: if one firm can secretly lower prices, steal sales, or evade the rules of the cartel, then the cartel is likely to be ineffective and dissolve.

Successful cartels attain their success by forcing cartel members to obey cartel rules and by making it impossible for new firms to join the cartel except at high cost. The market structure of the cartel is a prime determinant of the cartel's ability to force its members to conform and its ability to keep unwanted members out.

A number of facets of market structure are critically important to a cartel's operation.

Number of Firms Successful cartels seldom have a large number of member firms. When the number of cartel members is small, the behavior of cartel members can more easily be policed. Therein lies a portion of the NCAA's troubles. The NCAA has well over 600 members, and the activities of all of these members are virtually impossible to monitor effectively. While the success of the monitoring effort may increase under the three-division structure, the size of each division is still such as to limit cartel control.

Number of Points of Initiative Successful cartels are usually characterized by few points of initiative in the markets the cartel faces. That is, the number of points where competition, purchasing, and selling can take place is limited. A limited number of points of initiative means that it is much easier for the cartel to observe the behavior of its members. Once again, the NCAA falls short here, for the number of points of initiative is almost limitless. A large number of student-athletes exists, to say nothing of the large number of alumni and friends of university-firms that might violate rules. Furthermore, there is no need for the university-firm that wishes to cheat to do so on the university campus. Hence, transactions can take place nearly any place, at any time, and among sometimes unknown individuals.

Transactions Publicized Internally If all transactions made by cartel members are immediately publicized to the remainder of the cartel members, then it is unlikely that effective chiseling can take place. The NCAA, of course, attempts to publicize internal transactions such as the signing of a student-athlete, the payment of a fine, and so forth. Nonetheless, the NCAA is clearly incapable of reporting all transactions because of the large number of points of initiative in the market. Transactions by NCAA members simply are not reported immediately and openly to NCAA members in the fashion of the New York Stock Exchange. This makes chiseling easier and heightens the probability of ineffectiveness on the part of the NCAA.

Transactions Secret Externally A successful cartel ordinarily wishes its own members to be fully informed of transactions by its members, but at the same time wishes to hide its members' actions from outsiders. The cartel does not function effectively when its laundry is in public view. Public reporting of transactions, fines, and profits tends to attract interest, possible competition, and even governmental regulation. The NCAA is clearly deficient as a cartel in this respect. Its actions are reported far and wide in the press and those who dislike its rules and regulations have increasingly been seeking relief in the courts. Legislative investigative panels delve into the NCAA's affairs. Consequently, it is almost impossible for the NCAA to maximize profits and minimize costs blatantly or for the NCAA to chastise severely those who break its rules, because the NCAA is almost regarded as the public domain.

Existence of Barriers to Entry   The most successful cartels typically are beneficiaries of substantial barriers to the entry of new firms into the markets where the cartel members operate. That is, it is usually the case with successful cartels that newly entering firms would suffer some cost disadvantage which does not accrue to the firms already in the cartel. The NCAA also falls short here. It is indeed difficult for the NCAA to refuse membership to any university-firm that states that it will abide by the rules of the cartel. The public domain status of the NCAA makes it nearly impossible for the NCAA arbitrarily to state that a school will not be allowed to join the Association. Not only would such an action violate the slogans of the NCAA concerning the promotion of amateur athletics, but the action also would probably result in legislation or legal action which would force the NCAA's hand. Hence, nearly every university-firm can join the NCAA, and over 600 have.

Similarity of Member Interests and Costs   Cartels which contain members who have greatly dissimilar interests and costs generally are not effective because any rule which fits one type of member is often obnoxious to other members. Until recently the NCAA clearly was subject to this failing. University-firms, such as UCLA, which operate gigantic multi-million dollar athletic programs have little or nothing in common with university-firms such as Messiah College, which purchase no student-athletes and often charge no admission to athletic events. Consequently, a rule or regulation which was advocated by UCLA often would have been objected to by Messiah College. When dissimilar interest and costs structures characterize a cartel, that cartel either breaks up or becomes ineffective. The NCAA

has been largely characterized by ineffectiveness despite its domination by university-firms operating big-time programs. This situation supplied the major impetus for the recent reorganization of the NCAA into three divisions, which is intended to lessen the extent of dissimilarity within each decision-making body.

Purchasers Without Monopsony Power   A frequent characteristic of successful cartels is the fact that they sell their output to customers who are often small in size and have little economic clout or monopsony power. Such is largely the case with the NCAA. The single spectator to whom the NCAA sells its output has little influence over ticket prices or even the number of games played. Reversing the buyer-seller relationship for a moment, when the NCAA is the customer, it once again usually deals with sellers who have relatively little monopoly power. A single high school star may indeed be able to influence the price a university-firm pays him, but that is not the general case. The majority of student-athletes are purchased by university-firms in the NCAA for the standard "full ride" (tuition, room, board, books, and $15 per month for "laundry money"). Of course, the value of tuition, room, and board is not the same at all university-firms, and this does introduce a permissible element of price competition into the market.

In sum, the characteristics of market structure that most often are associated with successful cartels are frequently absent in the case of the NCAA. For a long time, the NCAA found it almost impossible to reconcile the conflicts inherent within its heterogeneous membership. As Darrell Royal, the well-known football coach of the University of Texas, so aptly put it, "Texas doesn't want Hofstra telling it what to do and vice-versa." The new divisional structure represents an attempt to respond to Royal's concern. But even if Texas and Hofstra belong to different divisions under the recent reorganization, the prevailing market structure makes it highly probable that considerable cheating would occur in any case and that the NCAA would face many of its present problems.

INTERNAL ADJUSTMENTS BY THE NCAA

It would be quite incorrect to imply that the NCAA has not made some attempts to lessen the stresses which are evident within it. The most important readjustment of the NCAA occurred at a special convention of the Association on August 6, 1973. The member colleges and universities subdivided the NCAA into three divisions, each of which will legislate its own rules of conduct relative to factors such as the number of scholarships, freshman eligibility, and the like. This proposal was successful even though an earlier proposal involving separation into two divisions was defeated at the January, 1973, Convention.

There are several reasons why the three-division plan was ultimately approved despite earlier opposition. First, the plan allows each university-firm to select freely the division in which it wishes to participate, with the exception of the 126 colleges rated major football institutions, which must join Division I. Second, each division will be able to write its own rules and will have only limited obligations to university-firms not in the same division. Third, and possibly most important, a number of large university-firms operating big-time programs have threatened to leave the NCAA and construct an organization which would negotiate with national television networks for the sole benefit of these university-firms. It is estimated that a television contract between a national television network and the fifty most prestigious football teams might be worth twenty-five million dollars. The current television contract which the NCAA has with the ABC network is for a lesser amount of money, primarily because ABC is forced to televise many games that it would not show if allowed to make the choices. Should the ABC television network be guaranteed, through a contract with a group of university-firms similar to the top fifty football schools mentioned above, that it could televise the most interesting contests without regard to regional considerations and NCAA politics, it would be willing to pay increased amounts of money for such a contract because of the high viewer ratings that would result.

Furthermore, the university-firms involved would be more satisfied because they would not be forced to split lucrative television revenues with the remainder of the NCAA membership.

One of the first rules that will probably be changed in Division I is the newly voted NCAA limitation upon the number of athletic scholarships that can be granted by any given university-firm. At its January, 1973, Convention, the NCAA voted to limit the overall number of athletic scholarships that can be in effect at a single university-firm to 229, with 75 scholarships being the limitation in football, and 13 scholarships being the limitation in basketball. Some university-firms currently have as many as 150 scholarships in effect in football, and the 75 scholarship limitation was passed over their protests. At the same time, the Division I members are likely to maintain scholarship limitations in the so-called minor sports, such as fencing and golf, in order to reduce costs of competition. In general, one can readily predict that those sports which generate spectator interest and revenues will be the least likely to have meaningful numerical scholarship limitations.

PREDICTED FUTURE BEHAVIOR

The reorganization eliminated a major source of discontent with the NCAA. Those university-firms which join Division I, however, will still face the perennial problem of matching expenditures to revenues. The major area where expenses might be reduced is in expenditures made in order to recruit and maintain student-athletes. The NCAA currently has no rule allowing one university-firm to sign a prospective student-athlete to a binding contract that prevents other NCAA members from negotiating with or utilizing him. Division I of the NCAA is likely to create its own national letter of intent for each sport and, in addition, designate a different signing date for each sport in order to reduce the time and expense incurred when the recruiting season is overly long.

There has also been talk in the NCAA of establishing a draft system for high school athletes similar to that carried out by admittedly professional leagues. Such a system is likely first to be established on a conference basis. The University of Michigan, for example, might obtain the right to negotiate with a given high school prospect, and no other Big Ten university-firm could compete with the University of Michigan for that individual's athletic services. A draft system would reduce recruiting costs and could lead to a conference-wide or nation-wide agreement concerning a reduction in the financial aid given student-athletes. The current free-wheeling competition among university-firms allows a prospective student-athlete to whipsaw one university-firm against another in order to obtain the most attractive terms.

The university-firms of the NCAA are often referred to as training grounds for admittedly professional athletics. The essence of this view is that the NCAA university-firms bear the cost of training prospective professional athletes and receive little in return from professional sports. This has led to the suggestion that the NCAA university-firm should be allowed to sign their student-athletes to long-term contracts for their services. Professional leagues or teams would then be compelled to purchase the contract of the student-athlete from the university-firms and would, as a result, be forced to assume a major portion of the costs of training him.

CONCLUSION

Despite its protestations, the NCAA does act as a cartel. The success of the cartel has been limited by the market structure of intercollegiate athletics, but there are signs that the restructuring of the NCAA will increase the effectiveness of its cartel. The stimulation for restructuring the NCAA has come from a host of legal actions taken against the Association, by its own members and by the athletes that it regulates, and from the threat of some members of the cartel to leave the NCAA and to construct their own organization which would be responsive to their needs and desires.

QUESTIONS

1. On what basis does Professor Koch make his case that the NCAA is a cartel? What behavior on the part of the NCAA would run counter to his thesis?
2. What are the aims of a cartel and what tactics are taken to secure these aims?
3. What does Professor Koch see as the primary "curse" of a cartel? What forms does this "curse" take in intercollegiate athletics? What forms might it take in a cartel of aluminum producers?

14 AN ALMOST PRACTICAL SOLUTION TO AIRLINE OVERBOOKING
Julian L. Simon

A Pareto optimal move, one of the subtlest concepts in economic science, basically means a move that economically benefits at least one person without making anyone else worse off. Below, Julian L. Simon illustrates a Pareto optimal policy with his unusual proposal to solve the problem of overbooking on airlines. Professor Simon has often combined his training in both economic theory and business administration in a skillful and innovative manner. He is on the faculty at the University of Illinois, Urbana and is particularly known for his research on advertising.

Perhaps the reader has suffered a fit of impotent rage at being told that he could not board an aeroplane for which he held a valid ticket. The explanation is clear, and no angry letter to the president of the airline will rectify the mistake, for mistake it was not. The airline gambles on a certain number of cancellations, and therefore sometimes sells more

Abridged from Julian L. Simon, "An Almost Practical Solution to Airline Overbooking," in *Journal of Transport Economics and Policy*, 2, no. 2 (May 1968), 1—2.

tickets than there are seats. Naturally there are sometimes more seat claimants than seats.

The solution is simple. All that need happen when there is overbooking is that an airline agent distributes among the ticket-holders an envelope and a bid form, instructing each person to write down the lowest sum of money he is willing to accept in return for waiting for the next flight. The lowest bidder is paid in cash and given a ticket for the next flight. All other passengers board the plane and complete the flight to their destination.

All parties benefit, and no party loses. All passengers either complete their flight or are recompensed by a sum which they value more than the immediate completion of the flight. And the airlines could also gain, because they would be able to overbook to a higher degree than at present, and hence fly their planes closer to seat capacity.

The level of optimum overbooking would be an easy computation, the parameters of which are only the probability of more claimants than seats at any given booking level, and the average low bid price. As a crude way of finding the optimum, an airline could first implement the bid system at present booking levels, and then increase the booking level in steps until the maximum net revenue point was reached. It is possible that the maximum might not be reached before all flights were filled to capacity.

One might wonder whether the lowest bid might not sometimes be so high as to make the scheme unprofitable for the airline. It seems unlikely that among a planeful of independent individuals there would not be one or two or three whose price would not be a tenth or a half or even the ticket price itself, and the airline would surely be ahead of the game even if the price were many times that high. An astronomical price would probably be the sign of a cartel, which would only be likely if an organization (such as a corporation) had bought all the seats on a flight and was in a position to enforce sanctions on a price cutter. It should be easy to prevent such exceptional situations by putting a high but not astronomical maximum on the winning bid price. And of course there is no danger from professional lottery players because the cost of a ticket

(for the plane and to the lottery) would make it a very poor bet.

If the innovating airline were particularly cautious it could begin the scheme with tourist-class passengers, whose bid price should be lower than that of first-class passengers.

This problem has the rare property that the solution is clearly closer to a Pareto optimum than is the present condition. All one is doing is to allow exchange (of time utilities) by auction, where no exchange is now possible. There are no trade-offs of utility between one group and another because no one is a loser.

But of course this scheme will not be taken up by the airlines. Why? Their first response will probably be "The administrative difficulties would be too great." The reader may judge this for himself. Next they will suggest that the scheme will not increase net revenue. But the *a priori* arguments to the contrary make the scheme worth a trial, and the trial would cost practically nothing and would require no commitment.

What are the real reasons why this scheme will not be adopted? Probably that "It just isn't done," because such an auction does not seem decorous; it smacks of the pushcart rather than the one price store; it is "embarrassing" and "crass," *i.e.,* frankly commercial, like "being in trade" in Victorian England.

Failure to adopt a scheme such as this, which would give a competitive advantage to the first adopter and then benefit all competitors, will give a further indication of the type of "competitive" atmosphere in which large companies such as the airlines live.

QUESTIONS

1. Why do airlines sometimes overbook the number of passengers for a given flight? What scheme does Professor Simon recommend for solving the overbooking problem? In what way might his proposal be superior to an outright prohibition on overbooking?

2. Professor Simon claims his proposal is Pareto

optimal in that no one is made any worse off because of its adoption and use. Why is the person who bids the lowest in the auction for available seats not made worse off? He or she will not, after all, be able to fly as first expected?

3. What other policy could you propose in any area of the economy that would have the attribute of being Pareto optimal?

15 THE SOCIAL RESPONSIBILITY OF BUSINESS IS TO INCREASE ITS PROFITS
Milton Friedman

Milton Friedman, of the University of Chicago, is one of the world's most widely read economists. Esteem for him comes from his well-known work in economic analysis; his notoriety stems from his entrenched defense of individualism and the free-market economy. He is both a former president of the American Economics Association and a Nobel laureate in economics. This essay, which should be read in conjunction with the following selection by Kenneth Arrow, argues that businesses should concentrate on increasing their profits. Indeed, Friedman maintains that businesspeople who encourage social responsibility in business are hypocrites, guilty of loose talk, or else puppets of those who would destroy the market mechanism.

When I hear businessmen speak eloquently about the "social responsibilities of business in a free-enterprise system," I am reminded of the wonderful line about the Frenchman who discovered at the age of 70 that he had been speaking prose all his life. The businessmen believe that they are defending free enterprise when they declaim that business is not concerned "merely" with profit but also with

Abridged from Milton Friedman, "The Social Responsibility of Business Is to Increase Its Profits," *The New York Times Magazine,* September 13, 1970. © 1970 by The New York Times Company. Reprinted by permission.

promoting desirable "social" ends; that business has a "social conscience" and takes seriously its responsibilities for providing employment, eliminating discrimination, avoiding pollution and whatever else may be the catchwords of the contemporary crop of reformers. In fact they are — or would be if they or anyone else took them seriously — preaching pure and unadulterated socialism. Businessmen who talk this way are unwitting puppets of the intellectual forces that have been undermining the basis of a free society these past decades.

In a free-enterprise, private-property system, a corporate executive is an employee of the owners of the business. He has direct responsibility to his employers. That responsibility is to conduct the business in accordance with their desires, which generally will be to make as much money as possible while conforming to the basic rules of the society, both those embodied in law and those embodied in ethical custom. Of course, in some cases his employers may have a different objective. A group of persons might establish a corporation for an eleemosynary purpose — for example, a hospital or a school. The manager of such a corporation will not have money profit as his objective but the rendering of certain services.

In either case, the key point is that, in his capacity as a corporate executive, the manager is the agent of the individuals who own the corporation or establish the eleemosynary institution, and his primary responsibility is to them.

What does it mean to say that the corporate executive has a "social responsibility" in his capacity as businessman? If this statement is not pure rhetoric, it must mean that he is to act in some way that is not in the interest of his employers. For example, that he is to refrain from increasing the price of the product in order to contribute to the social objective of preventing inflation, even though a price increase would be in the best interests of the corporation. Or that he is to make expenditures on reducing pollution beyond the amount that is in the best interests of the corporation or that is required by law in order to contribute to the social objective of improving the environment. Or that, at the expense of corporate profits, he is to hire "hard-core" unemployed instead of better-qualified available workmen to contribute to the social objective of reducing poverty.

In each of these cases, the corporate executive would be spending someone else's money for a general social interest. Insofar as his actions in accord with his "social responsibility" reduce returns to stockholders, he is spending their money. Insofar as his actions raise the price to customers, he is spending the customers' money. Insofar as his actions lower the wages of some employees, he is spending their money.

The stockholders or the customers or the employees could separately spend their own money on the particular action if they wished to do so. The executive is exercising a distinct "social responsibility," rather than serving as an agent of the stockholders or the customers or the employees, only if he spends the money in a different way than they would have spent it.

But if he does this, he is in effect imposing taxes, on the one hand, and deciding how the tax proceeds shall be spent, on the other.

We have established elaborate constitutional, parliamentary and judicial provisions to control these functions, to assure that taxes are imposed so far as possible in accordance with the preferences and desires of the public — after all, "taxation without representation" was one of the battle cries of the American Revolution. We have a system of checks and balances to separate the legislative function of imposing taxes and enacting expenditures from the executive function of collecting taxes and administering expenditure programs and from the judicial function of mediating disputes and interpreting the law.

Here the businessman — self-selected or appointed directly or indirectly by stockholders — is to be simultaneously legislator, executive and jurist. He is to decide whom to tax by how much and for what purpose, and he is to spend the proceeds — all this guided only by general exhortations from on high to restrain inflation, improve the environment, fight poverty and so on and on.

The whole justification for permitting the corporate executive to be selected by the stockholders is that the executive is an agent serving the interests of his principal. This justification disappears when the corporate executive imposes taxes and spends the proceeds for "social" purposes. He becomes in effect a public employee, a civil servant, even though he remains in name an employee of a private enterprise. On grounds of political principle, it is intolerable that such civil servants — insofar as their actions in the name of social responsibility are real and not just window-dressing — should be selected as they are now. If they are to be civil servants, then they must be selected through a political process. If they are to impose taxes and make expenditures to foster "social" objectives, then political machinery must be set up to guide the assessment of taxes and to determine through a political process the objectives to be served.

This is the basic reason why the doctrine of "social responsibility" involves the acceptance of the socialist view that political mechanisms, not market mechanisms, are the appropriate way to determine the allocation of scarce resources to alternative uses.

On the grounds of consequences, can the corporate executive in fact discharge his alleged "social responsibilities"? On the one hand, suppose he could get away with spending the stockholders' or customers' or employees' money. How is he to know how to spend it? He is told that he must contribute to fighting inflation. How is he to know what action of his will contribute to that end? He is presumably an expert in running his company — in producing a product or selling it or financing it. But nothing about his selection makes him an expert on inflation. Will his holding down the price of his product reduce inflationary pressure? Or, by leaving more spending power in the hands of his customers, simply divert it elsewhere?

The difficulty of exercising "social responsibility" illustrates, of course, the great virtue of private competitive enterprise — it forces people to be responsible for their own actions and makes it difficult for them to "exploit" other people for either selfish or unselfish purposes. They can do good — but only at their own expense.

Many a reader who has followed the argument this far may be tempted to remonstrate that it is all well and good to speak of government's having the responsibility to impose taxes and determine expenditures for such "social" purposes as controlling pollution or training the hard-core unemployed, but that the problems are too urgent to wait on the slow course of political processes, that the exercise of social responsibility by businessmen is a quicker and surer way to solve pressing current problems.

Aside from the question of fact — I share Adam Smith's skepticism about the benefits that can be expected from "those who affected to trade for the public good" — this argument must be rejected on grounds of principle. What it amounts to is an assertion that those who favor the taxes and expenditures in question have failed to persuade a majority of their fellow citizens to be of like mind and that they are seeking to attain by undemocratic procedures what they cannot attain by democratic procedures. In a free society, it is hard for "good" people to do "good," but that is a small price to pay for making it hard for "evil" people to do "evil," especially since one man's good is another's evil.

Precisely the same argument applies to the newer phenomenon of calling upon stockholders to require corporations to exercise social responsibility (the recent G.M. crusade, for example). In most of these cases, what is in effect involved is some stockholders trying to get other stockholders (or customers or employees) to contribute against their will to "social" causes favored by the activists. Insofar as they succeed, they are again imposing taxes and spending the proceeds.

The situation of the individual proprietor is somewhat different. If he acts to reduce the returns of his enterprise in order to exercise his "social responsibility," he is spending his own money, not someone else's. If he wishes to spend his money on such purposes, that is his right, and I cannot see that there is any objection to his doing so. In the process, he, too, may impose costs on employees and customers. However, because he is far less likely than a large corporation or union to have monopolistic power, any such side effects will tend to be minor.

Of course, in practice the doctrine of social responsibility is frequently a cloak for actions that are justified on other grounds rather than a reason for those actions.

To illustrate, it may well be in the long-run interest of a corporation that is a major employer in a small community to devote resources to providing amenities to that community or to improving its government. That may make it easier to attract desirable employees, it may reduce the wage bill or lessen losses from pilferage and sabotage or have other worthwhile effects. Or it may be that, given the laws about the deductibility of corporate charitable contributions, the stockholders can contribute more to charities they favor by having the corporation make the gift than by doing it themselves, since they can in that way contribute an amount that would otherwise have been paid as corporate taxes.

In each of these — and many similar — cases, there is a strong temptation to rationalize these actions as an exercise of "social responsibility." In the present climate of opinion, with its widespread aversion to "capitalism," "profits," the "soulless corporation" and so on, this is one way for a corporation to generate goodwill as a by-product of expenditures that are entirely justified in its own self-interest.

It would be inconsistent of me to call on corporate executives to refrain from this hypocritical window-dressing because it harms the foundations of a free society. That would be to call on them to exercise a "social responsibility"! If our institutions, and the attitudes of the public make it in their self-interest to cloak their actions in this way, I cannot summon much indignation to denounce them. At the same time, I can express admiration for those individual proprietors or owners of closely held corporations or stockholders of more broadly held corporations who disdain such tactics as approaching fraud.

Whether blameworthy or not, the use of the cloak of social responsibility, and the nonsense spoken in its name by influential and prestigious businessmen, does clearly harm the foundations of a free society. I have been impressed time and again by the schizophrenic character of many businessmen. They are capable of being extremely far-sighted and clear-headed in matters that are internal to their businesses. They are incredibly shortsighted and muddle-headed in matters that are outside their businesses but affect the possible survival of business in general. This shortsightedness is strikingly exemplified in the calls from many businessmen for wage and price guidelines or controls or incomes policies. There is nothing that could do more in a brief period to destroy a market system and replace it by a centrally controlled system than effective governmental control of prices and wages.

QUESTIONS

1. Articulate Friedman's view that corporate social responsibility is a form of taxation without representation. Do you agree?

2. What is the distinction between the socially responsible individual proprietor and the socially reponsible corporate executive?

3. "The political principle that underlies the market mechanism is unanimity. . . . The political principle that underlies the political mechanism is conformity." Comment.

4. Friedman argues that the conflict between social responsibility and increasing wealth is brought out more clearly in exhortations directed at union leaders than corporate executives. Do you agree? Why?

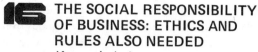

THE SOCIAL RESPONSIBILITY OF BUSINESS: ETHICS AND RULES ALSO NEEDED
Kenneth J. Arrow

This article is best read in response to the preceding one. The author of this reading on corporate behavior, just like the one before, is one of the United States' most decorated economists: president of the American Economic Association, president of the Econometric Society, a John Bates Clark medalist, and a Nobel laureate in economics. Kenneth Arrow teaches at Harvard University and is the author of over 100 articles, on subjects ranging from the frontiers of mathematical economic theory to literary propositions such as the one here reprinted from the Harvard journal Public Policy. *This is a revised version of the Carl Snyder Memorial Lecture Professor Arrow gave at the University of California at Santa Barbara.*

This paper makes some observations on the widespread notion that the individual has some responsibility to others in the conduct of his economic affairs. It is held that there are a number of circumstances under which the economic agent should forgo profit or other benefits to himself in order to achieve some social goal, especially, to avoid a disservice to other individuals. For the purpose of keeping the discussion within bounds, I shall confine my attention to the obligations that might be imposed on business firms. Under what circumstances is it reasonable to expect a business firm to refrain from maximizing its profits because it will hurt others by doing so?

First of all, it may be well to review what possible ways there are by which the economic activity of one firm may affect other members of the economy. A substantial list comes to mind; a few illustrations will serve. A firm affects others by competing with them in the product markets and in the factor markets, in the buying of labor, buying of

Abridged from Kenneth J. Arrow, "Social Responsibility and Economic Efficiency," in *Public Policy*, 21 (Summer 1973) pp. 303—316. Reprinted by permission.

other goods for its use, and in the selling of its products. It pays wages to others. It buys goods from others. It sets prices to its customers, and so enters into an economic relation with them. The firm typically sets working conditions, including — of greatest importance — conditions that affect the health and possibility for accident within the plant. We are reminded in recent years that the firm, as well as the private individual, is a contributor to pollution. Pollution has a direct effect on the welfare of other members of the economy. Less mentioned, but of the same type, are the effects of economic activity on congestion. Bringing a new plant into an already crowded area is bound to create costs, disservices, and disutilities to others in the area if by nothing else than by crowding the streets and the sidewalks and imposing additional burdens on the public facilities of the area. Indeed, although congestion has not been discussed as much as has pollution, it may have greater economic impact and probably even greater health costs. Certainly the number of automobile deaths arising from accidents far exceeds the health hazards arising from automobile pollution.

Let us first consider the case against social responsibility: the assumption that the firms should aim simply to maximize their profits. One strand of that argument is empirical rather than ethical or normative. It simply states that firms *will* maximize their profits. The impulse to gain, it is argued, is very strong and the incentives for selfish behavior are so great that any kind of control is likely to be utterly ineffectual. This argument has some force but is by no means conclusive. Any mechanism for enforcing or urging social responsibility upon firms must of course reckon with a profit motive, with a desire to evade whatever response of controls are imposed. But it does not mean that we cannot expect any degree of responsibility at all.

One finds a rather different argument, frequently stated by some economists. It will probably strike the noneconomist as rather strange, at least at first hearing. The assertion is that firms *ought* to maximize profits; not merely do they like to do so but there is practically a social obligation to do so. Let me briefly sketch the argument:

Firms buy the goods and services they need for production. What they buy they pay for and therefore they are paying for whatever costs they impose upon others. What they receive in payment by selling their goods, they receive because the purchaser considers it worthwhile. This is a world of voluntary contracts; nobody *has* to buy the goods. If he chooses to buy it, it must be that he is getting a benefit measured by the price he pays. Hence, it is argued, profit really represents the net contribution that the firm makes to the social good, and the profits should therefore be made as large as possible. Now, as far as it goes this argument is sound. The problem is that it may not go far enough.

Under the proper assumptions profit maximization is indeed efficient in the sense that it can achieve as high a level of satisfaction as possible for any one consumer without reducing the levels of satisfaction of other consumers or using more resources than society is endowed with. But the limits of the argument must be stressed. I want to mention two well-known points in passing without making them the principal focus of discussion. First of all, the argument assumes that the forces of competition are sufficiently vigorous. But there is no social justification for profit maximization by monopolies. Second, the distribution of income that results from unrestrained profit maximization is very unequal. The competitive maximizing economy is indeed efficient — this shows up in high average incomes — but the high average is accompanied by widespread poverty on the one hand and vast riches, at least for a few, on the other. To many of us this is a very undesirable consequence.

Profit maximization has yet another effect on society. It tends to point away from the expression of altruistic motives. Altruistic motives are motives whose gratification is just as legitimate as selfish motives, and the expression of those motives is something we probably wish to encourage. A profit-maximizing, self-centered form of economic behavior does not provide any room for the expression of such motives.

If the three problems above were set aside, many of the ways by which firms affect others should not be tampered with. Making profits by competition is, if anything, to be encouraged rather than discouraged. Wage and price bargains between the firm and uncoerced workers and customers represent mutually beneficial exchanges. There is, therefore, no reason within the framework of the discussion to interfere with them. But these examples far from exhaust the list of interactions with which we started. The social desirability of profit maximization does not extend to all the interactions on the list. There are two categories of effects where the arguments for profit maximization break down: The first is illustrated by pollution or congestion. Here it is no longer true (and this is the key to these issues) that the firm in fact does pay for the harm it imposes on others. When it takes a person's time and uses it at work, the firm is paying for this, and therefore the transaction can be regarded as a beneficial exchange from the point of view of both parties. We have no similar mechanism by which the pollution which a firm imposes upon its neighborhood is paid for. Therefore the firm will have a tendency to pollute more than is desirable.

The second category of effects where profit maximization is not socially desirable is that in which there are quality effects about which the firm knows more than the buyer. In my examples I will cite primarily the case of quality in the product sold, but actually very much the same considerations apply to the quality of working conditions. The firm is frequently in a better position to know the consequences (the health hazards, for example) involved in working conditions than the worker is, and the considerations I am about to discuss in the case of sale of goods have a direct parallel in the analysis of working conditions in the relation of a firm to its workers. Let me illustrate by considering the sale of a used car. (Similar considerations apply to the sale of new cars.) A used car has potential defects and typically the seller knows more about the defects than the buyer. The buyer is not in a position to distinguish among used cars, and therefore he will be willing to pay the same amount for two used cars of differing quality because he cannot tell the difference between them. As a result, there is an inefficiency in the sale of used cars. If somehow or other the cars were distinguished as to their quality, there would be some buyers who would prefer a

cheaper car with more defects because they intend to use it very little or they only want it for a short period, while others will want a better car at a higher price. In fact, however, the two kinds of car are sold indiscriminately to the two groups of buyers at the same price, so that we can argue that there is a distinct loss of consumer satisfaction imposed by the failure to convey information that is available to the seller.

Consider now any newly produced complex product, such as a new automobile. The seller is bound to know considerably more about its properties than all but a very few of its buyers. In order to develop the car, the producer has had to perform tests of one kind or another. He knows the outcome of the tests. Failure to reveal this knowledge works against the efficiency of satisfying consumers' tastes. The argument of course applies to any aspect of the quality of a product, durability or the ability to perform under trying circumstances or differing climatic conditions. Perhaps we are most concerned about the safety features of the automobile. The risks involved in the use of automobiles are not trivial, and the kind of withholding of safety information which has been revealed to exist in a number of cases certainly cannot be defended as a socially useful implication of profit maximization. The classical efficiency arguments for profit maximization do not apply here, and it is wrong to obfuscate the issue by invoking them.

Thus there are two types of situation in which the simple rule of maximizing profits is socially inefficient: the case in which costs are not paid for, as in pollution, and the case in which the seller has considerably more knowledge about his product than the buyer, particularly with regard to safety. In these situations it is clearly desirable to have some idea of social responsibility, that is, to experience an obligation, whether ethical, moral, or legal. Now we cannot expect such an obligation to be created out of thin air. To be meaningful, any obligation of this kind, any feeling or rule of behavior has to be embodied in some definite social institution. I use that term broadly: a legal code is a social institution in a sense. Exhortation to do good must be made specific in some external form, a steady reminder and perhaps enforcer of desirable values. Part of the need is simply for factual information as a guide to individual behavior. A firm may need to be told what is right and what is wrong when in fact it is polluting, or which safety requirements are reasonable and which are too extreme or too costly to be worth consideration. Institutionalization of the social responsibility of firms also serves another very important function. It provides some assurance to any one firm that the firms with which it is in competition will also accept the same responsibility. If a firm has some code imposed from the outside, there is some expectation that other firms will obey it too and therefore there is some assurance that it need not fear any excessive cost to its good behavior.

Let me [mention] some alternative kinds of institutions that can be considered as embodying the possible social responsibilities of firms. First, we have legal regulation, as in the case of pollution where laws are passed about the kind of burning that may take place, and about setting maximum standards for emissions. A second category is that of taxes. Economists, with good reason, like to preach taxation as opposed to regulation. The movement to tax polluting emissions is getting under way and there is a fairly widely backed proposal in Congress to tax sulfur dioxide emissions from industrial smokestacks. That is an example of the second kind of institutionalization of social responsibility. The responsibility is made very clear: the violator pays for violations.

A third very old remedy or institution is that of legal liability — the liability of the civil law. One can be sued for damages. Such cases apparently go back to the Middle Ages. Regulation also extends back very far. There was an ordinance in London about the year 1300 prohibiting the burning of coal, because of the smoke nuisance.

The fourth class of institutions is represented by ethical codes. Restraint is achieved not by appealing to each individual's conscience but rather by having some generally understood definition of appropriate behavior.

Let me turn to the fourth possibility, ethical codes. This may seem to be a strange possibility for an economist to raise. But when there is a wide difference in knowledge between the two sides of the market, recognized ethical codes can be, as has already been suggested, a great contribution to economic efficiency. Actually we do have examples of this in our everyday lives, but in very limited areas. The case of medical ethics is the most striking. By its very nature there is a very large difference in knowledge between the buyer and the seller. One is, in fact, buying precisely the service of someone with much more knowledge than you have. To make this relationship a viable one, ethical codes have grown up over the centuries, both to avoid the possibility of exploitation by the physician and to assure the buyer of medical services that he is not being exploited. I am not suggesting that these are universally obeyed, but there is a strong presumption that the doctor is going to perform to a large extent with your welfare in mind. Unnecessary medical expenses or other abuses are perceived as violations of ethics. There is a powerful ethical background against which we make this judgment. Behavior that we would regard as highly reprehensible in a physician is judged less harshly when found among businessmen. The medical profession is typical of professions in general. All professions involve a situation in which knowledge is unequal on two sides of the market by the very definition of the profession, and therefore there have grown up ethical principles that afford some protection to the client. Notice there is a mutual benefit in this. The fact is that if you had sufficient distrust of a doctor's services, you wouldn't buy them. Therefore the physician wants an ethical code to act as assurance to the buyer, and he certainly wants his competitors to obey this same code, partly because any violation may put him at a disadvantage but more especially because the violation will reflect on him, since the buyer of the medical services may not be able to distinguish one doctor from another. A close look reveals that a great deal of economic life depends for its viability on a certain limited degree of ethical commitment. Purely selfish behavior of individuals is really incompatible with any kind of settled economic life. There is almost invariably some element of trust and confidence.

Much business is done on the basis of verbal assurance. It would be too elaborate to try to get written commitments on every possible point.

Now I've said that ethical codes are desirable. It doesn't follow from that that they will come about. The code may be of value to the running of the system as a whole, it may be of value to all firms if all firms maintain it, and yet it will be to the advantage of any one firm to cheat — in fact the more so, the more other firms are sticking to it. But there are some reasons for thinking that ethical codes can develop and be stable. These codes will not develop completely without institutional support. That is to say, there will be need for focal organizations, such as government agencies, trade associations, and consumer defense groups, or all combined to make the codes explicit, to iterate their doctrine and to make

their presence felt. Given that help, I think the emergence of ethical codes on matters such as safety at least, is possible.

QUESTIONS

1. According to Professor Arrow, in what way does pollution or congestion or a lack of product quality call for a different motivation from the business sector than profit maximization?

2. What institutions can society devise to enhance the social responsibilities of business firms?

3. What evidence is there that ethical codes might be adopted by business firms to alleviate problems such as pollution, congestion, or poor product quality? What incentives, if any, would business firms have to adopt such codes?

PART FIVE

PUBLIC GOODS: GOVERNMENT BEHAVIOR

17 THE PROPER ROLE OF GOVERNMENT IN THE ECONOMY
George J. Stigler

How large the government should be and what tasks it should undertake are questions that have long occupied the attention of political philosophers and college students in bull sessions. Not surprisingly, economists are also concerned with this issue. George J. Stigler is the Walgreen Distinguished Service Professor of American Institutions at the University of Chicago, one of the nation's top microeconomic theorists, and one of the wittiest, as well. He offers a series of rules of government behavior and discusses the limited role the state can play. This essay should be read in conjunction with the one following by Paul A. Samuelson; they are drawn from a debate between these two economists at Swarthmore College. Discussion questions follow the second article.

There was an age when social dissatisfaction was kept in the house. All evils were ancient evils, and therefore necessary evils which served at least to keep men humble and patient. This resignation to imperfection has almost vanished in modern times — the hereafter in which all problems are solved has been moved up to two months after the next election. And government has become the leading figure in almost every economic reform. I propose to discuss what governments can do in economic life, and what they should do.

The question of what governments can do, what they are capable of doing, will strike many Americans, and for that matter most non-Americans, as an easy one. For it is a belief, now widely held and strongly held, that the government can, if it really puts its mind and heart to a task, do anything that is not palpably impossible. The government, we shall all admit, cannot really turn the number π into a simple fraction by legislative mandate, nor can a

Abridged from George J. Stigler, "The Government of the Economy," Selected Papers No. 7, *A Dialogue on the Proper Economic Role of the State,* Graduate School of Business, The University of Chicago, 1963, pp. 3–20.

joint resolution of the houses of Congress confer immortality. But with a will, the government can see to it that fully 85 percent of the male population, and a few women, are taught several infinite series for calculating π, and with a will, the government can prolong human life appreciably by suitable medical and social insurance programs.

AN ARTICLE OF FAITH

Our faith in the power of the state is a matter of desire rather than demonstration. When the state undertakes to achieve a goal, and fails, we cannot bring ourselves to abandon the goal, nor do we seek alternative means of achieving it, for who is more powerful than a sovereign state? We demand, then, increased efforts of the state, tacitly assuming that where there is a will, there is a governmental way.

Yet we know very well that the sovereign state is not omnipotent. The inability of the state to perform certain economic tasks could be documented from some notorious failures. Our cotton program, for example, was intended to enrich poor cotton farmers, increase the efficiency of production, foster foreign markets, and stabilize domestic consumption. It is an open question whether 28 years of our farm program have done as much for poor cotton farmers as the trucking industry. Again, the Federal Trade Commission is the official guardian of business morals, including advertising morals. I am reasonably confident that more would have been achieved if one of the F.T.C.'s 48 years of appropriations had been devoted to a prize for the best exposé of sharp practices.

That there should be failures of governmental policy is not surprising, nor will the failures lead us to a blanket condemnation of governmental activity in economic life. What is surprising is how little we know about the degree of success or failure of almost all governmental intervention in economic life. And when I say how little we know, I expressly include the people whose business it should be to measure the achievements, the professional economists.

When we have made studies of governmental controls that are sufficiently varied in scope and penetrating in detail, we may be able to construct a set of fairly useful generalizations about what the state can do. But society will not wait upon negligent scholars before meeting what seem to be pressing issues. The remainder of my talk cannot wait either, so I am driven to present what I consider plausible rules concerning feasible economic controls.

What economic tasks can a state perform? I propose a set of rules which bear on the answer to the question, but I shall not attempt a full argument in support of them — it must suffice to give an illustrative case, a plausible argument. It must suffice partly because full proofs have not been accumulated, but partly also because I wish to have time to discuss what the state should do, which is considerably less than what it can do.

RULE 1: *The state cannot do anything quickly.*

It would be unseemly to document at length the glacial pace of a bureaucracy in double step. Suffice it to say that if tomorrow a warehouse full of provisions labelled *"For General Custer: Top Priority"* were found, no one would have to be told whether the warehouse was publicly or privately owned.

A decent respect for due process lies behind some of the procedural delays, and poses a basic issue of the conflicting demands of justice and efficiency in economic regulation. But deliberation is intrinsic to large organizations: not only does absolute power corrupt absolutely; it delays fantastically. I would also note that initiative is the least prized of a civil servant's virtues, because the political process allots much greater penalties for failure than rewards for success.

SIZE VS. CONTROL

RULE 2: *When the national state performs detailed economic tasks, the responsible political authorities cannot possibly control the manner in which they are performed, whether directly by governmental agencies or indirectly by regulation of private enterprise.*

The lack of control is due to the impossibility of the central authority either to know or to alter the details of a large enterprise. An organization of any size — and I measure size in terms of personnel —

cannot prescribe conduct in sufficient detail to control effectively its routine operations: it is instructive that when the New York City subway workers wish to paralyze their transportation system, they can do so as effectively by following all the operating instructions in literal detail as by striking.

I estimate, in fact, that the federal government is at least 120 times as large as any organization can be and still keep some control over its general operations. It is simply absurd to believe that Congress could control the economic operations of the federal government; at most it can sample and scream.

UNIFORMITY OF TREATMENT

RULE 3: *The democratic state strives to treat all citizens in the same manner; individual differences are ignored if remotely possible.*

The striving for uniformity is partly due to a desire for equality of treatment, but much more to a desire for administrative simplicity. Thus men with a salary of $100,000 must belong to the Social Security system; professors in New York must take a literacy test to vote; the new automobile and the 1933 Essex must be inspected; the most poorly coordinated driver and the most skillful driver must obey the same speed limits; the same minimum wage must be paid to workers of highly different productivities; the man who gives a vaccination for smallpox must have the same medical credentials as a brain surgeon; the three-week-old child must have the same whiskey import allowance as a grown Irishman; the same pension must be given to the pilot who flew 100 dangerous missions as to the pilot who tested a Pentagon swivel chair; the same procedure must be passed through to open a little bank in Podunk and the world's largest bank in New York; the same subsidy per bale of cotton must be given to the hillbilly with two acres and the river valley baron with 5,000 acres. We ought to call him Uncle Same.

RULE 4: *The ideal public policy, from the viewpoint of the state, is one with identifiable beneficiaries, each of whom is helped appreciably, at the cost of many unidentifiable persons, none of whom is hurt much.*

The preference for a well-defined set of beneficiaries has a solid basis in the desire for votes, but it extends well beyond this prosaic value. The political system is not trustful of abstract analysis, nor, for that matter, are most people. A benefit of $50 to each of one million persons will always seem more desirable than a $1 benefit to each of 150 million people, because one can see a $50 check, and hence be surer of its existence.

RULE 5: *The state never knows when to quit.*

One great invention of a private enterprise system is bankruptcy, an institution for putting an eventual stop to costly failure. No such institution has yet been conceived of in the political process, and an unsuccessful policy has no inherent termination. Indeed, political rewards are more closely proportioned to failure than to success, for failure demonstrates the need for larger appropriations and more power. This observation does not contradict my previous statement that a civil servant must avoid conspicuous failure at all costs, for his failure is an unwise act, not an ineffectual policy.

The two sources of this tenacity in failure are the belief that the government must be able to solve a social problem, and the absence of objective measures of failure and success. The absence of measures of failure is due much more to the lack of enterprise of economists than to the nature of things. One small instance is the crop forecasting service of the Department of Agriculture. This service began shortly after the Civil War, and it eventually involved thousands of reporters and a secrecy in preparation of forecasts that would thwart Central Intelligence. It was not until 1917 that a Columbia professor, Henry Moore, showed that the early season forecasts were almost as good as flipping a coin, and the later season forecasts were almost as good as running a regression equation on rainfall. But as I have remarked, most public policies simply have not been studied from this viewpoint.

Let me emphasize as strongly as I can that each of these characteristics of the political process is a source of strength in some activities, as well as a limitation in other activities. If the state could move rapidly, contrary to Rule 1, and readily accepted abstract notions, contrary to Rule 4, our society would become the victim of every fad in morals and every popular fallacy in philosophy. If the state could effectively govern the details of our lives, no tyranny would ever have been overthrown. If the state were to adapt all its rules to individual circumstances, contrary to Rule 3, we would live in a society of utter caprice and obnoxious favoritism. If the state knew when to quit, it would never have engaged in such unpromising ventures as the American Revolution, not that I personally consider this our best war. But what are virtues in the preservation of our society and its basic liberties are not necessarily virtues in fixing the wages of labor or the number of channels a television set can receive.

STATE'S PROPER ECONOMIC ROLE

I turn now to our subject, the proper economic role for the state.

Class 1: Monopoly The fear of monopoly exploitation underlies a vast network of public regulation — the control over the so-called public utilities, including the transportation and communication industries and banking institutions, as well as traditional antitrust policies. The proper methods of dealing with monopoly, in their order of acceptability, are three:

1. The maintenance or restoration of competition by the suitable merger prevention policies, which we now fail to use in areas such as rail and air transport, and by the dissolution of monopolies. This method of once-for-all intervention provides the only really effective way of dealing with monopoly.

It will be said that for technological reasons even a modest amount of competition is unattainable in many areas. I believe these areas are very few in number. Even when a community can have only one electric company, that company is severely limited by the long-run alternatives provided by other communities.

2. Where substantial competition cannot be achieved — and I do not ask for perfect competition — the entry into the field is often controlled by the state — for example the TV channels are allocated by the FCC. Here auctioning off the channels seems

the only feasible method of capturing the inherent monopoly gains. The history of regulation gives no promise that such gains can be eliminated.

3.   In the few remaining cases in which monopoly cannot be eliminated or sold to the monopolist, monopolies should be left alone, simply because there is no known method of effective control.

Class 2:   Poverty   A community does not wish to have members living in poverty, whatever the causes of the poverty may be.   I consider treatment of poverty a highly proper function of the state, but would propose that it be dealt with according to two principles:

1.   Direct aid should take the form of direct grants of money, and only this form.   The present methods involve an unending chain of *ad hoc* grants in kinds: Some subsidized housing, some subsidized medical care, some subsidized food, some rigging of selling prices of cotton and wheat, some lunches for children, and so on.   Not only are many of these policies grossly inefficient, as when a farm support program hurts tenants and helps landowners or a minimum wage law leads to the discharge of the neediest workers, but also the policies impose gross limitations on the freedom of the poor.   If the poor would rather spend their relief checks on food than on housing, I see no reason for denying them the right.   If they would rather spend money on whiskey than on their children, I take it that we have enforceable laws to protect children.

2.   The basic problem of poverty from the social viewpoint, however, is not the alleviation of current need but equipping the people to become self-supporting.   Here we have been extraordinarily phlegmatic and unimaginative in acquiring understanding of the basic problem of low productivity and in devising methods of increasing the skills and opportunities of the poor.   The old English settlement laws sought to tie the poor to the native parish, and this utter perversity is presently approached by a relief and old age system which at times imposes marginal taxes in excess of 100 percent on earnings. We have become so single-minded in worshipping the curriculum of the good liberal arts college that we have only a primitive system of industrial train-

ing.   We tolerate widespread restrictionism on entry by unions, when it is the excluded entrants we should be worrying about.

In fact, so-called liberal policies in this area often seem to me to be almost studied in their callousness and contempt for the poor.

Class 3:   Economic Distress   I define economic distress as experiencing a large fall in income, or failing to share in a general rise, but without reaching some generally accepted criterion of poverty — of course the two differ only in degree.   Much of our farm program, our oil program, our protective tariff system, our regional development schemes, our subsidies for metals and soon for commuters, are so motivated.   Here my prescriptions would be:

1.   Compensation for losses in the cases in which the distress is clearly and directly caused by governmental policy.

2.   Exactly the same kind of treatment of distress as of poverty in other respects: Direct grants in the short-run; policies to foster the mobility of resources in the long-run.   I do not conceal the belief that many of these special aid programs are so indefensible that an open subsidy program could not survive.

Class 4:   Consumer and Worker Protection   Since unpunished fraud is profitable, it must be punished. I doubt whether many people realize how strong are the remedies provided by traditional law, and in particular how effective the actions of people who have been defrauded.   I am confident that research in this area would suggest methods of vastly increasing the role of self-policing in the economy.

It is otherwise with the alleviation of consumer incompetence: The belief is becoming strong that there is much fraud, or at least indefensible waste, that consumers are incompetent to discover.

My basic answer to this painful problem is: In order to preserve the dignity and freedom of the individual in my society, I shall if I must pay the price of having some fail wholly to meet the challenge of freedom.   I find it odd that a society which once a generation will send most of its young men against enemy bullets to defend freedom, will capitulate to a small handful of citizens unequal to its challenge.

This basic position does not imply that we should accept the institutions of 1900, or 1963, or any other year, as ideal in the protection they have given to men against fraud and danger. We should be prepared to examine any existing institution, or any proposal for change, with an open mind.

We should not, however, accept dramatic episodes as a measure of need; we should not simply assume that there is a useful law for every problem; and we should not lazily accept remedies which take freedom from 97 men in order to give protection to three.

These classes do not exhaust the range of functions undertaken by modern states, but they will suffice to illustrate the positions that seem to me to best meet the values of our society and the known limitations on its political processes.

And now I close. I consider myself courageous, or at least obtuse, in arguing for a reduction in governmental controls over economic life. You are surely desirous of improving this world, and it assuredly needs an immense amount of improvement. No method of displaying one's public-spiritedness is more popular than to notice a problem and pass a law. It combines ease, the warmth of benevolence, and a suitable disrespect for a less enlightened era. What I propose is, for most people, much less attractive: Close study of the comparative performance of public and private economy, and the dispassionate appraisal of special remedies that is involved in compassion for the community at large.

THE PROPER ROLE OF THE MARKET IN THE ECONOMY
Paul A. Samuelson

America's first Nobel Prize winner in economics, Paul A. Samuelson, is known to many students as a columnist and author of one of the best selling college textbooks ever. To economists he is known for his many contributions to economic theory. His collected scientific papers now run to three volumes. Samuelson began his teaching career at M.I.T., where he is now Institute Professor of Economics. In this essay, which should be read in conjunction with the one preceding, Samuelson considers the problem of delineating an appropriate role for the private and the public sectors. He also reflects on the nature of freedom in the economic sphere.

LINCOLN'S FORMULA

Some people begin the discussion of a concept by telling you how it is defined in Webster's dictionary. I follow the other fork and quote Abraham Lincoln. You may remember that the fellow who ran against Kennedy in 1960 quoted Lincoln on the proper role of government. It went something like the following.

I believe the government should do only that which private citizens cannot do for themselves, or which they cannot do so well for themselves.

One would think this is supposed to be saying something. Let us try it in its converse form.

I believe the private economy should be left alone to do those activities which, on balance after netting out all advantages and disadvantages, it can best do.

Obviously what I have stated is an empty tauto-

Abridged from Paul A. Samuelson, "The Economic Role of Private Activity," Selected Papers No. 7, *A Dialogue on the Proper Economic Role of the State,* Graduate School of Business, The Universtiy of Chicago, 1963, pp. 21—39.

logy. It is no more helpful than the usual answer from Dorothy Dix to a perplexed suitor that merely says, "Look into your own heart to see whether you truly love the girl. And then after you have made up your mind, I am sure it will be the right decision."

But are these mere tautologies? Do the two Lincolnesque statements say exactly the same thing? There is a certain literal sense in which they can be interpreted to be saying the same thing. But we all bring to the words we hear certain preconceptions and attitudes.

I think Lincoln meant to imply in his formulation that there is needed a certain burden of proof that has to be established by anyone who proposes that the government do something. The balance of advantage in favor of the government must be something a little more than epsilon or you should stand with the *status quo* of private enterprise.

Why? Lincoln does not say. But he takes it for granted that his listeners will understand that "personal liberty" is a value for its own sake and that some sacrifice of "efficiency" is worth making at the optimal point where activity is divided so as to maximize the total net advantage of "efficiency *cum* liberty" and vice versa.

The second statement that I have formulated also carries certain connotations. At a first hasty reading, it might suggest to some that the burden of proof is put on or against any proposal for *laissez faire* and individualism. And so it would be naturally construed in Soviet Russia.

After a second and more careful reading, it is seen to contain certain weasel words of qualification — such as "on balance," "netting" and "advantages" and "disadvantages." So interpreted, it can be made consistent with any desired emphasis on liberty as well as efficiency. So interpreted it could suffice for Stalin or Rousseau, for Keyserling or Friedman. And yet, even when almost completely emptied of its meaningful content, my formulation is left with a subtle connotation. It says, there are no absolutes here. The subject is an open one — open for debate and open to compromise. At some terms-of-trade, efficiency can be traded off against liberty. (Of course, Lincoln has already implied *this*, but not quite so strongly.)

OVERTURE TO THE PROGRAM

So much for introduction. My Act I has prepared the way for what is to follow. In Act II, I want to examine the conditions under which efficiency is realizable by free enterprise or *laissez faire*. This is familiar ground, but too familiar and needs reexamination.

Then in Act III, I want to raise some questions about the notion that absence of government means increase in "freedom." Is "freedom" a simply quantifiable magnitude as much libertarian discussion seems to presume?

Then I shall conclude on what may seem a *nihilistic* note, but which I hope is actually a *liberating* one.

TECHNICAL REQUIREMENTS FOR COMPETITIVE OPTIMALITY

Consider a society with limited resources. Let certain facts about technology be "known" (in varying degrees). Let there be more than one person, so that we can speak of society. Let people have their tastes and values. And if you like, let there be one or more sets of ethical beliefs in terms of whose norms various situations can be evaluated and ordered.

Now, to save time, we plunge into heroic assumptions.

1. Each person's tastes (and values) depend only upon his separable consumptions of goods. I.e., there must be no "consumption externalities."

2. Strict constant-returns-to-scale prevails.

3. Pefect competition, in senses too numerous to list here, prevails.

4. The interpersonal distribution of property (inclusive of personal attributes) is ethically correct initially or is to be made so by ideal lump-sum transfers of a perfectly non-distorting type.

Then, and only then, has it been rigorously proved that perfect competitive equilibrium is indeed optimal. So strict are these conditions that one would have thought that the elementary consideration that a line is infinitely thinner than a plane would make it a miracle for these conditions to be met. Real life optimality, or an approach to it, would seem to cry out — not merely for departure from *laissez faire* — but for never having been remotely near to *laissez faire*.

THE NATURE OF FREEDOM

But enough of these technicalities.

Adam Smith, our patron saint, was critical of state interference of the pre-Nineteenth Century type. And make no mistake about it: Smith was right. Most of the interventions into economic life by the State were then harmful both to prosperity and freedom. What Smith said needed to be said. In fact, much of what Smith said still needs to be said: Good intentions by government are not enough; acts do have consequences that had better be taken into account if good is to follow. Thus, the idea of a decent real wage is an attractive one. So is the idea of a low interest rate at which the needy can borrow. None the less the attempt *by law* to set a minimum real wage at a level much above the going market rates, or to set a maximum interest rate for small loans at what seem like reasonable levels, inevitably does much harm to precisely the people whom the legislation is intended to help. Domestic and foreign experience — today, yesterday and tomorrow — bears out the Smithian truth. Note that this is not an argument against *moderate* wage and interest fiats, which may improve the perfection of competition and make businessmen and workers more efficient.

Smith himself was what we today would call a pragmatist. He realized that monopoly elements ran through *laissez faire*. When he said that Masters never gather together even for social merriment without plotting to raise prices against the public interest, he anticipated the famous Judge Gary dinners at which the big steel companies used to be taught what every oligopolist should know. Knowing the caliber of George III's civil service, Smith believed the government would simply do more harm than good if it tried to cope with the evil of monopoly. Pragmatically, Smith might, if he were alive today, favor the Sherman Act and stronger antitrust legislation, or even public utility regulation generally.

THE INVISIBLE HAND AGAIN

One hundred percent individualists skip these pragmatic lapses into good sense and concentrate on the purple passage in Adam Smith where he discerns an Invisible Hand that leads each selfish individual to contribute to the best public good. Smith had a point; but he could not have earned a passing mark in a Ph.D. oral examination in explaining just what that point was. Until this century, his followers — such as Bastiat — thought that the doctrine of the Invisible Hand meant one of two things: (a) that it produced maximum feasible total satisfaction, somehow defined; or (b) that it showed that anything which results from the voluntary agreements of uncoerced individuals must make them better (or best) off in some important sense.

Both of these interpretations, which are still held by many modern libertarians, are wrong. They neglect Assumption 4 of my earlier axioms for nongovernment. This is not the place for a technical discussion of economic principles, so I shall be very brief and cryptic in showing this.

First, suppose some ethical observer — such as Jesus, Buddha, or, for that matter, John Dewey or Aldous Huxley — were to examine whether the total of social utility (as that ethical observer scores the deservingness of the poor and rich, saintly and sining individuals) was actually maximized by 1860 or 1962 *laissez faire*. He might decide that a tax placed upon yachts whose proceeds go to cheapen the price of insulin to the needy might increase the total of utility. Could Adam Smith prove him wrong? Could Bastiat? I think not.

Of course, they might say that there is no point in trying to compare different individuals' utilities because they are incommensurable and can no more be added together than can apples and oranges. But if recourse is made to this argument, then the doctrine that the Invisible Hand maximizes total utility of the universe has already been thrown out the window. If they admit that the Invisible Hand will truly maximize total social utility *provided the state intervenes so as to make the intitial distribution of dollar votes ethically proper,* then they have abandoned the libertarian's position that individuals are not to be coerced, even by taxation.

In connection with the second interpretation that anything which results from voluntary agreements is in some sense, *ipso facto,* optimal, we can reply by pointing out that when I make a purchase from a monopolistic octopus, that is a voluntary act: I can always go without Alka Seltzer or aluminum or nylon or whatever product you think is produced by a monopolist. Mere voluntarism, therefore, is not the root merit of the doctrine of the Invisible Hand; what is important about it is the system of checks and balances that comes under perfect competition, and its measure of validity is at the technocratic level of efficiency, not at the ethical level of freedom and individualism. That this is so can be seen from the fact that such socialists as Oscar Lange and A. P. Lerner have advocated channeling the Invisible Hand to the task of organizing a socialistic society efficiently.

THE IMPERSONALITY OF MARKET RELATIONS

Just as there is a sociology of family life and of politics, there is a sociology of individualistic competition. It need not be a rich one. Ask not your neighbor's name; enquire only for his numerical schedules of supply and demand. Under perfect competition, no buyer need face a seller. Haggling in a Levantine bazaar is a sign of less-than-perfect competition. The telephone is the perfect go-between to link buyers and sellers through the medium of an auction market, such as the New York Stock Exchange or the Chicago Board of Trade for grain transactions. Two men may talk hourly all their working lives and never meet.

These economic contacts between atomistic individuals may seem a little chilly or, to use the language of wine-tasting, "dry." This impersonality

has its good side. Negroes in the South learned long ago that their money was welcome in local department stores. Money can be liberating. It corrodes the cake of custom. Money does talk. Sociologists know that replacing the rule of status by the rule of contract loses something in warmth; it also gets rid of some of the bad fire of olden times.

Impersonality of market relations has another advantage, as was brought home to many "liberals" in the McCarthy era of American political life. Suppose it were efficient for the government to be the one big employer. Then if, for good or bad, a person becomes in bad odor with government, he is dropped from employment, and is put on a black list. He really then has no place to go. The thought of such a dire fate must in the course of time discourage that freedom of expression of opinion which individualists most favor.

Many of the people who were unjustly dropped by the federal government in that era were able to land jobs in small-scale private industry. I say small-scale industry because large corporations are likely to be chary of hiring names that appear on anybody's black list. What about people who were justly dropped as security risks or as members of political organizations now deemed to be criminally subversive? Many of them also found jobs in the anonymity of industry.

WHEAT GROWERS ANONYMOUS

Many conservative people, who think that such men should not remain in sensitive government work or in public employ at all, will still feel that they should not be hounded into starvation. Few want for this country the equivalent of Czarist Russia's Siberia, or Stalin Russia's Siberia either. It is hard to tell on the Chicago Board of Trade the difference between the wheat produced by Republican or Democratic farmers, by teetotalers or drunkards, Theosophists or Logical Positivists. I must confess that this is a feature of a competitive system that I find attractive.

We have seen how a perfect model of competitive equilibrium might behave if conditions for it were perfect. The modern world is not identical with that model. As mentioned before, there never was a time, even in good Queen Victoria's long reign, when such conditions prevailed.

Whatever may have been true on Turner's frontier, the modern city is crowded. Individualism and anarchy will lead to friction. We now have to co-ordinate and cooperate. Where cooperation is not fully forthcoming, we must introduce upon ourselves coercion.

MARKETPLACE COERCION, OR THE HEGELIAN FREEDOM OF NECESSITY

Libertarians fail to realize that the price system is, and ought to be, a method of coercion. Nature is not so bountiful as to give each of us all the goods he desires. We have to be coerced out of such a situation, by the nature of things. That is why we have policemen and courts. That is why we charge prices, which are high enough relative to limited money to limit consumption. The very term "rationing by the purse" illustrates the point. Economists defend such forms of rationing, but they have to do so primarily in terms of its efficiency and its fairness. Where it is not efficient — as in the case of monopoly, externality, and avoidable uncertainty — it comes under attack. Where it is deemed unfair by ethical observers, its evil is weighed pragmatically against its advantages and modifications of its structure are introduced.

Classical economists, like Malthus, always understood this coercion. They recognized that fate dealt a hand of cards to the worker's child that was a cruel one, and a favorable one to the "well-born." John Stuart Mill in a later decade realized that mankind, not Fate with a capital F, was involved. Private property is a concept created by and enforced by public law. Its attributes change in time and are man-made, not Mother-Nature-made.

Nor is the coercion a minor one. Future generations are condemned to starvation if certain supply-and-demand patterns rule in today's market. Under the freedom that is called *laissez faire*, some worthy men are exalted; and so are some unworthy ones. Some unworthy men are cast down; and so are some

worthy ones. The Good Man gives the system its due, but reckons in his balance its liabilities that are overdue.

Anatole France said epigrammatically all that needs to be said about the coercion implicit in the libertarian economics of *laissez faire*. "How majestic is the equality of the Law, which permits both rich and poor alike, to sleep under the bridges at night." I believe no satisfactory answer has yet been given to this. It is certainly not enough to say, "We made our own beds and let us each lie in them." For once Democracy rears its pretty head, the voter will think: "There, but for the Grace of God and the Dow-Jones averages, go I." And he will act.

The whole matter of proper government policy involves issues of ethics, coercion, administration, incidence, and incentives that cannot begin to be resolved by semantic analysis of such terms as "freedom," "coercion," or "individualism."

A FINAL LAW

At the end I must lay down one basic proposition. If you remember only one thing of what I say, let it be this. If you don't remember anything of what I say, let this be the last thing you forget.

There are no rules concerning the proper role of government that can be established by a priori reasoning.

QUESTIONS

1. What are the "Stigler Rules"? Do they have exceptions?
2. Contrast the positions of Stigler and Samuelson on the appropriate tasks of the state. Are their differences based on different uses of economic principles or differing value judgments (or both)?
3. Under what conditions will laissez-faire, that is, the absence of government intervention, lead to a social optimum?
4. In what sense, if any, are individuals "more free" under a system of markets than under one of government planning?

19 GOVERNMENT REGULATION IN THE PUBLIC INTEREST: THE U.S. EXPERIENCE
Mark Green and Ralph Nader

Ralph Nader needs no introduction to college audiences. Ever since his book, Unsafe At Any Speed, *was published, he has been a prominent critic of business and government behavior. In this article he and Mark Green, a younger colleague (neither likes the term "raider"), survey the history of government regulation of business and describe those areas where less government regulation is needed and those areas where more is required. This article should be read along with the one following by Ralph K. Winter. Messrs. Green and Nader are both graduates of Harvard Law School, Green is the director of the Corporate Accountability Research Group in Washington, D.C. Discussion questions follow the second article.*

Despite contrary speeches on the corporate hustings, our free enterprise economy has yielded to a mixed economy of public regulation and private industry. Yet because public policymakers have not confronted fundamental questions about its purpose, present economic regulation lacks both a comprehensive theory and a consistent goal.

DEFECTS OF DESIGN AND PROCESS

Design While the historical origins and constitutional basis of economic regulation are relatively clear, its economic rationale is not. The most common justification for regulation is *natural monopoly.* This situation arises when efficiency requires very large economies of scale; when due to large, fixed costs, unit costs decline as the scale of production increases. The installation of telephone lines and water mains are classic examples.

There are problems, however, with this concept

Reprinted by permission of The Yale Law Journal Company and Fred B. Rothman & Company from *The Yale Law Journal,* Vol. 82 (1973), pp. 871–889.

and its application. First, it is not clear what constitutes a natural monopoly. Most observers assume interstate telephoning is one, yet microwave technology and satellite communications have challenged that view. The Post Office, long considered a classic natural monopoly, is now facing competition in the delivery of mail. Thus, some care must be taken in defining natural monopoly, for what may appear to be an inevitable state of non-competition may be nothing more than a lack of imagination or an insensitivity to new technology.

Second, in its application, the grasp of natural monopoly can exceed its reach. Assuming *arguendo* that AT&T does have a natural monopoly in interstate telephone communications, the manufacture of telephone equipment is decidedly not part of it; yet AT&T's telephones are provided by Western Electric, its wholly owned subsidiary. While there are large economies of scale in the *generation* and *transmission* of electric power, they do not exist in its *distribution,* but the large scales of the former are often used to justify unnecessarily large scale in the latter. Finally, whatever the original reason for regulating the railroads, truck transportation is as close to the model of pure competition as exists in the economy; yet the regulation of railroads led Congress to approve the regulation of this competing mode. In sum, ill-defined natural monopoly situations are often used to justify the regulation of non-natural monopoly markets.

Besides natural monopoly, other controversial public interest rationales are offered for economic regulation. *Economic failure* may be judged too damaging to be tolerated. Here some would cite banking as a prime example. Others, however, believe more competition in banking could benefit the consumer by raising interest rates on deposits, creating more convenient locations, and encouraging the type of higher-risk loans which over-cautious loan officials avoid. *Limited space,* historically true for airlines as well as radio and television spectrums, supposedly requires government allocation among applicants. Yet both cable and satellite advances have antiquated the concept of spectrum scarcity. *Destructive competition,* which in a capital-intensive industry can lead to below-cost (predatory) pricing and deterioration of quality, is another justification for economic regulation. While this phrase is sometimes used by industrialists today to mean stiff competition, and while this did occur to some extent in the early days of preregulation, contemporary commentators question its present day likelihood in many industries. More importantly, the antitrust laws already proscribe destructive and monopolistic competition. Finally, *guaranteeing service* to sparsely populated areas may require regulation. Thus, long-distance, well-traveled air routes are overcharged in order to subsidize shorter, less popular ones. Yet if a route is considered in the public interest, it would seem the burden should fall on all equally via a subsidy from general tax revenues rather than from an implicit tax on certain commuters hundreds of miles away. Moreover, as such subsidies are created by agency action without public hearing or comment, there is little guarantee that wise economic decisions result.

In short, since little is known about how regulation affects the market performance of an industry, and since Congress has often failed to give any guidance to the courts or agencies other than admonitions to act in the public interest, our government has little idea of when to regulate. Consequently, like an architect without blueprints, economic regulation is unsure of itself and confused about its purpose.

At least two conclusions emerge about our present system of economic regulation. First, the monopolistic practices and results of economic regulation exact their tribute from the American economy and consumer. Excessive rates mean higher consumer prices for both products and services — prices which may bar the lower-income citizen entirely. Second, because we have no clear understanding of whom or when to regulate, we have regulated too much.

PROPOSALS FOR REFORM

If the problem is over-regulation based on irrational economics, then the most effective remedy is deregulation. Where there would be a viable, competitive market but for economic regulation, the industry should be freed from all such restraint. By this standard, trucking, air, and water transport, radio and television could return to the open market. Where economic regulation substitutes for the kind of managerial decisions, such as pricing, which are usually within the domain of private competitive firms, deregulation should also occur. Thus, railroad, transoceanic shippers, and airlines should no longer be able to price-fix with (or without) agency approval, though in certain limited situations, maximum rates might still be necessary. They could then compete on price, instead of on the color of their planes or the hemline of their stewardesses' skirts. The savings generated by such reform should be enormous.

But deregulation, if it is to occur, has a number of necessary preconditions and qualifications. First, a viable competitive market must be able to exist; if a well-defined "natural monopoly" or "natural oligopoly" characterizes the market, then the deregulation cure may prove no better than its regulatory disease. Second, antitrust policy and enforcement must be well-funded and vigorous to deter collusion or concentration and achieve effective competition. Third, since the introduction of competition will cause the closing of some inefficient facilities, a complementary program must underwrite the relocation and retraining of displaced employees. Finally, deregulation should be administered with a scalpel, not a scythe. It should not be applied to non-economic regulation which aims to complement, rather than replace, a market system incompetent or uninterested in fulfilling certain social needs. Several regulatory areas would be covered by this standard.

AREAS OF NEEDED REGULATION

Safety regulation explicitly assumes that the market will not adequately protect consumers against certain product hazards. Such laws are based on the rationale that it is better to prevent consumer harm than to compensate it later. The harm inflicted may simply be unacceptable to its victims, as in deaths from dangerous drugs or crashing airplanes. Or it may be unrealistic to assume that a manufacturer will compensate victims: Not only may court costs pose a serious entry barrier to individually small (but collectively large) damage claims, but corporations can also employ a variety of litigative tactics to discourage meritorious claims. Examples of this type of regulation include food and drug safety, airline safety, auto crashworthiness, flammable fabrics, and radiation levels.

Regulation of non-market externalities would cover damage caused to third parties who neither bought nor sold the product inflicting the damage. For example, while dangerous cars may be sold through the market system, no one can be said to have "bought" auto pollution. The same is true for the risk of radiation poisoning from a nuclear reactor. In short, producers lack a market incentive to contain certain harms, including environmental and land use effects. Here government standards are necessary to protect the public.

Enabling regulation establishes the necessary preconditions for competitive enterprise to succeed. Antitrust law establishes the borders and rules for economic contest. Anti-discrimination laws, occupational health and safety requirements, and unemployment compensation establish minimal standards for the protection of the individual in the production process. Similarly, corporate and product disclosure requirements are *sine qua nons* for investor knowledge and consumer sovereignty. The corporate balance sheet should be made public so the capital market can reward and sanction firms accordingly. At the same time product information — e.g., nutritional labeling, code dating, truth in lending provisions — provide consumers with the intelligence necessary for rational purchasing.

Yardstick enterprise might also have to be provided by the government when industry withdraws from a market because it is perceived as unprofitable. Such public enterprise could fulfill a public need and, if properly circumscribed and wisely implemented, set an example for private enterprise. For instance, railroads wish to curtail passenger service; private insurance firms have shied away from flood and crime insurance; and because of oversupply, oil firms for years have not been interested in develop-ing commercially viable processes for extracting oil from shale.

CONSUMER PROTECTION AGENCY

Finally, aided by more liberal standing decisions and increased access to agency data under the Freedom of Information Act, citizen suits could raise regulatory issues which the agencies shun. "Public interest" legal counsel, or a Consumer Protection Agency, could also represent previously ignored consumer interests. For years the regulatory agencies acceded to producer demands partly because that was the way of avoiding the embarrassment of public criticism or reversals on appeals brought by displeased producers. With citizen advocates now pressing their views on the agencies, they are less prone to defer to the judgment of their "client" industries. And so as the advocacy process becomes more competitive, so may agency policies.

20 NADERISM AND THE PUBLIC INTEREST: THE U.S. EXPERIENCE
Ralph K. Winter, Jr.

This article appeared in the Yale Law Journal *as a critical response to the policy suggestions made by Green and Nader. Ralph Winter, a professor of law at Yale University, argues that the consistent failings of government regulation, which have been unveiled by Nader and others, should not lead them to recommend larger and additional government agencies. This article should be read with the preceding one. Although the authors of both pieces are trained in law, a perusal of the articles in their unabridged form reveals their heavy reliance on economic literature in their own research and analysis.*

The unqualified statements that "present economic regulation lacks both a comprehensive theory and a consistent goal . . ." and "that our unguided regulatory system undermines competition and entrenches monopoly at the public's expense . . ." are obvious conclusions to be drawn from the so-called "Nader Reports." It is significant, however, that Mr. Nader and Mr. Green have categorically drawn them, for their credibility with some parts of our society may counteract the widespread conviction that faith in economic regulation is the mark of the educated Twentieth Century man.

Economic regulation has proven to be a noble but futile endeavor. The catalog of fiascos collected by Mr. Nader and Mr. Green demonstrates that proposition, and it is by no means exhaustive.

Mr. Nader and Mr. Green correctly identify one source of regulatory failure as the misuse of economic theory. All too often the underlying justification for government regulation has been theoretically defective or distortions of theory have been used to justify regulatory fiat aiding special interests. They might well have added two other common er-

rors made by advocates of regulation, common enough that Mr. Nader and Mr. Green occasionally commit them themselves. The first is assuming that any departure from the economist's model of perfect competition justifies regulation. Of course it does not. The model is but an abstraction designed solely as an analytic or pedagogic tool. Because no claim is made that it accurately describes reality or that only perfect competition maximizes consumer welfare, a departure from the model is not itself proof of a net injury to consumers. For example, no one contends that consumers have perfect knowledge in the real world, even though it is frequently assumed in the model for analytic purposes. This divergence between reality and academic assumptions, however, is not itself sufficient to make a case for regulation. Because the collection and transmittal of knowledge consumes society's resources, it is not costless, and may itself be a commodity best allocated by the market. Similarly, the model of perfect competition does not describe the only circumstances in which consumer welfare is maximized. Industrial concentration may in fact be better for consumers than atomistic competition when there are economies of scale.

Something more than a departure from the abstraction of perfect competition must thus be shown to justify government intervention. The kind of market failure which may call for regulation involves a failure of competition (natural monopoly), free rider effects (national defense), externalities (auto pollution), or the like — cases in which voluntary exchange is thought to be inhibited rather than facilitated by free markets.

The second error is failing to distinguish between regulation of this sort, which expedites free exchange (market supporting), and that which inhibits it for ethical reasons or personal preference (market supplanting). Mr. Nader and Mr. Green sometimes seem to advocate the former, sometimes the latter, without pausing to distinguish between them. Indeed, for all the economic gloss of their article, most of their suggestions for regulation appear to be based on their own value preferences rather than established market failure — preferences which they spend little time explaining, much less justifying.

Reprinted by permission of The Yale Law Journal Company and Fred B. Rothman & Company from *The Yale Law Journal,* Vol. 82 (1973), pp. 890–902.

Mr. Nader and Mr. Green are thus to be applauded for concluding that substantial deregulation is essential. Their other proposals for reform, however, entail regulation which is in principle indistinguishable from that which they condemn.

Once we make the assumption that the free market is to serve as the principal coordinator of economic activity, a theory of regulation must be two-pronged: First, it must establish those cases of market failure sufficiently serious to justify intervention, along with the goals such regulation should strive to achieve; second, it should describe the legal processes appropriate to the various kinds of regulation.

Since an important reason for choosing the market is to serve individual consuming tastes, a theory of regulation ought, where possible, transcend the preferences of particular individuals. A preference for the welfare of certain groups or for conduct which appeals to one's personal tastes is simply not a general theory of economic regulation.

SAFETY REGULATION

Consider, for example, safety regulation. Mr. Nader has been criticized for imposing on consumers his preferences as to the proper trade-off between risks and the costs of avoiding them. The justification for safety regulation Mr. Nader and Mr. Green now offer seeks to avoid such criticism by arguing that "it is better to prevent consumer harm than to compensate it later." To the extent that compensation through tort litigation is inadequate — whether because of legal sloth or an inability to calculate damages — the real cost of a risk will not be properly allocated. Nevertheless, if regulation is to be justified, it must be shown, first, that compensation is in fact inadequate in the case of the particular product, and, second, that the benefits lost by regulation are less than the difference between the compensation received by injured parties and that which adequately covers the loss.

If we apply this formula to one of Mr. Nader and Mr. Green's examples, drug regulation, the difficulty of making such a showing is evident. Let us assume that the damages paid in tort by drug manufacturers are less than the cost of the injuries caused. Mr. Nader and Mr. Green would require drug regulation in such circumstances. Yet recent findings have demonstrated that rigorous drug regulation significantly impedes the rate of introduction of new drugs and thus prevents beneficial as well as harmful drugs from entering the market. And those who suffer from the absence of beneficial drugs get *no compensation at all.* That the cost-effectiveness argument supports the call for regulation thus seems on the available facts anything but self-evident.

The second justification offered for safety regulation — that "the harm inflicted may simply be unacceptable to its victims" — is, save where externalities are present, simply no theory at all. Mr. Nader and Mr. Green would make autos crashworthy, but how does one explain *compulsory* seat belts in terms of consumer judgments as to unacceptable risks? After all, consumers who find the risk "unacceptable" can have seat belts installed and hardly need a loud, continuous buzzer to torment them into buckling up. Clearly, the judgment of acceptability stems from the preferences of Mr. Nader and Mr. Green, rather than from those of auto buyers.

In light of the campaigns mounted in the name of consumerism, the rhetoric of cost effectiveness and unacceptability is thus just so much boilerplate justifying the imposition of the campaigners' preferences. Neither rationale supports, for example, the campaign over the sturdiness of automobile bumpers. Similarly, while the Nader Report on the F.D.A. criticizes white bread because it is less nutritious than other breads, it concedes that less nutritious breads may be more profitable. The only explanation for that phenomenon, of course, is consumer choice.

Mr. Nader and Mr. Green make much of the fact that existing economic regulation has been turned to the advantage of special interest groups. There is nothing inherent in safety regulation, however, that makes it immune from such manipulation. Product safety regulation is, in fact, well suited for use as a weapon against one's competitors. Indeed, it is merely one form of restriction on entry. Had Mr. Nader been the force in the 50's that he is today, it is likely that he would have made strange bedfellows with the American auto industry in its battle against the small (and less safe) foreign car.

EXTERNALITIES

Citing auto pollution as an example, Mr. Nader and Mr. Green also call for the regulation of externalities where persons not a party to an economic transaction are injured by it. No one would deny, of course, that externalities are an example of market failure, but Mr. Nader and Mr. Green overstate the extent to which they serve as a guide for regulation. The externality formula does tell us which parties will benefit from regulation but precious little about whether, when, or how we ought to go about it.

In fact, almost any economic regulation may be justified by externality theory. Those who say they suffer psychic harm from the mere thought of others watching obscene movies can make a case for regulating the sale of pornography, just as Mr. Nader and Mr. Green presumably can make a case for seat belts on the grounds that they cannot bear the thought of people risking life and limb. Calling something an externality, therefore, merely throws us back on our personal value systems.

I am not arguing that we should not regulate activities entailing significant externalities. They are a type of market failure and thus carry no presumption with them. Nevertheless, regulation entails difficult cost-benefit judgments as well as normative or distributional decisions favoring some groups over others — issues which are often obscured and never resolved by saying that regulation is needed "to protect the public."

ENABLING REGULATION

Mr. Nader and Mr. Green also approve of something called enabling regulation as a theoretically valid form of market control. Their description is, however, so broad and so vague as to drain the phrase of meaning.

If enabling regulation is merely market supporting such as is contract and proper antitrust law, it may have some theoretical basis. But Mr. Nader and Mr. Green in effect call any laws they like enabling regulation. Anti-discrimination laws, occupational health and safety requirements, and unemployment compensation may be good laws and may arguably be grounded in economic efficiency. To lump them together as Mr. Nader and Mr. Green do, however, is simply to abandon the search for theory. Advocates of the farm program and the Lockheed loan, after all, rely heavily on the need to protect individuals in the productive process. Indeed, there are few instances of economic regulation that cannot be justified on such grounds so long as they are consistent with one's preferences.

Similarly, most of Mr. Nader and Mr. Green's proposals for increasing the flow of information seem based on personal preference, rather than market failure. For example, absent some showing of market failure, there is no reason to treat information differently than any other commodity. Competition rewards those who provide the information desired by consumers. One can expect entrepreneurs to establish independent testing organizations where the value of information to consumers is greater than the cost of collection and transmittal.

YARDSTICK ENTERPRISE

The final circumstance in which Mr. Nader and Mr. Green call for economic regulation involves what they term yardstick enterprise. Again, all of their talk of "public need" and setting "an example for private enterprise" comes down to the proposition that the government ought to engage in certain activities which Mr. Nader and Mr. Green personally find worthy. One will recall how heavily "yardstick" arguments were relied on by proponents of the supersonic transport and the space program. I do not know whether Mr. Nader and Mr. Green support those particular endeavors, but, given the right personal preferences, those projects certainly fall within their definition of yardstick enterprise.

The one major change in regulatory process Mr. Nader and Mr. Green suggest is the establishment of a Consumer Protection Agency to represent consumers before other federal agencies. Since it is thought that the other agencies have failed in part because only special interests appear before them, it is hoped that this new agency will improve overall regulatory performance. Unless there is truly magic in a name, however, we must conclude that the reasons this agency will be able to avoid the pitfalls which have downed its predecessors are anything but self-evident. Sloth, inefficiency, and responsiveness to special interests can prey on it as easily as they have preyed on its brethren. Indeed, the very argument that widespread agency failure can be cured by the creation of yet another agency seems to answer itself.

Such an agency, moreover, seems wrong in concept. Legal representation can be effective only when there is a single interest to represent. Where, as with consumers, there is no homogeneous, single interest, representation is impossible. Consumer tastes vary widely as to products, appearance, quality, safety, durability, price, and so on. Every purchase involves innumerable trade-offs among such matters; a single agency can represent only the views of certain consumers.

It is interesting to speculate on whether the "consumer tastes" such an agency is likely to represent are those of the upper-income consumer. While consumerism appears as an anti-establishment movement, a closer examination suggests it may be largely the ideological handiwork of the liberal, upper-middle class. To be sure, law can compel the production of "better" products, but only by increasing their cost. It can also compel, at a cost, the dissemination of detailed product information which is of greatest value to the highly educated. All these measures must decrease output and in particular decrease the production of cheap, mass produced goods. It is all very well for middle and higher income groups to call for more quality and safety when they can afford it. Laws compelling greater production of "better" goods may, because of economies of scale, make such goods less expensive. But such laws may also eliminate the even cheaper products the poor can now afford. We have had much experience in the past with producer groups seeking governmental protection from competition. Can one now make the argument that consumerism is unique in seeking a monopoly for the consuming tastes of its members, the upper-middle class?

QUESTIONS

1. What do Nader and Green mean by deregulation? In what way do they recommend the deregulation of American industry? In their view what areas are still in need of regulation and what forms should this regulation take?

2. Contrast the views of Nader and Green with those taken by Winter regarding safety legislation. How can safety legislation be designed to protect consumers without impinging upon their freedom of choice?

3. Discuss the case for and against a consumer protection agency. Has your view changed (if you had one) on this political issue since reading these essays?

4. Evaluate the charge that the consumer protection movement is a class movement representing primarily the white upper-middle class.

PART SIX

PROBLEMS IN PRODUCT MARKET BEHAVIOR

21 WHAT IS A MARKET . . .
AND WHAT IS A MONOPOLY?
Justice Reed Versus Justice Warren

*In the early 1950s, the Justice Department's Anti-
trust Division charged the du Pont corporation with
violating the Sherman Act by monopolizing the sale
of cellophane. The trial court found for the de-
fendant and the government took its appeal to the
Supreme Court. As often happens in antitrust law,
the decision depended heavily on the definition of
the "relevant market" in which du Pont's business
was to be examined. The Court split on this definition 4–3; what follows is the opinion, delivered by
Justice Reed, and the dissent, delivered by Chief
Justice Warren. Note the use of the language of
economics by the justices — antitrust law permits a
fascinating application of economic analysis. A
good way to read Justices Reed and Warren's efforts
is to take the role of judge and evaluate these two
opinions as if they were briefs, each advocating a
different view. Then decide the case yourself.*

THE OPINION OF THE COURT

During the period that is relevant to this action, du
Pont produced almost 75 percent of the cellophane
sold in the United States, and cellophane constituted less than 20 percent of all "flexible packaging
material" sales.

The Government contends that, by so dominat-
ing cellophane production, du Pont monopolized a
"part of the trade or commerce" in violation of § 2
[of the Sherman Act] . . . . The court below found
that the "relevant market for determining the extent of du Pont's market control is the market for
flexible packaging materials," and that competition
from those other materials prevented du Pont from
possessing monopoly powers in its sales of cellophane.

MONOPOLIZATION

The only statutory language of § 2 pertinent on this
review is: "Every person who shall monopolize . . .

Abridged from *United States* v. *du Pont de Nemours & Co.*,
351 U.S. 377 (1956), pp. 379–426.

shall be deemed guilty. . . ." Our cases determine
that a party has monopoly power if it has, over
"any part of the trade or commerce among the several States," a power of controlling prices or unrea-
sonably restricting competition.

Determination of the competitive market for
commodities depends on how different from one
another are the offered commodities in character or
use, how far buyers will go to substitute one commodity for another. For example, one can think of
building materials as in commodity competition but
one could hardly say that brick competed with steel
or wood or cement or stone in the meaning of Sherman Act litigation; the products are too different.
On the other hand, there are certain differences in
the formulae for soft drinks but one can hardly say
that each one is an illegal monopoly. Whatever the
market may be, we hold that control of price or
competition establishes the existence of monopoly
power under § 2. Our next step is to determine
whether du Pont has monopoly power over cellophane: that is, power over its price in relation to or
competition with other commodities. The charge
was monopolization of cellophane. The defense,
that cellophane was merely a part of the relevant
market for flexible packaging materials.

THE RELEVANT MARKET

In considering what is the relevant market for determining the control of price and competition, no
more definite rule can be declared than that commodities reasonably interchangeable by consumers
for the same purposes make up that "part of the
trade or commerce," monopolization of which may
be illegal.

Cellophane differs from other flexible packaging
materials. From some it differs more than from
others. . . . Comparative characteristics have been
noted thus:

*Moistureproof cellophane is highly transparent,
tears readily but has high bursting strength, is highly
impervious to moisture and gases, and is resistant to
grease and oils. Heat sealable, printable, and adapted to use on wrapping machines, it makes an excel-*

lent packaging material for both display and protection of commodities.

Other flexible wrapping materials fall into four major categories: (1) opaque nonmoistureproof wrapping paper designed primarily for convenience and protection in handling packages; (2) moistureproof films of varying degrees of transparency designed primarily either to protect, or to display and protect, the products they encompass; (3) nonmoistureproof transparent films designed primarily to display and to some extent protect, but which obviously do a poor protecting job where exclusion or retention of moisture is important; and (4) moistureproof materials other than films of varying degrees of transparency (foils and paper products) designed to protect and display.

> [Stocking and Mueller, "The Cellophane
> Case," *American Economic Review,*
> *45, n. 29 (1955)*]

Cellophane's principal uses are analyzed in the Appendix. Food products are the chief outlet, with cigarettes next. The Government makes no challenge that cellophane furnishes less than 7 percent of wrappings for bakery products, 25 percent for candy, 32 percent for snacks, 35 percent for meats and poultry, 27 percent for crackers and biscuits, 47 percent for fresh produce, and 34 percent for frozen foods. Seventy-five to 80 percent of cigarettes are wrapped in cellophane. Thus, cellophane shares the packaging market with others. The over-all result is that cellophane accounts for 17.9 percent of flexible wrapping materials, measured by the wrapping surface.

Moreover a very considerable degree of functional interchangeability exists between these products. . . . It will be noted that except as to permeability to gases, cellophane has no qualities that are not possessed by a number of other materials. Meat will do as an example of interchangeability. Although du Pont's sales to the meat industry have reached 19,000,000 pounds annually, nearly 35 percent, this volume is attributed "to the rise of self-service retailing of fresh meat." In fact, since the popularity of self-service meats, du Pont has lost "a considerable proportion" of this packaging business

to Pliofilm. Pliofilm is more expensive than cellophane, but its superior physical characteristics apparently offset cellophane's price advantage. While retailers shift continually between the two, the trial court found that Pliofilm is increasing its share of the business. One further example is worth noting. Before World War II, du Pont cellophane wrapped between 5 and 10 percent of baked and smoked meats. The peak year was 1933. Thereafter du Pont was unable to meet the competition of Sylvania and of greaseproof paper. Its sales declined and the 1933 volume was not reached again until 1947.

An element for consideration as to cross-elasticity of demand between products is the responsiveness of the sales of one product to price changes of the other. If a slight decrease in the price of cellophane causes a considerable number of customers of other flexible wrappings to switch to cellophane, it would be an indication that a high cross-elasticity of demand exists between them; that the products compete in the same market. The court below held that the "[g]reat sensitivity of customers in the flexible packaging markets to price or quality changes" prevented du Pont from possessing monopoly control over price.

It is the variable characteristics of the different flexible wrappings and the energy and ability with which the manufacturers push their wares that determine choice. A glance at "Modern Packaging," a trade journal, will give, by its various advertisements, examples of the competition among manufacturers for the flexible packaging market. The trial judge visited the 1952 Annual Packaging Show at Atlantic City, with the consent of counsel. He observed exhibits offered by "machinery manufacturers, converters and manufacturers of flexible packaging materials." He states that these personal observations confirmed his estimate of the competition between cellophane and other packaging materials.

The "market" which one must study to determine when a producer has monopoly power will vary with the part of commerce under consideration. The tests are constant. That market is composed of products that have reasonable interchangeability for the purposes for which they are produced — price, use and qualities considered. While the application of the tests remains uncertain, it seems to us that du Pont should not be found to monopolize cellophane when that product has the competition and interchangeability with other wrappings that this record shows.

On the findings of the District Court, its judgment is

Affirmed.

APPENDIX TO THE OPINION OF THE COURT

[Sales in] 1949 . . . of 19 major representative converters whose business covered a substantial segment of the total converting of flexible packaging materials for that year showed the following [see Table 1] as to their sales of flexible packaging materials, classified by end use.

THE DISSENTING OPINION

This case, like many under the Sherman Act, turns upon the proper definition of the market. In defining the market in which du Pont's economic power is to be measured, the majority virtually emasculate § 2 of the Sherman Act. They admit that "cellophane combines the desirable elements of transparency, strength and cheapness more definitely than any of" a host of other packaging materials. Yet they hold that all of those materials are so indistinguishable from cellophane as to warrant their inclusion in the market. We cannot agree that cellophane . . . is "the selfsame product" as glassine, greaseproof and vegetable parchment papers, waxed papers, sulphite papers, aluminum foil, cellulose acetate, and Pliofilm and other films.[1]

[T]he record provides convincing proof that businessmen did not so regard these products. Dur-

[1]In *Times-Picayune Publishing Co.* v. *United States*, 345 U.S. 594, 612, note 31, the Court said: "For every product, substitutes exist. But a relevant market cannot meaningfully encompass that infinite range. The circle must be drawn narrowly to exclude any other product to which, within reasonable variations in price, only a limited number of buyers will turn; in technical terms, products whose 'cross-elasticities of demand' are small."

Table 1. *Sale of Flexible Packaging Materials, by End Use*

	Quantity (Millions Sq. In.)	Percent of Total End Use
Bakery products		
Cellophane	109,670	6.8
Foil	2,652	0.2
Glassine	72,216	4.4
Papers	1,440,413	88.6
Films	215	0.0
Total	1,625,166	100.0
Candy		
Cellophane	134,280	24.4
Foil	178,967	32.5
Glassine	117,634	21.4
Papers	119,102	21.6
Films	484	0.1
Total	550,467	100.0
Snacks		
Cellophane	61,250	31.9
Foil	1,571	0.8
Glassine	120,556	62.8
Papers	8,439	4.4
Films	79	0.1
Total	191,895	100.0
Meat and poultry		
Cellophane	59,016	34.9
Foil	88	0.1
Glassine	4,524	2.7
Papers	97,255	57.5
Films	8,173	4.8
Total	169,056	100.0
Crackers and biscuits		
Cellophane	29,960	26.6
Foil	192	0.2
Glassine	11,253	10.0
Papers	71,147	63.2
Films	8	0.0
Total	112,560	100.0
Fresh produce		
Cellophane	52,828	47.2
Foil	43	0.1
Glassine	96	0.1
Papers	51,035	45.6
Films	7,867	7.0
Total	111,869	100.0
Frozen food excluding dairy products		
Cellophane	31,684	33.6
Foil	629	0.7
Glassine	1,943	2.1
Papers	56,925	60.3
Films	3,154	3.3
Total	94,335	100.0

ing the period covered by the complaint (1923–1947) cellophane enjoyed phenomenal growth. Du Pont's 1924 production was 361,249 pounds, which sold for $1,306,662. Its 1947 production was 133,502,858 pounds, which sold for $55,339,626. Yet throughout this period the price of cellophane was far greater than that of glassine, waxed paper or sulphite paper. . . . [I]n 1929 cellophane's price was seven times that of glassine; in 1934, four times, and in 1949 still more than twice glassine's price. . . . [C]ellophane had a similar price relation to waxed paper and sulphite paper sold at even less than glassine and waxed paper. We cannot believe that buyers, practical businessmen, would have bought cellophane in increasing amounts over a quarter of a century if close substitutes were available at from one-seventh to one-half cellophane's price. That they did so is testimony to cellophane's distinctiveness.

The inference yielded by the conduct of cellophane buyers is reinforced by the conduct of sellers other than du Pont. . . . Sylvania, the only other cellophane producer, absolutely and immediately followed every du Pont price change, even dating back its price list to the effective date of du Pont's change. Producers of glassine and waxed paper, on the other hand, displayed apparent indifference to du Pont's repeated and substantial price cuts. . . . [F]rom 1924 to 1932 du Pont dropped the price of plain cellophane 84 percent, while the price of glassine remained constant. And during the period 1933–1946 the prices for glassine and waxed paper actually increased in the face of a further 21 percent decline in the price of cellophane. If "shifts of business" due to "price sensitivity" had been substantial, glassine and waxed paper producers who wanted to stay in business would have been compelled by market forces to meet du Pont's price challenge just as Sylvania was. The majority correctly point out that:

An element for consideration as to cross-elasticity of demand between products is the responsiveness of the sales of one product to price changes of the other. If a slight decrease in the price of cellophane causes a considerable number of customers of other flexible wrappings to switch to cellophane, it would be an indication that a high cross-elasticity of demand exists between them; that the products compete in the same market.

Surely there was more than "a slight decrease in the price of cellophane" during the period covered by the complaint. That producers of glassine and waxed paper remained dominant in the flexible packaging materials market without meeting cellophane's tremendous price cuts convinces us that cellophane was not in effective competition with their products.

Certainly du Pont itself shared our view. From the first, du Pont recognized that it need not concern itself with competition from other packaging materials. For example, when du Pont was contemplating entry into cellophane production, its Development Department reported that glassine "is so inferior that it belongs in an entirely different class and has hardly to be considered as a competitor of cellophane."[2] This was still du Pont's view in 1950 when its survey of competitive prospects wholly omitted reference to glassine, waxed paper or sulphite paper and stated that "Competition for du Pont cellophane will come from competitive cellophane and from noncellophane films made by us or by others."[3]

Du Pont's every action was directed toward maintaining dominance over cellophane. Its 1923 agreements with La Cellophane, the French concern which first produced commercial cellophane, gave du Pont exclusive North and Central American rights to cellophane's technology, manufacture and sale, and provided, without any limitation in time, that all existing and future information pertaining to the cellophane process be considered "secret and confidential," and be held in an exclusive common

---

[2] The record contains many reports prepared by du Pont from 1928 to 1947. They virtually ignore the possibility of competition from other packaging materials.

[3] It is interesting to note that du Pont had almost 70 percent of the market which this report considered relevant.

pool.[4] In its subsequent agreements with foreign licensees, du Pont was careful to preserve its continental market inviolate. In 1929, while it was still the sole domestic producer of cellophane, du Pont won its long struggle to raise the tariff from 25 percent to 60 percent, ad valorem, on cellophane imports,[5] substantially foreclosing foreign competition. When Sylvania became the second American cellophane producer the following year and du Pont filed suit claiming infringement of its moistureproof patents, they settled the suit by entering into a cross-licensing agreement. Under this agreement, du Pont obtained the right to exclude third persons from use of any patentable moistureproof invention made during the next 15 years by the sole other domestic cellophane producer, and, by a prohibitive royalty provision, it limited Sylvania's moistureproof production to approximately 20 percent of the industry's moistureproof sales. The record shows that du Pont and Sylvania were aware that, by settling the infringement suit, they avoided the possibility that the courts might hold the patent claims invalid and thereby open cellophane manufacture to additional competition. If close substitutes for cellophane had been commercially available, du Pont, an enlightened enterprise, would not have gone to such lengths to control cellophane.

As predicted by its 1923 market analysis, du Pont's dominance in cellophane proved enormously profitable from the outset. After only five years of production, when du Pont bought out the minority stock interests in its cellophane subsidiary, it had to pay more than fifteen times the original price of the stock. But such success was not limited to the period of innovation, limited sales and complete domestic monopoly. A confidential du Pont report shows that during the period 1937–1947, despite great expansion of sales, du Pont's "operative return" (before taxes) averaged 31 percent, while its average "net return" (after deduction of taxes, bonuses, and fundamental research expenditures) was 15.9 percent. Such profits provide a powerful incentive for the entry of competitors. Yet from 1924 to 1951 only one new firm, Sylvania, was able to begin cellophane production. And Sylvania could not have entered if La Cellophane's secret process had not been stolen.[6] It is significant that for 15 years Olin Industries, a substantial firm, was unsuccessful in its attempt to produce cellophane, finally abandoning the project in 1944 after having spent about $1,000,000.

The trial court found that

Du Pont has no power to set cellophane prices arbitrarily. If prices for cellophane increase in relation to prices of other flexible packaging materials it will lose business to manufacturers of such materials in varying amounts for each of du Pont cellophane's major end uses.

This further reveals its misconception of the antitrust laws. A monopolist seeking to maximize profits cannot raise prices "arbitrarily." Higher prices of course mean smaller sales, but they also mean higher per-unit profit. Lower prices will increase sales but reduce per-unit profit. Within these limits a monopolist has a considerable degree of latitude in determining which course to pursue in attempting to maximize profits. The trial judge thought that, if du Pont raised its price, the market would "penalize" it with smaller profits as well as lower sales. Du Pont proved him wrong. When 1947 operating earnings dropped below 26 percent for the first time in 10 years, it increased cellophane's price 7 percent and boosted its earnings in 1948. Du Pont's division manager then reported

---

[4] The agreement of June 9, 1923, in which the parties agreed to divide the world cellophane market, is illegal *per se*. . . . The supplementary agreement providing for the interchange of technological information tightened the cellophane monopoly and denied to others any access to what went into the common pool. . . .

[5] On appeal from an adverse decision by the Commissioner of Customs, du Pont persuaded the United States Customs Court to order reclassification of cellophane.

[6] In 1924 two of La Cellophane's principal officials absconded with complete information on the cellophane process. A Belgian concern was then set up to use this process in making cellophane, and it later organized Sylvania as an American affiliate.

that "If an operative return of 31 percent is considered inadequate then an upward revision in prices will be necessary to improve the return." It is this latitude with respect to price, this broad power of choice, that the antitrust laws forbid. Du Pont's independent pricing policy and the great profits consistently yielded by that policy leave no room for doubt that it had power to control the price of cellophane. The findings of fact cited by the majority cannot affect this conclusion. For they merely demonstrate that, during the period covered by the complaint, du Pont was a "good monopolist," i.e., that it did not engage in predatory practices and that it chose to maximize profits by lowering price and expanding sales. Proof of enlightened exercise of monopoly power certainly does not refute the existence of that power.

We would reverse the decision below and remand the cause to the District Court with directions to determine the relief which should be granted against du Pont.

QUESTIONS

1. What is the definition of "monopoly power" under the Sherman Antitrust Act? Is this definition consistent with economic analysis?

2. Both the Antitrust Division and du Pont agreed that if cellophane were the relevant market, then du Pont's 75 percent share of that market would be evidence of monopoly power and a violation of the Sherman Act. Do you agree? Why is a share of 100 percent not required? If du Pont had 50 percent of the cellophane market, and you were convinced that cellophane was in fact a relevant market, would you then argue that du Pont had monopoly power? How would you determine the "threshold" percentage?

3. What is cross-elasticity of demand? What use is made of it in this trial? What data are relevant in using cross-elasticity in a problem of this sort? What weight would you place on the impressions the trial judge received from visiting the packaging trade show?

4. The dissenting opinion considers the du Pont profits on cellophane as evidence of cellophane's monopoly position. How much weight would you give to profit levels in determining the extent of monopoly power?

5. Which opinion is correct?

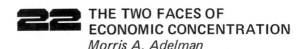

THE TWO FACES OF ECONOMIC CONCENTRATION
Morris A. Adelman

Economic concentration is a "glandular term" in that it can arouse passions and stimulate adrenalin flow. In this article Morris A. Adelman of M.I.T. endeavors to examine the extent of economic concentration in the United States and its effect on competition. Professor Adelman is known for his contributions on the measurement of concentration and antitrust policy. He is also one of the world's leading economic experts on petroleum economics and energy policy.

"Economic concentration" or "concentration of economic power" calls up a vision of a corporation, with billions in assets, thousands of employees, elaborate staff planning, etc., etc. It "dominates" its market and decides prices and outputs, either alone or in concert with one or two of its fellow giants. Such "concentration" and "domination," presumably, is the typical pattern, or at least "the wave of the future." The "grand sweep" of the 20th century is away from competition and into the new era of the big firm, etc. All this is a good story but not necessarily a true story. An effort to see and analyze what is actually happening in the world makes it apparent that "economic concentration," so far from being a simple, massive phenomenon, is actually a vague phrase applied to two different kinds of measurement of two different phenomena. One is

Reprinted with permission of M. A. Adelman from *The Public Interest*, No. 21, Fall 1970, 117—126. Copyright © 1970 by National Affairs Inc.

that of bigness, the other of market concentration, but the relation between the two is quite complicated.

CONCENTRATION RATIOS

The statistics of *market concentration* exist because economists have tried to put numbers into their analysis of monopoly and competition. Theory and observation seem to prove that it does make a difference whether there are few or many firms in a market. The ultimate in fewness is monopoly, where a single firm can do what is best for the industry as a whole because it *is* the industry as a whole. It has the power to control output: to let only so much of production on to the market as will yield the greatest money profit, or perhaps the most quiet managerial life. Short of actual monopoly, the fewer the firms, the easier it is for them to collaborate, to align prices and production so as to travel much or all the way toward monopoly. The more firms, the harder is such collaboration, and the more are they forced willy-nilly to act independently. At the extreme of such competitiveness, each firm always seeks its own profit, neither trying to serve the group industrial interest nor expecting anyone else to do so. Of course, even a very large number of firms can be regimented into monopoly through detailed agreements tolerated or enforced by government. But if these cannot be made, there is no control of supply, and no market power. Output is higher, prices are lower, and resources better used.

All this seems simple enough. But it isn't. To begin with, trying to measure the manyness or fewness of firms in an industry is difficult. Companies are usually of such unequal size that a simple headcount is useless. Suppose one firm had 95 per cent of a market and 100 other firms have the other 5 per cent. There would be literally 101 sellers. But it would be nearer the truth to call this a one-firm industry. Both statements would be imprecise, but the first would be wildly wrong in its implications.

In the 1930's, the Census Bureau first tabulated something called the "concentration ratio": the sales of the largest four companies in each industry as a percentage of total sales of all companies in that industry. Since 1947, the Census of Manufactures has regularly collected and published concentration ratios for each of 450-odd manufacturing industries, further subdivided into about a thousand product classes.

Now, manufacturing is certainly the heart of what is usually called "the industrial economy." But it is well to keep in mind that manufacturing represents only about 35 per cent of the private economy; we have no such systematic data for mining, construction, wholesale and retail trade, services, or the "public utilities" of transportation, communication, and electric power. Thus, the very biggest (e.g., A.T.&T.) and the very smallest companies fall outside of the range of what is periodically canvassed and reported by the Census.

Moreover, the concentration ratio — the sales of the largest four as a per cent of the total — is no precise measure. A concentration ratio of 50 could mean that the single largest company had 49 per cent of the sales, while the three next largest had 1/3 per cent each. A concentration ratio of 50 could also mean that the largest four had respectively 13, 13, 12 and 12.

A far more important limitation of the concentration ratio is the uncertain denominator, "total industry sales." The boundaries of the "industry" or "market" are often fuzzy. If much of a product used in this country is imported or exported, the American sellers and customers are part of a worldwide market, and figures on domestic activity are only a truncated fragment of a larger whole. Inside the United States, there may be a substitution from similar or identical products which happen to be classified as belonging to another industry, or from facilities which can easily be converted.

Finally, a concentration ratio is a snapshot and gives no indication of the way an industry is going. In a concentrated market, but a growing one to which entry is relatively easy, rewards to those who grab the largest share may be so great that an attempt to hold the line on prices cannot succeed. Prices and outputs may be highly competitive. But if entry into this growing market is difficult (e.g., because of patents), there may be less competition than there seems.

THE FACTS OF MARKET CONCENTRATION

In any given instance, therefore, a concentration ratio may not mean anything. But what cannot be said of any individual in a group may be truthfully said of a group. A single concentration ratio tells us little about a given industry at a given time, but much may be learned from analysis of groups of industries over time, or among countries or regions. So the close attention to dusty detail is bound together with broad comparisons in time and space. The most important contribution of the statistics is perhaps not in the detailed numbers but the way of looking at industries. We see some familiar terrain in a new light and the single stereotype of "big business" disintegrates into a more difficult but more interesting universe.

For example, the "third world" of the less-developed countries is almost surely the most highly concentrated and monopolized. Because incomes are low, most markets are extremely small, with room for few rivals. Capital, skilled labor and know-how are scarce, innovation is risky, and starting new enterprises is that much harder. Hence, vested interests are that much more safe from new entrants.

In such countries as Great Britain and France, companies tend to be much smaller than in the United States, but markets are very much smaller, so that in any given market, concentration tends to be higher than in the United States. (The European Economic Community is now providing much bigger markets, within which the rivals will be bigger but also more numerous and hence more competitive.) Japan is, as in so many other respects, in a class by itself. Concentration seems to run higher than in the United States, but the importance of foreign trade is so much greater that the conclusion is in doubt.

In the United States, one can study concentration over time. A comparison between manufacturing around 1900 and in 1947 seems to show a substantial drop. But given the unsystematic data for 1900, it seems better to make a sure bet on a milder proposition: concentration could not have increased. Between 1947 and 1966, individual industries or products often change, but the ups balance the downs, and there is no net total change in industrial concentration.

Attempts have also been made to relate concentration to other economic variables. The more concentrated an industry, for instance, the less competitive it presumably is, and the more profitable it ought to be. And so it appears in fact. But the relation is a weak one at best, and the odds are only a little over 50—50 that a more concentrated industry will be more profitable than a less concentrated one. This mild signal is actually reassuring. For if higher industry concentration were associated with *lower* profits, one would have to ask — on the assumption that businessmen are not as a class insane — whether concentration data made much sense.

THE LARGEST 100—200-ETC.

These facts on industry concentration get no headlines. What we mostly hear about is "aggregate concentration" (or "overall concentration" or "super-concentration"), which is the percentage of total manufacturing — all industries added together — that is accounted for by the largest 50 or 100 or 200 firms, regardless of industry.

A few comparisons over time are possible. In 1935, the largest 50 companies accounted for somewhere around 22 per cent of total Census manufacturing "value-added" (i.e., the margin between purchases and sales); in 1947, only 17 per cent; in 1954, 23 per cent, and in 1966, 25 per cent. Another way to measure big-company participation is by the proportions of corporate assets owned. Assets are harder to measure and more risky to compare, because of variations in accounting rules, which moreover have changed over time. But the figures on assets show a parallel movement to the figures on "value-added." According to the statistics of the Internal Revenue Service, the largest 139 manufacturing corporations had 47 per cent of all corporate assets in 1931 and the largest 141 had 48 per cent in 1963. Measuring on a different basis,

Professor Charles Berry has estimated the share of the largest 100 at 44 per cent in 1948 and 48 per cent in 1964; applying his methods to later years, the figure is seen to be 50 per cent in 1968.

It is reassuring that both value-added and asset figures agree in broad outline: a decrease from the early 1930's to the late 1940's; then a restoration; then an even further increase.

The trend can be embellished, for polemical purposes, by measuring from low to high, i.e., comparing 1948 with 1968, rather than from high to high (or at least earliest to latest), i.e., comparing 1931 with 1968. It is a bit like comparing department store sales, August with December, to show that sales are doing fine. Extrapolate the 1948–1968 "trend" by twenty or fifty years, and there is as much to view with alarm as there was decades ago; only a spoilsport would ask what happened to those earlier predictions of an imminent monopolistic economy.

The increased share of the largest 50 or 100, etc., has come about largely because the industries composed of big companies have grown faster than industries with smaller companies. (These industries of big companies, it should be noted, are *not* the industries with the highest concentration ratios. And within these big-company industries, there was actually some decrease in concentration ratios during 1947-1966.) The minor reason for the higher aggregate concentration has been mergers, some conglomerate some not, though such terms are highly imprecise.

But the most important question is the relevance of "superconcentration." Statistics do not speak for themselves. One needs a theory to show that a given set of numbers has a given meaning. A private-enterprise economy works well or badly through the network of markets which compose it. But there is no linkage between "aggregate concentration" and any market in the real world. At the limit, concentration ratios could be declining in every industry, and the less concentrated industries growing more rapidly, yet if those were big-company industries, "aggregate concentration" would increase.

The two biggest manufacturing companies are Standard Oil (New Jersey) and General Motors, with respectively $17 billion and $14 billion of assets. GM has about 55 per cent of U.S. automotive production. (The largest four automobile producers account for practically all domestic output.) Yet as we warned earlier, a concentration ratio of 100 *exaggerates*. (GM, Ford, Chrysler, and American Motors do not in fact have the entire market.) Jersey Standard, although bigger than GM, has only about 9 per cent of domestic oil refining, and less of production. *The huge size of a given company tells nothing about the rivalry it faces, the kind of market it lives in, or its price-output pattern.*

The attention and publicity given to "aggregate concentration" derives partly from the belief that "the big firm" has basic advantages in the market place. It can outlast, outlose, outfight, outspend, etc., and thereby drive smaller rivals out of its respective markets without resort to anything so crude and costly as predatory warfare. (The belief is even stronger in Europe, despite the loss of export markets by American companies to much smaller European and Japanese firms.) The theory is general, and presumes to hold as well for the United States 70 years ago as for now. If it is correct, one should see an updrift in concentration ratios, as the firms which were largest in total size took over more and more of the markets in which they operated. The tendency would be stronger in some places, weaker in others, but over a long period of time it would be a tide lapping steadily upward and onward over the land. But as seen earlier, there is no such tendency; the chief problem is why industry concentration has remained so stable for so long, through stronger and weaker antitrust enforcement; through war, depression, and boom.

Plainly the theory is wrong, and size alone does not convey an inherent advantage. There are two mistakes in supposing that big and richer companies can elbow smaller rivals out of the market merely because they are big. First, investment for profit is not like spending for personal need or pleasure. If Mr. A and Mr. B both bid for the same painting, and Mr. A has ten times as much income and assets, he has the power to outbid and take the picture. But if Corporation X has a cash flow ten times that of Corporation Y, it has about ten times as many claims on it. There is no presumption that Corporation X can obtain more money more easily than Corporation Y for the particular purpose of improving its position in Y's market. Other markets may offer more lucrative opportunities — and such a comparison is bound to be made by management, the firm's creditors, and the investing public. Possibly the big firm can borrow more cheaply, though the advantage is never great and above a certain point, perhaps $50 million in assets, it goes to zero. Furthermore, most capital is equity capital, and the more profitable company can sell equity securities on better terms.

This brings us to the second and perhaps more basic mistake in supposing that larger companies can outlose or outbid smaller ones. Business firms only want money in order to make more. The firm which stands to gain more from an expenditure can offer more for the use of money. In any given market, therefore, the more efficient firm will tend to outbid its less efficient rival. The more profitable companies will tend to grow faster than the less profitable. If the process continues for some time, the biggest companies in any given industry may well end up being the ones who are the most profitable — but this hardly proves that size as such brings high profits.

Public opinion has been, not hostile to big business, but at least cool and critical of it. It is no bad thing, in my opinion, that generations of big business executives have learned that they live in a goldfish bowl, more subject to taxes and regulations and prohibitions than smaller firms. But like all good things, this public opinion has its price, which is confusion and ambivalence, admiration and mistrust often equally misplaced.

Perhaps bigness is much more important, sociologically or politically, than is revealed by measuring economic quantities to understand market facts. If that is the case, it should be studied directly, and not be confused with economic concentration, a market phenomenon.

QUESTIONS

1. What distinction does Professor Adelman draw between market concentration and aggregate concentration?

2. What difficulties exist in using Census Bureau statistics to describe an industry's structure?

3. What has been the trend of concentration in the American economy?

4. What is the relationship between the size of a company's sales and competition in its market? What relationship does the author see between competition in an economy and the extent of aggregate concentration?

23 POLLUTION: AN ECONOMIC PROBLEM
Larry Ruff

Among the flood of articles on pollution, one of the finest is Larry Ruff's analysis of the economic aspects of the problem. Ruff was director of the Washington Environmental Research Center of EPA and is now with the Resources and Environment Program of the Ford Foundation.

We are going to make very little real progress in solving the problem of pollution until we recognize it for what, primarily, it is: an economic problem, which must be understood in economic terms. Of course, there are *noneconomic* aspects of pollution, as there are with all economic problems, but all too often, such secondary matters dominate discussion. Engineers, for example, are certain that pollution will vanish once they find the magic gadget or power source. Politicians keep trying to find the right kind of bureaucracy; and bureaucrats maintain an unending search for the correct set of rules and regulations. Those who are above such vulgar pursuits pin their hopes on a

Abridged from Larry Ruff, "The Economic Common Sense of Pollution," *The Public Interest,* no. 19 (Spring 1970), 69–85. © National Affairs, Inc., 1970. Reprinted by permission.

moral regeneration or social revolution, apparently in the belief that saints and socialists have no garbage to dispose of.   But as important as technology, politics, law and ethics are to the pollution question, all such approaches are bound to have disappointing results, for they ignore the primary fact that pollution is an economic problem.

Before developing an economic analysis of pollution, however, it is necessary to dispose of some popular myths.

First, pollution is not new. Spanish explorers landing in the sixteenth century noted that smoke from Indian campfires hung in the air of the Los Angeles basin, trapped by what is now called the inversion layer. Before the first century B.C., the drinking waters of Rome were becoming polluted.

Second, most pollution is not due to affluence, despite the current popularity of this notion. In India, the pollution runs in the streets, and advice against drinking the water in exotic lands is often well taken. Nor can pollution be blamed on the self-seeking activities of greedy capitalists. Once-beautiful rivers and lakes which are now open sewers and cesspools can be found in the Soviet Union as well as in the United States, and some of the world's dirtiest air hangs over cities in Eastern Europe, which are neither capitalist nor affluent. In many ways, indeed, it is much more difficult to do anything about pollution in noncapitalist societies. In the Soviet Union, there is no way for the public to become outraged or to exert any pressure, and the polluters and the courts there work for the same people, who often decide that clean air and water, like good clothing, are low on their list of social priorities.

In fact, it seems probable that affluence, technology, and slow-moving, inefficient democracy will turn out to be the cure more than the cause of pollution. After all, only an affluent, technological society can afford such luxuries as moon trips, three-day weekends, and clean water, although even our society may not be able to afford them all; and only in a democracy can the people hope to have any real influence on the choice among such alternatives.

What *is* new about pollution is what might be called the *problem* of pollution. Many unpleasant phenomena — poverty, genetic defects, hurricanes — have existed forever without being considered problems; they are, or were, considered to be facts of life, like gravity and death, and a mature person simply adjusted to them. Such phenomena become problems only when it begins to appear that something can and should be done about them. It is evident that pollution has advanced to the problem stage. Now the question is what can and should be done?

Most discussions of the pollution problem begin with some startling facts: Did you know that 15,000 tons of filth are dumped into the air of Los Angeles County every day? But by themselves, such facts are meaningless, if only because there is no way to know whether 15,000 tons is a lot or a little. It is much more important for clear thinking about the pollution problem to understand a few economic concepts than to learn a lot of sensational-sounding numbers.

MARGINALISM

One of the most fundamental economic ideas is that of *marginalism,* which entered economic. theory when economists became aware of the differential calculus in the nineteenth century and used it to formulate economic problems as problems of "maximization." The standard economic problem came to be viewed as that of finding a level of operation of some activity which would maximize the net gain from that activity, where the net gain is the difference between the benefits and the costs of the activity. As the level of activity increases, both benefits and costs will increase; but because of diminishing returns, costs will increase faster than benefits.   When a certain level of the activity is reached, any further expansion increases costs more than benefits. At this "optimal" level, "marginal cost" — or the cost of expanding the activity — equals "marginal benefit," or the benefit from expanding the activity. Further expansion would cost more than it is worth, and reduction in the activity would reduce benefits more than it would save costs. The net gain from the activity is said to be maximized at this point.

This principle is so simple that it is almost embarrassing to admit it is the cornerstone of economics. Yet intelligent men often ignore it in discussion of public issues. Educators, for example, often suggest that, if it is better to be literate than illiterate, there is no logical stopping point in supporting education. Or scientists have pointed out that the benefits derived from "science" obviously exceed the costs and then have proceeded to infer that their particular project should be supported. The correct comparison, of course, is between *additional* benefits created by the proposed activity and the *additional* costs incurred.

The application of marginalism to questions of pollution is simple enough conceptually. The difficult part lies in estimating the cost and benefits functions, a questions to which I shall return. But several important qualitative points can be made immediately. The first is that the choice facing a rational society is *not* between clean air and dirty air, or between clear water and polluted water, but rather between various *levels* of dirt and pollution. The aim must be to find that level of pollution abatement where the costs of further abatement begin to exceed the benefits.

The second point is that the optimal combination of pollution control methods is going to be a very complex affair. Such steps as demanding a 10 percent reduction in pollution from all sources, without considering the relative difficulties and costs of the reduction, will certainly be an inefficient approach. Where it is less costly to reduce pollution, we want a greater reduction, to a point where an additional dollar spent on control anywhere yields the same reduction in pollution levels.

MARKETS, EFFICIENCY, AND EQUITY

A second basic economic concept is the idea — or the ideal — of the self-regulating economic system. Adam Smith illustrated this ideal with the example of bread in London: the uncoordinated, selfish actions of many people — farmer, miller, shipper, baker,

grocer — provide bread for the city dweller, without any central control and at the lowest possible cost. Pure self-interest, guided only by the famous "invisible hand" of competition, organizes the economy efficiently.

The logical basis of this rather startling result is that, under certain conditions, competitive prices convey all the information necessary for making the optimal decision. A builder trying to decide whether to use brick or concrete will weigh his requirements and tastes against the prices of the materials. Other users will do the same, with the result that those whose needs and preferences for brick are relatively the strongest will get brick. Further, profit-maximizing producers will weigh relative production costs, reflecting society's productive capabilities, against relative prices, reflecting society's tastes and desires, when deciding how much of each good to produce. The end result is that users get brick and cement in quantities and proportions that reflect their individual tastes and society's production opportunities. No other solution would be better from the standpoint of all the individuals concerned.

This suggests what it is that makes pollution different. The efficiency of competitive markets depends on the identity of *private* costs and *social* costs. As long as the brick-cement producer must compensate somebody for every cost imposed by his production, his profit-maximizing decisions about how much to produce, and how, will also be socially efficient decisions. Thus, if a producer dumps wastes into the air, river, or ocean; if he pays nothing for such dumping; and if the disposed wastes have no noticeable effect on anyone else, living or still unborn; then the private and social costs of disposal are identical and nil, and the producer's private decisions are socially efficient. *But if these wastes do affect others, then the social costs of waste disposal are not zero. Private and social costs diverge, and private profit-maximizing decisions are not socially efficient.* Suppose, for example, that cement production dumps large quantities of dust into the air, which damages neighbors, and that the brick-cement producer pays these neighbors nothing. In the social sense, cement will be over-produced relative to brick and other products because users of the products will make decisions based on market prices which do not reflect true social costs. They will use cement when they should use brick, or when they should not build at all.

This divergence between private and social costs is the fundamental cause of pollution of all types, and it arises in any society where decisions are at all decentralized — which is to say, in any economy of any size which hopes to function at all. Even the socialist manager of the brick-cement plant, told to maximize output given the resources at his disposal, will use the People's Air to dispose of the People's Wastes; to do otherwise would be to violate his instructions. And if instructed to avoid pollution "when possible," he does not know what to do: how can he decide whether more brick or cleaner air is more important for building socialism? The capitalist manager is in exactly the same situation. Without prices to convey the needed information, he does not know what action is in the public interest, and certainly would have no incentive to act correctly even if he did know.

Although markets fail to perform efficiently when private and social costs diverge, this does not imply that there is some inherent flaw in the idea of acting on self-interest in response to market prices. Decisions based on private cost calculations are typically correct from a social point of view; and even when they are not quite correct, it often is better to accept this inefficiency than to turn to some alternative decision mechanism, which may be worse. Even the modern economic theory of socialism is based on the high correlation between managerial self-interest and public good. There is no point in trying to find something — some omniscient and omnipotent *deus ex machina* — to replace markets and self-interest. Usually it is preferable to modify existing institutions, where necessary, to make private and social interest coincide.

And there is a third relevant economic concept: the fundamental distinction between questions of efficiency and questions of equity or fairness. A situation is said to be efficient if it is not possible to rearrange things so as to benefit one person without harming any others. That is the *economic*

equation for efficiency. *Politically,* this equation can be solved in various ways; though most reasonable men will agree that efficiency is a good thing, they will rarely agree about which of the many possible efficient states, each with a different distribution of "welfare" among individuals, is the best one. Economics itself has nothing to say about which efficient state is the best. That decision is a matter of personal and philosophical values, and ultimately must be decided by some political process. Economics can suggest ways of achieving efficient states, and can try to describe the equity considerations involved in any suggested social policy; but the final decisions about matters of "fairness" or "justice" cannot be decided on economic grounds.

ESTIMATING THE COSTS OF POLLUTION

Both in theory and practice, the most difficult part of an economic approach to pollution is the measurement of the cost and benefits of its abatement. Only a small fraction of the costs of pollution can be estimated straightforwardly. If, for example, smog reduces the life of automobile tires by 10 percent, one component of the cost of smog is 10 percent of tire expenditures. It has been estimated that, in a moderately polluted area of New York City, filthy air imposes extra costs for painting, washing, laundry, etc., of $200 per person per year. Such costs must be included in any calculation of the benefits of pollution abatement, and yet they are only a part of the relevant costs — and often a small part. Accordingly it rarely is possible to justify a measure like river pollution control solely on the basis of costs to individuals or firms of treating water because it usually is cheaper to process only the water that is actually used for industrial or municipal purposes, and to ignore the river itself.

The costs of pollution that cannot be measured so easily are often called "intangible" or "noneconomic," although neither term is particularly appropriate. Many of these costs are as tangible as burning eyes or a dead fish, and all such costs are relevant to a valid economic analysis. Let us therefore call these costs "nonpecuniary."

The only real difference between nonpecuniary

costs and the other kind lies in the difficulty of estimating them. If pollution in Los Angeles harbor is reducing marine life, this imposes costs on society. The cost of reducing commercial fishing could be estimated directly: it would be the fixed cost of converting men and equipment from fishing to an alternative occupation, plus the difference between what they earned in fishing and what they earn in the new occupation, plus the loss to consumers who must eat chicken instead of fish. But there are other, less straightforward costs: the loss of recreation opportunities for children and sports fishermen and of research facilities for marine biologists, etc. Such costs are obviously difficult to measure and may be very large indeed; but just as surely as they are not zero, so too are they not infinite. Those who call for immediate action and damn the cost, merely because the spiney starfish and furry crab populations are shrinking, are putting an infinite marginal value on these creatures. This strikes a disinterested observer as an overestimate.

The above comments may seem crass and insensitive to those who, like one angry letter-writer to the Los Angeles *Times,* want to ask: "If conservation is not for its own sake, then what in the world *is* it for?" Well, what *is* the purpose of pollution control? Is it for its own sake? Of course not. If we answer that it is to make the air and water clean and quiet, then the question arises: what is the purpose of clean air and water? If the answer is, to please the nature gods, then it must be conceded that all pollution must cease immediately because the cost of angering the gods is presumably infinite. But if the answer is that the purpose of clean air and water is to further human enjoyment of life on this planet, then we are faced with the economists' basic question: given the limited alternatives that a niggardly nature allows, how can we best further human enjoyment of life? And the answer is, by making intelligent marginal decisions on the basis of costs and benefits. Pollution control is for lots of things: breathing comfortably, enjoying mountains, swimming in water, for health, beauty, and the general delectation. But so are many other things, like good food and wine, comfortable housing and fast transportation. The question is not which of these desirable things we should have, but rather what combination is most desirable. To determine such a combination, we must know the rate at which individuals are willing to substitute more of one desirable thing for less of another desirable thing. Prices are one way of determining those rates.

But if we cannot directly observe market prices for many of the costs of pollution, we must find another way to proceed. One possibility is to infer the costs from other prices, just as we infer the value of an ocean view from real estate prices. In principle, one could estimate the value people put on clean air and beaches by observing how much more they are willing to pay for property in nonpolluted areas. Such information could be obtained; but there is little of it available at present.

Another possible way of estimating the costs of pollution is to ask people how much they would be willing to pay to have pollution reduced. A resident of Pasadena might be willing to pay $100 a year to have smog reduced 10 or 20 percent. In Barstow, where the marginal cost of smog is much less, a resident might not pay $10 a year to have smog reduced 10 percent. If we knew how much it was worth to everybody, we could add up these amounts and obtain an estimate of the cost of a marginal amount of pollution. The difficulty, of course, is that there is no way of guaranteeing truthful responses. Your response to the question, how much is pollution costing *you,* obviously will depend on what you think will be done with this information. If you think you will be compensated for these costs, you will make a generous estimate; if you think that you will be charged for the control in proportion to these costs, you will make a small estimate.

In such cases it becomes very important how the questions are asked. For example, the voters could be asked a question of the form: Would you like to see pollution reduced x percent if the result is a y percent increase in the cost of living? Presumably a set of questions of this form could be used to estimate the costs of pollution, including the so-called "unmeasurable" costs. But great care must be taken in formulating the questions. For one thing, if the voters will benefit differentially from the activity, the questions should be asked in a way which reflects this fact. If, for example, the issue is cleaning up a river, residents near the river will be willing to pay more for the cleanup and should have a means of expressing this. Ultimately, some such political procedure probably will be necessary, at least until our more direct measurement techniques are greatly improved.

Let us assume that, somehow, we have made an estimate of the social cost function for pollution, including the marginal cost associated with various pollution levels. We now need an estimate of the benefits of pollution — or, if you prefer, of the costs of pollution abatement. So we set the Pollution Control Board (PCB) to work on this task.

The PCB has a staff of engineers and technicians, and they begin working on the obvious question: for each pollution source, how much would it cost to reduce pollution by 10 percent, 20 percent, and so on. If the PCB has some economists, they will know that the cost of reducing total pollution by 10 percent is *not* the total cost of reducing each pollution source by 10 percent. Rather, they will use the equimarginal principle and find the pattern of control such that an additional dollar spent on control of any pollution source yields the same reduction. This will minimize the cost of achieving any given level of abatement. In this way the PCB can generate a "cost of abatement" function, and the corresponding marginal cost function.

While this procedure seems straightforward enough, the practical difficulties are tremendous. The amount of information needed by the PCB is staggering; to do this job right, the PCB would have to know as much about each plant as the operators of the plant themselves. The cost of gathering these data is obviously prohibitive, and, since marginal principles apply to data collection too, the PCB would have to stop short of complete information, trading off the resulting loss in efficient control against the cost of better information. Of course, just as fast as the PCB obtained the data, a technological change would make it obsolete.

The PCB would have to face a further complication. It would not be correct simply to determine how to control existing pollution sources given their existing locations and production methods. Although this is almost certainly what the PCB would do, the resulting cost functions will overstate the true social cost of control. Muzzling existing plants is only one method of control. Plants can move, or switch to a new process, or even to a new product. Consumers can switch to a less-polluting substitute. There are any number of alternatives, and the poor PCB engineers can never know them all. This could lead to some costly mistakes. For example, the PCB may correctly conclude that the cost of installing effective dust control at the cement plant is very high and hence may allow the pollution to continue, when the best solution is for the cement plant to switch to brick production while a plant in the desert switches from brick to cement. The PCB can never have all this information and therefore is doomed to inefficiency, sometimes an inefficiency of large proportions.

Once cost and benefit functions are known, the PCB should choose a level of abatement that maximizes net gain. This occurs where the marginal cost of further abatement just equals the marginal benefit. If, for example, we could reduce pollution damages by $2 million at a cost of $1 million, we should obviously impose that $1 million cost. But if the damage reduction is only $1/2 million, we should not and in fact should reduce control efforts.

This principle is obvious enough but is often overlooked. One author, for example, has written that the national cost of air pollution is $11 billion a year but that we are spending less than $50 million a year on control; he infers from this that "we could justify a tremendous strengthening of control efforts on purely economic grounds." That *sounds* reasonable, if all you care about are sounds. But what is the logical content of the statement? Does it imply we should spend $11 billion on control just to make things even? Suppose we were spending $ 11 billion on control and thereby succeeded in reducing pollution costs to $50 million. Would this imply we were spending too *much* on control? Of course not. We must compare the *marginal* decrease in pollution costs to the *marginal* increase in abatement costs.

DIFFICULT DECISIONS

Once the optimal pollution level is determined, all that is necessary is for the PCB to enforce the pattern of controls which it has determined to be optimal. (Of course, this pattern will not really be the best one, because the PCB will not have all the information it should have.) But now a new problem arises: how should the controls be enforced?

The most direct and widely used method is in many ways the least efficient: direct regulation. The PCB can decide what each polluter must do to reduce pollution and then simply require that action under penalty of law. But this approach has many shortcomings. The polluters have little incentive to install the required devices or to keep them operating properly. Constant inspection is therefore necessary. Once the polluter has complied with the letter of the law, he has no incentive to find better methods of pollution reduction. Direct control of this sort has a long history of inadequacy; the necessary bureaucracies rarely manifest much vigor, imagination, or devotion to the public interest. Still, in some situations there may be no alternative.

A slightly better method of control is for the PCB to set an acceptable level of pollution for each source and let the polluters find the cheapest means of achieving this level. This reduces the amount of information the PCB needs, but not by much. The setting of the acceptable levels becomes a matter for negotiation, political pull, or even graft. As new plants are built and new control methods invented, the limits should be changed; but if they are, the incentive to find new designs and new techniques is reduced.

A third possibility is to subsidize the reduction of pollution, either by subsidizing control equipment or by paying for the reduction of pollution below standard levels. This alternative has all the problems of the above methods, plus the classic shortcoming which plagues agricultural subsidies:

The old joke about getting into the not-growing-cotton business is not always so funny.

Clearly, the PCB has a big job which it will never be able to handle with any degree of efficiency. Some sort of self-regulating system, like a market, is needed, which will automatically adapt to changes in conditions, provide incentives for development and adoption of improved control methods, reduce the amount of information the PCB must gather and the amount of detailed control it must exercise, and so on. This, by any standard, is a tall order.

PUTTING A PRICE ON POLLUTION

And yet there is a very simple way to accomplish all this. *Put a price on pollution.* A price-based control mechanism would differ from an ordinary market transaction system only in that the PCB would set the prices, instead of their being set by demand-supply forces, and that the state would force payment. Under such a system, anyone could emit any amount of pollution so long as he pays the price which the PCB sets to approximate the marginal social cost of pollution. Under this circumstance, private decisions based on self-interest are efficient. If pollution consists of many components, each with its own social cost, there should be different prices for each component. Thus, extremely dangerous materials must have an extremely high price, perhaps stated in terms of "years in jail" rather than "dollars," although a sufficiently high dollar price is essentially the same thing. In principle, the prices should vary with geographical location, season of the year, direction of the wind, and even day of the week, although the cost of too many variations may preclude such fine distinctions.

Once the prices are set, polluters can adjust to them any way they choose. Because they act on self-interest they will reduce their pollution by every means possible up to the point where further reduction would cost more than the price. Because all face the same price for the same type of pollution, the marginal cost of abatement is the same everywhere. If there are economies of scale in pollution control, as in some types of liquid waste treatment, plants can cooperate in establishing joint treatment facilities. In fact, some enterprising individual could buy these wastes from various plants (at negative prices — i.e., they would get paid for carting them off), treat them, and then sell them at a higher price, making a profit in the process. (After all, this is what rubbish removal firms do now.) If economies of scale are so substantial that the provider of such a service becomes a monopolist, then the PCB can operate the facilities itself.

Obviously such a scheme does not eliminate the need for the PCB. The board must measure the output of pollution from all sources, collect the fees, and so on. But it does not need to know anything about any plant except its total emission of pollution. It does not control, negotiate, threaten, or grant favors. It does not destroy incentive because development of new control methods will reduce pollution payments.

As a test of this price system of control, let us consider how well it would work when applied to automobile pollution, a problem for which direct control is usually considered the only feasible approach. If the price system can work here, it can work anywhere.

Suppose, then, that a price is put on the emissions of automobiles. Obviously, continuous metering of such emissions is impossible. But it should be easy to determine the average output of pollution for cars of different makes, models, and years, having different types of control devices and using different types of fuel. Through graduated registration fees and fuel taxes, each car owner would be assessed roughly the social cost of his car's pollution, adjusted for whatever control devices he has chosen to install and for his driving habits. If the cost of installing a device, driving a different car, or finding alternative means of transportation is less than the price he must pay to continue his pollution, he will presumably take the necessary steps. But each individual remains free to find the best adjustment to his particular situation. It would be remarkable if everyone decided to install the same devices which some states currently require; and yet that is the effective assumption of such requirements.

Even in the difficult case of auto pollution, the price system has a number of advantages. Why should a person living in the Mojave desert, where pollution has little social cost, take the same pains to reduce air pollution as a person living in Pasadena? Present California law, for example, makes no distinction between such areas; the price system would. And what incentive is there for auto manufacturers to design a less polluting engine? The law says only that they must install a certain device in every car. If GM develops a more efficient engine, the law will eventually be changed to require this engine on all cars, raising costs and reducing sales. But will such development take place? No collusion is needed for manufacturers to decide unanimously that it would be foolish to devote funds to such development. But with a pollution fee paid by the consumer, there is a real advantage for any firm to be first with a better engine, and even a collusive agreement wouldn't last long in the face of such an incentive. The same is true of fuel manufacturers, who now have no real incentive to look for better fuels. Perhaps most important of all, the present situation provides no real way of determining whether it is cheaper to reduce pollution by muzzling cars or industrial plants. The experts say that most smog comes from cars; but *even if true, this does not imply that it is more efficient to control autos rather than other pollution sources.* How can we decide which is more efficient without mountains of information? The answer is, by making drivers and plants pay the same price for the same pollution, and letting self-interest do the job.

In situations where pollution outputs can be measured more or less directly (unlike the automobile pollution case), the price system is clearly superior to direct control. A study of possible control methods in the Delaware estuary, for example, estimated that, compared to a direct control scheme requiring each polluter to reduce his pollution by a fixed percentage, an effluent charge which would achieve the same level of pollution abatement would be only half as costly — a saving of about $150 million. Such a price system would also provide incentive for further improvements, a simple method of handling new plants, and revenue for the control authority.

In general, the price system allocates costs in a manner which is at least superficially fair: those who produce and consume goods which cause pollution, pay the costs. But the superior efficiency in control and apparent fairness are not the only advantages of the price mechanism. Equally important is the ease with which it can be put into operation. It is not necessary to have detailed information about all the techniques of pollution reduction, or estimates of all costs and benefits. Nor is it necessary to determine whom to blame or who should pay. All that is needed is a mechanism for estimating, if only roughly at first, the pollution output of all polluters, together with a means of collecting fees. Then we can simply pick a price — any price — for each category of pollution, and we are in business. The initial price should be chosen on the basis of some estimate of its effects but need not be the optimal one. If the resulting reduction in pollution is not "enough," the price can be raised until there is sufficient reduction. A change in technology, number of plants, or whatever, can be accommodated by a change in the price, even without detailed knowledge of all the technological and economic data. Further, once the idea is explained, the price system is much more likely to be politically acceptable than some method of direct control. Paying for a service, such as garbage disposal, is a well-established tradition, and is much less objectionable than having a bureaucrat nosing around and giving arbitrary orders. When businessmen, consumers, and politicians understand the alternatives, the price system will seem very attractive indeed.

SOME OBJECTIONS AREN'T AN ANSWER

There are some objections that can be raised against the price system as a tool of pollution policy. Most are either illogical or apply with much greater force to any other method of control.

For example, one could object that what has been suggested here ignores the difficulties caused by fragmented political jurisdictions; but this is true for any method of control. The relevant question is: what method of control makes interjurisdictional cooperation easier and more likely? And the answer is: a price system, for several reasons. First, it is probably easier to get agreement on a simple schedule of pollution prices than on a complex set of detailed regulations. Second, a uniform price schedule would make it more difficult for any member of the "cooperative" group to attract industry from the other areas by promising a more lenient attitude toward pollution. Third, and most important, a price system generates revenues for the control board, which can be distributed to the various political entities. While the allocation of these revenues would involve some vigorous discussion, any alternative methods of control would require the various governments to raise taxes to pay the costs, a much less appealing prospect; in fact, there would be a danger that the pollution prices might be considered a device to generate revenue rather than to reduce pollution, which could lead to an overly-clean, inefficient situation.

Another objection is that the Pollution Control Board might be captured by those it is supposed to control. This danger can be countered by having the board members subject to election or by having the pollution prices set by referendum. With any other control method, the danger of the captive regulator is much greater. A uniform price is easy for the public to understand, unlike obscure technical arguments about boiler temperatures and the costs of electrostatic collectors versus low-sulfur oil from Indonesia; if pollution is too high, the public can demand higher prices, pure and simple. And the price is the same for all plants, with no excuses. With direct control, acceptable pollution levels are negotiated with each plant separately and in private, with approved delays and special permits and other nonsense. The opportunities for using political influence and simple graft are clearly much larger with direct control.

A different type of objection occasionally has been raised against the price system based essentially on the fear that it will solve the problem. Pollution, after all, is a hot issue with which to assault

The Establishment, Capitalism, Human Nature, and Them; any attempt to remove the issue by some minor change in institutions, well within The System, must be resisted by The Movement. From some points of view, of course, this is a perfectly valid objection. But one is hopeful that there still exists a majority more concerned with finding solutions than with creating issues.

"IF WE CAN GO TO THE MOON, WHY . . . ETC?"

"If we can go to the moon, why can't we eliminate pollution?" This new, and already trite, rhetorical question invites a rhetorical response: "If physical scientists and engineers approached their tasks with the same kind of wishful thinking and fuzzy moralizing which characterizes much of the pollution discussion, we would never have gotten off the ground." Solving the pollution problem is no easier than going to the moon, and therefore requires a comparable effort in terms of men and resources and the same sort of logical hard-headedness that made Apollo a success. Social scientists, politicians, and journalists who spend their time trying to find someone to blame, searching for a magic device or regulation, or complaining about human nature, will be as helpful in solving the pollution problem as they were in getting us to the moon. The price system outlined here is no magic formula, but it attacks the problem at its roots, and has a real chance of providing a long-term solution.

QUESTIONS

1. What are the implications of marginal analysis in analyzing pollution problems?
2. Can all problems of pollution be considered as cases of divergence between private and social costs?
3. A recent *Annual Report* of the President's Council of Economic Advisers suggested consideration of "prices" for the right to pollute air and water — that is, a potential polluter would have to pay a certain price per unit of pollutant emitted. Would such a system contribute to a more efficient solution to the pollution problem than a system that simply ordered all polluters to cut their emissions by some fixed percent? Explain.

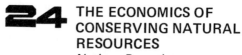

24 THE ECONOMICS OF CONSERVING NATURAL RESOURCES
Nathan Rosenberg

What are the chances of the United States running out of oil, wood, coal, or any other natural resource? What social institutions work to protect or augment the supply of these materials? Drawing on both economic analysis and economic history, Rosenberg explores the topical issue of conserving natural resources. And in so doing he attacks some of the shibboleths of particular segments of the conservation movement by arguing that the market mechanism automatically does a great deal to conserve natural resources. Rosenberg is professor of economics at Stanford University. One of his research specialties is the history of economic development and the effect of institutions on economic growth.

The central concern of this paper is with the adequacy of natural resource supplies to support an indefinite continuation of high rates of economic growth in advanced industrial economies. It is inspired — if that is the right word — by a recent spate of apocalyptic literature purporting to show that natural resource constraints impose an insuperable obstacle to such growth. I will suggest that this extreme pessimism is unwarranted because it attaches insufficient weight to an impressive array of adaptive mechanisms through which a market economy responds to shifting patterns of resource scarcity. Most important, I will argue that technological change is, in the long run, the most powerful mechanism of response.

Abridged from Nathan Rosenberg, "Innovative Responses to Material Shortages," *American Economic Review Papers and Proceedings,* 63, no. 2 (May 1973), 111–118.

Some disclaimers are in order. It should be obvious that no amount of historical analysis can provide an adequate basis for optimism concerning our *future* prospects. Evidence of past successes in dealing with natural resource constraints cannot, by itself, disprove the possibility that we may now have arrived at some crucial turning point or reached the end of an historical epoch. Equally obviously, arguments drawn from the past history of countries which have demonstrated a high degree of technological innovativeness are not likely to be directly applicable to countries where such skills and talents have been notably lacking. The purpose of my recourse to history is, therefore, relatively modest. It is simply to provide some insight into the manner in which economies possessed of a high degree of technological versatility have adapted to changing patterns of resource scarcities. History can, I believe, enlarge our awareness of the nature and possible range of these mechanisms. In so doing, it can also suggest the reasonableness of a number of possible alternative scenarios to the essentially Malthusian one which is currently receiving so much uncritical acclaim.

Let me first sketch out some basic historical trends. A broad view of the long-term trends in American natural resource use (agriculture, timber products, minerals) reveals a substantial upward movement in resource consumption. An index of consumption of resources (1947–49 = 100) rose from 17 in 1870 to 41 in 1900 to 110 in 1954. When consumption is expressed in per capita terms, the rise is far more modest, growing from $174 in 1870 to $221 in 1900 and to $279 in 1954 (all in 1954 dollars). If, over this period, the growing scarcity of resources had been acting as a serious constraint upon economic growth, this role would presumably have become apparent in the form of an increase in the relative prices of extractive products and a rising share of GNP consisting of the output of resources. In fact, however, this has not been the case. Since 1870 there have been extreme short-run fluctuations in the prices of extractive products relative to the general wholesale price index. But, at most, one can argue that there is some evidence of a slight upward drift in the long-term trend. There is, however, one important exception to this statement: timber product prices have moved sharply and unmistakably upward, roughly quadrupling between 1870 and the 1950's. Timber products, therefore, offer an excellent opportunity for studying the nature of the economy's response to a rapid increase in the relative price of a major class of raw material inputs, both because the price increase has been very substantial and because the materials involved are of a class upon which the economy was once heavily dependent.

American inventive effort in the early decades of the nineteenth century focused heavily upon developing techniques for exploiting her abundant forest resources. By the 1850's American woodworking machinery was generally acknowledged by Europeans to be the most sophisticated and advanced in the world. The relatively limited degree to which these machines were adopted in Europe, however, seems to have reflected the fact that they were, in many ways, wasteful of wood — a consideration much less important in the United States than in Great Britain in the first half of the nineteenth century. American circular saws, for example, while very fast, had thicker blades, with their teeth spaced widely apart, and they converted a distressingly large portion of the log into sawdust instead of lumber. Indeed, an observer writing in the early 1870's, who was intimately familiar with British and American woodworking methods, stated categorically that "Lumber manufacture, from the log to the finished state, is, in America, characterized by a waste that can truly be called criminal . . . ." This characterization might have been reasonable had American techniques been employed in Britain. Given the relative factor scarcities in the United States, however, these techniques, by substituting abundant, cheap wood for scarce and expensive labor, may well have been optimal. In England, by contrast, handicraft technology, which amounted to the substitution of relatively cheap labor for relatively expensive wood, continued to prevail.

A similar profligacy in wood consumption persisted within the household so long as wood supplies were locally abundant. Under these circumstances, fireplaces were designed to accommodate large logs, an arrangement which was wasteful of fuel wood but economized upon the labor-intensive activities of cutting or chopping wood. (Stoves, which utilized wood supplies more efficiently, but were more expensive and raised the labor cost of preparing the wood, became increasingly popular whenever and wherever wood prices began to rise substantially.) America's abundance of forest resources, in fact, led to innumerable adaptations which involved substituting natural resource inputs for other, scarcer factors of production. The American builder relied on wood, a highly tractable material, in uses where his European counterpart would have employed stone, iron, or other materials. In the construction of houses, this led to the development in the 1830's of a distinctively American technique of housebuilding: the balloon-frame design, which was not only highly utilitarian, but the method of construction of which was uniquely suited to a labor-scarce, resource-abundant society. Similar adaptations took place elsewhere. Americans employed wood in uses which astonished European visitors — not only in building bridges and aqueducts, but in more improbable uses such as the framing of steam engines, canal locks, and pavements. They even — *mirabile dictu!* — built roads (the famous plank roads) out of wood.

The increase in the relative prices of forest products and the cheapening of coal and iron in mid-nineteenth century America signaled a shift away from the use of wood both as a fuel and as a building material. In 1850 mineral fuels still supplied less than 10 percent whereas wood supplied more than 90 percent of all fuel-based energy. In the second half of the nineteenth century, however, the changes in the relative costs of fuel sources as well as technological changes favoring the use of mineral resources both in the manufacture of iron and steel and the production of steam power brought about a rapid shift to coal. Subsequent decades are largely the story of the declining importance of coal — a decline in which dieselization in transportation and the loss of household markets played major roles — and the rise of liquid and gaseous fuels. Just as fuel-

wood was rapidly displaced by coal as an energy source in the second half of the nineteenth century, so coal was displaced by oil and natural gas in the half century after the First World War.

This drastic reduction in the reliance upon increasingly expensive wood as a fuel source had a direct counterpart with respect to the use of wood as an industrial raw material. The price of timber products, unlike the prices of agricultural products and minerals, has risen dramatically, quadrupling between 1870 and 1950. This increase has triggered off substitution of other inputs, including that of minerals, and appears to have induced significant technological changes which have limited the utilization of timber. Iron and steel were substituted for wood across a whole range of investment goods in the nineteenth century, going back to the pre-Civil War period. Machinery, ships, and bridges which were made of wood in 1800 were made of iron or steel in 1900. In construction, by far the largest consumer of lumber, there has been an increasing reliance upon traditional masonry and other mineral building materials and upon aluminum. More recently, technological change has produced plastics and fiber glass materials which have served as substitutes for wood. New materials, such as plastics and aluminum foil, and older ones, such as glass, have replaced forest products as a packaging material. Further technological changes have also generated methods which economize upon wood requirements without the substitution of competitive materials, or which substitute cheaper woods for more expensive woods — for example, in the cases of plywood and wood veneers. (In addition, wood waste is now utilized in the manufacture of fiber board and synthetics.) Other technological changes, such as the self-powered chain saw, the tractor, and the truck have reduced the cost of extracting and transporting the timber from its forest stands. Finally, other technological changes have, in effect, significantly increased the size of our forest resource base by making possible the utilization of low-grade materials which previously had gone unused. Until the 1920's the woodpulp industry utilized only the spruce and fir trees of the northern portions of the country. Improvements in sulphate pulping technology during the 1920's made possible the exploitation of faster growing southern pine which was previously unusable, as a result of which the South accounted for over half of the country's woodpulping capacity by the mid-1950's.

The discussion up to this point has obviously been illustrative rather than exhaustive. Let me now advance the generalization that this sort of experience has, in fact, been quite representative of the experience of industrial economies in dealing with shifting patterns of resource availability. Modern industrial economies possess a remarkably wide range of options with respect to the exploitation of the natural resource environment. At any one time the range of substitution possibilities among material resource inputs is far higher than is generally recognized. From a historical point of view, these possibilities are, in large measure, the product of past technological change which has produced new substitute inputs or raised the productivity of old ones. The ways in which it has done this defy simple categorization, but they have included the following:

1. Raising output per unit of resource input — as, for example, the decline in the amount of coal required to generate a kilowatt-hour of electricity, which fell from almost seven pounds in 1900 to less than nine-tenths of a pound in the 1960's.

2. Development of totally new materials — synthetic fibres, plastics, etc.

3. Raising the productivity of the extractive process.

4. Raising the productivity of the process of exploration and resource discovery.

5. Development of techniques for the reuse of scrap or waste materials.

6. Development of techniques for the exploitation of lower-grade, or other more abundant, resources.

One of the main effects of these technological developments is to reduce the economy's dependence upon any specific resource input and to widen progressively the possibilities of materials substitution. As a result, although particular resources of specified quality do inevitably become increasingly scarce,

the threat of a *generalized* natural resource constraint upon economic growth by no means follows from this. It now seems clear that the discussion of the role of natural resource constraints upon economic growth cannot be usefully pursued within the framework of asking how long it will be before we "run out" of specific resource inputs defined and estimated in physical units. That is simply not an interesting question, partly because there are seldom sharp discontinuities in nature, and partly because, by making it possible to exploit resources which could not be exploited before, technological change is — in economic terms if not in geological terms — making continuous *additions* to the resource base of the economy. What we are more normally confronted with are limited deposits of high quality resources and then a gradually declining slope toward lowergrade resources, which typically exist in abundance. The much greater profusion in the earth's crust of low-grade resources than high-grade resources is one of those geological facts of life which we can — and, if the past is any guide at all, will — learn to live with. Our technological adjustment to this fact has been apparent in recent decades. As the high quality Mesabi iron ores approached exhaustion, the major steel companies not only turned increasingly to foreign sources, but directed their research toward the exploitation of the enormous deposits of hard, low-grade taconites. Similarly, although we import large quantities of bauxite because our domestic reserves of high-grade bauxite are now inadequate, alternative sources of aluminum such as clays are, quite simply, immense. As a matter of fact, the earth's crust contains far more aluminum than it does iron.

Although there is cause for pessimism over the long-term prospects for crude oil, in spite of great improvements in techniques of oil exploration and extraction, oil may also be recovered from other sources, such as shale. Indeed, the technical feasibility of such a process has already been established and these deposits are estimated to be several times as great as the combined total of petroleum and natural gas reserves. Beyond this alternative loom the possibilities of producing oil from coal — a much more abundant resource — or tar sands. And beyond all fossil fuels, of course, looms the eventual prospect of widespread reliance upon atomic energy. These alternatives may, in spite of technological change, turn out to be more costly than our present arrangements, but it should be apparent that the *cost* of alternative sources of fuel is the question that needs to be addressed and not the prospect of resource exhaustion. Elementary though it may seem, it would constitute a major step forward in the public discussion of long-term growth prospects if the focus could be shifted from the prospects (imminent or remote) for resource *exhaustion* to the prospects for significant alterations in the resource costs of alternative technologies. Even in the absence of further technological change, it must be noted, the question of what constitutes a recoverable natural resource may be extremely sensitive to price changes. It was estimated for the Paley Commission, for example, that, at cost levels prevailing in 1951, our recoverable coal reserves amounted to some 30 billion tons. However, at prices 50 percent above those prevailing at the time, it was estimated that reserves which were worth recovering were no less than twenty times greater than the 30 billion tons estimate.

There is no obvious reason why the further growth of technological skills should not make it possible to continue the shift from dependence upon scarce sources of materials to dependence upon more abundant sources — a shift already dramatized in the present century by the extraction of nitrogen from the air and magnesium from seawater. Indeed, the ability to manipulate the raw material inputs of nature has been multiplied several times in the past century by fundamental advances in our knowledge of the physical world.

QUESTIONS

1. Why is the economist often viewed as an anti-conservationist? Is the charge true?

2. Are Americans consuming more natural resources today than a century ago?

3. Why was American "waste" of wood once referred to as "criminal"? In what sense, if any, would the adoption of European woodworking techniques

in this country have been "wasteful"?

4. As a resource becomes scarcer, and hence more expensive, what responses by modern industrial economies are predicted by Rosenberg?

THE ECONOMICS OF URBAN RENEWAL
Otto A. Davis and Andrew B. Whinston

Urban renewal has become a topic of serious study in economics — indeed, many departments of economics now offer courses in urban economics. Professors Otto Davis of Carnegie-Mellon University and Andrew Whinston of Purdue University offer one explanation of urban blight, and argue that the unfettered market mechanism may not be sufficient to effectuate the renewal of urban areas. Note the use of a central policy concept of economic analysis — Pareto optimality.

In light of two implications of urban renewal, it is not at all surprising that this phenomenon provides an excellent area for the application of welfare economics. These implications are: First, that the market mechanism has not functioned "properly" in urban property; and second, that positive action can "improve" the situation. The propositions of welfare economics provide some tools for judging public policy measures such as urban renewal. But since these propositions themselves are based upon ethical postulates, it seems desirable that we begin our discussion of urban renewal by stating explicitly what we consider the role of the economist to be in this situation.

WELFARE ECONOMICS AND URBAN RENEWAL

Welfare economics itself provides one criterion, the Pareto condition, for judging public policy measures.

Abridged from Otto A. Davis and Andrew B. Whinston, "The Economics of Urban Renewal," *Law and Contemporary Problems*, 26, no. 1 (Winter 1961), 105–112. Reprinted with permission from a symposium, Urban Renewal, Part II; copyright, 1961, by Duke University.

The Pareto condition states that a social policy measure can be judged "desirable" if it results in either (1) everyone being made better off, or (2) someone being made better off without anyone being made worse off. This rule is, of course, an ethical proposition, but it requires a minimum of premises and should command wide assent.

On the other hand, the economist need not be limited solely to the Pareto condition in giving policy advice. This becomes especially true when the objective ambiguity of the terms "better off" and "worse off" is considered. Indeed, the role of the economist in the formation of social policy may be compared to that of the consultant to an industrial firm. The consultant to a firm serves two functions. First, given the goals of the firm, he tries to find the best or most efficient means of achieving these goals. The second function of the consultant is equally important; he must try to clarify vague goals by pointing out possible inconsistencies and determining implications in order that re-evaluations and explicit statements can be made.

We conceive of the role of the economist as quite similar to that outlined for the consultant. First, the economist may try to clarify social goals by pointing out inconsistencies and determining implications of possible social rules. Second, if a goal happens to be given and agreed upon — i.e., if a social welfare function is defined — then the economist might try to advise the body politic by proposing policies for the attainment of the defined goals.

It is in the above spirit that we consider the problem of urban renewal. Granted the individualistic basis of Western civilization, it seems reasonable to assume that any action which satisfies the Pareto condition would improve social welfare and, therefore, should be desired by society. On the other hand, society might desire, granted the institutional form of political decision-making, certain actions which violate the narrowly conceived Pareto condition. Certainly income redistribution would fit this category. And so may urban renewal.

THE PRICE MECHANISM AND URBAN BLIGHT

Having stated the position from which we shall make policy judgments, we now must examine the question of why urban renewal is necessary. In other words, why do "blighted" areas develop and persist? Why do individuals fail to keep their properties in "acceptable" states of repair?

Several arguments may be advanced as answers to the above questions. For example, it has been asserted that property owners have exaggerated notions of the extent and timing of municipal expansion. Hence they may neglect possible improvements of existing structures in anticipation of the arrival of more intensive uses which might bring capital gains. Note that even if this argument is accepted as plausible — and the reason why property owners might have exaggerated notions about municipal expansion is by no means evident — it does not constitute an argument for urban renewal. Instead, one might infer that, given sufficient time, a transition to intensive and profitable uses would take place. Then too, it can be argued that there is no reason to expect governmental authorities to have better judgment than individual entrepreneurs.

Aside from the previous "mistaken judgments" argument, it might seem plausible at first glance to believe on the basis of price theory and the profit maximization assumption that urban blight could not occur. After all, would not profit-maximizing individuals find it to their advantage to keep their property in a state of repair? Certainly it seems reasonable to suppose that if individual benefits from repair or redevelopment exceed individual costs, then individual action could be expected and no social action would be necessary. We shall now attempt to demonstrate why rational individual action might allow property to deteriorate and blight to occur.

First of all, the fact that the value of any one property depends in part upon the neighborhood in which it is located seems so obvious as hardly to merit discussion. Yet, since this simple fact is the villain of the piece, further elaboration is warranted. Pure introspective evidence seems sufficient to indicate that persons consider the neighborhood when deciding to buy or rent some piece of urban property. If this is the case, then it means that externalities are present in utility functions; that is to say, the subjective utility or enjoyment derived from a property depends not only upon the design, state of repairs, and so on of that property, but also upon the characteristics of nearby properties. This fact will, of course, be reflected in both capital and rental values. This is the same as saying that it is also reflected in the return on investment.

THE PRISONER'S DILEMMA

In order to explain how interdependence can cause urban blight, it seems appropriate to introduce a simple example from the theory of games. This example, which has been developed in an entirely different context and is commonly known as "The Prisoner's Dilemma," appears to contain the important points at issue here.[1] For the sake of simplicity, let us consider only two adjacent properties. More general situations do not alter the result but do complicate the reasoning. Let us use the labels Owner I and Owner II. Suppose that each owner has made an initial investment in his property from which he is reaping a return, and is now trying to determine whether to make the additional investment for redevelopment. The additional investment will, of course, alter the return which he receives, and so will the decision of the other owner.

The situation which they might face can be summarized in the following game matrix:

		Owner II	
		Invest	Not Invest
	Invest	[.07, .07]	[.03, .10]
Owner I			
	Not Invest	[.10, .03]	[.04, .04]

[1]The reason for the intriguing title of this type of game theory analysis is interesting in itself. The name is derived from a popular interpretation. The district attorney takes two suspects into custody and keeps them separated. He is sure they are guilty of a specific crime but does not have adequate evidence for a conviction. He talks to each separately and tells them that they can confess or not confess. If neither confesses, then he will book them on some minor charge and both will receive minor punishment. If both confess, then they will be prosecuted but he will recommend less than the most severe sentence. If either one confesses and the other does not, then the confessor will receive lenient treatment for turning state's evidence, whereas the latter will get "the book" slapped at him. The Prisoner's Dilemma is that without collusion between them, the individually rational action for each is to confess.

The matrix game is given the following interpretation: Each property owner has made an initial investment and has an additional sum which is invested in, say, corporate bonds. At present, the average return on both these investments, the property and the corporate bonds considered together, is four percent. Thus if neither owner makes the decision to sell his corporate bonds and make a new investment in the redevelopment of his property, each will continue to get the four percent average return. This situation is represented by the entries within brackets in the lower right of the matrix where each individual has made the decision "Not invest." The left-hand figure in the brackets always refers to the average return which Owner I receives, and the right-hand figure reflects the return of Owner II. Thus for the "Not invest, Not invest" decisions, the matrix entry reflects the fact that both owners continue to get a four percent return.

On the other hand, if both individuals made the decision to sell their bonds and invest the proceeds in redevelopment of their property, it is assumed that each would obtain an average return of seven percent on his total investment. Therefore, the entry in the upper left of the matrix, the entry for the "Invest, Invest" decisions, has a seven percent return for each owner.

The other two entries in the matrix, which represent the situation when one owner invests and the other does not, are a little more complicated. We assumed, as was mentioned earlier, that externalities, both external economies and diseconomies, are present. These interdependencies are reflected in the returns from investment. For example, consider the entries in the brackets in the lower left corner of the matrix. In this situation, Owner I would have decided to "Not invest" and Owner II would have decided to "Invest."

Owner I is assumed to obtain some of the benefits from Owner II's investment, the redevelopment contributing something to a "better neighborhood." For example, if the two properties under consideration happened to be apartment buildings, the decision of Owner II to invest might mean that he would demolish his "outdated" apartment building and construct a new one complete with off-street parking and other amenities. But this would mean that the tenants of Owner I would now have an easier time finding parking spaces on the streets, their children might have the opportunity of associating with the children of the "higher class" people who might be attracted to the modern apartment building, and so forth. All this means that (as soon as leases allow) Owner I can edge up his rents. Thus his return is increased without having to make an additional investment. We assume that his return becomes ten percent in this case, and this figure is appropriately entered in the matrix. Owner II, on the other hand, would find that, since his renters also consider the "neighborhood" (which includes the ill effects of Owner I's "outdated" structure), his level of rents would have to be less than would be the case if his apartment building were in an alternative location. Thus we assume that the return on his total investment (the investment in the now-demolished structure plus the investment in the new structure) falls to three percent. This figure is also appropriately entered in the matrix. For simplicity, the reverse situation, where Owner I decides to invest and Owner II decides not to invest, is taken to be similar. Thus the reverse entries are made in the upper right corner of the matrix.[2]

Having described the possible situations which the two owners face, consider now the decision-making process. Both owners are assumed to be aware of the returns which are available to themselves in the hypothesized situations. Owner I will be considered first. Owner I must decide whether to invest or not invest. Remember that the left-hand

[2]Economists might think that we have used inappropriate and sleight-of-hand methods by lumping together old and new investments, and also by considering the average rate of return instead of marginal rates. Actually these methods are completely appropriate here due to the way we have simplified the problem to make the exposition of the game theory easier. The old investment does not represent a sunk cost, since it is yielding a return and thus has economic value. Both owners are assumed to have precisely the amount of money in bonds that is required for the redevelopment of their property. The rate of return on the bonds can be assumed to be the "social rate of return" and the best alternative available to the two individuals. Since the owners are interested in maximizing the total income from their capital, the above assumptions allow us to lump together and to use average rates.

entries in the brackets represent the possible returns for Owner I. Two possible actions of Owner II are relevant for Owner I in his effort to make his own decision. Therefore, Owner I might use the following decision process: Assume, first, that Owner II decides to invest. Then what decision would be the most advantageous? A decision to invest means only a seven percent return on Owner I's capital, whereas the decision not to invest would yield an average return of ten percent of the total relevant amount of capital. Therefore, if Owner II were to decide to invest, it would certainly be individually advantageous to Owner I not to invest. But suppose that Owner II decided not to invest. Then what would be the most advantageous decision for Owner I? Once again the results can be seen from the matrix. For Owner I the decision to invest now means that he will receive only a three percent return on his capital, whereas the decision not to invest means that he can continue to receive the four percent average return. Therefore, if Owner II were to decide not to invest, it would still be individually advantageous to Owner I not to invest.

The situation for Owner II is similar. If Owner I is assumed to invest, then Owner II can gain a ten percent average return on his capital by not investing and only a seven percent return by investing. If Owner I is assumed not to invest, then Owner II can gain only a three percent return by investing, but a four percent average return by not investing. Therefore, the individually rational action for Owner II is also not to invest.

The situation described above means, of course, that neither Owner I nor Owner II will decide to invest in redevelopment. Therefore, we might conclude that the interdependencies summarized in the Prisoner's Dilemma example can explain why blighted areas can develop and persist. Before concluding the analysis, however, we might try to answer some questions which may at this point be forthcoming.

PROBLEMS WITH THE MODEL

First of all, it might be suggested that we have imposed an unrealistic condition by not allowing the two owners to coordinate their decisions. After all, does it not seem likely that the two owners would get together and mutually agree to invest in the redevelopment of their properties? Not only would such action be socially desirable, but it would seem to be individually advantageous. Note that while it might be easy for the two property owners in our simple example to communicate and coordinate their decisions, this would not appear to be the case as the number of individuals increased. If any single owner were to decide not to invest while all other owners decided to redevelop, then the former would stand to gain by such action. The mere presence of many owners would seem to make coordination more difficult and thus make our assumption more realistic. Yet, this is precisely the point; it is the objective of social policy to encourage individuals in such situations to coordinate their decisions so that interdependencies will not prevent the achievement of a Pareto welfare point. In this regard, it is worthwhile to note that, if coordination and redevelopment do take place voluntarily, then no problem exists and urban renewal is not needed.

Second, it might be observed that, if coordinated action does not take place, incentive exists for either Owner I, Owner II, or some third party to purchase the properties and develop both of them in order that the seven percent return can be obtained. And certainly, it cannot be denied that this often occurs in reality. However, it is necessary to point out here that, because of the institutional peculiarities of urban property, there is no assurance that such a result will always take place. Consider, for example, an area composed of many holdings. Suppose that renewal or redevelopment would be feasible if coordination could be achieved, but that individual action alone will not result in such investment due to the interdependencies. In other words, the situation is assumed to be similar to the previous example except that many owners are present. Incentive exists for some entrepreneur to attempt to purchase the entire area and invest in redevelopment or renewal.

Now suppose that one or more of the owners of the small plots in the area became aware of the entrepreneur's intentions. If the small plots were so located as to be important for a successful project, then the small holders might realize that it would be possible to gain by either (1) using their position to expropriate part of the entrepreneur's expected profits by demanding a very high price for their properties, or (2) refusing to sell in order to enjoy the external economies generated by the redevelopment. If several of the small holders become aware of the entrepreneur's intentions, then it is entirely possible, with no communication or collusion between these small holders, for a situation to result where each tries to expropriate as much of the entrepreneur's profit as possible by either of the above methods. This competition can result in a Prisoner's Dilemma type of situation for the small holders. Individually rational action on their part may result in the cancellation of the project by the entrepreneur. Indeed, anyone familiar with the functioning of the urban property market must be aware of such difficulties and of the care that must be taken to prevent price-gouging when an effort is made to assemble some tract of land.

If the above analysis is correct, then it is clear that situations may exist where individually rational action may not allow for socially desirable investment in the redevelopment of urban properties. Now such situations need not — indeed, in general will not — exist in all urban properties. The results of the analysis not only required special assumptions about the nature of investment returns caused by interdependencies, but it was also shown that, due to the special institutional character of tract assembly, the presence of numerous small holdings can block entrepreneurial action for redevelopment. These two conditions may or may not be filled for any given tract of land. However, we now may use the above results to *define* urban blight. Blight is said to exist whenever (1) strictly individual action does not result in redevelopment, (2) the coordination of decision-making via some means would result in redevelopment, and (3) the sum of benefits from renewal could exceed the sum of costs.

Note that we have defined blight strictly in relation to the allocation of resources. The fact that the properties in an area have a "poor" appearance may or may not be an indication of blight and the malallocation of resources. For several factors, aside from tastes, help to determine the appearance of properties. The situation which we have described, where individually rational action may lead to no investment and deterioration, is only one type of case. Another may be based on the distribution of incomes. Poor classes can hardly be expected to afford the spacious and comfortable quarters of the well-to-do. Indeed, given the existence of low income households, a slum area *may* represent an efficient use of resources. If the existence of slums per se violates one's ethical standards, then, as economists, we can only point out that for elimination of slums the main economic concern must be with the distribution of income, and urban renewal is not sufficient to solve that problem. Indeed, unless some action is taken to alter the distribution of income, the renewal of slum areas is likely to lead to the creation of slum areas elsewhere. It is to be emphasized that slums may or may not satisfy the definition of a blighted area. On the other hand, the mere fact that the properties in some given area appear "nice" to the eye is not sufficient evidence to indicate that blight (by our definition) is absent.

QUESTIONS

1. What is a "Pareto optimal" social policy? Is the principle of Pareto optimality a useful one in formulating public policy? Can you imagine a Pareto optimal piece of legislation? Can you imagine a Pareto optimal policy which you would not support?

2. Can you construe any examples, hypothetical or real, of the Prisoner's Dilemma?

3. Why does simple communication not solve or remove the Prisoner's Dilemma in urban renewal?

26 RACE AND THE MARKET
Thomas Sowell

Do racial minorities fare better in the private or the public sector? Are ethnic groups better off dealing with competitors or monopolists? Are ghetto markets exploitative? These questions are addressed in this selection from Race and Economics, *Thomas Sowell's well-known book on race, ethnicity, and economic advancement. The author's conclusions will be unsettling to many readers. Professor Sowell is a professor of economics at UCLA and the author of books on black education and the ideas of the classical economists.*

Race is a factor in many kinds of markets. The most obvious is the employment market, where in the past such phrases as "white only" or "no Irish need apply" were commonplace. The passing of such explicit phrases did not of course mean that the policies and attitudes behind such phrases had completely passed as well. Race is also an important factor in housing markets — not only as regards whether individuals from different ethnic groups have the same opportunity to buy or rent desirable housing, but also as to whether the *terms* on which they may buy or rent are equal. Finally, in the purchase of everyday consumer goods, the price and quality of such goods often vary by neighborhood, with the highest prices and/or lowest quality often being in black ghettos, Puerto Rican barrios, and other neighborhoods inhabited by poor or minority groups.

Whatever the merits of moral or philosophical arguments, cause-and-effect analysis is needed to analyze the scope, magnitude, and variation of discrimination over time, the degree to which various market and nonmarket forces intensify or reduce discrimination, the extent to which various behavior patterns within a minority group advance or retard its economic progress, and to judge the consequences of various possible approaches to dealing with the problem. Causal analysis requires much more precise terms than moral judgments. Terms such as "discrimination," "equality," or "exploitation" may be sufficiently meaningful to express moral feelings, but specific analysis of causation requires much more precise definition.

This analysis tacitly assumes that (1) employers are attracted by prospects of unusually high profits and that (2) there is no effective general collusion against a particular group. If employers were indifferent to opportunities for high profit or if the rate of profit they could earn was externally controlled, then any opportunities, to hire members of ethnic groups whose pay was lower than their productivity could be passed up. There is little indication that most employers are unconcerned as between making more money and making less money. What does happen in a number of situations is that they are prevented from earning more by government agencies — regulatory commissions such the ICC or FCC — or may be legally nonprofit, as with schools, foundations, hospitals, etc. When this is so, then there is no real opportunity to earn more profit by hiring misjudged minorities or in any other way. In such circumstances, the employer can hire according to his own prejudices without paying any price in terms of foregone profits.

Economic theory would lead to an expectation of more discrimination in markets with externally controlled and externally limited profit rates than in unstructured and uncontrolled competitive markets. In general, this is what is found. The railroad industry, which is tightly regulated by the Interstate Commerce Commission, has long been one of the most discriminatory industries in the United States — hiring *no* Negroes at all, for decades, in many skilled jobs, and hiring substantial numbers only as Pullman porters. In the middle of the nineteenth century, before regulation, Negroes dominated railroad occupations in the South, except for conductors. The communications industry, whose profit is regulated by the Federal Communications Commission and by state regulatory agencies, likewise has a long history of discriminatory hiring far more severe than that in the economy as a whole. Other highly controlled areas of the economy, such as banking,

likewise exhibit a pattern of extreme discrimination, not only against Negroes, Jews and other minorities, but even against nonconformist personality types. It would be hard to explain this pattern by personal prejudice alone, for there is no special reason why employers in regulated industries should happen to have *more* prejudice than employers in other industries. What is different in the regulated industries is that the *cost* of discrimination is reduced or eliminated.

Regulated industries are of course regulated by politically appointed commissioners, so that while their hiring policies have fewer *economic* constraints (such as those which force more competitive industries to hire minorities), they are even more subject to *political* constraints. This means that while there is likely to be more racial discrimination in a regulated industry than in an unregulated industry during periods when there is no great public outcry against discrimination, the regulated industries would be forced to make a more sudden about-face on discrimination than the unregulated industries when political forces attack discrimination. An example of this is the telephone industry, a highly regulated industry which has long had an extremely low percentage of Negro employees, even in jobs such as operators and linemen, which require no special education or experience. Yet when employment discrimination became a major political issue in the 1960s, there were great increases in the hiring of Negroes in the telephone industry — even in occupations where the total number of jobs was declining. In the South, where political pressures were not comparable, there was virtually no increase in the proportion of Negroes hired, even though the industry's employment was growing fastest in the South. In the North, *one-third* of the *new* employees hired between 1966 and 1968 were Negroes. Among electric and gas utilities also, Negro employment gains were concentrated in the North. All these public utilities are primarily *state*-regulated; more so than federally regulated.

In short, empirical evidence confirms what economic analysis would predict: that regulated industries have *more* discrimination than unregulated industries when this depends only on economic considerations, but reverse themselves more rapidly than unregulated industries when discrimination becomes a political issue.

A legally nonprofit organization is in a very similar position to the firm whose profits are limited by a regulation. It too pays no economic cost for discrimination, and could therefore be expected to be more discriminatory than unregulated, profit-seeking organizations — as long as public opinion is not aroused. But since it is typically dependent upon public contributions, grants from the government, or at least needs its tax-exempt status, it too is likely to change more drastically when the climate of opinion changes on racial discrimination. The academic world is a classic example here. In 1936, only three Negro Ph.D. holders were employed by all white colleges and universities in the United States. By contrast, more than three hundred Negro chemists alone were employed in private industry in 1940. Just one generation later, after public opinion became aroused against racial discrimination — all this was reversed. White colleges and universities began hiring black faculty members en masse — and lectured private industry on the need to end discrimination! It is also significant that black breakthroughs in the academic world first occurred in the money-making part of the college — varsity athletics. Hospitals are another large area of nonprofit organizations, and one which, until relatively recent times also practiced extreme exclusion and discrimination against doctors who were Jewish or black. This often extended to patients as well.

In general, job discrimination has a cost, not only to those discriminated against and to society, but also to the person who is discriminating. He must forgo hiring some employees he needs, or must interview more applicants in order to get the number of qualified workers required, or perhaps offer higher wages in order to attract a larger pool of applicants than necessary if hiring on merit alone. These costs do not necessarily eliminate discrimination, but discrimination — like everything else — tends to be more in demand at a low price than at a high price. The cost, of course, is of no concern to a businessman who is personally unconcerned about profit,

but such businessmen are rare to begin with, and tend to get eliminated through competition, for their financial backers and creditors care about profitability even if they do not. Nonprofit organizations, however, can ignore the economic cost of discrimination — though not the cost of antagonizing the public, if the public is actively opposed to discrimination.

CONSUMER GOODS MARKETS

Numerous studies have indicated that prices of goods tend to be higher and the average quality lower in low-income ethnic neighborhoods. In addition, numerous schemes to defraud the less-knowledgeable people in such neighborhoods have flourished for many years, probably as long as such neighborhoods have existed. In the nineteenth century, Irish immigrants were cheated and swindled before they even got off the boat, and the process continued on the docks, in the roominghouses in which they usually spent their first days in America, and among travel agents who sold them fraudulent tickets to their destinations. The nineteenth-century Italian immigrants were similarly exploited in innumerable ways by travel agents, landlords, bankers, labor contractors, etc. In the twentieth century, the victims are more often Negro, Puerto Rican, or Mexican-American.

In Los Angeles, for example, a clock-radio selling for $19 elsewhere in the city was sold for $42 in the Mexican-American community. Gas ranges selling for $110 elsewhere sold for $200 in the Mexican-American community — and a portable television set selling for $230 in the Mexican-American community sold for $270 in Watts. Comparison shoppers in New York found that the same item in the same store sold for different prices to whites, Puerto Ricans, and blacks. According to another study, "In East Harlem, there are hardly any 'one price' stores." East Harlem has a variety of ethnic groups, with many individuals being very new to the city. A common feature of fraudulent stores in ethnic neighborhoods is the absence of price tags, for this very reason. In still another study, the Federal Trade Commission found an item selling for

$165 in the regular shopping areas of Washington that was selling for $250 in a store specializing in low-income customers.

The question is not whether fraud is practiced on ethnic minorities, but how much of the price and quality differences in ethnic communities is solely a result of fraud rather than many other economic factors. What is physically the same product may have different costs of delivery to the customer, depending upon the conditions of delivery. Supermarkets, for example, are able to operate profitably selling a standard product for less than the price charged at a small grocery store, which may be making little or no profit. This is largely because the *turnover* is faster in the supermarket; the item sits on the shelf a much shorter time before it is sold, so that a given investment in a shelf full of goods earns a return many more times in the course of a year, even if each individual return is slightly lower than in the corner grocery store, where the goods turn over fewer times a year. Low-income ethnic neighborhoods typically have relatively more small grocery stores and relatively fewer major supermarkets. Even if each item sold for the same price in ethnic neighborhood grocery stores as in other grocery stores, and the same price in ethnic neighborhood supermarkets as in other supermarkets, the average price paid in the ethnic neighborhoods would still be higher than elsewhere, simply because the mixture of grocery stores and supermarkets is different in such neighborhoods.

There are reasons why low-income communities have a different mixture of small and large stores. Major supermarket chains have lower costs of delivering goods to the customer because of a higher volume of business for each hour that a store is open — that is, for each hour that they are paying salaries to their employees. The more hours they stay open, the harder it is for them to have as high a volume of business per hour and per employee. Ghetto supermarkets are usually not open as many hours per day as the local grocery stores. Obviously they eliminate those hours which bring in the least revenue in proportion to cost. Evening hours are especially costly because of overtime pay or night differential pay for supermarket employees, or because the store may operate less efficiently after the manager has gone home, or because of the higher cost of getting a good manager who is willing to stay in the store extra long hours. Evening hours are also more costly in terms of an increased probability of getting robbed at night. Supermarkets therefore tend to do a high volume of business per hour during the day and then close — especially in high crime areas.

While there is a demand for supermarket services in low-income ethnic neighborhoods, there are more people in such neighborhoods who cannot rely wholly on supermarkets. People who arrive home in the evening after a day of work — especially at manual labor — may lack the time or energy to get to the supermarket before it closes. A smaller proportion of the families have wives who are at home during the day to do supermarket shopping. A smaller proportion have automobiles, so that the distance to the store is more of a factor. Because of sporadic unemployment and other financial problems, a certain proportion of the residents of low-income ethnic communities use credit in buying grocery items. Supermarkets do a cash business, eliminating the time and paperwork of credit transactions, the cost of collection agencies, and the losses from unpaid debts. Such credit arrangements are left to the small grocery store, or at least to some of them. In short, although the supermarket may deliver the same physical package as the small grocery store, it does not deliver it at the same time, or as close to home, or under the same arrangements, so that the total service sold may be very different and have different costs, which are passed on to the consumer. Even when the service is no different, the fact that the goods on the shelf turn over at different rates means that different prices are required to cover operating costs, which are based on time (rent, salaries, electricity, etc.). If a supermarket sells twenty refrigerators full of beer in the same time it takes a local grocery store to sell 10 refrigerators full of beer, then it has cost the local grocery store twice as much to refrigerate each can of beer. The same principle applies to operating costs in general.

In addition to different kinds of stores that are represented in low-income neighborhoods, there are generally different costs for any given kind of store. Insofar as such neighborhoods are less attractive to potential employees or managers (justifiably or not does not matter in cause-and-effect terms), the cost of operating and managing stores tends to rise. Theoretically, this could take the form of paying higher salaries to get the same quality of personnel in the ethnic community stores as in other stores. However, since companies tend to maintain standard salaries, it is more likely to take the form of attracting less efficient employees and managers for the same pay. In either case, the net result is a higher cost of operation.

There is no principle of justice which causes consumers to pay the costs associated with the neighborhood. The bulk of the population, even in crime-ridden areas, are law-abiding people. It is not equity but economics which forces up the prices they pay. The differences in prices between ethnic ghettoes and middle-class suburbs cannot be explained by stores charging "all that the traffic will bear" in one case and not in the other. Stores charge all that the traffic will bear in *both* cases. The traffic will just not bear as much in the middle-class suburb — and the *reason* for this is that there are so many more *competing* stores. Those businesses are *able* to operate at lower costs because they can more readily attract efficient workers, management, capital, and low-cost insurance. They are *forced* to operate at lower cost because there are so many firms competing with one another.

For the low-income ghetto workingman who has to pay more for the same can of beer chilled to the same temperature as the beer bought by a middle-class suburbanite, it may seem like pointless hair-splitting whether the situation is explained economically or is simply called "exploitation." And if he has to pay more money for a lower quality beer than the suburbanite pays for premium beer, then he may be even more likely to prefer the latter label. The fact is, if he were not black, or Mexican, or Puerto Rican, etc. he would not have to pay as much for what he buys. Economic analysis is not philosophic justification, nor is that its purpose.

What economics can do is help predict the consequences of various possible ways of dealing with the problem.

QUESTIONS

1. In which type of employment situation does economic theory suggest there is likely to be more racial or ethnic discrimination, a nonprofit government agency or a profit-making business enterprise? Why?

2. What evidence would support the conclusion that ghetto consumers are exploited? How do you define the term exploitation?

3. "A supermarket chain that sells the same brand of bread at a higher price in the inner city than at its suburban store locations is discriminating against inner-city residents." Comment.

PART SEVEN

LABOR MARKET BEHAVIOR

THE UNIONIZATION OF THE GOVERNMENT

Everett M. Kassalow

Perhaps no topic in labor relations arouses so much controversy as the role of the union in government employment. This is the topic of Everett Kassalow's article. Professor Kassalow teaches at the University of Wisconsin at Madison, and is a frequent writer on the economics of the labor sector. Prior to his career in education, he was on the staff of a number of labor union organizations.

Strikes of public employees, once a novelty, are no longer unusual. During one three-month period, not so long ago, a casual check showed social workers' strikes in Chicago, Sacramento, and White Plains; slowdowns of firefighters in Buffalo and of policemen in Detroit; strikes among university maintenance employees at Ohio State, Indiana, and the University of Kansas Medical Center; a three-day "heal-in" by the interns and residents of the Boston City Hospital; "informational" picketing, with a strike threat, by the Philadelphia School Nurses' Association; teachers' strikes in a dozen communities, ranging from West Mifflin, Pennsylvania, and Gibraltar, Ohio, to South Bend, Indiana, and Baltimore, Maryland. Such strikes and slowdowns among teachers, policemen, firemen, etc. have become daily occurrences. Because there had been a growing feeling that industrial relations were becoming more "mature," strikes of this sort in sectors hitherto unidentified with unionism have led to confusion. Large-scale unionization of government workers is a relatively new phenomenon in this country, although it has been common in almost all other democratic industrial countries of the world. That large-scale public-employee unionism was also inevitable in the United States at some time is clear. But why now? What new forces account for the current upsurge of public unionism?

Abridged from Everett M. Kassalow, "Trade Unionism Goes Public," *The Public Interest,* no. 14 (Winter 1969), 118–130. © National Affairs, Inc., 1969. Reprinted by permission.

THE RESPECTABILITY OF UNIONS

The first of these forces has been the institutionalization of trade unionism in American life. Unions date back more than 150 years in the United States. But large-scale unionism dates only from the late 1930s, and it has only been in the past decade or so that collective bargaining has become widely accepted as the appropriate way to settle wages and working issues. During this decade unionists have become respectable. Union leaders have been named to innumerable presidential commissions dealing with every conceivable problem area of the country's foreign and domestic business.

It is not surprising thus that, despite the revelations in the senate investigations of the malfeasance of Jimmy Hoffa and a few other union leaders, public opinion surveys show that union officers have registered a significant gain in occupational prestige between 1947 and 1963. This gain is clearly attributable to the widespread acceptance of the basic value of unionism in society, and this legitimacy is being transferred to public employees as well. For this reason, unionism among government workers has begun to advance rapidly and there is every prospect it will continue to grow.

There is a second, more specific reason for the recent growth of government unionism, and this is Executive Order 10988 issued by President John F. Kennedy in January 1962, which encouraged unionism in the federal service. In its support of public unionism, this order was as clear and unequivocal as the Wagner Act of 1936 had been in its support for unions and collective bargaining in the private sector. It declared that "the efficient administration of the government and the well-being of employees require that orderly and constructive relationships be maintained between employee organizations and management."

In New York City, earlier orders issued by Mayor Robert Wagner resulted in the "breakthrough" of unionism in 1961 among 44,000 teachers. Kennedy's order has a spillover effect in legitimating unionism in states and local public service. Further, the reapportionment of state legislatures seems to have had a generally liberalizing effect, and a flow of new

Table 1. *Public Employment Trends (in hundreds)*[1]

	1947	1967
All public employment	5,474	11,616
Federal employment	1,892	2,719
State and local employment	3,582	8,897

[1] The public employment increase since 1947 has been primarily in the state and local sector. According to U.S. Labor Department projections, between 1965 and 1975 this same sector will increase by an additional 48 percent, whereas total private employment will only grow some 24 percent.

legislation in a dozen states has expedited public employee bargaining.

The enormous growth in public employment has also acted to transform the status of the government worker. Between 1947 and 1967, the number of public employees increased over 110 percent (see Table 1). (During the same period, private nonagricultural employment increased only 42 percent.) Clearly, the day has passed when being a civil servant is a prestigious matter. At a time when unions and bargaining have become increasingly accepted elsewhere in the society, this expansion of public employment, with its consequent bureaucratization and depersonalization of relationships, has undoubtedly encouraged unionization in the public sector.

A NEW KIND OF WORKER

The spread of unionism among government civil servants and teachers is a partial answer to the old question of whether substantial numbers of white-collar employees can be unionized. It is true that much of the growth of public unionism, principally the American Federation of State, County and Municipal Employees and the American Federation of Government Employees (which operates at the federal level) has been among blue-collar employees. (Over two-thirds of the AFL-CIO's State, County and Municipal Employees union, for example, are blue-collar workers.) But some important footholds have been gained among white-collar workers and (because teachers are the largest number unionized) among professionals.

Between 20 and 25 percent of all local and state employees are teachers, and it is among them that the significant contest in unionization has been taking place. For the organization of teachers has had its impact not only in traditional union circles, but also among other associations of public service employees that formerly limited themselves to fraternal and professional questions. Prominent among these is the National Education Association (NEA). Under competition from the AFL-CIO American Federation of Teachers (AFT), the NEA has radically altered its views on bargaining in recent years. From a reluctant acceptance of only "professional negotiations," combined with opposition to strikes, the NEA now is at the point where some of its affiliates sign full-scale collective agreements. At its convention in 1967, the NEA even came to accept strikes, where circumstances render them necessary. In the fall of 1967, the Governor of Florida was led to denounce NEA activities in that state for seeking "blackboard power."

In the large cities, such as New York, Chicago, Detroit, Boston, and Philadelphia, the AFT has won bargaining rights. In smaller cities the NEA has led the way and has won sole bargaining rights in Denver, Milwaukee, Niagara Falls, and a few other fairly middle-sized cities. Some NEA officials argue that the turn of teachers to AFL-CIO unionism in the large cities reflects administrative breakdown in those areas where educational systems are contracting, equipment is aged, and population is fleeing to the suburbs. The NEA points out that in far western cities such as Seattle, San Diego, Portland, and Los Angeles, where educational systems are still expanding and plant is still relatively new, the AFT has not made serious inroads. These cities as well as some others in the Middle West that are still unorganized (such as, for example, Minneapolis and St. Paul) are the likely battlegrounds in the next few years of teacher unionism. The likelihood is that the AFT will become dominant in the large, urban areas, whereas the NEA will hold its strength in smaller towns and possibly generally in the South. Some top AFT leaders have begun to talk about greater cooperation and even a possible merger with the NEA. The NEA with a membership close to a million will, in any case, be of continuing national influence on educational policy.

Like the NEA, other independent state and local public employee associations whose activities until recently have largely been limited to welfare and fraternal programs, are now turning their attention to collective bargaining. These associations, strong among white-collar employees, include, at the state level alone, over 400,000 members who, in turn, are loosely grouped into a national joint body. These associations have the additional advantage, in some states, of being favored by public managers.

As is clear from the many strikes reported, a great many different groups in the public sector are on the move. To the extent that one can judge, the new unrest seems to be greatest among those who have very clearly identifiable professions and/or strategic occupations. Teachers, for example, have clearly been in the forefront of public employee labor agitation in the past few years. Nurses have begun to make demands in the large cities. Social workers, a group with old traditions in public employee bargaining, are extending their organization significantly. Firemen and policemen have been revealing a new militancy. In their summer 1968 conventions the AFL-CIO's fireman's union and the independent American Nurses Association both removed clauses prohibiting strikes from their respective constitutions. In contrast, such professional groups as engineers and architects (admittedly employed on a much smaller scale in the public sector than either teachers or nurses) are much less affected. These occupations continue to enjoy a generally more favorable labor market than the other professions, and this would seem to be a clue to the difference.

Because it is likely that legislation encouraging collective bargaining in the near future will be enacted in more states, unionism at this level will clearly grow. The Department of Labor has projected that local and state employment will exceed 10 million by 1970, and unionism in this sector must almost inevitably grow in importance on the American labor scene.

UNIONS IN PUBLIC EMPLOYMENT

The sharp increase in collective bargaining in the public service has served to offset the decline in traditional unionism. Whereas union membership in the private sector actually fell from 17.189 million to 16.467 between 1956 and 1964, union membership among government workers increased from .915 million to 1.453 million during the same period. The economic boom since 1964 has led to a broad increase in national union membership, but union membership continues to grow more rapidly in government than in the private economy.

Three public unions have been in the forefront of this general advance: As a percentage of total union membership, government unions rose from approximately 5 percent in 1956 to 8 percent in 1964, and 9 percent in 1966.

Thus between 1956–1957 and 1966–1967 the AFL-CIO as a whole (including its rapidly growing government unions) made a modest recovery from its decline to the early 1960's and managed to increase its membership by 7 percent. But during this same ten-year period public employee unions have doubled and tripled their membership. Even these figures, based as they are on biennial averages, understate the current membership *for public employee unions*. By the end of 1968 the American Federation of Government Employees (AFGE), which organized federal workers, had jumped to 300,000. Some of AFGE's victories in bargaining rights elections such as a 21,000 employee air base unit in September 1968 have been reminiscent of the CIO's organization of mass production industries of the late 1930's. The progress of the State, County, and Municipal Workers (AFSCME) has been made in smaller units, but it had reached 400,000 late in 1968.

The rapid expansion of membership among the federal unions, state, county, and municipal and teachers' unions has been accompanied by the sort of internal turmoil that usually goes with growth. Major conflicts for top union leadership positions have erupted in all three of these public employee unions during the past half dozen years. As membership rolls and treasuries expanded, moreover, and full-time elected and appointive posts opened up, struggles also occurred at the regional and local levels. With the prospect for continuing, substantial membership growth, we can expect relatively high instability and at least a fair amount of election conflict to continue among the officials of these unions.

STRIKES IN THE PUBLIC SERVICE

No subject in recent years has provoked as much heat as the matter of strikes among public employees. It is probably the most difficult problem in the public employee field. Even expert arbitrators and mediators, men of hard-headed, pragmatic experience, have taken surprisingly rigid, ideological positions on this matter.

Curiously, this issue is being debated as though the American experience was unique. But the fact is that many other countries have faced this same problem, and a wide range of solutions have been tried. Some countries have substituted compulsory arbitration for the right to strike, thereby presumably offering the unions a fair alternative to break "impasse" situations. Other countries have widely conceded public employees the right to strike, though a few groups such as policemen, firemen, or the military may be excepted by law or voluntary agreement.

Before taking hard and arbitrary positions, it is well to put strikes in a proper perspective. Over the past two decades or so, strikes in the United States have generally been declining. Occasional upsurges occur, particularly during periods of war or defense-induced inflation, but generally the number of strikes have declined as union-management relations have matured. There is good reason to believe that, once the organizing phase is over, public employee unions will prove even less strike prone than those in private industry. For one thing, working conditions are generally more secure and often more pleasant and less onerous than in private industry. For this reason it is important to note that as unionism and the bargaining process is extended for the first time to millions of new employees and new institutions (public agencies) considerable fric-

tion and tension will occur. The very inexperience of the new union leaders and the public managers guarantees this. But neither should the historic trajectory of unionism be ignored either.

Because there are inherent difficulties in the adjustment to new bargaining public officials need to approach these difficulties with caution, rather than be obsessed with strikes and punishment for strikes. Admittedly, in today's transition period, most cities or states are not likely to concede the right to strike to public employees. However, rather than setting forth elaborate punishment systems for strikes which may occur, officials should take positive steps, wherever possible, to improve relations.

THE NEED FOR PROCEDURES

New unions are generally very much concerned about their own security and legitimacy. Public authorities, by law and by practice, ought to expedite ways and means of extending recognition, and exclusive recognition where the union demonstrates its majority status. Attempts to provide for clumsy proportional representation of employee groups by competing unions or associations should be avoided. The principle of granting a union that represents a majority sole and exclusive bargaining rights has been found to work best, by far, in the United States, and becomes the eventual guarantee of mature relationships.

But even with the best of intentions there will be some impasses and some seemingly irreconcilable conflicts. To deal with these, state and/or local legislation has to spell out, in advance, the kinds of procedures open to parties to resolve these difficulties. If the procedures are known before, there will be fewer "crises," for it is when procedures must be improvised at the last moment that one side or the other feels "put upon." Some states have had success with provisions that stipulate that, in the event of an impasse, the parties accept a fact-finding inquiry. Such recommendations often carry great weight in inducing the parties to accept a settlement. Arbitration may be a possible solution for public employee-management disputes in critical areas. Even though this would involve a break with the tradition of bargaining in the private sector, such history cannot be a direct guide for public bargaining. The almost accidental way in which New York City's sanitation strike, early in 1968, ended in a *joint* submission to arbitration is an indication that new pressures can lead to the acceptance of hitherto rejected solutions.

The operation of the so-called Taylor Law in New York State illustrates the problem with punitive legislation. Despite provisions banning public employee strikes, with penalties such as dismissal or the withdrawal of recognition or check-off rights from the unions, etc., the law did not head off the New York City teachers' strike or the sanitation strike. If anything the withdrawal of the teachers' union check-off of dues and the eventual imprisonment of the local union's president Albert Shanker for fifteen days, in the wake of the 1967 New York City strike, seems to have kept union militancy at a high pitch long after the strike was over.

It does not seem that the strike issue will be important in *federal* labor-management relationships. A liberal managerial policy, including important wage and benefit improvements in the past decade, has set a good framework. In his recent appearance before a special government committee reviewing experience to date under Federal Executive Order 10988, AFL-CIO President George Meany concluded that the order "has brought significant improvements in labor relations within the federal government." Although Meany recommended a number of changes in the workings of the new system, he did not question the legislative ban on strikes in the federal service. Nor did the AFL-CIO December 1967 convention resolution on federal employee bargaining say anything about the existing legal prohibition on strikes by federal government employees. Most of the unions which deal with federal employees have a voluntary ban provision in their constitutions.

At the state and local level, where organizing has met with more resistance, the strike issue remains more troublesome. Even here, in the words of AFSCME President Wurf, whose own union jealously defends the right to strike, at least

The debate [now] seems to center around the right

to strike, rather than the right to organize and bargain. . . . It seems only yesterday . . . that the right to bargain was at stake. . . . Now the right to strike is what is being discussed. . . . As painful as the situation is at times, it is an important step forward.

From what has already been suggested, bargaining in the public sector has to be viewed as an evolving process. What might seem to be best today, is likely to be obsolete tomorrow. The first written agreement between General Motors Corporation and the United Automobile Workers Union signed some thirty years ago was a one-page memorandum. Twenty-five years later it was a printed contract running 200 printed pages.

At present, general wage and hour conditions are not subject to negotiations in most public employee bargaining relationships. Both in the case of classified federal civil servants and a large proportion of state and local employees, these matters are reserved to the legislators. It seems difficult to believe that public employees, once their unions are established, will be content with a situation in which bargaining over the most basic issues is outside their purview. The general management attitude that, "We can talk about individual workers' problems, or the lights or noise in this room, but general wages and hours are out — left solely to the legislature," won't go down well. Here again the United States can look to the experience of other countries. The typical European nation entered the modern era with civil servants regarded as part of "His Majesty's Service." The private, let alone the public lives of these servants was subject to close and highly arbitrary scrutiny by the government. Personal oaths to king or emperor were given as a condition of employment. The Europeans have passed from these quaint and paternalistic times to a situation where full bargaining rights are now accorded to public employee unions. Their activities and rights now run to bargaining power over general wage and hour changes, holidays, vacations, and most of the economic benefits that one associates with a private sector collective agreement in the United States.

PUBLIC EMPLOYEE BARGAINING AND JOINT MANAGEMENT

In the present era there is probably an unparalleled opportunity to make public employee union-management relationships something new and unique in American labor history. In the United States there has been an important scaling upward of educational attainments in the past twenty years. As a result of this and other factors, one finds, especially among many white collar employees, a growing desire for wider participation in the decision making processes. If public managers turn their thoughts on how to *widen,* rather than limit, the scope of management-union relationships, to embrace serious consultation with their employees on policy matters and the organization of their agencies, all sorts of new possibilities may be opened. The public sector may provide a useful training ground for what in other countries has been variously termed co-determination, joint-consultation or workers' participation in management. Obviously these possibilities vary from agency to agency and from union to union, and there may be greater possibilities in state and local service than at the federal level. But the potentialities for new types of relationships based as much, and possibly more, on cooperative rather than conflicting bonds are formidable in the public service. As yet, however, the public managers have been more fearful than expansive in their reactions to the "new unionism."

The demands of many professional employees, most notably teachers and nurses, have from the very beginning gone far beyond wages and hours. Their very professionalism turns them to the substantive policy questions affecting the agencies that employ them. Curriculum content, the size of classes, the organization of the educational system — these and other matters run to the heart of a teacher's interests, and one can list similar professional areas for nurses.

In the long run, indeed, if public managers are to carry forward the process of enlarging the scope of union-management relationships, the unions might find it difficult to depend upon *traditional union* member loyalty patterns and appeals. The increasing professionalization of society may be the beginning of a new kind of role for organized labor, not the guild socialism once proposed by G. D. H. Cole, but some new form of participation in authority. That is one of the aspects of what Daniel Bell has called the "post-industrial" society, the coming of a new society in which professionalization becomes the commonplace mark of skilled employment. A large-scale society of professionals inevitably means a reduction of that status. But it also means the upgrading of an older worker status, and this adds to the importance of the sweeping new public employee unionism in the United States.

QUESTIONS

1. What factors account for the growing unionization of government employees? What factors, if any, inhibit this trend?

2. What government occupation accounts for the bulk of union organization activity?

3. Kassalow shows a rather optimistic and lenient view of strikes in the public sector. Do you share his view? Why or why not? Do you see the issue as primarily one of economic policy or broader social matters involving concepts such as liberty and justice?

4. Some observers have argued that strikes in the public sector should be allowed only in nonessential occupations. Do you agree? Could you reach a consensus with three friends on the meaning of nonessential? Some occupations you might begin with: transit workers, garbage collectors, police, teachers, secretaries and clerks at the Pentagon, maintenance men at the water works, congressmen, firemen, judges.

5. "Strikes and collective bargaining in the public sector are not at all analogous to those in the private sector. Public officials need not consider costs when bargaining with a union in the sense that a businessman does and when a government union strikes, users of that public good or service have nowhere to turn. Consequently collective bargaining and the strike, while perhaps appropriate for the private sector, have no place in the government." Comment.

28 THE ECONOMICS OF UNION ENTRY RESTRICTIONS
Gary S. Becker

Gary Becker, University Professor of Economics at The University of Chicago, was awarded a John Bates Clark medal for his ingenious ability to apply economic theory to social phenomena. The applications have been to racial discrimination, crime and punishment, household behavior, and even an economic theory of marriage! In this article Becker demonstrates the usefulness of the principles of demand and supply in explaining union behavior regarding racial discrimination and high initiation fees.

Economists have long been concerned with the economic power of unions,[1] and in the last twenty years have attempted to determine this power empirically. The principal measure used has been a ratio of the union's wage rate to one that would exist in the union's absence. Most economists would agree that union power has been imperfectly estimated, partly because this measure ignores union effects on nonpecuniary and future income, and partly because it has been difficult to determine wages, especially wages that would exist in the union's absence. The probability of serious error would be reduced if other independent measures were also used. In this chapter, two measures are developed that frequently can be used either to check a relative wage estimate or to measure union power when a relative wage estimate is unavailable. Both incorporate the fact that unions affect the level of employment and the attractiveness of an occupation as well as wages. A union that raises wages attracts people to the union from other

[1] Throughout this chapter the word "union" refers to both trade unions and organizations which are in similar economic positions, such as the American Medical Association.

Abridged from Gary S. Becker, "Union Restrictions on Entry," in Philip D. Bradley, ed., *The Public Stake in Union Power* (Charlottesville: University of Virginia Press, 1959), pp. 209–224. Reprinted by permission.

occupations, and it becomes necessary to ration entry to the union. One measure of union power is associated with the use of nonprice techniques to ration entry, the other with the use of "high" initiation or entrance fees to ration entry.

These two methods of rationing entry not only produce different measures of union power, but also other important differences in admission policies. For example, there is more discrimination against minority groups and more nepotism toward relatives and friends in unions that restrict entry with nonprice techniques. The degree of power being the same, unions charging high initiation fees tend to reject fewer applicants. The first section of this chapter relates union power to restrictions on entry and discusses several differences between price and nonprice rationing. The second section uses the analysis of the first to understand the actual policies of a few unions.

These two sections seem to demonstrate that union members are better off if initiation fees are used to ration entry, yet it is evident that trade unions rely almost exclusively on nonprice rationing. The third and final section tries to reconcile this apparent conflict between actual and rational trade union policy.

THE ADMISSION OF APPLICANTS

Consider Figure 1, where the curves *DD* and *SS* represent, respectively, the demand for and supply of a particular factor as a function of its relative wage. In the absence of unions and monopsonists, equilibrium would occur at Point *P*, with *PQ* the wage rate and *OQ* the quantity employed. If a union did not change the location of the demand curve it would move along *DD* to a point like *P'* with *P'Q'* the new wage rate and *OQ'* the new quantity employed. The quantity *OA* measures the amount that wants to be employed at the union wage rate. The quantity *Q'A* therefore measures the gap between the quantity available and the quantity demanded. This gap can be closed in three different ways: (a) All applicants could be admitted, but the number of hours worked by the typical union member reduced, (b)

Figure 1.

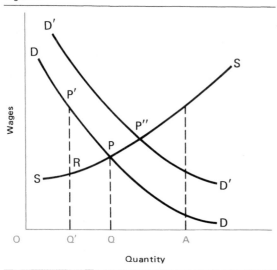

some applicants could be arbitrarily excluded, or (c) the number of applicants could be reduced by "high" initiation fees. These three are discussed in turn.

If all applicants were admitted, supply being adjusted entirely through reductions in hours worked, it might be impossible to increase the real income of a typical member. To take an extreme example, let us suppose the supply of persons to a union was infinitely elastic at the income level prevailing under competitive conditions. Then, no matter what the increase in wages, the increase in the number of union members would reduce hours sufficiently to maintain the real incomes prevailing under competitive conditions. In general, the greater the elasticity of supply of persons to a union, the more difficult it is to increase income by reducing hours. Since the long-run supply elasticity to an occupation or industry is probably very high, a reduction in hours would not be a promising way to raise the long-run incomes of union members. The available evidence appears to support this conclusion, for large declines in hours worked by trade union members appear to occur primarily during sharp cyclical or secular declines in demand. Under these conditions a reduction in hours seems like a natural way to ration the limited work available. Reductions in hours to raise long-run incomes appear to be much less common,

although it must be admitted that only limited quantitative evidence is available, and I have not systematically examined what is available.[2]

If unions do not reduce long-run supply through a reduction in hours, they must do it through a reduction in numbers. A common way to reduce numbers is to reject arbitrarily some applicants. A strong union — one not faced with much competition from other labor or machinery — would reject many applicants since, over a wide range, income of the average member would be negatively related to the number in the union. There would likewise be an incentive to reduce the number over time by not replacing members who die or retire. On the other hand, a weak union — one faced with intense competition from other labor and machinery — would not reject a large number of applicants, since doing so would cause a reduction in the average member's income. Even a strong union can go too far in the rejection of applicants, for excessive rejections can stimulate the competition from non-union labor. In both strong and weak unions the equilibrium number of members is reached when a further reduction in numbers would reduce the income of the average member.

A union will not move along a given demand curve if it can shift the demand curve, say to $D'D'$ in Figure 1. Both employment and income could be raised without raising the value of this relative quantity measure, as illustrated by point P''. This is unlikely, however, because a union has an incentive to move along $D'D'$ away from P''. A movement away from P'' creates a gap between the quantity of labor demanded and supplied, and thus increases the number of applicants per member. So, even if a union could shift the demand curve for its services, there would still be a positive correlation between the increase in wages and the number of applicants per member.

A union that restricts entry by the "arbitrary" rejection of some applicants does not necessarily select members at random. On the contrary, the union would consider any differences among appli-

[2] The building, printing, and a few other unions have negotiated contracts calling for relatively short working days, but white collar workers, most of whom are non-union, have shorter working days than most union members.

cants in choosing among them. For example, if a union did not want colored people in the union, colored applicants would tend to be rejected. If a union preferred sons and nephews of present or former members, they would be admitted more easily than others. Discrimination and nepotism such as this would not cost union members anything as long as the number rejected or accepted because of discrimination or nepotism was less than the number that would be accepted or rejected if new members were chosen at random. This condition is more fully realized in strong unions, since they reject more applicants than do weak unions. When a union can engage in costless discrimination and nepotism, there is every incentive for it to do so. Hence we would expect discrimination and nepotism to be more prevalent in strong unions.

A union might restrict entry not only by excluding some applicants but also by reducing their number. Suppose a union decided to admit thirty new members from a group of one hundred homogeneous applicants. It could select thirty applicants at random and admit them, or it could substitute an admissions fee for this random mechanism. If the fee were too "low," more than thirty persons would apply and the union would have to select at random thirty persons. If it were too "high," fewer than thirty persons would apply and the union would be unable to secure the desired number. If it were set just "right," exactly thirty persons would apply, and no further rationing would be necessary. Thus an admissions fee could reduce the number of applicants to the desired number. The proceeds, which presumably would be distributed to union members, represent an additional return to the union's economic power.

This equilibrium admissions fee would equal the difference between the present value of the income stream received by a union member and the present value received in the next best occupation. If it were greater, too few people would want to join the union. If it were less, too many people would want to join, with the result that the union could raise the fee and still admit the desired number. Therefore, this fee is an excellent index of a union's economic power, measuring future as well as present income, and implicitly estimating the income expect-

ed in comparable occupations. Union economic power would be positively correlated with the size of admissions fees, rather than with the number of applicants per member.

If a union used nonprice rationing, rejected applicants might offer bribes to those administering the admissions program. Presumably, the amount offered would be directly related to the union's power. In very strong unions these bribes might be large enough to constitute a major temptation. There is less scope (or perhaps less need) for bribery in a union using price rationing, for if the fee was appropriately set, nothing would be paid sub rosa for admission. Moreover, it would be difficult to show any favoritism not sanctioned by union members, since this would be relatively easily uncovered by an audit of the books of those in charge.

A union using an admissions fee to ration entry could discriminate against minorities and show favoritism towards relatives, but it would have to pay for this privilege. Consider the union that set an admissions fee high enough to reduce the number of applicants to thirty, the desired number of new members. If the union did not want any colored members and if some of these thirty applicants were colored, it would be necessary to lower the fee in order to secure thirty white applicants. The difference between these two fees would measure the cost of its discrimination against colored people. The amount of discrimination "consumed" is presumably negatively related to its cost or "price." Therefore, the lower the price at which thirty white applicants could be obtained, the greater the incentive to admit colored applicants. Since discrimination is free to unions using nonprice rationing, these unions can be expected to discriminate more than other unions.

I have implicitly assumed that the number of persons in a union is independent of admission policies, but I now show that this number varies directly with the degree of price rationing. Under nonprice rationing, increased competition from other factors is the only cost of restricting entry. At the margin this cost is balanced against the gain (higher wages) from a reduction in numbers. Under price rationing, foregone admission fees are an additional cost, so that at the margin these two costs must be balanced against the gain from a reduction in numbers. If a union converted from non-price to price rationing it would thus increase the marginal cost of a reduction in numbers — approximately by the size of the admissions fee[3] — and this provides an incentive to increase its numbers. It might appear paradoxical that an increase in the entrance fee can result in more, not fewer, admissions. The appearance of a paradox probably stems from an implicit comparison of unions that ration by charging entrance fees with unions that do not ration entry at all. The actual comparison, however, is between unions that use different kinds of rationing. Once this is recognized, the result should not be surprising.

APPLICATION OF THE ANALYSIS

We find, then, that unions using price to ration entry systematically differ from other unions in a few major respects: (1) The present value of their monopoly power can be measured by the size of the admissions fee, while the monopoly power of other unions can be measured by the number of applicants per member; (2) bribery, discrimination, and nepotism would be less important, insofar as admissions are concerned, than in other unions; (3) the relative number rejected would be fewer than in other unions. I now examine several unions and focus my attention on these different effects of price and nonprice rationing.

Entry to Medical School The American Medical Association uses nonprice methods to restrict entry, and the extent of the restriction is exhibited by the large number of applicants rejected from medical schools. This has been used as evidence of substantial economic power. Medical schools have been accused, with some justification, I believe, of discrimination against minority groups and of favoritism towards relatives of AMA members. Perhaps this explains why doctors' sons more frequently seem to follow in their fathers' footsteps than do sons of other professional men. Bribes to secure entry to medical schools have also been reported. It is im-

possible to determine whether the number admitted to the schools is less than it would be if price were used to ration entry.

Immigration The United States uses nonprice rationing to restrict the entry of persons from other countries. There is no need to dwell on the large number of persons denied entry, or to spell out the implication that real incomes in the United States are considered substantially higher than elsewhere. The discrimination and nepotism in the immigration laws are apparent to all, as exemplified by the almost total exclusion of Asians and the preferential treatment given relatives of United States citizens. It seems likely that immigration restrictions would be weakened if each immigrant were required to pay a "large" entrance fee.

Licensing Licenses are required for many activities, such as the sale of liquor, the use of the air waves for radio and television, and the operation of taxicabs. Because new licenses are usually rationed by non-price methods, the economic value of a license can be measured by the relative number of applicants. If old licenses were transferable, the economic value could also be measured by the price of old licenses (see my discussion of taxicabs). Recent Congressional hearings uncovered bribery, favoritism and discrimination in the issuance of television licenses by the FCC. Periodic investigations by state and municipal committees disclose similar practices in the issuance of liquor and cab licenses. These practices could be predicted from a knowledge that new licenses are retained by non-price methods.

Labor Union Membership If, as is generally believed, most trade unions use nonprice rationing to restrict entry, their economic power could be measured by the number of applicants per member. Such evidence would indicate that craft unions have more economic power than industrial unions, since it is more difficult to enter craft unions. Direct evidence on the income of industrial and craft unionists tends to support this conclusion. Discrimination against minorities and nepotism towards relatives also appear to be greater in craft unions and greatest in the strongest craft unions. Some exclude minorities

---

[3] I say "approximately" because account would be taken of the change in the admissions fee as the number admitted changed.

(especially Negroes) by constitutional provision, and in some entry is impossible for persons unrelated to a craftsman. "The building trades unions in St. Louis have a very definite policy of keeping the trade in the family and enforce it to such an extent that a boy has as good a chance to get into West Point as into the building trades unless his father or uncle is a building craftsman!"

A trade union may raise wages but have no control over the distribution of new jobs. In a union shop contract this power is nominally[4] controlled by employers. Since a new union member may have no reasonable expectation of finding employment, easy entry would not necessarily indicate that wages have not been raised. The trade union's power would have to be measured by the number of applicants for employment per employed person. The employer, rather than the trade union, would ration entry and could discriminate and show favoritism at no cost to himself. I concluded that craft unions have more power than industrial unions because they reject more applicants and discriminate more. The possibility remains, however, that industrial unions have had the power to raise wages, but have lacked the power to ration jobs.

These four examples are very similar in spite of apparent diversity. Immigration, medicine, television stations and trade unions appear to have little in common, and indeed, discussions of entry into each usually emphasize unique considerations. Yet unique considerations do not seem so important, as these similarities could be predicted from the knowledge that nonprice rationing is used in all four cases.

Taxicab Medallions In New York City a medallion is required to operate a cab,[5] and it is usually transferable from one individual (or company) to another. Since few new medallions are issued[6] the principal way to enter this industry is to buy an old medallion. The price of an old medallion, therefore,

should approximate the present value of the additional income from operating a cab. In the last few years medallions have sold for about $17,000. At an interest rate of 7 percent this is equivalent to an annual income of $1,200, implying that the city's reluctance to issue new medallions has raised the income of an owner-operator[7] by about $1,200 per annum. This $1,200 is about 20 percent of the income he could have earned in another occupation. Although this increase has been gained with but little publicity, it is as large as — and possibly larger than — the increase estimated for a few of the strongest trade unions. There is reason to believe that this simple estimate of the gain to cab operators is more reliable than many estimates of the gains to trade unions. This estimate measures real income and not wages alone, takes account of expected future income as well as present income, and implicitly uses the best estimate of the income that would be received if there were no restrictions on entry.[8]

The sale of medallions seems less affected by discrimination and nepotism than is membership in those trade unions with an equal amount of economic power. Since price is used to ration medallions but not to ration membership in trade unions, this difference is entirely consistent with our earlier analysis.

Union Initiation Fees Although trade unions appear to rely primarily on nonprice rationing, initiation fees are also used to ration entry. These fees are greater in craft unions than in industrial ones, thus supporting my earlier conclusion that craft unions have the greater economic power. There is likewise a tendency for stronger craft unions to charge higher fees than others. Some initiation fees amount to several hundred dollars and one, reported for the Chicago glaziers in the early 1940s, would equal about $3,000 in today's prices.

---

[4] I say "nominally" because many contracts are written as union shop contracts to comply with the Taft-Hartley Act, but are in effect closed shop contracts.

[5] This is not the same as the license required to *drive* a cab.

[6] The number of medallions outstanding evidently has declined during the last few years.

[7] The number of individual owners is regulated: a medallion owned by an individual can be sold only to another individual.

[8] The discussion here also brings out one advantage that price rationing has for policy: it provides a direct and simple measure of economic power. The high price of a medallion informs the city that its restrictions have created a large monopoly income for cab operators.

A trade union often receives substantial government assistance because the occupation of its members is closely related to the health and safety of the public. As government intervention is assumed to be in the public's interest, a union must avoid giving the impression that it greatly benefits from the intervention. A high initiation fee is prima facie evidence of personal gain, while nepotism and discrimination are not easily distinguished from selection by "quality." The control of the AMA over the certification of medical schools would be rapidly revoked if medical schools had to pay the AMA thousands of dollars in order to be certified. Moreover, government assistance is frequently combined with an implicit outlawing of admissions fees. The AMA controls the licensing of doctors, and in many states the plumbers' union controls the licensing of plumbers, but these licenses cannot be sold. This reliance on government assistance is probably a sufficient explanation of the low initiation fees in many trade unions. Others, however, such as the typographical union, seem to be far enough removed from direct government assistance to have less reason to fear government reaction. And although cab operators in New York are entirely dependent on government assistance, for several years they have managed to charge more than $10,000 for a medallion. It would appear, then, that the connection between economic power and government assistance partly, but not entirely, explains the persistence of low initiation fees in strong trade unions.

Initiation fees may be low because trade unions are not interested in pecuniary income alone. For example, fees would be low if union members believed it was "wrong" to require new members to buy their way in, perhaps because many new members would be related to present members. Surely, few Americans want to charge immigrants substantial entrance fees, the reason presumably being that the sale of citizenship is morally repugnant. A similar objection may prevent trade unions from charging high fees. Admittedly, trade unions may have to forfeit more than a year's income, but a substantial amount is also forfeited because entrance fees are not collected from immigrants. It is often asserted, but rarely demonstrated, that trade union decisions are strongly influenced by nonpecuniary motives.

If this explanation of low initiation fees is even partly valid, there would be evidence that trade unions *are* willing to forfeit pecuniary income for non-pecuniary income, and it would suggest that the same may also be true of other trade union decisions. It must be emphasized, however, that this discussion of the use of price rationing by trade unions is highly conjectural and tentative. A fuller consideration of the problem may cast doubt on the factors stressed here and uncover others completely ignored.

To summarize:

1. The number of persons trying to enter a union varies directly with its economic power. Since a strong union can only admit some applicants, entry must be rationed. If nonprice rationing is used, the union's power can be measured by the number of applicants per member; if price rationing is used, by the admissions fee. These measures are in many ways better than the usual measure of union power, which is the ratio of union wages to the wages that would exist in the union's absence.

2. If nonprice rationing is used, strong unions can discriminate against minorities and show favoritism to relatives and friends at no cost to themselves. This explains why such unions greatly discriminate and show much favoritism. If price rationing is used, unions must pay for discrimination and favoritism, and this discourages such behavior.

If price rationing is used, an admissions fee is received from each new member, and this provides an incentive to admit new members which other unions do not have. It is, therefore, natural to expect unions using price rationing to be less restrictive than other unions with equal power.

3. An examination of several actual unions clearly showed that the technique used to ration entry not only determined how a union's power could be measured, but also determined the amount of discrimination, favoritism, and exclusiveness in a union.

4. Price rationing would seem to be the most "rational" union policy, yet trade unions seldom use it. Two ways to reconcile this apparent conflict between actual and rational policy merit further consideration. One emphasizes that trade union power is often based on government aid, and argues

that this aid would be withdrawn if trade unions charged high fees. The other emphasizes that trade union decisions are strongly affected by nonpecuniary factors, and argues that trade unions are unwilling to sell the privilege of membership. There is only limited evidence for either explanation and much further work is needed.

QUESTIONS

1. What is the "principal measure" used to measure the union impact on wages? What flaws does this measure have?
2. What other techniques are suggested for measuring a union's economic power?
3. If economic analysis demonstrates the "rationality" of strong unions charging high initiation fees, why is the phenomenon so seldom observed?

THE ECONOMICS OF WOMEN'S LIBERATION
Barbara R. Bergmann

The feminist movement has not escaped the scrutiny of economic analysis. In the following article the economics of women's liberation is discussed by an especially well-qualified economist. Barbara Bergmann is a professor of economics at the University of Maryland and is director of the Project on the Economics of Discrimination there.

It will take a lot of changes if equal participation in the American economy for women is to become a reality. In the feminists' vision of a better future there would be, with few exceptions, no "men's occupations" and "women's occupations"; women would get equal pay for equal work; they would do less unpaid work at home, and men would do more. I want to consider two sets of issues concerning the postliberation world. First, I shall explore the nature and strength of the economic forces blocking the way to the development of a world in which

Abridged from Barbara R. Bergmann, "The Economics of Women's Liberation," *Challenge* (May/June 1973), 11—17.

women would have (and would take advantage of) equal opportunities for paid work. Second, I shall try to describe some of the changes in economic and social arrangements which a more equal participation of women in the economy and a more equal participation of men in the home would entail.

WHAT'S BLOCKING WOMEN'S LIBERATION?

Aside from inertia, there are four factors which have been alleged to be at work to keep things as they are: (1) discrimination against women in employment and promotion due to male prejudice or malevolence; (2) inferior job performance by women; (3) the disinclination of many women to enter into what they view as men's roles; and (4) the profits to be made by business from keeping women in their present roles. Not all of these factors are of equal importance, as we shall see.

When we speak of employer prejudice against women we generally do not mean feelings of hatred or a desire to refrain from association with them. After all, most men are very glad to have a woman secretary right outside their office door. The most important manifestation of employer prejudice against women is a desire to restrict them to spheres which are viewed as proper for them. Everybody knows which jobs are "fit" for women: domestic and light factory work for the least educated ones; clerical and retail sales work for the high-school graduates; and teaching, nursing, and social work for those with professional inclinations.

The economist Victor R. Fuchs of the National Bureau of Economic Research, who is one of the pioneers in research on women's role in the labor market, finds occupational segregation by sex to be far more extreme than occupational segregation by race. In a 1970 study he says, ". . . one of the most striking findings is how few occupations employ large numbers of both sexes. Most men work in occupations that employ very few women and a significant fraction of women work in occupations that employ very few men." Fuchs attributes occupational segregation and the low pay for women it entails largely to the conditioning of women by society to avoid certain fields.

Up to now, the relative importance of discrimination in filling these high paying jobs and the relative importance of women's failure to compete for them in explaining occupational segregation by sex have not really been carefully measured by anyone. In the end, it may prove statistically impossible to separate out the precise importance of the various factors. However, there is considerable evidence that discrimination is far from a negligible factor.

The economic results of occupational segregation for women are low wages. Women are relegated for the most part to those occupations in which experience adds very little to the status and productivity of the worker as she advances in age. After a year or two a secretary is about as good as she will ever be, while her junior executive boss, who may have the same formal education as she, continues to gain in confidence, knowledge and technical competence, and of course makes commensurate advances in pay.

Since the boundaries separating the men's occupational preserve from the women's are economically speaking artificial and not easily changed, the women's preserve may tend to get overcrowded, especially if the proportion of women in the labor force increases. This is exactly what has been occurring. Between 1950 and 1970, the number of men working increased by 15 percent, while the number of women working increased by 70 percent.

Into what kinds of jobs did these women go? Because of employer discrimination and their own limited horizons, millions of them went into the traditional women's preserve — clerical work. In that 20-year period, there was a very great increase in the number of women clerical workers: they more than doubled their numbers. About one quarter of women workers were in the clerical category in 1950, and by 1970 more than one in three working women were clerical workers. There was no change in the nature of the economy to require such a dramatic upsurge in clerical employment. On the contrary, computerization tends to reduce the demand for clerks. These extra women were absorbed through the classic mechanism of a flexible economy — clerks lost ground in pay, and took on lower-priority work. That clerical jobs of the type filled by women became relatively overcrowded is shown by the fact that, during this period, wage rates in this relatively poorly paid occupation lagged still farther behind all other occupational groups for men and women.

Interestingly, some progress apparently was made in the professional and technical group and the service worker group during the fifties and sixties. Women increased their representation in these occupations substantially, yet enjoyed better than average increases in pay rates. I take this as evidence of expanding demand for women in these fields, possibly involving some desegregation of employment in the particular jobs which make up these two large occupational groups.

Allegations concerning women's inferior job performance center on the lower commitment of some women to the labor market. Many women do leave jobs for prolonged periods to give birth to and take care of babies, or to follow their husbands to another city. At any given age they have less work experience, on the average, than men of the same age. A great deal has been made of women's relative lack of experience, but the truth is that in the kinds of jobs women are mostly consigned to, experience counts for very little in terms of skill or pay.

Women have been quitting jobs at a higher rate than men (the latest figures, for 1968, show quit rates of 2.6 percent per month for women in manufacturing and 2.2 percent for men). But calculations by Professor Isabel Sawhill of Goucher College indicate that about half of the gap in quit rates is due to the fact that women are heavily employed in the kinds of occupations in which *men and women* tend to quit more often, whereas men are heavily employed in the kinds of jobs in which stability of employment is rewarded.

We come finally to the allegation, usually made by radicals out to discredit capitalism, that women's subjection is all a capitalist plot. Who benefits financially from maintenance of the *status quo*? The most obvious beneficiaries of prejudice against women are male workers in those occupations in which women are not allowed to compete. This lack of competition raises pay and in certain circumstances may reduce unemployment in an occupation largely reserved for males. Of course, wives who have a stay-at-home ideology also gain when women are excluded from their husbands' occupations. This undoubtedly accounts for some of the social pressure against women's liberation.

Will capitalism collapse if women don't stay home and spend their time purchasing consumer goods? In fact, women who stay home are a poorer market for capitalist enterprise's products than women who go to work. Women who stay at home bake cakes and make dresses. Women who go to work patronize bakeries and dress shops more. A woman who leaves the home for a job will undoubtedly spend less time thinking about and seeking the detergent that will leave her clothes whiter than white, but she will probably buy the same amount of detergent, unless she starts patronizing a commercial laundry, in which case it will be the laundry that buys the detergent.

WHAT WOULD THE POSTLIBERATION ECONOMY LOOK LIKE?

One of the most dramatic effects of women's liberation would be the change in the size and pay of occupations from which women had been excluded or had excluded themselves. Assuming, for example, that the number of places in medical schools will in the future be responsive to the number of qualified applicants, the number of physicians might in time double, and the income of physicians would surely come down at least relatively. The benefits to nonphysicians in terms of better services and cheaper health care are quite obvious. The financial losses to the present members of of the medical profession (and their stay-at-home wives) are also obvious, but even they might enjoy the shorter workweek and lower patient load.

After a discussion of women as physicians it is only fair to discuss women as streetcleaners. The Soviet Union is always held up as a horrible example of what happens when women's liberation is tried; we have all seen the pictures of elderly women, scarves tied around their heads, sweeping the streets in the Moscow winter. These pictures and their captions are supposed to make us feel sorry for the women in a way we would not feel sorry for male

streetcleaners. But I don't think we should shrink from the notion of streetcleaning as an occupation appropriate to the physically fit of both sexes. Streetcleaning is probably healthier and more interesting than clerical work; and when these jobs are well paid, they are much sought after.

Professor Estelle James of Stony Brook made some calculations of the effect of wage rates that a relaxation of occupational segregation by sex would entail. She assumed that women would compete on an equal footing with men of the same educational achievement. Occupations having similar requirements in terms of education, intelligence, skill, and experience would not have different pay scales, as they now do, depending on whether they are in the men's or women's preserve. Occupations previously reserved for women, which currently command low pay, would shrink in size as the rate of pay in them rose. Women would shift to those occupations previously reserved for men, which would increase in size, and which would experience a fall in pay. For example, in jobs held by those with a high-school diploma or better, she estimates that previously male occupations would increase in size by almost 15 percent and that wage rates in these occupations would decrease by about 15 percent. Employment in previously female occupations would be cut about 35 percent, and the pay would increase about 55 percent. Let me hasten to add that the decreases in wage rates projected for men would in actuality be translated in most cases into low or zero rates of increase, because the transition would occur only gradually and would be mitigated by increases in productivity. Despite this fact, Professor James' calculations suggest that womens' liberation would bring a radical change in the lineup of occupational wage rates.

One of the benefits of the achievement of women's liberation would be a reduction in the incidence of poverty. One-third of poverty families are those the Census Bureau defines as "headed by women." When a man leaves his family or dies, the family loses the worker who was discriminated against least. The low pay of most of the jobs open to women means that when the woman goes out to work she has a poor chance of earning an income above the poverty level. The boring nature of many of these jobs, plus the lack of incentive that the low pay entails, induces many women who have lost their husbands through separation or death to languish at home on welfare payments. Thus, in the United States, discrimination against women combined with a high incidence of marital instability has helped to increase the incidence of poverty. We have estimated that about two-thirds of the poverty among black and/or female-headed families in which the head of the family works is due to discrimination.

The achievement of women's liberation obviously involves changed distribution of work in the home. Arrangements may be made for outside paid help in cooking, dishwashing, shopping, child care, and cleaning chores, but family members are still going to have to do a considerable amount of unpaid domestic work. Norton Dodge's monumental study *Women in the Soviet Economy* shows that Soviet men have taken over some of the housework, but probably far from a fair share of it. Russian men who work an eight-hour day spend an average of one and a half hours a day on household chores, whereas women who work an eight-hour day spend three and seven-tenths hours a day on such chores.

But all of this is, so far as I can see, grossly unlikely. If the current level of interest in women's liberation were to continue for decades, then the transformations I have been describing would occur. But that is a very big "if." In the meantime, individual women who want to do work other than full-time unpaid domestic labor will just have to go on bucking the prejudice of employers, fighting their own laziness and sense of insufficiency, and nagging their husbands to help them with the dishes.

QUESTIONS

1. In the past two decades, have males or females entered the marketplace at a more rapid rate? What might account for this differential?

2. What hypotheses are most commonly used to explain why women tend to receive lower wages than men? What policies, taken either by business or government, could eliminate the wage differential?

3. If women's liberation becomes an even more prominent and established social movement, what changes are going to evolve in the running of businesses and the operation of homes?

4. Is women's liberation in any way a threat to the free-enterprise system?

THE ECONOMIC THEORY OF BRUSHING ONE'S TEETH
Alan S. Blinder

Human capital theory concerns the behavior of individuals as they augment their income—earning potential through education, training, health care, and the like. Princeton's Alan S. Blinder here examines, tongue in cheek, whether the human capital approach applies to the brushing of teeth. Dr. Blinder's more sober scholarly efforts relate to the economics of income distribution and stabilization policy.

The ever-growing literature on human capital has long recognized that the scope of the theory extends well beyond the traditional analysis of schooling and on-the-job training. Migration, maintenance of health, crime and punishment, even marriage and suicide, are all decisions which can usefully be considered from the human capital point of view. Yet economists have ignored the analysis of an important class of activities which can and should be brought within the purview of the theory. A prime example of this class is brushing teeth.

The conventional analysis of toothbrushing has centered around two basic models. The "bad taste in one's mouth" model is based on the notion that each person has a "taste for brushing," and the fact that brushing frequencies differ is "explained" by differences in tastes. Since any pattern of human behavior can be rationalized by such implicit theo-

Abridged from the *Journal of Political Economy*, 82 (July/August 1974), 887–891. Copyright © 1974 by The University of Chicago.

rizing, this model is devoid of empirically testable predictions, and hence uninteresting.

The "mother told me so" theory is based on differences in cultural upbringing. Here it is argued, for example, that thrice-a-day brushers brush three times daily because their mothers forced them to do so as children. Of course, this is hardly a complete explanation. Like most psychological theories, it leaves open the question of why mothers should want their children to brush after every meal. But it does at least have one testable implication: that individuals from higher social classes will brush more frequently.

In these pages I describe a new model which is firmly grounded in economic theory and which generates a large number of empirically testable hypotheses. I then show that the predictions of the model are supported by the data.

The basic assumption is common to all human capital theory: that individuals seek to maximize their incomes. It follows immediately that each individual does whatever amount of toothbrushing will maximize his income. The "mother told me so" model can be considered as a special case where the offspring only does as he or she is told, but the mother's decisions are governed by income maximization for the child. Thus, offspring will behave *as if* they maximized income.

An example will illustrate the usefulness of the model. Consider the toothbrushing decisions of chefs and waiters working in the same establishments. Since chefs generally come from higher socioeconomic strata, the "mother told me so" model predicts that they will brush more frequently than waiters. In fact, it has been shown that the reverse is true. Of course, the human capital model predicts precisely this behavior. On the benefits side, chefs are rarely seen by customers and work on straight salary. Waiters, by contrast, are in constant touch with the public and rely on tips for most of their income. Bad breath and/or yellow teeth could have deleterious effects on their earnings. On the cost side, since wages for chefs are higher, the opportunity cost of brushing is correspondingly higher. Thus, the theory predicts unambiguously that chefs will brush less.

REVIEW OF THE LITERATURE

A substantial literature on dental hygienics exists. It is ironic that economists are almost completely unaware of these studies, despite the fact that most economists brush their teeth.

The best empirical study was conducted by a team of researchers at the University of Chicago Medical Center in 1967. They compared toothbrushing habits of a scientifically selected sample of 27 sets of twins who had appeared in Wrigley's chewing gum commercials with a random sample of 54 longshoremen. The twins brushed their teeth an average of 3.17 times per day, while the longshoremen brushed only 0.76 times daily. The difference was significant at the 1 percent level. As noneconomists, the doctors advanced two possible explanations for this finding: either twins had a higher "taste for brushing" than nontwins, or the Wrigley Company deliberately set out to hire people with clean teeth. Further study, they concluded, would be needed to discriminate between these two hypotheses. The human capital viewpoint makes the true explanation clear enough. Earnings of models depend strongly on the whiteness of their teeth. On the other hand, no direct connection has ever been established between the income of longshoremen and the quality of their breath.

Another recent contribution was a survey of professors in a leading Eastern university. It was found that assistant professors brushed 2.14 times daily on average, while associate professors brushed only 1.89 times and full professors only 1.47 times daily. The author, a sociologist, mistakenly attributed this finding to the fact that the higher-ranking professors were older and that hygiene standards in America had advanced steadily over time. To a human capital theorist, of course, this pattern is exactly what would be expected from the higher wages received in the higher professorial ranks, and from the fact that younger professors, looking for promotions, cannot afford to have bad breath.

A Theoretical Model of Toothbrushing   Let w be the wage rate of an individual; let J be an index of his job; and let B be the time spent brushing his teeth. With no loss of generality, I can reorder the jobs so that jobs with higher J are the jobs where clean teeth are more important. The assumed wage function is therefore

$$w = w(J, B), \quad w_B \geqslant 0,$$
$$w_{BJ} = w_{JB} \geqslant 0. \tag{1}$$

Since jobs have been reordered, there is no a priori presumption about the sign of w_J. It is also assumed that $w(\, \cdot \,)$ is continuous, twice differentiable, and semistrictly quasi-concave in the nonnegative orthant.

Each individual is assumed to maximize his income:

$$Y = w(J, B)(T - B) + P, \tag{2}$$

where T is the fixed amount of time per period available for working or brushing and P is the (exogenously determined) amount of unearned income. That is, each individual selects a value of B to maximize (2). The necessary condition for a maximum is

$$w_B(J, B)(T - B) - w(J, B) = 0. \tag{3}$$

Several important implications follow from (3). First, since both w and w_B are presumptively positive, (3) implies that $T - B$ must be positive. In words, the theory predicts that no person will spend every waking hour brushing his teeth — an empirically testable proposition not derivable from either the "bad taste" or "mother told me" models.

Second, (3) can be rewritten

$$\frac{B}{T - B} = \frac{Bw_B}{w} \tag{4}$$

In words, the ratio of brushing to nonbrushing time is equated to the partial elasticity of the wage with respect to brushing time. So individuals in jobs where wages are highly sensitive to brushing will devote more time to brushing than will others — as indicated in the verbal discussion. Also, for any two jobs with equal w_B's but unequal w's, (3) implies that the higher-wage person will brush less due to his greater opportunity cost.

Finally consider the important case where (1) is linear in B (though possibly nonlinear in J):

$$w = \alpha(J) + \beta(J)B, \quad \alpha \geqslant 0, \quad \beta \geqslant 0 \tag{1'}$$

Substituting into (3) and solving yields

$$B = \frac{T}{2} - \frac{\alpha}{2\beta}. \tag{5}$$

In jobs where brushing is immaterial to success, $\beta \to 0$, so (5) calls for a corner maximum with $B = 0$. Thus, we have a second strong prediction from the model: such persons will never brush. At the other extreme, as the ratio α/β approaches zero, (5) implies $B \to T/2$. In words, individuals whose wages depend almost exclusively on the whiteness of their teeth (M.C.'s of television quiz shows are a good example) will spend approximately half their lives brushing. Again, no sociological theory can generate predictions as strong as this.

QUESTIONS

1. The "human capital view," which Professor Blinder here satirizes, has illuminated much behavior previously thought to be outside the domain of economics. For example, one economist has predicted that married children from wealthy families will visit their parents more often than will the children of poorer parents. Why?

2. In Professor Blinder's schema of human motivation, can it be unambiguously predicted whether doctors or shoe clerks would spend more time in the brushing of teeth? Explain your answer.

PART EIGHT

MICROECONOMIC POLICY: SHOULD THE MARKET PRICE RULE?

31 WHAT SHOULD BE THE PRICE OF A GALLON OF GASOLINE?
Armen Alchian

At a time of energy shortages and crude oil restrictions by the OPEC nations, is it fair to allow gasoline to be priced via the unfettered market system? Or should price controls or rationing prevail? Armen Alchian, professor of economics at UCLA, argues that everyone's interests are best served without government interference in the allocation of this product. Professor Alchian's scholarly writings are widely known not only among economists but also to those involved in the study of law. His path-breaking work on the economics of property rights has made an imprint on both economic and legal research.

"Fuel is scarcer: use it wastefully!" Those who propose governmental allocations and rationing of fuel and energy are saying, in effect, precisely that. Surely fuel should be assigned to its most beneficial uses; every gallon of fuel should be employed where the benefits of using it exceed those of all other possible uses. It would hardly seem necessary to state so basic a principle. Yet the most beneficial use of fuel is exactly what rationing, allocations, and price controls prevent.

It is remarkable that many people do not understand this. They are usually ignorant of two crucial facts about the market economy: 1) free market prices direct fuel to more important, higher valued uses; 2) free markets compensate people who transfer fuel from less important to more important uses.

How would rationing and price controls defeat both of these desired effects? When all men receive equal amounts of fuel, their needs remain unequal (N.B.: there is no necessary relation between need and wealth; a poor man may need his quota of a given good either more or less than a rich man). Peter's last gallon, useful as it may be for his own

From Armen Alchian, "There's Gas in Your Future," *National Review* (January 4, 1974). Reprinted by permission of National Review, 150 East 35 Street, New York, New York, 10016.

purposes, may be worth still more to Paul. But if they can neither measure the relative values of the fuel nor transfer it, the misallocation will remain undetected and uncorrected. If, however, the market price is allowed to serve as a measure of that fuel's value to Paul as against its value to Peter, the appropriate allocation can be made by simple exchange: Peter can sell to Paul. The buyer finds the fuel more useful than the goods he forsook to get it; the seller finds the goods he received more useful than the fuel. The public generally ignores this effective direction of fuel and goods toward their most valued uses, since the whole process occurs dispersedly, in thousands of independent market transactions, rather than as the result of deliberate government actions or conscious social control, which, if less efficient, are at least more obvious.

Both effects — allocation to better uses, and compensation for forsaking inferior ones — are achieved by permitting sale at free market prices. Both are prevented by price controls, rationing, and governmental allocations. And so strong is the desire for better allocation (and for its concomitant compensations) that all such controls will be violated at every chance, as each man sees that it is sensible — even if illegal — to violate them. Bad laws make for bad citizens as well as poor production. (If you think market values are not good or appropriate measures of value of uses, read on — we shall come to that problem later.)

The damage done by rations and allocations — their stifling of the efficient distribution of available fuel — can be somewhat reduced if recipients are permitted to sell and transfer them at free market prices. But the sad irony is that proponents of rationing rarely provide for that critical transferability. Why not? Some conjectures are possible.

IS IT A RIP-OFF?

One cynical conjecture is that advocates of rationing want to disrupt our economic system, gain control over our lifestyles, and destroy our free, liberal society. A more respectful conjecture is that they don't comprehend the real consequences of their schemes. Why should they? Economic wisdom is not instinctive or inherited. You pay taxes to hire economists to teach these simple principles to college students. If they were all that obvious, why pay to have them taught? The second conjecture is both more charitable and more probable.

But let us face up to the confiscation issue, and to the argument that higher prices could hurt the poor disproportionately. Honesty compels us to acknowledge that stockowners of U.S. fuel companies are people like everyone else, poor, middle class, and rich: they are taxpayers, your neighbors and friends. If their wealth is confiscated and given to others, why are the recipients more deserving of it? That is a question for the conscience.

But moral considerations aside, permitting the sale and transfer of quotas would dispose of the objection that higher market prices for fuel would hurt the poor most. The freedom to sell one's rations would be an *advantage* — to everyone, rich and poor. Instead of being stuck with an assigned amount of fuel, unalterable regardless of its value to him, the poor man would be free to exchange as much of his quota as he saw fit for other more desirable goods, thereby releasing so much fuel to higher valued uses. He would in fact be better off than he had been without transferable rations at free market prices. Since transferability, as against nontransferability, is a boon to everyone, the poor would be disproportionately *helped*.

Again, to summarize, if quotas, rationing, and controls are imposed, it would at least help minimize the harm they do to permit quotas to be purchasable or divisible and transferable at free market prices. For fuel would then tend to go to its highest valued uses; nobody would willingly put fuel to uses worth less than either any other use to which it could be put, or the goods that could be had in exchange for it. So if we must restrict oil stockholders' wealth, at least let us transfer the wealth to poorer ration recipients without preventing the available fuel from finding its most valuable uses. Taxing oil companies for the sake of the poor need not, after all, condemn what fuel *is* available to bad or wasteful uses.

Even if we have the minimal wisdom to allow the sale of whatever rations we adopt, increased production of fuel will still not be properly encouraged.

We shall have reduced people's incentive to direct their wealth and efforts toward finding and producing the fuels we most desire. In trying to effect the "equitable" distribution of a scarce commodity, we will condemn ourselves to a longer period of greater scarcity. Why handicap our efforts to get more fuel with a scheme that doesn't really protect the poor, but does discourage production?

A better, simpler, proven method exists, which not only helps the poor, but also fosters the production (and productive use) of more fuel: higher market prices. If, for example, we insist that poorer gasoline users must not be required to pay what the fuel is worth in the free market, it is still better to permit prices to rise to whatever heights they will, and *then* take supplementary government action: subsidize the "poor" who are most heavily dependent on purchasing fuel for their livelihood, perhaps by giving them fuel stamps (like food stamps) which they can either use to defray part of the higher price of fuel, or sell as they please. The cost of such supplements should be covered out of general tax revenues (as is done with food stamps).

And if we fear that these supplements would permit stockholders to gain "unjustly," we can still impose a per cent-of-excess-profits tax on the oil companies. This would restrict output less than an excise tax of so much per gallon of gasoline. An excise tax levied on each unit of fuel would not encourage increased productivity; but the per cent-of-excess-profits tax would, by increasing the after-tax profits of those who expand fuel production.

RICH V. POOR

The question remains: is market value an appropriate value? Some will object to our proposition that fuel, on the open market, will be transferred to its 'best" uses; a rich man, they will argue, would use fuel for a faster drive or a pleasure trip, while the poor man who gives up some fuel to the rich man would suffer by having to find other means of getting to work. And surely (and here's the clincher) the rich man's whims are not as important as a poor man's transportation to work!

But this does not effect our argument, for two reasons:

1. We did not say they *were* as important. What we did say was that both the rich man and the poor man would agree that it is better to be free to transfer their rationed amounts than to be forbidden to do so. Again: if the available gallon of gasoline is worth more to Peter than the goods he must give up to get it, he will want to exchange; and if Paul wants to gain possession of those goods more than he wants to keep the gallon, he will agree to the exchange. The prohibition of that exchange by a third party — the state — would prevent that direction of the fuel and other goods to the highest valued uses as judged by the parties to the exchange themselves. And since society is made up of just such parties, society at large suffers under such prohibitions.

2. It is true that a poor man's consumption values, as expressed in the market, do reflect his poverty. Having said this, we must distinguish between the interpersonal distribution of general wealth (*how much* men have) and the interpersonal mixture of goods (*what* they have). We may think the present distribution of general wealth is unjust by this or that criterion, and that a fuel scarcity will exacerbate the injustice. Even so, forbidding the transfer of rations would diminish the freedom (and, concretely, the wealth) of all, including the poor, by preventing each person from using his available wealth to secure the particular mixture of goods that suits him best according to his personal preference and lifestyle. Rationing, allocations, and price controls would freeze some goods in uses worth less to the recipient than a) what he could get for them and b) their value to another consumer. Who profits by this? Only an authoritarian controller.

To prevent free market prices from allocating goods (whether or not some redistributionist supplement like fuel stamps is used) is to prevent fuel from finding its more important and beneficial uses. To deny this is to contend that political authorities should decide what uses are "more important and beneficial"; a contention which, for consistency's sake, requires the further contention that political authorities should also decide which TV news programs are "beneficial and important" enough to

merit allocation of energy, or which newspapers and magazines deserve the allocation of paper. The scarcity of fuel (or any other good) relative to demand is not a valid reason for imposing government controls. We have used for centuries a method consistent with — indeed a foundation for — a free society. It is both more effective in adapting to changes in supply, and more consistent with the rights we treasure. Why abandon that method at exactly the moment when it is most useful?

QUESTIONS

1. For what reason does Alchian argue that price controls would be inefficient?
2. "The fair thing to do is to calculate how much gasoline we have and distribute it equally among the citizenry." Comment on the economic implications of this statement. In what sense, if any, would an equal distribution be fair?
3. Professor Alchian argues that if rationing of gasoline is to be adopted, recipients of ration "coupons" should be able to sell them to others if they choose. What purpose, in his view, is served by allowing such sales to be made?

32 WHAT SHOULD BE THE PRICE OF A MULE?
Thomas Wolfe

Thomas Wolfe, one of America's greatest novelists, draws upon his youth in North Carolina to portray a commonplace event with the "Men of Old Catawba." The event illustrates the moral dilemma some people face with voluntary exchange in a price system.

The Catawba people are great people for all manner of debate and reasoned argument. Where the more fiery South Carolinian or Mississippian will fly into a rage and want to fight the man who doubts his word or questions his opinion, the eye of the Catawban begins to glow with a fire of another sort — the lust for debate, a Scotch love of argument. Nothing pleases a Catawban better than this kind of dispute. He will say persuasively, "Now let's see if we can't see through this thing. Let's see if we can't git to the bottom of this." A long, earnest, and even passionate discussion will ensue in which the parties on both sides usually maintain the utmost good temper, kindliness, and tolerance, but in which they nevertheless pursue their arguments with great warmth and stubbornness. In these discussions several interesting traits of the Catawban quickly become manifest: the man is naturally a philosopher — he loves nothing better than to discuss abstract and difficult questions such as the nature of truth, goodness, and beauty, the essence of property, the problem of God. Moreover, in the development of his arguments the man loves the use of homely phrases and illustration, he is full of pungent metaphors drawn from his experience and environment; and in discussing an ethical question — say, the "moral right" of a man to his property, and to what extent he may profit by it — the Catawban may express himself somewhat in this manner:

"Well, now, Joe, take a case of this sort: suppose I buy a mule from a feller over there on the place next to mine, an' suppose I pay a hundred and fifty dollars fer that mule."

"Is this a one-eyed mule or a two-eyed mule you're buyin'?" Joe demands with a broad wink around at his listening audience.

"It's a two-eyed mule," the first man says good-humoredly, "but if you've got any objections to a two-eyed mule, we'll make it a one-eyed mule."

"Why, hell, no! Jim," the other man now says, "I ain't got no objections, but it seems to me if you're goin' to have a two-eyed mule you ought to have something better than a one-eyed argyment."

There is a roar of immense male laughter at this retort, punctuated with hearty slappings of thigh and knee, and high whoops in the throat.

"'Od-damn!" one of the appreciative listeners cries, when he can get his breath, "I reckon that'll hold 'im fer a while."

The story of the "two-eyed mule and the one-eyed argyment" is indeed an immense success, it is the kind of phrase and yarn these people love, and it is destined for an immediate and wide circulation all over the community. It may even be raised to the dignity of proverbial usage, so that one will hear men saying, "Well, that's a two-eyed mule an' a one-eyed argyment if I ever saw one," and certainly the unfortunate Jim may expect to be greeted for some time to come in this way:

"Howdy, Jim. I hear you've gone into the mule business," or, "Hey, Jim, you ain't bought no two-eyed mules lately, have you?" or, "Say, Jim: you ain't seen a feller with a one-eyed argyment lookin' fer a two-eyed mule, have you?"

Jim knows very well that he is "in" for this kind of treatment but he joins in the laughter good-humoredly, although his clay-red face burns with a deeper hue and he awaits the resumption of debate with a more dogged and determined air.

"Well, that's all right about that," he says, when he can make himself heard. "Whether he's a one-eyed mule or a two-eyed mule is neither here nor there."

"Maybe one eye is here, an' t'other there," some one suggests, and this sets them off again at Jim's expense. But Jim has the determination of the debater and the philosopher, and although his face is pretty red by now, he sticks to his job.

"All right," he says at length, "say I got a mule, anyway, an' he's a good mule, an' I paid one hundred and fifty dollars fer him. Now!" he says, pausing and lifting one finger impressively. "I take that mule an' work him on my farm fer *four* years. He's a *good* mule an' a *good* worker an' durin' that time he pays fer himself *twice* over! Now!" he declares again, pausing and looking triumphantly at his opponent, Joe, before resuming his argument.

"All right! All right!" Joe says patiently with an air of resignation. "I heard you. I'm still waitin'. You ain't *said* nothin' yet. You ain't *proved* nothin' yet."

"Now!" Jim continues slowly and triumphantly. "I gave one hundred and fifty dollars fer him but he's earned his keep an' paid fer himself *twice* over."

"I heard you! I heard you!" says Joe patiently.

"In other words," some one says, "you got back what you paid fer that mule with one hundred and fifty dollars to boot."

"Egs-actly!" Jim says with decision, to the group that is now listening intently. "I got back what I put into him an' I got one hundred fifty dollars to boot. Now here comes another feller," he continues, pointing indefinitely towards the western horizon, who *needs* a good mule, an' he sees *my* mule, an' he *offers to buy it!*" Here Jim pauses again, and he turns and surveys his audience with triumph written on his face.

"I heard you. *I'm* listenin'," says Joe in a patient and monotonous voice.

"How much does *he* offer you?" some one asks.

"Now, wait a minute! I'm comin' to that," says Jim with a silencing gesture. "This here feller says, 'That's a perty good mule you got there!' 'I reckon he'll do!' I say. 'I ain't got no complaint to make!' 'I'm thinkin' of buyin' a mule myse'f,' he says. 'That so?' I say. 'Yes,' he says, 'I could use another mule on my farm. You ain't thinkin' of sellin' that mule there, are you?' 'No,' I say 'I ain't *thinkin'* of it.' 'Well,' he says, 'would you consider an offer fer him?' 'Well,' I say, 'I might an' I might not. It all depends.' 'How much will you take fer him?' he

says. 'Well,' I say, 'I ain't never thought of sellin' him before. I'd rather you'd make an offer. How much will you give?' 'Well,' he says, 'how about three hundred dollars?'"

There is a pause of living silence now while Jim turns finally and triumphantly upon his audience.

"*Now!*" he cries again, powerfully, and decisively, leaning forward with one big hand gripped upon his knee and his great index finger pointed toward them.

"I'm *listenin'*," Joe says in a calm but foreboding tone.

"I *got* my money back out o' that mule," Jim says, beginning a final recapitulation.

"Yes, an' you got another hundred an' fifty to boot," some one helpfully suggests.

"That makes *one* hundred per cent clear profit on my 'riginal investment," Jim says. "Now here comes a feller who's willin' to pay me three hundred dollars on top of that. That makes *three* hundred per cent."

He pauses now with a conclusive air.

"Well?" says Joe heavily. "Go on. I'm still waitin'. What's the argyment?"

"Why," says Jim, "the argyment is this: I *got* my money back——"

"We all *know* that," says Joe. "You got your money back and a hundred per cent to boot."

"Well," says Jim, "the argyment is this: Have I any *right* to take the three hundred dollars that feller offers me?"

"Right?" says Joe, staring at him. "Why, what are you talkin' about? Of course, you got the right. The mule's yours, ain't he?"

"Ah!" says Jim with a knowing look, "that's just the point. *Is* he?"

"You *said* you bought an' *paid* fer him, didn't you?" some one said.

"Yes," said Jim, "I did that, all right."

"Why hell, Jim," some one else says, "you just ain't talkin' sense. A man's got the right to sell his own property."

"The *legal* right," Jim says, "the *legal* right! Yes! But I ain't talkin' about the *legal* right. I'm talkin' about the *mawral* right."

They gaze at Jim for a moment with an expression of slack-jawed stupefaction mixed with awe. Then he continues:

"A man's got a right to buy a piece of property an' to sell it an' to git a fair profit on his investment. I ain't denyin' that. But has *any* man," he continues, "a right — a mawral right — to a profit of three hundred per cent?"

Now Jim has made his point, he is content to rest for a moment and await the attack that comes, and comes immediately: after a moment's silence there is a tumult of protest, derisive laughter, strong cries of denial, a confusion of many voices all shouting disagreement, above which Joe's heavy baritone finally makes itself heard.

"Why, Jim!" he roars. "That's the damndest logic I ever did hear. I did give you credit fer havin' at least a *one*-eyed argyment, but I'm damned if this argyment you're given' us has any eyes a-tall!"

Laughter here, and shouts of agreement.

"Why, Jim!" another one says with solemn humor, with an air of deep concern, "you want to go to see a doctor, son: you've begun to talk funny. Don't you know that?"

"*All* right. *All* right!" says Jim doggedly. "You can laugh all you please, but there's two sides to this here question, no matter what you think."

"Why, Jim!" yet another says, with a loose grin playing around his mouth. "What you goin' to do with that two-eyed mule? You goin' to *give* him away to that feller simply because you got your money out of him?"

"I ain't sayin'!" says Jim stubbornly, looking very red in the face at their laughter. "I ain't sayin' what I'd do. Mebbe I would and mebbe I wouldn't."

There is a roar of laughter this time, and the chorus of derisive voices is more emphatic than ever. But for some moments now, while this clamor has been going on, one of the company has fallen silent, he has fallen into a deep study, into an attitude of earnest meditation. But now he rouses himself and looks around with an expression of commanding seriousness.

"Hold on a moment there, boys," he says. "I'm not so sure about all this. I don't know that Jim's such a fool as you think he is. 'Pears to me there may be something in what he says."

"Now!" says Joe, with an air of finality. "What did I tell you! The woods are full of 'em. Here's another 'un that ain't all there."

But the contest is now just beginning in earnest: it goes on furiously, but very seriously, from now on, with these two Horatiuses holding their bridge valiantly and gaining in strength and conviction at each assault. It is a remarkable circumstance that at almost every gathering of Catawbans there are one or more of these minority warriors, who become more thoughtful and dubious as their companions grow more vociferous in their agreement and derision, and who finally, from a first mild expression of doubt, become hotly embattled on the weaker side, and grow in courage and conviction at every breath, every word they utter, every attack they make or repel.

QUESTIONS

1. Is the fact that the mule "earned his keep and paid for himself twice over" relevant in determining its selling price? Why? Is the price of a used car a function of the worth of the car to its previous owner?

2. If a man does not have a moral right to earn a profit of 300 percent, what is the highest profit he may morally earn?

3. The fellow with the "loose grin" asked what other price or allocation system Jim would use to dispose of his mule. If you agree that accepting the $300 for the mule is immoral, what other allocative mechanism would you recommend? What if there were two strangers offering $300 for the mule?

4. Where is Catawba?

PART NINE

MACROECONOMICS: THE NATIONAL ECONOMY

33 THE AMAZING IMPACT OF LORD KEYNES
Time

Bertrand Russell claimed that John Maynard Keynes was the most brilliant man he had ever met. Certainly the ideas of Lord Keynes have had a profound impact upon events in the twentieth century. Though introductory classes in economics seldom deal in biography, Keynes warrants exception. The following article from Time *is a readable account of Keynes and his influence.*

The ideas of economists and political philosophers, both when they are right and when they are wrong, are more powerful than is commonly understood. Indeed the world is ruled by little else. Practical men, who believe themselves to be exempt from any intellectual influences, are usually the slaves of some defunct economist.

—The General Theory of
Employment, Interest and Money

Concluding his most important book with those words in 1935, John Maynard Keynes was confident that he had laid down a philosophy that would move and change men's affairs. Today, some 20 years after his death, his theories are a prime influence on the world's free economies, especially on America's, the richest and most expansionist.

FROM MISCHIEF TO ORTHODOXY

When Keynes first propagated his theories, many people considered them to be bizarre or slightly subversive, and Keynes himself to be little but a left-wing mischief maker. Now Keynes and his ideas, though they still make some people nervous, have been so widely accepted that they constitute both the new orthodoxy in the universities and the touch-

Abridged from "We Are All Keynesians Now," from "U.S. Business in 1965," TIME (December 31, 1965). Reprinted by permission from TIME, *The Weekly Newsmagazine;* copyright Time, Inc., 1965.

stone of economic management in Washington. They have led to a greater degree of government involvement in the nation's economy than ever before in time of general peace.

That legacy was the product of a man whose personality and ideas still surprise both his critics and his friends. Far from being a socialist left-winger, Keynes (pronounced canes) was a high-cast Establishment leader who disdained what he called "the boorish proletariat" and said: "For better or worse, I am a bourgeois economist." Keynes was suspicious of the power of unions, inveighed against the perils of inflation, praised the virtue of profits. "The engine which drives Enterprise," he wrote, "is not Thrift but Profit." He condemned the Marxists as being "illogical and so dull" and saw himself as a doctor of capitalism, which he was convinced could lead mankind to universal plenty within a century. Communists, Marxists and the British Labor Party's radical fringe damned Keynes because he sought to strengthen a system that they wanted to overthrow.

TRUTH & CONSEQUENCES

Keynes was born the year Marx died (1883) and died in the first full year of capitalism's lengthy postwar boom (1946). The son of a noted Cambridge political economist, he whizzed through Eton and Cambridge, then entered the civil service. He got his lowest mark in economics. "The examiners," he later remarked, "presumably knew less than I did." He entered the India Office, soon after became a Cambridge don. Later, he was the British Treasury's representative to the Versailles Conference, and saw that it settled nothing but the inevitability of another disaster. He resigned in protest and wrote a book, *The Economic Consequences of the Peace,* that stirred an international sensation by clearly foretelling the crisis to come.

He went back to teaching at Cambridge, but at the same time operated with skill and dash in business. The National Mutual Life Assurance Society named him its chairman, and whenever he gave his annual reports to stockholders, the London Money Market suspended trading to hear his forecasts for interest rates in the year ahead. He was also editor of the erudite British *Economic Journal,* chairman of the *New Statesman and Nation* and a director of the Bank of England.

Keynes began each day propped up in bed poring for half an hour over reports of the world's gyrating currency and commodity markets; by speculating in them, he earned a fortune of more than $2,000,000. Money, he said, should be valued not as a possession but "as a means to the enjoyments and realities of life." He took pleasure in assembling the world's finest collection of Newton's manuscripts and in organizing London's Camargo Ballet and Cambridge's Arts Theater. Later, the government tapped him to head Britain's Arts Council, and in 1942 King George VI made him a lord.

Part dilettante and part Renaissance man, Keynes moved easily in Britain's eclectic world of arts and letters. Though he remarked that economists should be humble, like dentists, he enjoyed trouncing countesses at bridge and Prime Ministers at lunch-table debates. He became a leader of the Bloomsbury set of avant-garde writers and painters, including Virginia and Leonard Woolf, Lytton Strachey and E. M. Forster. At a party at the Sitwells, he met Lydia Lopokova, a ballerina of the Diaghilev Russian ballet. She was blonde and buxom; he was frail and stoop-shouldered, with watery blue eyes. She chucked her career to marry him. His only regret in life, said Keynes shortly before his death of a heart attack, was that he had not drunk more champagne.

THE WHOLE ECONOMY

The thrust of Keynes's personality, however strong, was vastly less important than the force of his ideas. Those ideas were so original and persuasive that Keynes now ranks with Adam Smith and Karl Marx as one of history's most significant economists. Today his theses are the basis of economic policies in Britain, Canada, Australia and part of Continental Europe, as well as in the U.S.

Economics is a young science, a mere 200 years old. Addressing its problems in the second half of its second century, Keynes was more successful than his predecessors in seeing it whole. Great theorists

before him had tried to take a wide view of economic forces, but they lacked the 20th century statistical tools to do the job, and they tended to concentrate on certain specialties. Adam Smith focused on the marketplace, Malthus on population, Ricardo on rent and land, Marx on labor and wages. Modern economists call those specializations "microeconomics"; Keynes was the precursor of what is now known as "macroeconomics" — from the Greek *makros,* for large or extended. He decided that the way to look at the economy was to measure all the myriad forces tugging and pulling at it — production, prices, profits, incomes, interest rates, government policies.

For most of his life, Keynes wrote, wrote, wrote. He was so prolific that a compendium of his books, tracts and essays fills 22 pages. In succession he wrote books about mathematical probability (1921), the gold standard and monetary reform (1923), and the causes of business cycles (1930); each of his works further developed his economic thinking. Then he bundled his major theories into his magnum opus, *The General Theory*, published in 1936. It is an uneven and ill-organized book, as difficult as *Deuteronomy* and open to almost as many interpretations. Yet for all its faults, it had more influence in a shorter time than any other book ever written on economics, including Smith's *The Wealth of Nations* and Marx's *Das Kapital.*

PERMANENT QUASI-BOOM

Keynes perceived that the prime goal of any economy was to achieve "full employment." By that, he meant full employment of materials and machines as well as of men. Before Keynes, classical economists had presumed that the economy was naturally regulated by what Adam Smith had called the "invisible hand," which brought all forces into balance and used them fully. Smith argued, for example, that if wages rose too fast, employers would lay off so many workers that wages would fall until they reached the point at which employers would start rehiring. French Economist Jean Baptiste Say embroidered that idea by theorizing that production always creates just enough income to consume whatever it produces, thus permitting any excesses of demand to correct themselves quickly.

Keynes showed that the hard facts of history contradicted these unrealistic assumptions. For centuries, he pointed out, the economic cycle had gyrated from giddy boom to violent bust; periods of inflated prosperity induced a speculative rise, which then disrupted commerce and led inexorably to impoverished deflation. The climax came during the depression of the 1930s. Wages plummeted and unemployment rocketed, but neither the *laissez-faire* classicists nor the sullen and angry Communists adequately diagnosed the disease or offered any reasonable remedies.

By applying both logic and historical example to economic cycles, Keynes showed that the automatic stabilizers that economists had long banked on could actually aggravate rather than prevent a depression. If employers responded to a fall-off in demand by slicing wages and dumping workers, said Keynes, that would only reduce incomes and demand, and plunge production still deeper. If bankers responded to a fall-off in savings by raising interest rates, that would not tempt penniless people to save more — but it would move hard-pressed industrialists to borrow less for capital investment. Yet Keynes did not despair of capitalism as so many other economists did. Said he: "The right remedy for the trade cycle is not to be found in abolishing booms and keeping us permanently in a semi-slump; but in abolishing slumps and thus keeping us permanently in a quasi-boom."

MANAGEMENT OF DEMAND

The key to achieving that, Keynes perceived, is to maintain constantly a high level of what he called "aggregate demand." To him, that meant the total of all demand in the economy — demand for consumption and for investment, for both private and public purposes. His inescapable conclusion was that, if private demand should flag and falter, then it had to be revived and stimulated by the only force strong enough to lift consumption: the government.

The pre-Keynesian "classical" economists had

thought of the government too. But almost all of them had contended that, in times of depression, the government should raise taxes and reduce spending in order to balance the budget. In the early 1930s, Keynes cried out that the only way to revive aggregate demand was for the government to cut taxes, reduce interest rates, spend heavily — and deficits be damned. Said Keynes: "The State will have to exercise a guiding influence on the propensity to consume partly through its scheme of taxation, partly by fixing the rates of interest, and partly perhaps, in other ways."

A few other economists of Keynes's time had called for more or less the same thing. Yet Keynes was the only one with enough influence and stature to get governments to sit up and pay attention. He was the right man at the right time, and his career and fame derived largely from the fact that when his theories appeared the world was racked by history's worst depression and governments were desperately searching for a way out.

Contrary to the Marxists and the socialists, Keynes opposed government ownership of industry and fought those centralists who would plan everything ("They wish to serve not God but the devil"). While he called for conscious and calculated state intervention, he argued just as passionately that the government had no right to tamper with individual freedoms to choose or change jobs, to buy or sell goods, or to earn respectable profits. He had tremendous faith that private men could change, improve and expand capitalism.

QUESTIONS

1. What opinion, if any, did you have of Keynes and his economic thinking prior to your course in economics? What opinion, if any, do your parents hold? Since Keynes was obviously no socialist or Marxist, what accounts for the dislike that much of the political right seems to have for him?

2. What is the essence of Keynesian economics? What does macroeconomics mean?

34 GNP: A MEASURE OF AMERICA'S OUTPUT?
Arthur M. Okun

The Department of Commerce's Survey of Current Business *is the most authoritative source of the gross national product of the United States. But the Commerce Department has been criticized for generating a figure which, while prominent and newsworthy, allegedly has little social value. Arthur Okun, writing on the occasion of the fiftieth anniversay of these national income accounts, describes the value and limitations of these statistics. Okun is a Senior Fellow at the Brookings Institution, was a member of the Council of Economic Advisors under President Johnson, and is an advisor to President Jimmy Carter.*

Happy fiftieth birthday to the *Survey of Current Business*. Long may it roll off the presses, recording and analyzing the growth of national income and product. Your national accounts system is a great accomplishment of modern quantitative economics; it supplies an intelligible, integrated, and invaluable body of information about the functioning of the Nation's economy. Its big summary number, gross national product, has become a household word and has even been enshrined in a clock.

GNP NO MEASURE OF WELFARE

Yet at a time when your numbers are experiencing greater use and greater attention than ever before, they also are getting more fundamental criticism than ever before. Put simply (perhaps to the point of caricature), the criticism is that, even after correction for price and population change, the gross national product does not yield an unambiguous measure of national welfare; a rise in real GNP per capita does not necessarily mean that the Nation has

Abridged from Arthur M. Okun "Social Welfare Has No Price Tag," *Survey of Current Business*, 51, no. 7, part 2, U.S. Department of Commerce (July, 1971), 129–133.

become better off, nor does a decline imply that it has become worse off. This diagnosis may be followed by either of two prescriptions: (a) ignore GNP, or (b) fix GNP so that it does measure social welfare.

I know you will not ignore the GNP. I urge you to bear the criticism with pride as a symptom and symbol of your success. I urge that you not try to "fix it" — to convert GNP into a purported measure of social welfare. Producing a summary measure of social welfare is a job for a philosopher-king, and there is no room for a philosopher-king in the Federal Government.

It is hard to understand how anyone could seriously believe that GNP could be converted into a meaningful indicator of total social welfare. Obviously, any number of things could make the Nation better off without raising its real GNP as measured today: we might start the list with peace, equality of opportunity, the elimination of injustice and violence, greater brotherhood among Americans of different racial and ethnic backgrounds, better understanding between parents and children and between husbands and wives, and we could go on endlessly. To suggest that GNP could become *the* indicator of social welfare is to imply that an appropriate price tag could be put on changes in all of these social factors from one year to the next. This is hardly a minor modification of the national accounts. It is, as I have suggested, asking the national income statistician to play the role of a philosopher-king, quantifying and evaluating all changes in the human scene. And it is absurd to suggest that, if the national income statistician can't do that job, the figure he writes for GNP is not interesting.

We all display better sense in judging family welfare, avoiding verdicts intoxicated with the brew of economic determinism. We know that income is an important attribute of any family: the size of its income is an excellent indicator of whether the family is likely to be suffering from malnutrition, to be having difficulty in realizing the full educational potential of its children, etc. If any man on the street were asked to judge a family's welfare, he would want to know a lot of other things about its members too — facts about their health, about their relations to one another, and to their jobs, their friends, and their society. Even our cliches remind us that the best things in life are free and that there are things like love and good health that money can't buy. These lessons are equally important and equally applicable in the evaluation of social well-being.

MARKET-ORIENTED PRODUCTION

What you can and do measure as national income statisticians is the output resulting from market-oriented activity. The key to market-oriented activity is the presence of price tags. These are the essential ingredient in any objective standard of measurement that you can apply. Price tags enable you to sum up in a meaningful way physicians' prescriptions and phonograph records and pounds of steak and packages of beans. You can add up all the things that money can buy. But if you were to be seduced by your critics into inventing price tags which neither exist nor can be reasonably approximated for things which money can't buy, you will have sacrificed any objective yardstick.

Let me run through some examples of changes you should *not* make.

HOUSEWIVES' SERVICES AND LEISURE

For good reasons, you violate the normal institutional boundary line between business and consumers when you impute the rental value of owner-occupied housing. You do this because the owner-occupant is short-circuiting the market that tenants go through. You do the same thing for food which farmers produce and consume within their own households rather than sending to market. Why, the argument goes, should you not treat the housewife similarly, as short-circuiting the market and providing services which other families obtain by hiring domestic workers? I find it a compelling argument that a housewife is not a maid — and that this difference is of a higher order of magnitude than the difference between the title to a house and a lease. The activity of a housewife is not that of a maid, and valuation of the housewife's hourly services in terms of the wage rate of maids, or any multiple thereof, would not translate her activity meaningfully into dollars and cents.

I have never been disturbed by the well-known paradox that, when the bachelor marries his cook the national product goes down. The GNP is measuring the output of market-oriented activity, and market-oriented activity is reduced by the cook's marriage. Whatever she does as the mistress of the household is a different type of activity, oriented toward different objectives than receiving her pay at the end of the week. Why is this any more paradoxical than the fact that the national product will go down if I take a month's unpaid vacation in order to travel around the world? In both cases, the marketable output of the Nation is reduced, but that doesn't mean that welfare is reduced. If I made a rational decision, the psychic value of that trip must have exceeded the sacrifice of income. But if on that account it is argued that the GNP must not be allowed to fall, then I must ask how to evaluate the same trip if I had made it on paid vacation and had not had to sacrifice income.

The vacation example gets us into the largest element of what might conceivably be viewed as potentially marketable services that do not show up in the national accounts, i.e., time allocated to everything but work. I suspect that, if we lived in a world in which everyone had the option of working precisely as many hours as he wanted every week at a fixed and known wage schedule, a plausible — although still not compelling — argument could be made for evaluating leisure as a consumption good. In such a world, one might argue that the individual must explicitly decide to withhold some portion of his potentially marketable services, and thus to sell that time to himself for consumption purposes. But the real world has more or less standard workweeks and imperfect opportunities for moonlighting. In the real world, the current practice of ignoring leisure in the GNP is the only sound and sensible treatment. Leisure is a good thing, but it is one of the many good things which do not bear a reasonably determinate price tag. It is an important subject for analysis and evaluation and research, but it does not belong in the GNP.

"REGRETTABLE NECESSITIES"

It is obvious that many of the things consumers buy are not intended for pure enjoyment, but rather are a means of avoiding discomfort or preventing deterioration of physical and human capital. Yet you count them all as final product. You have been urged to try to eliminate "regrettable necessities" from final product and thus to classify them as a cost of living rather than a source of satisfaction. Don't start down that path. If you should do so, regrettable and unnecessary as it would be, you would find it winds along forever. Physicians' services and all other medical care costs are obvious regrettable necessities. So are the services of lawyers, policemen, firemen, sanitation workers, and economists (including national income statisticians). So are heating and air-conditioning outlays. Except for the few people who live to eat rather than eat to live, food is a regrettable necessity. Indeed, it is hard to imagine any output which clearly serves the purpose of pure, unmitigated enjoyment. But even if you could invent some arbitrary definition that kept final-product consumption from falling to zero, the exclusion of regrettable necessities would make no sense. It would deny the distinction between meeting one's necessities and failing to meet them.

EXTERNALITIES

It is obvious that the producer does not incur all the costs of producing certain types of output, nor does the consumer get all the benefits. The producer who belches forth smoke or who sends effluent into the rivers is imposing a cost on society which is not reflected in his private costs of production. On the other hand, the clearing of a swamp or the creation of a park may generate benefits which are equally absent in your measure of the gross national product. Although externalities obviously go both ways as costs and benefits, there is no reason to believe that they balance out on the average or even that their net balance is small. Why, then, it can be argued, should you not try to estimate the net deterioration (or improvement) of the environment as a cost of productive activity, netting it out of GNP?

Again, I must ask how such a valuation could be made if the market and the democratic process don't generate the price tags. Following your present rules, you will reflect the costs and benefits that society recognizes and responds to. If a ban is placed on activity that is inherently dangerous, or fees and taxes are imposed, you will follow the signals and properly reflect them in your valuation of output. If society changes its mind, you will make some rather puzzling changes in your definition and coverage of outputs. But any puzzles that arise concern the volatility of the Nation's collective judgment.

MEASURING SOCIAL PERFORMANCE

Let me make clear that these possible conceptual revisions would not seriously impair the usefulness of the national accounts for the analysis of economic fluctuations and growth. Even if you did all the things I am telling you not to do, I could still get what I need out of the national accounts. Yet I urge against such changes with conviction because, as I see it, the big danger is that, by taking a few steps in the direction of an allegedly more comprehensive measure of welfare, a reformulation of the accounts might mislead the Nation into supposing that GNP was at last measuring social welfare. And that would impede the progress which we so urgently need toward better measurement and evaluation of various changes in our social and physical environment, our health, and the diffusion of well-being across our society.

QUESTIONS

1. At a time when GNP statistics have attained great prominence in the news, the figures are also receiving considerable criticism. Of what sort?

2. What does GNP measure? To what extent is its growth consistent with improvements in social welfare and to what extent could a rise in GNP be accompanied by a worsening social situation? How do you define "social welfare" and "social situation"?

35 MEASURING AMERICA'S WEALTH
John W. Kendrick

A nation's wealth is conceptually different from a nation's output of goods and services. The former represents income potential; the latter indicates results. John W. Kendrick, formerly of George Washington University and now the chief economist of the U.S. Department of Commerce, has been a pioneer in the development of data that measure the wealth of the United States. He is also an authority on comparisons of the productivity of different economies. Below he presents his estimates of the wealth of the U.S. economy.

Wealth is productive power. It represents capacity to produce output and income. By a broad definition, wealth includes human resources in addition to man-made structures, equipment and inventories, and natural resources.

Despite the importance of national wealth estimates for macro-economic and industry analyses, they are not yet prepared as a regular part of official national accounts. Eventually annual estimates of national wealth, by major sector and type, will be published as a regular complement to the official national income and product accounts. To fill the gap meanwhile — and to supplement the planned Commerce Department series — I have recently completed estimates of national wealth.

NATIONAL WEALTH, TOTAL AND PER CAPITA

At the end of 1975, net national wealth — or net worth — is estimated at close to $5,700 billion. This tremendous sum is easier to grasp when it is averaged out to $26,530 for each of the men, women, and children residing in the United States, or about $106,000 for the typical family of four. The per-capita numbers relate not only to the direct holdings of individuals in the personal sector, which compose about 40% of the net national wealth

Abridged from John W. Kendrick, "Measuring America's Wealth," *The Morgan Guaranty Survey* (May 1976), 5–13.

(NNW), but also to their share of business and public domestic wealth plus net foreign assets.

In light of the bicentennial, it may be of interest to compare the current national wealth with an estimate for 1775, based on data assembled by economic historians from probate inventories and accounts of estate executors or administrators in sample counties of the thirteen colonies. Estimated wealth at that time amounted to a bit under $4 billion, or $1,550 per capita (in 1975 prices). Thus, while population grew by about ninety-fold, from under 2½ million in 1775, over the two centuries, real wealth per capita grew seventeen-fold, which works out to a 1.4% average annual rate of increase. In other words, real NNW per capita more than doubled every 50 years, on average.

During the most recent half-century, 1925–1975, real worth grew at an average annual rate of 2½%, or 1.3% per capita (see the table below). But the growth of wealth was severely retarded by the Great Depression of the 1930s, and the postwar record was decidedly better. Between 1948 and 1973, total real NNW grew fairly steadily at a pace of about 3½% a year, almost 2% per annum faster than population. The relatively strong growth of wealth in the postwar period reflects the generally strong advance of output and income since World War II and the relative mildness of the economic contractions that have been experienced.

COMPOSITION BY SECTOR AND TYPE

There were pronounced shifts in the sectoral composition of real GNW (gross national wealth) as indicated by the accompanying table:

	Percentages of Real GNW		
	1925	1948	1975
Personal Sector	29.5	28.6	40.3
Business Sector	56.4	39.6	37.3
Government Sector	12.0	29.8	21.3
Net Foreign Assets	2.1	2.0	1.2

The strong relative growth of personal-sector wealth since 1948 is particularly noteworthy. By 1975 real wealth in the personal sector exceeded that of the business sector. Most of the decline in the business proportion of total wealth had occurred by the end of World War II, when the strong relative expansion of government assets reached its peak. Since then the public share has receded, but by 1975 it was still much higher than in the 1920s. The growth of net foreign assets since 1948 has been less than the growth of domestic wealth, and by 1975 net foreign assets composed only 1.2% of the national total.

There also were marked shifts in the composition of real gross domestic wealth (GDW) by type, as indicated by the following table:

Percentages of Real GDW			
	1925	1948	1975
Equipment	19.9	31.3	36.5
Structures	55.8	48.3	44.9
Land	15.9	12.7	10.1
Inventories	8.4	7.7	8.5

The proportion of equipment, including consumer durables, rose markedly, while the relative declines in both structures and land reduced the real estate component of real GDW from more than 71% in 1925 to 55% a half century later. In current prices, however, the real estate proportion remained constant due to a relative increase in prices of land and structures. The share of equipment rose to a lesser extent based on current value measures, while the inventory proportion fell somewhat since the prices of goods entering inventories rose less than capital-goods prices. Although the proportions of wealth by type differ somewhat among the several sectors, the compositional changes for each were generally in the same directions as for the aggregate.

CAPITAL REQUIREMENTS: 1980 AND BEYOND

A major use of estimates of real stocks of capital is for projections of investment requirements in future years. These estimates can be converted to an average annual requirements basis.

The projections indicate that the cumulative gross investment requirements for the five-year period 1976–1980 would somewhat exceed 12% of projected GNP, compared with 10.4% in the prior decade. Even if corporate profits and cash flow continue to recover smartly from the recent recession, it is doubtful if fixed investment demand will grow as much relative to GNP as the Commerce Department projections indicate is needed, unless special investment incentives are provided.

This is not the place to discuss the various tax and other incentives that have been proposed to stimulate private investment. Suffice it to note that if after-tax profit rates are not adequate, the growth of captial per person engaged in production will be less than in the past, which will tend to reduce the growth of labor productivity and real income per capita.

QUESTIONS

1. What is the definition of an economy's wealth? How does this differ from the economy's income? Does per capita wealth in the U.S. exceed per capita income?
2. What sector of the U.S. economy has the largest percentage of the nation's wealth? The fastest growing percentage?
3. "Most of America's wealth is in the form of land." Comment.

36 ECONOMETRIC FORECASTING: CAN ECONOMISTS PREDICT THE ECONOMY'S FUTURE?
Deborah DeWitt

More and more business firms and government agencies purchase the predictions of economic forecasters — in spite of a prognostication track record that is far from perfect. Deborah DeWitt, an associate economist with the Chase Manhattan Bank, here examines the building of mathematical models which predict the economy's future behavior. Her article focuses on the dean of American forecasters, the University of Pennsylvania's Lawrence Klein, who is also one of President Jimmy Carter's economic advisors. Dr. Klein holds a coveted Benjamin Franklin professorship at the university Mr. Franklin founded.

Despite the infamous record compiled by numerous economic forecasters in recent years, the demand for forecasts — in striking contrast to the demand for everything else — has been flourishing. Forecasts based on econometric models seem to be especially in demand. It must surely be sinking in on many businessmen, and ordinary readers of the financial pages, that more and more of those numbers they're being exposed to come from models and are being spat out by computers.

A rather extraordinary effort has gone into producing those numbers. They are the final product of a formal system of equations representing a model-builders' effort to simulate the workings of the U.S. economy. Once the system has been developed and programmed for a computer, the model is ordinarily capable of converting current data into new forecasts at a prodigious rate: quarter by quarter, and often sector by sector, the forecasts of real growth, inflation, interest rates, employment and unemployment, productivity, profit and wage gains, and quite a bit more, come pouring out of the computer.

Abridged from Deborah DeWitt, "Lawrence Klein and His Forecasting Machine," *Fortune* (May 1975), 152–157.

The acknowledged dean of U.S. model-builders is Lawrence Klein, fifty-four, Benjamin Franklin Professor of Economics at the University of Pennsylvania's Wharton School. Klein has been building models of the U.S. economy for thirty years. His influence on the art and science of model-building is reflected in the prestige of the Wharton model, which he closely monitors, and whose forecasts are always among the most widely quoted. But his influence can also be discerned in many of the models on which he has not worked directly.

Klein's reputation is worldwide, and he spends a fair amount of time racing around the globe in an effort to stay abreast of — and enlighten others about — the latest ideas in econometric thinking.

IT'S SIMPLER WITH SUNSPOTS

A model of the economy is, in effect, a hypothesis about how the economy works. In principle, the hypothesis might be stated in ordinary declarative sentences, but most model-builders prefer the brevity and precision of equations. Highly mathematical economic models are described as "econometric," a word that came into use in the 1930s and that refers to the union of economics, mathematics, and statistics.

If the model-builder has some very simple view of what makes the economy run — e.g., everything depends on the cycle of sunspots — only a few equations may be needed. But most economists use a lot of them; the Wharton model, for example, has 400 equations. This means that the "Wharton forecast" actually involves hundreds of forecasts of matters as diverse as the Treasury bill rate and new-car sales. Indeed, seven different elements, or "variables," go into the model's prediction of new-car sales, including consumer income, the price of cars compared to prices of other consumer goods, and the unemployment rate. Even then, Wharton's forecast of car sales has on average been off by some 5 percent.

The amount of detail in a model will also vary with its purpose. An economist who is interested in forecasting only the major components of G.N.P. —

personal-consumption spending, business spending, government spending, and net exports — may need only ten or twelve equations. If he is planning to sell the forecasts to businessmen, he probably will want a host of detail on industry sales and earnings. And an economist building a model for government policymakers would probably want still more detail, so that the users could simulate the precise effects of different policy proposals — e.g., the effect of a 10 percent tax cut on consumer spending.

DOES WEALTH MAKE A DIFFERENCE?

The most important differences between models concern, not the number of equations in them, but what the equations say. It is no secret that economists disagree about numerous fundamental matters. One major disagreement has to do with the effect on consumer spending of changes in individuals' wealth (for instance, because of stock-market fluctuations). The Wharton model links consumer spending closely to changes in disposable personal income and largely ignores changes in wealth. The Federal Reserve model, however, assumes that wealth has a great deal of impact on spending.

There is, as all model-builders are keenly aware, a great circularity in economic relationships. For example, practically every model has an equation in which consumer spending is shown to depend on income. But the same model will also have an equation in which income is shown to depend on G.N.P. — of which consumer spending is a major component. Thus consumption must be known in order to forecast income, and income must be known in order to forecast consumption. Since just about every economic variable is at least indirectly linked to every other one, the circularity is by no means confined to income and consumption.

Thus one of the major problems involved in building models is finding values that are internally consistent for the different variables. The problem is ordinarily worked out by a trial-and-error search in the computer. In the Wharton model some 170 variables, ranging from spending on clothing to spending on plant and equipment, must be simultaneously determined by this process.

Even when the modeler is rid of the inconsistencies in his variables, his troubles are not over. Periodically, some equations kick out numbers that generally make no sense. Last summer, for example, the equation in the Wharton model that projects the Treasury bill rate wasn't working well. If it had been left alone, it would have forecast a rate of 16 percent on three-month Treasury bills (the rate in fact never rose above 9.5 percent). The solution to this problem was fairly straightforward. As any other modelers would have done in the circumstances, the forecasters at Wharton simply adjusted the rate downward every time they prepared a forecast. They concluded that their Treasury bill equation was going awry in part because it had no way of predicting the sudden explosion of Arab demand for U.S. debt instruments. After some experimentation, the Wharton team finally came up with an equation that has been successful.

But some variables are always apt to be in trouble, and the Wharton model, like just about all others, is endlessly subject to "adjustment." The notion that models are challenging human judgment has some validity to it some of the time. But a lot of the time the process is reversed — i.e., the model's findings are themselves being challenged and overridden.

SELLING IT TO BUSINESSMEN

The Wharton model is used for a good deal more than academic research. It is one of several models whose findings are available to businessmen for a fee. Its principal competitors are Data Resources, Inc., headed by Otto Eckstein of Harvard, who was a member of the Council of Economic Advisers in 1964—66; and Chase Econometric Associates, headed by Michael Evans, a former colleague of Klein's at Wharton.

There are, however, significant differences in goals. Wharton Econometric Forecasting Associates is not trying to make any money for Klein or the Wharton School. A nonprofit operation, W.E.F.A. was originally launched in 1963 with financial support from Bethlehem Steel, Deere, I.B.M., G.E., and Jersey Standard (now Exxon). They had separately approached Wharton for help in building econometric models of their own, and Klein had talked them into sharing the cost of a new model that he would build. W.E.F.A. now has about 150 subscribers, who pay $7,500 a year for its quarterly forecasts and for the right to attend its seminars.

Data Resources, founded by Eckstein in 1968, has made a major effort to relate macroeconomic data to the particular problems of businessmen in different industries. "When I left the council and began consulting," says Eckstein, "I discovered that businessmen were having a hard time relating G.N.P. forecasts to decisions on how much steel to buy."

The firm now has more than 300 subscribers, who pay a minimum of $12,000 a year for quarterly G.N.P. forecasts, access to a vast data bank, and twelve days' worth of consulting. Data Resources encourages its subscribers to hook up their time-sharing terminals to its two computers, and the firm helps them to run their own G.N.P. forecasts based on their own assumptions about government policies.

Chase Econometric's basic service — monthly forecasts of G.N.P. and quarterly seminars — costs $6,000 a year. For another $2,500, a subscriber can get access to the firm's data base and can use its model to make forecasts based on his own assumptions. Evans has also built a monthly-interest-rate model, an industrial-production model, and a model of U.S. agriculture, all of which may be purchased separately. Some 500 clients are currently paying an average of $10,000 a year for these services.

Right now only two U.S. government agencies have full-scale econometric models of the U.S. economy. The Commerce Department's Bureau of Economic Analysis has a model — an updated version of an early Wharton model — that was designed to examine the effects of proposed changes in fiscal policy. And the Federal Reserve has a model, completed in 1968, which places heavy emphasis on the effects of monetary policy.

The Council of Economic Advisers has never had a formal model of its own. Its annual forecasts are generally an amalgam of judgment and forecasts prepared for them by the commercial firms. But the lack of their own model seems to be getting bothersome to council members.

A good deal of what's happening among model-builders today can be traced back to Klein's thinking during his student days. He graduated from the University of California at Berkeley in 1942, with highest honors in economics and a Phi Beta Kappa key. He then studied under Paul Samuelson at the Massachusetts Institute of Technology, where he completed his Ph.D. in just two years. That happens to be the record for the fastest doctorate in the history of M.I.T.'s economics department.

Klein was not the first econometric model-builder. The Dutch economist, Jan Tinbergen, is actually considered the father of model-building. Tinbergen constructed a number of models of the Dutch economy in the 1930's, and a descendant is currently being used by the Central Planning Bureau at the Hague. Tinbergen and the Norwegian economist Ragnar Frisch won a Nobel prize in 1969 for their work in econometrics.

But there is no doubt that Klein introduced model-building to the U.S. Soon after he got his Ph.D., when he was just twenty-four, he prepared a twenty-equation model of the U.S. economy for the Cowles Commission at the University of Chicago. The model indicated that there would be a vast surge of economic activity after the war. But Klein never had much luck peddling this forecast to government officials. "I was very young then," he recalls, "and they all gave me the brush-off."

This first effort was soon followed by a far more ambitious one. In 1951, when Klein was teaching at the University of Michigan, he was largely responsible for a historic work that has come to be called the Klein-Goldberger model (Arthur Goldberger was one of Klein's graduate students). This model is generally thought of as the grandfather of just about all contemporary models.

LINKING UP THE WORLD

Right now the most ambitious project on Klein's agenda is something called Project Link, which is an effort to develop a model of the world economy. For the past six years, he has been supervising the efforts of a group of model-builders from different countries. The idea is to integrate their different models and study the "transmission mechanisms" by which the economies of the world affect one another.

Right now the basic elements of Link include large-scale econometric models for Japan and twelve Western industrial countries, four smaller regional models of developing nations, and one large model of the Soviet-bloc countries. China, North Vietnam, and North Korea are treated only superficially in the system. When all the models are hooked up, the system has some 3,000 equations.

Although Link is still in a development stage, it has already been pressed into service. In December, 1973, the U.S. Treasury asked Klein to crank up the model for a quick reading on the extent to which various countries would be affected by the oil embargo. Link predicted that oil shortages would reduce still further the slow growth foreseen for the world's economies. The model did not project a cumulative deterioration. "But from the financial viewpoint, our projections were scary," says Klein.

The Link project gives Klein a marvelous excuse to travel; meetings are generally held twice a year, with sites rotating among the sponsors' countries. However, Klein has another pretty good excuse in a project of his that is separate from Link: building an econometric model of the Soviet Union. To support this effort, he has put together a team that includes Russian scholars from the Stanford Research Institute and the University of Pennsylvania and econometricians at Wharton.

Building a model of a completely planned economy presents a number of unusual problems. Ordinarily, model-builders do a lot of research in order to develop equations that accurately reflect the way people behave when they are given certain choices. But in the Soviet Union, many transactions do not really reflect individuals' choices; some of the time, at least, people buy certain goods, not because they really want them, or because the price is right — but because there is literally no other choice. "There are some economists who think model-building won't work in economies where there is so little market choice," says Klein. "But we think there is enough."

Klein originally thought that the Soviet model would be small, but it already has more than eighty equations and is still growing. Klein and associates unveiled the model last fall on their mission to the Soviet Union. The reaction of the Soviet economists who looked it over was guarded.

BUT DOES IT REALLY WORK?

Given the vast prestige and commercial success of econometric models, it might be assumed that their superiority over conventional forecasting methods is firmly established. Oddly enough, it isn't at all established. Consider, for example, the record of the econometric models in forecasting last year's economy.

At the end of 1973, Wharton was projecting a 0.6 percent increase in real growth for 1974 and a 7.2 percent increase in G.N.P. prices. Chase weighed in with a forecast of 0.7 percent real growth and a 6.6 percent increase in prices. D.R.I. had a 1.2 percent growth in output and a 6.5 percent price rise. In fact, real G.N.P. actually declined by 2.2 percent last year, and prices rose by 10.2 percent. Thus Wharton did the best of the three models — which still wasn't very good.

It is true, of course, that the "judgmental" forecasters had a rough time last year too. But there is no good evidence that they did worse than the model-builders. Nor is there any such evidence for other years. In September, 1973, Stephen McNees, an economist then with the Federal Reserve Bank of Boston, published a study comparing forecasts that had been made by D.R.I., Wharton, and Chase between 1970 and mid-1973. McNees examined projections made by each model of nominal G.N.P. and its components, real G.N.P., and inflation rates, over spans of one to five quarters during the three and one-half years. It turned out that Chase had the best record in predicting current-dollar G.N.P. during the entire period. D.R.I. had the best inflation forecasts. And Wharton had the best estimate of real G.N.P.

But when McNees compared the forecasts of the models with those made in the same period by thirty-six economists who primarily relied on their judgment, he found that neither method was proved superior. The median forecasts of current-dollar G.N.P., inflation rates, and real G.N.P. made by the thirty-six were typically less accurate than the two best econometric forecasts. But they were more accurate than the worst.

SEARCHING FOR THE STRUCTURE

Neither Klein nor Eckstein will admit to being particularly dismayed by these results. According to Klein, the real search is not for better forecasts, but "for the structure of the system." He adds: "Given the uncertainty of the base figures, we have probably gone as far as we can go in the closeness of estimates of G.N.P." Eckstein argues that, regardless of accuracy, econometric forecasting has been successful "because models build consistent logic." Supporters of models can also make a point that is often made about computers generally: the process of working with them, in business or government, obliges their users to be explicit and quantitative about many matters previously dealt with in only the vaguest terms. There is, presumably, a case for being clear about things.

Still, it does seem odd that all these insights into the "structure of the system" haven't demonstrably paid off in better forecasts. Ordinarily, any claim to superior understanding — of a person, or a theory, or a government policy — is supposed to be validated by superior predictions. And so the failure of the model-builders to demonstrate any special predictive advantages must at least raise a question about their understanding of the economy.

A more sympathetic judgment is possible, however. It may well be that, in retrospect, we will look back upon the model-builders of the mid-1970's as still pioneering in a great intellectual adventure. It may be that bigger and better models will produce better forecasts in the future. And meanwhile, it does seem possible that the disciplines imposed on economics by the model-builders are improving the work of forecasters who rely on their own judgment; it is, at least, harder to get away with vagueness in

the forecasting business these days. In any case, it seems reasonable to hope that the intellectual prodigies performed by Klein and his colleagues will somehow pay off in a big way.

QUESTIONS

1. What are the purposes of a model of an economy?

2. In what way is it more difficult to "model" a planned economy such as the Soviet Union's? What are the principal difficulties in building a model of any industrialized economy?

3. What functions are served by econometric models of the United States?

PART TEN

REDISTRIBUTING THE NATIONAL INCOME

37 DOES MONEY BUY HAPPINESS?
Richard A. Easterlin

Does money bring happiness? Philosophers have tended to answer "no," but millions of nonphilosophers have acted as though it does (or could if they only had more). Richard A Easterlin, professor of economics at the Wharton School of Finance and Commerce at the University of Pennsylvania, has tried to use empirical studies to answer the question. His conclusion: money does buy happiness — but there's a catch.

For many Americans, the pursuit of happiness and the pursuit of money come to much the same thing. More money means more goods (inflation aside) and thus more of the material benefits of life. As it is for the individual, so it is for society as a whole. National economic growth — a steady upward march in average income, year after year, decade after decade — means, it is supposed, greater well-being and a happier society.

There have always been those who questioned, on moral or philosophic grounds, the identification of human well-being with material pursuits. More recently, the goal of economic growth has been increasingly questioned chiefly because of growing awareness of adverse side effects of growth, such as pollution and congestion. But the question of what the evidence is on the relation between money and happiness has remained, with a few exceptions, untouched. Are the wealthier members of society usually happier than the poorer? Does raising the incomes of all increase the happiness of all?

Doubtless, the main reason for neglect of this basic factual question has been the absence of data on happiness. Since World War II, however, reports on personal happiness have been obtained in a number of national population surveys here and abroad. Recently, I brought together, for a scholarly article, the data from 30 surveys conducted in 19 developed and less developed countries and analyzed the rela-

The Public Interest, No. 30 (Winter 1973), pp. 3–10, copyright © by National Affairs Inc., 1973.

tion between reported happiness and income. Because these data and this area of research are so new, the findings can only be considered tentative. But the results are provocative and the implications worthy of more general discussion — hence this brief summary for a wider audience. The concern here, it should be emphasized, is not with moral judgments about the view that money will make one happy. The question simply is: Given the prevalence of this view, do the facts actually indicate that people who get more money typically feel happier?

The conclusions to which the evidence points, in brief, are these. *In all societies, more money for the individual typically means more individual happiness. However, raising the incomes of all does not increase the happiness of all.* The happiness-income relation provides a classic example of the logical fallacy of composition — *what is true for the individual is not true for society as a whole.*

The resolution of this paradox lies in the relative nature of welfare judgments. Individuals assess their material well-being, not in terms of the absolute amount of goods they have, but relative to a social norm of what goods they ought to have. At any given time, those above the norm typically feel happier than those below. Over time, however, the process of economic advance leads, not only to a general increase in incomes, but also to a corresponding rise in the social norm by which material well-being is judged. This increase in material aspirations in a society, itself produced by material progress, thus negates the positive impact of income growth on happiness that one might have expected from the happiness-income relation among individuals prevailing at any point of time.

WHAT IS HAPPINESS?

Happiness is not, of course, simply a matter of material well-being, even to the "common man." When assessing their happiness — for example, whether they are very happy, fairly happy, or not so happy — survey respondents are frequently asked to explain what they mean by happiness. At first glance, one might expect this to produce as many definitions as there are individuals — and indeed there are differences in the replies. But more impressive is the striking similarity, not only within countries, but also among countries. If the replies are grouped into broad classes, one finds that usually each of three concerns is mentioned at least a majority of times in personal happiness judgments — economic matters, family considerations, and health, with economic concerns being most frequently cited. Other considerations, such as social or political conditions, are mentioned much less often — by perhaps only one person in 10, or less. On reflection, the similarity among people in arriving at happiness judgments makes sense. What concerns people most are the matters of their everyday experience. In all cultures the way in which most adults spend most of their time is the same — working, trying to provide for and raise a family, dealing with family problems and sickness. Hence the kinds of things people mention when asked about happiness are similar. Needless to say, within these general categories the specifics frequently differ. For example, while economic concerns are important to people in both developed and less developed countries, the particular goods they want are strikingly different, a point to which I shall return later.

Self-reports on happiness, then, are dominated by the "homey" concerns of everyday life. But is reported happiness credible — can people assess their own happiness? Will they tell the truth, or merely say what they think the interviewer wants to hear? These questions lead into technical matters in the evaluation of survey data which I cannot go into here. Those who have investigated these issues typically conclude that while there are biases in the data, the responses do bear a real relation to the respondents' subjective feelings. In particular, the data can be used to throw meaningful light on the question posed here of the relation between happiness and income.

THE EVIDENCE ON HAPPINESS AND INCOME

What do the data show on the comparative happiness of income groups within a country at a given time? Does greater happiness go with higher income? The answer is, quite clearly, yes. This does not mean there are no unhappy people among the rich and no happy people among the poor. On the average, however, higher-income people are happier than the poor. For example, in a December 1970 survey of the American population, not much more than a fourth of those in the lowest income group (under $3,000 annual income) reported that they were "very happy." In the highest income group identified in the survey (over $15,000) the proportion that was "very happy" was almost twice as great. In successive income groups from low to high, the proportion "very happy" rose steadily. For the typical individual, it would seem, more money brings with it more happiness.

This positive relation between happiness and income appears in every single one of the 30 national population surveys studied. Eleven of these surveys relate to the United States between 1946 and 1970, and 19 to other countries, including three communist nations (Poland, Yugoslavia, and Cuba) and 11 countries in Asia, Africa, and Latin America. Note that the association between greater individual happiness and more money appears without exception in widely different countries and social systems — in non-Western as well as Western societies, poor as well as rich countries, Communist as well as non-Communist nations. Happiness appears to be related also to marital status, age, and education; however, the influence of income is apparent independently of these other factors, and it seems to have the strongest and most consistent association with happiness.

The data thus show a statistical association between income and emotional well-being; the present discussion, however, has adopted a causal interpretation, namely, that higher income makes for greater happiness. A question may be raised whether the converse may not be true. Perhaps happier people are more productive and thus likely to make more money. It would be naive to suppose that the causal relation must run in one direction only. One reason, however, for thinking that there is a relation going from income to happiness appears in the respondents' own statements on happiness. As I have noted, when people are asked about the things that make them happy or unhappy, their responses indicate that economic, family, and health concerns are foremost. These concerns are expressed by both lower and higher income groups. The evidence shows, however, that the lower income group differs most from the higher in that the prevalence of worries about money is more frequent. This suggests that higher income, by reducing one major source of worry, is a cause of greater happiness.

NATIONAL WEALTH AND INDIVIDUAL HAPPINESS

The repeated evidence of a positive point-of-time relation between happiness and income within countries suggests that if incomes increase generally in the population, there will be a rise in the average level of happiness. Is this in fact the case?

To answer this, we have available two types of data. One shows the historical trend for a given country in the average level of happiness as average income grows. On this, there is evidence for only one nation, the United States, since 1946. The other is point-of-time data for countries at different income levels. Since the populations of more developed nations have higher average incomes than those of less developed nations, we can ask whether their average level of happiness is also greater. Such international comparisons are available for several dates in the postwar period, the most comprehensive and intensive study by far being that done by Hadley Cantril for the period around 1960.

The showing of both sets of data — international and historical — does *not* conform to what one would expect on the basis of the positive relation between happiness and income prevailing *within* countries. Richer countries are not typically happier than poorer ones. In the United States, the average level of happiness in 1970 was not much different from that in the late 1940's, though average income, after allowance for taxes and inflation, could buy over 60 percent more. By and large, the evidence indicates no relation — positive or negative — between happiness and national income. Whether the people in a particular time or place are comparatively happy is seemingly independent of the average level of income.

THE UNDERLYING REASONS

How can one explain this paradoxical result? If for the individual more money typically means more happiness, why not for society as a whole? The answer lies in the way that people form their welfare judgments. The satisfaction one gets from his material situation depends not on the absolute amount of goods he has, but on how this amount compares with what he thinks he needs. A lot of goods relative to perceived needs makes for a lot of material satisfaction and thus greater happiness; if goods are low compared with needs, the result is relatively less happiness.

A crucial question, then, is how are needs determined. If perceived needs were essentially the same for all people in all times and places, being determined, say, primarily by physiological considerations, then more money would mean more happiness, not only among individuals at a given time, but also in those societies which grow richer over time.

In fact, however, what people perceive as their needs is socially determined, and those who live in richer times and places perceive their needs in more ambitious terms than those in poorer societies. Needs, or material aspirations, are formed as the result of prior and on-going experience in a society — in the language of sociology, through the socialization experience of the individual. Thus what one "needs" as he reaches adulthood typically depends on the impressions he has formed of "how to live" from observing life around him and in his society while growing up. This is not to say that all individuals in a society conceive their needs identically. There are many personal and social reasons why differences exist; for example, peer group influences doubtless make for greater perceived needs among the rich than the poor, even in a given society. But because of the common experiences people share as members of the same society and culture, there is also considerable similarity in their perceptions of needs — there is, in effect, a social norm.

In general, then, the reason why higher income for a society does not typically mean more happiness is that the general level of needs, relative to which material well-being is judged, grows along with and as a result of income growth in the society. At any given time, however, the needs perceived by the members of a society are sufficiently similar so that those better able to satisfy those needs — that is, those with more money — are typically happier.

Are we then trapped in a material rat-race, "hooked" on what Philip Brickman and Donald T. Campbell more euphemistically call a "hedonic treadmill"? The argument points to this uncomfortable conclusion. Each persons acts on the assumption that more money will bring more happiness; and, indeed, if he does get more money, and others do not (or get less), his happiness increases. But when everyone acts on this assumption and incomes generally increase, no one, on the average, feels better off. Yet each person goes on, generation after generation, unaware of the self-defeating process in which he is caught up. To the outside observer, economic growth appears to be producing an ever more affluent society, but to those involved in the process, affluence will always remain a distant, urgently sought, but never attained goal.

QUESTIONS

1. Summarize and discuss the methodology used by Easterlin to answer the question, Does money buy happiness? Can you think of any other empirical methods to test the correlation between wealth and happiness?

2. What is the relationship between rising individual wealth and rising national wealth to the phenomenon of happiness? What role does the fallacy of composition play in this issue?

3. Would your minister, priest, or rabbi (if you have one — if not, substitute a philosophy professor) agree with Easterlin's conclusions?

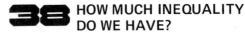 **HOW MUCH INEQUALITY DO WE HAVE?**
Lester C. Thurow and Robert E. B. Lucas

The "pocketbook" issue in economics is income distribution and the policies that redistribute such monies. This issue figured prominently in the last two presidential campaigns and is an economic question about which everyone has views, often strongly held. In this article, written for the Joint Economic Committee of the U.S. Congress, Lester C. Thurow and Robert E. B. Lucas summarize data on the American distribution of income and recommend taxes to alter the existing pattern. Rhodes scholar Lester Thurow is professor of management and economics at M.I.T. His coauthor, Robert Lucas, who holds an M.I.T. doctorate in economics, is on the economics faculty at UCLA. This article should be read in conjunction with the one following.

THE ROLE OF MONEY INCOMES

All of the axioms that are used to praise market economies depend upon a fundamental condition. If a market economy starts with an optimum distribution of income, then a market economy will efficiently and equitably produce and distribute goods and services. Other conditions are necessary to insure that market economies really work, but the whole structure of justifications for market economies depends upon this initial condition. If the condition is not met, the most perfectly functioning market economy will be inefficient and unjust. It is simply starting out with the wrong distribution of economic voting power.

One of the main functions of government is to establish the right distribution of economic voting power. Not only must it establish such a distribution initially, it must continually re-establish such a distribution. Market economies will efficiently and equitably produce and distribute goods and services

Abridged from Lester C. Thurow and Robert E. B. Lucas, *The American Distribution of Income: A Structural Problem* (Washington, D.C.: U.S. Government Printing Office, March 17, 1972) 3—14.

if they start with the optimum initial distribution of economic voting power, but market economies will not automatically regenerate such a distribution. Using tax and transfer policies, governments must be continually modifying market distributions of income.

But what is the right, optimum, or desired distribution of income? Fundamentally, the answer cannot be found in economic analyses. It is a moral problem that revolves around our collective judgments as to the proper degree of equality or inequality. Some individuals may want a society with complete equality in private purchasing power; others may want a large degree of inequality. In essence the fights over progressive versus regressive tax structures, level of welfare, and social security benefits are all disputes over the optimum distribution of money incomes. Living in one society, however, we must all agree on some common degree of equality.

Economics' only contribution to such a political discussion is a factual analysis of how the division of the economic pie affects the size of the economic pie. Do higher taxes cause individuals to work more or less (they may do either since higher taxes lower take-home wage rates and after-tax standards of living)? What effects do transfer payments have on individuals' work habits? Knowing the answers to such questions, it is possible to estimate how the division of America's gross national product affects the size and rate of growth of its gross national product. Knowing the answer to this question does not, however, determine the optimum distribution of income. It is merely one of many factors that the body politic may wish to weigh in making its ultimate decisions. It is perfectly rational to opt for a degree of equality that will retard the rate of growth as long as society is aware of what it is doing.

Most of the existing literature on work incentives focuses on the activities of high income managers and self-employed professionals. These are the working individuals who are thought to have the capability of altering their work habits. Such analysis found that high income individuals with the capability of altering their work habits seemed to work harder or longer as a result of higher marginal tax rates.

Economic analysis of labor force participation rates confirms this result for the general population. For the labor force as a whole, income effects seem to dominate substitution effects. When taxes are raised and incomes fall, individuals work more not less.

The effect of transfer payments is much less well known. In the past most transfer payments went to individuals who could not work or to individuals who had legal restrictions on their working opportunities (the aged, etc.). Transfer systems also operated with effective tax rates of 100 percent. A dollar earned was one less dollar in the welfare check. Under any theoretical framework, transfer payments coupled with 100 percent tax rates should discourage work effort. Such a conclusion, however, does not prove that transfer payments coupled with something less than 100 percent tax rates discourage work.

At the moment the federal government is in the process of investigating the work impacts of transfer payments in a variety of negative income tax experiments. Early evidence seems to indicate that these transfers do not materially affect the work incentives of low income individuals, but definitive evidence will simply have to wait for these experiments to be completed and anlyzed.

Although foreign examples and experiences do not provide conclusive proof as to how the American population would react to different distributions of income, they provide information on the response patterns of other human beings. Interestingly, the pre-tax distributions of income in Sweden, the United Kingdom, and West Germany are not noticeably different from that in the United States. All four countries seem to have approximately an 8 to 1 ratio between the average income of the richest quintile of the population and the poorest quintile of the population. Surprisingly, the country with by far the most rapid rate of growth has the most equal distribution of pre-tax income. In Japan the average income of the richest quintile is less than 5 times as large as that of the poorest quintile. In at least one culture, the world's highest rate of economic growth and a relatively equal distribution of market incomes seems compatible.

Analysis should, however, focus on post- rather than pre-tax incomes. Substantial equalization may come about in the process of taxation or in the process of distributing public goods and services. In the U.S. the pre- and post-tax distributions of income are not noticeably different. When all of our taxes (local, state, and federal) are added together, progressive taxes seem to be cancelled by regressive taxes leaving a proportional tax system. As a result, taxes reduce everyone's income by the same percentage and leave relative incomes unchanged. Either pre- or post-tax the richest quintile has approximately 8 times as much income as the poorest quintile. In contrast, in Sweden substantial equalization in living standards comes about through the distribution of public goods and services. Although U.S. public expenditures are also redistributive, they are nowhere near as redistributive as those in Sweden. In the United Kingdom a much more progressive income tax leads to a more equal distribution of post-tax income.

Depending upon the tastes of the American body politic, the U.S. may have three distinguishable income redistribution goals. First, it may seek to alter the distribution of income — to make it more equal or more unequal. Second, it may wish to alter the distributions of minority and majority incomes so that they are indistinguishable — to make the black income distribution identical with the white income distribution. Third, it may wish to increase economic mobility — to insure that a son's income is not determined by his father's income or to insure that the poorest man this year is not the poorest man next year.

The poverty program is a current program for altering the distribution of income. If it were to succeed, the percentage of total income going to those now in poverty should rise from 2.8 to 4.6 percent in 1970. Equal opportunity programs are designed to bring minority and majority income distributions into conformity. If they were to succeed, a white family's probability of having an income over $25,000 per year would be equal to that of a black family rather than five times as high. Public education is to some extent designed to improve economic mobility. Children from poor families are

to be educated to prevent them from also being poor.

Until each of these three possible income redistribution goals have been set, it is not possible to design actual plans and policies for altering the distribution of income. It is possible, however, to analyze the techniques by which the distribution of income might be altered if society were to choose to do so. If the body politic is satisfied with the existing distribution of income, such techniques are merely of theoretical interest. If the body politic is not satisfied with the existing distribution of income (the existence of a poverty program and an equal opportunity program indicate some official interest in altering the distribution of income) such techniques are the basic ingredients for constructing plans and programs for altering the distribution of income.

To aid in making the necessary value judgments, this paper outlines the current pattern and recent trends in the distribution of income and wealth. To make value judgments as to how income should be redistributed it is necessary to know how it is currently distributed and what changes are likely to occur in the absence of explicit government programs to alter the distribution of income. If the current distributions are society's desired distributions or if the current distributions are rapidly moving toward society's desired distributions, overt government programs to alter the distribution of income are unnecessary. If current distributions are not satisfactory, governmental programs must be designed to transform the current distributions.

There are two methods for redistributing income and wealth. In the first approach the federal government simply uses its tax rates and transfer system (negative taxes) to transform any market distribution of income into its desired distribution of income. If the market place does not generate enough equality, a progressive tax system is adopted to create equality. If the market place generates too much equality, a regressive tax system is adopted to create inequality. In the second approach the federal government adopts policies to alter the market distribution of income itself. Policies to improve the education of low (or potentially low) income individuals are an example of such approaches. By reducing educational differentials the country seeks to reduce income differentials.

THE AMERICAN DISTRIBUTION OF INCOME AND WEALTH

Family Incomes In the 22 years from 1947 to 1969 the median American family income has risen from $4,972 to $9,433 (in 1969 dollars). While summary measures of relative dispersion, such as the GINI coefficient, seem to indicate little change in the distribution of income these measures can be misleading. The income distribution has been basically stable in the post-war period but there have been noticeable changes. Whether they are significant depends upon the view of the beholder. (See Table 1.) The average income of the richest 20 percent of all families has fallen from 8.6 to 7.3 times that of the poorest 20 percent of all families. The average income of the richest 5 percent of all families has fallen from 36.6 to 21.6 times that of the poorest 5 percent of all families.

Relative incomes are only one measure of dispersion, however. Constant and even falling relative differences are compatible with increasing absolute differences in a world with rising incomes. In 1947 the average income of the richest 20 percent of all families was $10,565 higher than that of the poorest 20 percent of all families; in 1969 it was $19,071 higher (in 1969 dollars). The real gap between the poorest and richest 5 percent of all families rose from $17,057 to $27,605 (in 1969 dollars) despite the sharply declining difference in relative incomes.

Analysis of the family income distribution indicates that all income classes seem to be sharing in the fruits of economic growth. Incomes seem to be growing at about the same rate in most income classes. Measured in relative terms some equalization of the distribution of income is occurring; measured in absolute terms some further dispersion of income is occurring.

Within the distribution of family earning, wives are playing an increasingly important role. The probability of having a working wife rises as a husband's earnings rise until his earnings reach the average level for husbands. As his earnings continue to rise, her probability of working declines. Measured in relative terms working wives make the distribution of income more equal. The relative differences in female earnings across male earnings classes are simply not as great as those in male earnings. The maximum average contribution for a wife is only 2.4 times as large as that of the wives in the lowest income class. In addition, husbands with high earnings have wives with lower average earnings than that of the poorest husbands.

Working wives make the absolute income gap between poor and middle income families larger, but reduce the income gap between middle and high income families. The largest contribution to family earnings ($2,075 per year) is made by wives of husbands earning $8,000 to $10,000 per year, while wives with husbands at the bottom of the earnings distribution earn $879 and wives with husbands at the top of the earnings distribution earn $570.

Post-war increases in female participation rates have resulted in some relative equalization of the distribution of income. They have reduced the absolute income gaps between middle and upper income families, but they have also increased the ab-

Table 1. *Percentage Share of Aggregate Before-Tax Income Going to Families [In Percent]*

	1947	1950	1956	1960	1965	1969
Lowest 5th	5.0	4.5	5.0	4.9	5.3	5.6
2d 5th	11.8	12.0	12.4	12.0	12.1	12.3
Middle 5th	17.0	17.4	17.8	17.6	17.7	17.6
4th 5th	23.1	23.5	23.7	23.6	23.7	23.4
Highest 5th	43.0	42.6	41.2	42.0	41.3	41.0
Top 5 percent	17.2	17.0	16.3	16.8	15.8	14.7
Bottom 5 percent	0.47 . . . . 0.68					

U.S. Bureau of the Census, "Current Population Reports, Consumer Income, 1969," Washington, D.C., 1970, page 56.

solute income gaps between poor and middle income families. Given the existing distribution of female participation rates by their husbands' earning class, the areas with the greatest potential for further increases are at the top and the bottom of the income distribution. If improvements in job opportunities were to entice these wives into the labor force, poor family incomes would rise relative to middle class family incomes but rich family incomes would also rise relative to middle class family incomes.

If income opportunities were opened so that women had the same potential earning capabilities as males, the impact would depend on the extent of selective mating. To the extent that males with high potential earning capabilities marry females with high potential earning capabilities and males with low potential earning capabilities marry females with low potential earning capabilities, equal income opportunities for women would make the family income distribution more disperse. Since actual mating habits are not apt to match males with higher earning capabilities with females with low earning capabilites, increasing female income opportunities will probably make the actual distribution of family incomes more disperse. This would occur unless high income males choose to select wives who are willing to stay at home.

Minority Groups   Minority groups are participating in the same general growth in incomes as the white majority. While average white family incomes were growing from $5,194 to $9,764, the average family incomes of Negroes and other races were growing from $2,660 to $6,191 (from 51 percent to 63 percent of white incomes). (See Table 2.)

Based on econometric analyses of the relationships between black incomes and the business cycle, black incomes might have been expected to rise to about 57 percent of white incomes in 1969 but not to 63 percent. The difference is an indication of some movement toward more income equality for minority groups. Once again, however, relative improvements are compatible with absolute deteriorations. From 1947 to 1969 the absolute difference

Table 2.   *Ratio of Negro and Other Races to White Median Incomes*

Year:	Percent	Year—Continued	Percent
1947	51	1963	53
1949	51	1965	55
1952	57	1966	60
1954	55	1967	62
1958	51	1968	63
1960	55	1969	63

U.S. Bureau of the Census, "Current Population Reports, Consumer Income, 1969," Washington, D.C., 1970, page 25.

between black and white family incomes rose from $2,534 to $3,603 (in 1969 dollars).

In terms of income distributions, the distribution of income among Negroes and other races is slightly more unequal than the distribution of income among whites. (See Table 3.) While the richest 20 percent of all black families have 43.1% of all black family income the richest 20 percent of white families have 40.4% of all white family income.

The major source of income gains for minority groups has been geographic mobility. Blacks have increasingly moved out of the south where their relative incomes are low to the north and west where their relative incomes are higher. In 1970 blacks earned 57 percent of white incomes in the south, 71 percent in the northeast, 73 percent in the north central region, and 77 percent in the west. Based on the geographic movements that have actually taken place among blacks between 1950 and 1970, black incomes should have risen by about 12 percentage points relative to white incomes. In fact, they have risen by about 10 percentage points. Thus geographic movement more than accounts for the ob-

Table 3.   *Percentage Shares of Aggregate Incomes in 1969*

	White	Negro and Other Races
Lowest 5th	6.0	4.7
2d 5th	12.6	10.8
Middle 5th	17.6	16.9
4th 5th	23.4	24.4
Highest 5th	40.4	43.1
Top 5 percent	14.8	14.7

Lester C. Thurow, "Poverty and Discrimination," the Brookings Institution, Washington, D.C., 1969, page 26.

served relative increase in black incomes. Up to 1969 anti-discrimination programs seemed to be having little impact on average black incomes. Although geographic movement can be a powerful source of relative income gains, it is inherently limited. If all black families were to move out of the south, black incomes would still only be about 75 percent of white incomes.

Improvements in female incomes and job opportunities will also tend to lead to a widening gap between black and white family incomes. In 1969, 53 percent of all black wives were working in the paid labor force while only 38 percent of all white wives were doing so. At high incomes the difference is even more extreme. Seventy-three percent of all black families with incomes over $15,000 had a wife in the paid labor force while only 48 percent of all white families with incomes over $15,000 per year had a wife in the paid labor force. As a consequence, better income opportunites for existing female workers would tend to equalize black and white incomes, but better income and job opportunities that succeeded in attracting more female workers into the labor force would tend to increase the dispersion between black and white incomes. There are simply more white wives remaining to be attracted into the labor force.

In addition to blacks, Spanish speaking Americans and American Indians are the principal groups with below average incomes. The average income for Spanish speaking Americans is $5,641 (in 1969), or $350 less than that of blacks. American Indians make even less (probably around $3,000 per family). Although Americans of recent European descent often consider themselves to be subject to discrimination, all of the major ethnic groups have average incomes above those of white Americans who arrived earlier. In 1969 the range was from $11,554 for Russian American families to $8,127 for Irish Americans. In contrast other Americans (natives) had average incomes of only $7,671.

Female Incomes Almost no changes have occurred in the relative earnings of males and females since 1939. In 1939 year-around full-time female work-

ers earned 58 percent of male earnings; in 1969 they earned 59 percent. Once again constant relative differences imply increasing absolute differences. In 1939 the real income gap was $1,570 (in 1969 dollars) between year-around full-time male and female workers; in 1969 it was $3,526.

The overall consistency masks quite dramatic changes for black females. Between 1939 and 1969 year-around full-time white female earnings fell from 61 to 58 percent of their male counterparts while the earnings of year-around full-time black female earnings rose from 51 percent to 69 percent of their black male counterparts. Since year-around full-time black male earnings were rising from 45 percent to 69 percent of their white male counterparts (most of this increase occurred during World War II), year-around full-time black female workers earnings rose from just 38 percent of their white counterparts to 82 percent.

Family incomes, however, did not equalize at the same rate. White women were moving into the year-around full-time labor force much faster than black women. Rising white female participation rates managed to offset much of the income gains of black workers.

Age and Income With an increasing tendency for young people to stay in school (to be part-time rather than full-time workers), the age distribution of income has become more unequal in the post-war period. Individuals less than 24 years of age have significantly lower incomes relative to average incomes. Other than this general change, however, the male distribution of income has been remarkably stable across age classes. In addition to the general deterioration in the position of young women, women above the age of 45 made particularly sharp gains. Women 45–54 years of age witnessed an increase in their incomes from 121 percent to 167 percent of average female incomes.

Wealth Distributions of wealth are available less frequently than those of income, but occasional measurements have been made. In 1962 the Federal Reserve Board conducted a survey of the ownership

Table 4. *Family Distribution of Net Worth in 1962*

	Cumulative Distribution of Families	Cumulative Distribution of Total Net Worth
Net worth class (thousands):		
Negative	8.1	−0.2
0 to $1	25.4	0
$1 to $5	42.7	2.1
$5 to $10	56.9	6.6
$10 to $25	81.3	23.8
$25 to $50	92.5	40.9
$50 to $100	97.6	55.9
$100 to $200	98.6	61.3
$200 to $500	99.5	74.2
$500 and over	100.0	100.0

Federal Reserve Bulletin, "Survey of Financial Characteristics," March 1964, Washington, D.C., page 291.

of all private assets. At that time, the wealthiest 20 percent of the population owned over 75 percent of all private assets while the poorest 25 percent of all families had no net worth (their debts equaled their assets). (See Table 4.) The wealthiest 8 percent of the population owned 60 percent of all private assets; the wealthiest 1 percent owned over 26 percent of all private assets.

As these data indicate, the distribution of wealth is much more unequal than the distribution of income. While the richest 20 percent of all families have 41 percent of total income they own 75 percent of all assets. While the poorest 20 percent have 5.6 percent of total income, they have no net worth.

Economic Mobility What is the probability of individuals moving from one point on the income distribution to another over the course of a year, a lifetime, or a generation? What is the conditional probability of a son's income given his father's income? With perfect intergenerational mobility, knowing a father's income provides no information as to his son's income. With no intergenerational mobility, knowing a father's income provides all of the information necessary to predict a son's income. Economic mobility of this type is important since society's value judgments about the equity or inequity of a particular income distribution may depend upon the degree of economic mobility (annual, lifetime, or

intergenerational) within it. A high degree of economic mobility may make us more willing to tolerate inequalities at any point in time. If incomes were given out on a lottery basis, any annual income distribution, no matter how unequal, could be consistent with a completely equal lifetime income.

Studies of poverty families indicate that about 70 percent of the families that were in poverty last year are in poverty this year. Of the remaining 30 percent, 11 percent were dissolved from death and other causes and 19 percent escaped from poverty. Of the 19 percent who escaped, 8 percent were still within $1,000 of the poverty line, 4 percent were within $2,000 of the poverty line, and 7 percent were more than $2,000 away from the poverty line. Families who escape from poverty in any one year also have a significant probability of falling back into poverty in succeeding years. As a consequence, poverty data would seem to indicate a low degree of economic mobility among the poverty population. Such evidence, however, does not prove a low degree of economic mobility for other parts of the income distribution.

Intergenerational economic mobility is even less well charted. Sociologists rather than economists have studied intergenerational mobility. They have focused on occupational mobility rather than on economic mobility partly because of their interests and partly because of a lack of data of intergenerational economic mobility. Given the wide ranges of incomes within occupations, the lack or presence of occupational mobility indicates little about economic mobility. Intergenerational occupational mobility is not high, but this conclusion does not necessarily lead to the same conclusion for economic mobility.

Future Trends In the absence of governmental policies to the contrary, future trends in the distribution of income are apt to mirror the trends of the post-war period. These trends seem firmly established in the American economy. Without government actions to alter them, they can be expected to continue.

Given post-war changes in the distribution of income and the likelihood that the same types of changes will occur in the immediate future, the body politic must explicitly decide whether it wants changes in the distribution of income. Without such decisions and programs to bring the desired changes about, the distribution of income will not be noticeably different than it now is. Every group seems to be participating in economic progress to the same degree. Average incomes are rising, but the distribution of income around this average is not changing.

A NECESSARY ROLE FOR TAXATION

Market redistributions of income are inherently limited in terms of what they can accomplish. They cannot affect the earnings of those who are outside of the labor forces and they can only slowly affect the existing distribution of wealth. As a consequence, any systematic effort to raise the incomes of low income individuals or to alter the distribution of wealth must rely on the tax transfer system.

To raise low incomes some variant of the negative income tax (sometimes known as the family assistance plan or the guaranteed annual income) *is essential.* The aged, the ill, the handicapped, and the mentally retarded are only a few of the groups that cannot possibly earn a satisfactory income in the market place.

QUESTIONS

1. What guidelines or assistance can economics offer to the policy question of income redistribution?
2. What evidence is uncovered by the authors on the propensity of housewives to work? Why do you suppose the pattern they find exists? If more housewives entered the labor market, what would that do to the black—white family income differential?
3. Upon reading the article by Professor Edgar Browning (Reading 39), what criticisms, if any, would you make of the statistics used by the authors of this article?

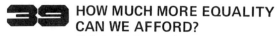

39 HOW MUCH MORE EQUALITY CAN WE AFFORD?
Edgar K. Browning

Can the American economy afford more income redistribution? Professor Edgar K. Browning examines first the extent of present redistributional policies and then explains the economic obstacles to additional such efforts. Professor Browning is at the University of Virginia, where he has authored a remarkable quantity of scholarly articles on social insurance, externalities, and public finance. This reading provoked nationwide television attention and should be read in tandem with the preceding article.

It is probably true, as *Business Week* recently reported, that "the greatest single force changing and expanding the role of the federal government in the United States today is the push for equality." Although some government statistics misleadingly indicate otherwise, it is clear that the distribution of income has become dramatically more equal in recent years as a result of egalitarian policies. Moreover, the massive redistribution currently taking place each year makes it very costly to attempt to move still further toward equality. I will show why by examining the economic and ethical implications of additional redistribution.

HOW UNEQUAL ARE INCOMES?

One popular index of inequality is the number of Americans officially classified as poor. In 1973, there were 23 million people classified as poor, only one third less than the 33 million in 1965. Yet there has been a tremendous expansion in government programs designed to aid the poor during this period: Social welfare expenditures by all levels of government rose from $77 billion in 1965 to $215 billion in 1973. Many people have been troubled over how such a massive commitment of resources

Reprinted with permission of Edgar K. Browning from *The Public Interest*, No. 43, Spring 1976, 90—110. Copyright © 1976 by National Affairs, Inc.

could produce such a small reduction in the number of poor Americans.

The major reason for the apparent persistence of poverty in the face of such expenditures lies in the definition of poverty itself. A family is officially poor when its *money* income falls below a certain level — $4250 annually for a family of four in 1973, for example. Thus, because government programs dispensing benefits in the form of specific goods and services ("in-kind" transfers) do not and cannot raise *money* incomes, they are unable to move families out of poverty, so defined. Interestingly, government in-kind transfers have expanded at a much more rapid rate in recent years than have cash transfers, following the growth of medicare, medicaid, food stamps, housing assistance, and job training programs. To see clearly why the number of poor Americans has not declined more rapidly, note that in-kind transfers per poor person rose from $42 to $657 between 1964 and 1973 — or by 1464 per cent! These resources are not counted as income in the official definitions of poverty. In contrast, cash transfers, which are counted as income, rose by only 172 per cent.

Clearly in-kind transfers should be counted as income in defining poverty. If a $1000 cash transfer to a poor person — who proceeds to spend it on food, housing, and medical care — reduces poverty, then so does $1000 worth of these goods provided outright (or at subsidized prices). When in-kind transfers (exclusive of public education provided by state and local governments) are counted as income, the average poor family in 1973 had an income that was approximately 30 percent *above* the poverty line. In terms of the average income of officially poor families, there is practically no poverty — statistically speaking — in the United States today, and, indeed, there has not been for several years. It only remains for our accounting procedures to be modified to record this achievement.

Many people object to an emphasis on the number of poor Americans because the poverty lines are fixed in terms of real incomes. Consequently, a poverty-level income falls as a percentage of average income when the average rises over time as a result of economic growth. This suggests that it may be

Table 1. *Relative Income Distribution (Expressed as Percentage Share of Total Money Income Received by Families, by Quintile)*

Year	Lowest Quintile	Second Quintile	Third Quintile	Fourth Quintile	Highest Quintile
1952	4.9	12.2	17.1	23.5	42.2
1962	5.0	12.1	17.6	24.0	41.3
1972	5.4	11.9	17.5	23.9	41.4

Source: United States Bureau of the Census, "Money Income in 1972 of Families and Persons in the United States," *Current Population Reports,* series P-60, No. 90 (1973), Table 16.

better to consider what happens to the incomes of poor people relative to the incomes of others. Table 1 shows a popular method of looking at the relative distribution of income. It gives the share of total money income received by families whose incomes place them in the lowest 20 per cent (lowest quintile) of the income distribution, the second lowest quintile, and so on. Not only do these figures suggest a large degree of inequality in each year, but, of more interest, they indicate that the shares of income received by the various quintiles have changed remarkably little over this 20-year period. It is this distribution which has led many observers to conclude that the distribution of income has not become significantly more equal since World War II.

This conclusion is, however, almost certainly wrong. Once again, a major part of the problem is that the Census Bureau's measures of income are based on a definition that includes only money incomes, and excludes in-kind transfers and benefits of public education. In addition, the figures are based on incomes before payment of direct personal taxes, and no adjustment is made for differences in average family size among the quintiles. Table 2

Table 2. *Adjusted Relative Income Distribution (Expressed as Percentage Share of Income Received by Quintile)*

Year	Lowest Quintile	Second Quintile	Third Quintile	Fourth Quintile	Highest Quintile
1952	8.1	14.2	17.8	23.2	36.7
1962	8.8	14.4	18.2	23.1	35.4
1972	11.7	15.0	18.2	22.3	32.8

Source: Derived from estimates presented in my "The Trend Toward Equality in the Distribution of Net Income," *Southern Economic Journal.*

gives the percentage shares received by quintiles after adding in-kind transfers and education, subtracting income and social security taxes, and converting to a per capita distribution. As shown in Table 2, the distribution of income is much more equal than the Census figures in Table 1 suggest. In 1972, for example, the adjustments more than double the share of the lowest quintile, raising it from 5.4 to 11.7 per cent.

Not only is the distribution of income more equal in each year than is indicated by the Census figures, but there has also been a marked trend towards equality over the 20-year period. This is particularly apparent for the lowest quintile, whose share rose from 8.1 per cent in 1952 to 11.7 per cent in 1972, an improvement of 44 per cent in the relative position of low-income families. Most of this gain occurred since 1962, largely as a result of the expansion of education benefits and in-kind transfers. In fact, by 1972 government transfers had become the largest source of income for low-income families. More than two thirds (about $50 billion) of the net income of families in the lowest quintile was in the form of cash transfers, education benefits, and in-kind transfers.

INCENTIVES AND MARGINAL TAX RATES

Of the many factors to consider in evaluating redistributive programs, none is more important than the impact on the incentives of taxpayers and transfer recipients to continue producing income. If incentives are dulled sufficiently, the outcome is a reduction in the total size of the income "pie," and more equal shares of a smaller total can result in lower incomes for taxpayers and transfer recipients alike. The most common way tax and transfer programs affect incentives is through the application of high marginal tax rates to income. To understand why, it is necessary to distinguish clearly between *marginal* and *average* tax rates.

Suppose the government wishes to collect $4000 in taxes from a person earning $20,000. It can set out to accomplish this by exempting $15,000 (so taxable income is $5000) and applying a flat rate tax of 80 per cent on taxable income. If the person continues to earn $20,000 he will pay $4000 in taxes. Thus his average tax rate is 20 per cent; however, his marginal tax rate is 80 per cent — i.e., for each additional dollar earned above $15,000, the taxpayer keeps only 20¢. To illustrate the relationship between high marginal tax rates and work incentives, note that if the taxpayer earns $5000 less, his taxes *fall* by $4000. Thus, by sacrificing only $1000 in net income he could take a vacation for a fourth of the year. In this way high marginal tax rates make it much less expensive for a person to earn less — that is, they weaken the incentive to continue expending as much effort to acquire income. Average tax rates may also have some independent effect, but it is high marginal tax rates that are most likely to undermine incentives. As we shall see, redistributive programs usually involve extremely high marginal tax rates, even though average tax rates may be relatively low.

High marginal tax rates are often applied to beneficiaries of government transfers, but these rates are usually hidden in the benefit structure of the program. If the transfer a family receives is reduced when family income is increased, then this reduction in benefits has exactly the same effect as a marginal tax rate applied to income. Suppose, as is actually true in several programs, that the transfer received is reduced by $1 for every $2 earned. Then when earnings increase by $2, disposable income goes up by only $1, exactly the same as when a 50 per cent marginal tax rate is applied to earnings.

In terms of marginal tax rates, a policy of complete equality implies marginal tax rates of 100 per cent for everyone. In this case, a person's net income would not increase if he earned more and would not fall if he earned less, or even if he earned nothing. Thus, there would be no financial incentive for anyone to work. It is an understanding of the full implications of this that has led most scholars to conclude that marginal tax rates must be kept well below 100 per cent to preserve adequate incentives. This, of course, is tantamount to concluding that complete equality is undesirable.

I have been emphasizing how marginal tax rates tend to weaken work incentives of both taxpayers and transfer recipients. Actually, high marginal tax rates are inimical to productivity in general, and not just to the amount of time people work. Consider a few examples of other types of incentives that can be undermined by high marginal tax rates. The incentive to undertake job training or get a good education is weakened since the student will get to keep only part of the higher income that a better education makes possible. Insofar as the return to savings is also subject to tax, the flow of savings, so important to economic growth, can be adversely affected by high marginal tax rates. Occupational choices can also be influenced: People will be led to take lower paying jobs that do not involve as much risk or responsibility. Earlier retirement, longer vacations, and lower labor-force participation by secondary workers are other plausible responses to high rates. Greater conversion of income into nontaxable forms (through the use of tax loopholes), and even emigration to other countries can result when the tax rates get high enough, as has recently been the case in England.

THE IMPACT ON LOW-INCOME FAMILIES

As a result of the multitude of tax and transfer programs now in existence, marginal tax rates are already very high for most people, but especially for those with very high and very low incomes. Before explaining how high the rates are, it should be stressed that the marginal tax rate relevant for incentives is the combined rate which results from all the separate taxes and transfer programs applied to a family. As an example, a family in a 20-per-cent federal income tax bracket and a five-per-cent state income tax bracket is subject to an effective marginal tax rate of 25 percent, and it is this rate that is instrumental in affecting its economic behavior.

Since federal, state, and local taxes combined are now 35 per cent of net national product (national income), it seems clear that many taxpayers face marginal tax rates approaching 50 per cent. (Marginal rates will often be higher than this overall average rate of 35 per cent due to progressivity in the tax system.) Effective marginal tax rates are probably lowest for families with incomes near the average of about $15,000, but even at this income

level, the combined effect of federal and state income taxes, social security, sales, excise, and property taxes will produce rates of at least 35 per cent. At higher income levels, effective rates will be even higher, perhaps reaching 60 per cent for a relatively few families. Most upper-income families, are probably confronted with rates in the neighborhood of 40 to 50 per cent, however.

Therefore, effective marginal tax rates are already quite high for middle-income and upper-income families, ranging between 35 and 50 percent, with a small proportion paying still higher rates. As high as these rates are, however, low-income families are paying even higher marginal tax rates!

The major reason low-income families face higher marginal tax rates than most other Americans is that poor families receive numerous transfers that are inversely related to their incomes. As pointed out earlier, when the amount of assistance falls as a family's own income increases, this is equivalent to applying a marginal tax rate on income. There has been a substantial growth in programs of this type in recent years. The more important of these programs are food stamps, housing subsidies, medicaid, Aid to Families with Dependent Children, Supplemental Security Income, and Social Security. The implicit marginal tax rates used, of course, vary among these programs. Housing subsidies typically use a rate of 25 per cent, Supplemental Security Income a rate of 50 per cent, and Aid to Families with Dependent Children, a rate of 67 per cent.

The individual rates in these programs are fairly high, but the effective rates for most low-income families can be even higher, for two reasons. First, low-income families also pay explicit taxes in the form of social security taxes, sales taxes, and so on. Second, and becoming increasingly important, many families are receiving benefits from several transfer programs simultaneously. As an example, a family receiving food stamps, with the implicit marginal tax rate of 25 to 30 per cent, will still pay social security, excise, sales, and possibly state income and other taxes. As a result, the effective marginal tax rate would be about 45 per cent. Even though this family may have an income too low to be subject to the federal income tax, its effective tax rate exceeds that of most middle-income and upper-income families. For families receiving transfers from other programs, and especially when a family receives aid from more than one program, effective marginal tax rates can exceed 70 and even 80 per cent.

At present, then, effective marginal tax rates are already very high, especially for low-income families. Additional redistribution will produce surprisingly large increases in these rates, both for taxpayers and recipients, as we shall see.

THE EFFECTS OF REDISTRIBUTION

That a greater volume of redistribution would result in higher marginal tax rates is obvious, but the exact relationship between the amount of redistribution and the necessary rate increases is far from obvious. Many observers of American society have implied that our wealthy society could easily afford to redistribute another, say, one or two per cent of national income to low-income families. Yet redistributing even one per cent more will probably require marginal tax rates to rise by at least 10 percentage points for most, and possibly all, families. It may appear surprising that transferring only one per cent of national income to low-income families would lead to such an increase in tax rates, and that is why it is worth considering the relationship in some detail.

It may help to begin with an example. Suppose transfers totaling one per cent of national income are made to families with income below $5000. Suppose further that these families have incomes averaging $3000, and that one per cent of national income will finance a transfer of $2000 per family. What this implies is that one per cent of national income is sufficient to raise every family with an income below $5000 up to $5000. In other words, we could make a transfer of $5000 to a family with no income of its own, a transfer of $4000 to a family with a $1000 income, and so on up to a transfer of $1 to a family with $4999. Note that this describes a transfer program with a marginal tax rate of 100 per cent; the transfer falls by a dollar for every dollar of additional earnings. Thus, when we attempt to concentrate a seemingly small propor-tion of national income on a relatively small number of low-income families, the impact on their marginal tax rates can be surprisingly great. Although the numbers chosen are hypothetical, they do represent fairly accurately the true nature of the problem.

It might be felt that a different type of transfer program would not require marginal rates of 100 per cent. For instance, suppose that a transfer of exactly $2000 is made to every family with income below $5000. A family with a zero income would receive $2000 and so would a family with $5000, thus implying a zero marginal tax rate; benefits don't fall with income. Is this a way to avoid the incentive problem? As long as we are considering a redistribution only to families with incomes below $5,000, the answer to this question is definitely no. The incentive difficulties are just shifted to a different income range. Note that, under this scheme, a family with $5000 earned income would have a net income of $7000, but families earning from $5001 to $6999 would actually have lower net incomes, since they would receive no transfers. Not only is this inequitable, but it creates a tremendous incentive for all those earning between $5000 and $7000, as well as some earning above $7000, to reduce their earnings to $5000 and collect a $2000 transfer. The abrupt termination of transfer payments at $5000 creates what is called a "notch" problem, indicating the discontinuity in the relationship between earned and net income that occurs at $5000. Most analysts agree that the consequences of such "notches," both for equity and efficiency, are worse than the high marginal tax rates that they only seem, on a superficial inspection, to avoid.

To avoid such a notch at $5000, the transfer per family must be gradually tapered off until it ultimately reaches zero when family income reaches $5000. It is this gradual tapering off of the transfer payment that produces the marginal tax rate in the program. And when transfers are made only to low-income families, the transfer must be reduced very rapidly as income rises, to make sure the transfer falls to zero at the "breakeven income level" (the income level at which the net transfer is zero) of $5000. Hence, the marginal tax rate in such a program will then tend to be very high.

As long as transfers are to be made only to families with incomes below a relatively low level, like $5000, any substantial redistribution implies either very high marginal tax rates or a "notch" problem, which is just as bad. This should explain why the tax rates are so high for low-income families in the United States. The high rates are simply the inevitable consequences of concentrating sizable transfers on these families. It will be recalled that the marginal tax rate for the average low-income family is probably about 65 per cent, even though only about four per cent of national income is being redistributed to families in the lowest quintile of the income distribution.

THE COSTS OF REDISTRIBUTION

Now that we understand why tax rates of recipients are so sensitive to the amount redistributed, we can move from our hypothetical example to the actual situation in the United States. Suppose, then, that we wish to redistribute one per cent more of national income to families in the lowest 20 per cent of the income distribution. One per cent of national income is $13 billion, an average of about $1200 per family for the 11 million families in the lowest quintile. This group contains families with money incomes below approximately $7000 (but net incomes including in-kind transfers would be higher), and these families now face a wide range of marginal tax rates that average about 65 per cent. How high must marginal tax rates rise with an additional redistribution of $13 billion? By now, perhaps, it will come as no surprise to learn that marginal rates would have to rise to approximately 100 per cent, or slightly more. I do not think it is necessary to belabor the point that the economic effects — not to mention the social and political ones — of such high rates would be unacceptable. Thus, given the present size of the United States welfare system, any substantial additional redistribution concentrated on the lowest quintile would result in prohibitively high marginal tax rates.

There is one way to redistribute more to low-income families without such a great increase in their tax rates, and that is to extend transfer payments to families with incomes above $7000. By raising the "breakeven income" of the additional redistribution, the transfer payment per family can be tapered off more gradually as income rises, thus implying a smaller increment in marginal tax rates. For example, we might redistribute an additional one per cent of national income to families with incomes below $10,000, thereby using a breakeven income of $10,000 instead of $7000. However, this program would still require marginal rates to rise by 15 percentage points for all families with incomes below $10,000. For low-income families the increase is from 65 per cent to 80 per cent, and for families close to $10,000, from about 35 per cent to 50 per cent. Even these rates raise very serious questions, especially since more than a third of all American families have incomes below $10,000. In my judgment, rates this high pose a danger of seriously undermining incentives that is too great to be acceptable.

HOW GREATER EQUALITY CAN INCREASE INEQUALITY

Most redistributive programs involve transferring resources from families with high money incomes to families with lower money incomes. It is often taken for granted that the result is a more equal distribution of income. Of course, money incomes become more equally distributed, but it is not obvious that the distribution of real income becomes more equal. For a variety of reasons, differences in money incomes among families do not necessarily imply a difference in real incomes. This poses a very difficult problem for the evaluation of policies that tend to equalize money incomes. A few examples will indicate the nature of the problem.

If we consider a group of people with equal abilities to earn income, their actual earnings may nonetheless differ quite widely as a result of differences in their preferences. Some people, for instance, may choose to become teachers even though they could have received a higher money income by working for a private business. In such a case, the difference in money income between teachers and business employees is called an "equalizing income differential." This means that a difference in money incomes is necessary to make the net attractiveness of the jobs equal — that is, to make real incomes equal. Many differences in money income are equalizing income differentials that simply reflect differences in the attractiveness of different jobs. When this is the case, equalization of money incomes implies disequalization of real incomes. If teachers and business employees have the same money income, the teachers would have higher real incomes: equal money incomes plus a job they consider more attractive.

Another way preferences can lead to different money incomes concerns the amount of leisure time (meaning all time not spent working for money wages) that families have. Of two people who can work at the same wage rate, one may choose to work shorter hours than the other because he values leisure more highly (or, equivalently, dislikes work more). There would be a difference in money incomes, but most of us would agree that their real incomes are the same. In short, leisure time is a valuable consumption item, and should be considered a part of a person's real income. In addition to different hours of work in different jobs, two significant sources of variation in leisure time deserve explicit mention, since they are easily overlooked: the retirement decision and the decision of several members of a family to work. Retirement is an explicit decision to sacrifice money income in return for more leisure, just as is the decision of a wife to work in the home rather than for money wages in the market. Both phenomena lead to differences in money incomes in some situations where real incomes are not different.

Another major source of differences in money incomes is the use of a one-year accounting period in the measurement of income. Two people may have unequal incomes in a given year, but their lifetime incomes can be identical. A person who goes to work after leaving high school will normally have a higher income at age 20 than his friend who attends college, but the reverse will probably be true 20 years later. Nevertheless, both may have the same lifetime incomes, especially when the cost of the college education is considered as a cost of the graduate's future income.

In general, incomes tend to rise with age up to about age 55, and then decline. The median income in 1972 of families headed by a person in the 14-to-24 age class was $7447, while for the 45-to-54 age class the median was nearly double, $14,056. Above age 65 the median was $5968. Comparing people of different ages can give a misleading impression of inequality. Note that a redistribution plan based on money income would, in part, transfer income from those of middle age to those who are younger. Yet certainly the average young family today will have a higher, not lower, lifetime income than the average middle-aged family. Not only will age and experience work to increase the young family's income in the future, but so too will economic growth. In all likelihood, by the time a young family today reaches middle age, the median income of middle-aged families will be at least $20,000.

While still other examples could be given, I think these suffice to make the point that differences in annual money incomes are not an accurate guide to differences in real economic position. In some cases, inequality in money income is consistent with equality in real income, and in other cases equality in money income is consistent with inequality in real income. Recognition of this has important implications for the ethical desirability of plans to produce greater equality in money incomes. Equalizing money incomes will, in many instances, produce greater inequality in real incomes.

For years, countless reformers have been urging the adoption of measures to produce a more equal distribution of income. The call is always for more equality than we now have, but seldom is the issue of exactly how much more equality is desirable faced squarely. Since we have gone quite far in equalizing incomes in recent years, now is an appropriate time to consider this fundamental question. It may be that we have gone far enough.

QUESTIONS

1. What is the distinction between a marginal and an average tax rate? What is the economic significance of each ?
2. Why does the enforcement of perfect income equality entail marginal tax rates of 100 percent?
3. How do in-kind transfers affect the distribution of income in the United States?

40 GOVERNMENT SPENDING: WHO GETS SUBSIDIZED?
Sheldon W. Stahl

The size of the federal government's budget remains a continual issue of social concern. This selection describes not only the size of the federal budget but also explores the meaning and extent of subsidies in the public sector. Sheldon W. Stahl, the author, is a staff economist with the Federal Reserve Bank of Kansas City.

If there is a negative overtone or stigma surrounding the word "subsidy" for many people today, it is interesting to reflect that such a negative attachment has not always been the case. In fact, the concept of the subsidy is almost as old as our nation itself. When the First Congress convened in 1789, its initial action was to devise a system for administering oaths of office. However, the next item of business was the enactment of a tariff law to protect and promote the new nation's agricultural and industrial development. Included in the legislation was a special subsidy feature designed to encourage the growth of an American merchant fleet. All goods imported into the United States in American vessels were to have their customs duties reduced by 10 per cent, and a tonnage tax favorable to American shipping interests was also made part of the law.

Abridged from Sheldon W. Stahl, "The Federal Subsidy Picture: A Blurred Image," Federal Reserve Bank of Kansas City *Monthly Review* (October, 1976) 12–20. Reprinted by permission.

From this early beginning, the Government has used the subsidy time and again, not only to influence the pace and direction of economic development, but for diverse other purposes, including the promotion of science and the arts, and to mitigate the normal workings of market demand and supply forces when deemed desirable.

One of the more frequently recurring themes on the contemporary political scene is the size and scope of the Federal Government and its effects upon the private lives of individuals or in their roles as business or professional persons. In general, many allege that the Government is too big and that its spending has contributed mightily to the problem of inflation in this country. The relative merits of such charges continue to be argued at length with considerable vigor. If the discussants have not yet been successful in convincing each other of the rectitude of their positions, at least the debate has generated one valuable consequence: The subject of Government spending is no longer confined to economists and/or those with an abiding interest in the field of fiscal finance. Rather, the topic is now one which is more generally discussed by the public at large. And, as a corollary, that same public is subjecting the spending process to closer scrutiny than ever before.

The basic reason for the growing wave of public interest in Federal spending would appear to be reasonably straightforward. The sheer volume of spending and its apparent inexorability makes it exceedingly difficult to ignore. For example, during World War II Federal outlays rose dramatically, increasing from less than $14 billion for the fiscal year 1941 to a peak level for that period of just under $93 billion in the 1945 fiscal year. The end of World War II brought a reversal of the growth in Federal outlays. For the fiscal years 1947 and 1948, spending fell to a range of approximately $30-$35 billion, and sizable budgetary surpluses were achieved. However, these developments were short-lived, and the period since then has been marked by continuous increases in Federal outlays. Not only have these expenditures grown almost uninterruptedly in absolute amounts — outlays for fiscal year 1977 will likely exceed $400 billion — but, as Table 1 shows, total

Table 1. *Federal Sector Expenditures as a Per Cent of GNP*

Description	1947 Actual	1957 Actual	1967 Actual	1977 Estimate
Defense purchases.	4.3	9.8	8.7	5.1
Nondefense purchases	1.7	1.3	2.5	2.5
Domestic transfer payments.	3.7	3.3	4.8	8.9
Foreign transfer payments.	.8	.4	.3	.2
Grants-in-aid to state and local governments.	.7	.9	1.9	3.2
Net interest paid	1.8	1.2	1.2	1.7
Subsidies less current surplus of Government enterprises	.3	.6	.7	.3
Total expenditures[1].	13.3	17.5	20.0	22.0

Source: Special Analyses, Budget of the United States Government, Fiscal Year 1977 (Washington: U.S. Government Printing Office, 1976), Table A-3, p. 12.

[1]Individual items may not add to totals due to rounding.

expenditures for the various Federal sectors have claimed an increasing share of the nation's gross national product (GNP).

In the face of these developments in overall Federal spending, a closer look at the subsidy picture might appear somewhat misplaced in terms of priorities. For example, during the 3 decades shown in Table 1, outlays for subsidies represented well under 1 per cent of GNP, and accounted for the same share of GNP — 0.3 per cent — in fiscal year 1977 as in fiscal year 1947. Indeed, in the last decade, the share of GNP accounted for by outlays on Federal subsidies has fallen by more than one-half.

ON DEFINING A SUBSIDY

The Office of Management and Budget (OMB) defines subsidy as "a monetary grant to a unit engaged in commercial activities." Thus, the rather modest scale of subsidy costs shown results from a narrow view of just what constitutes a subsidy. In this particular instance, nonmonetary benefits to recipients not engaged in commercial activities would not appear as subsidies for budget purposes. Such a definition is too confining given the wide range of Government activities which benefit varying groups in our society and which can and do take forms other than monetary grants.

Few would disagree that a subsidy involves a transfer of income either between Government and the private sector or between groups within the private sector. Furthermore, the transfer imposes costs upon the donor. The form of income transfer may involve money or some monetary equivalent. In either case, the increase in income by the recipient enhances his or her ability to satisfy economic demands or desires. A second characteristic of subsidy is that, insofar as a transfer of income occurs, it is a one-way transfer. This aspect of a subsidy undoubtedly has caused many people to view subsidy programs simply as giveaways, a view undoubtedly reinforced by another characteristic of subsidies. Subsidies are restricted in nature and accrue to a special group — a subgroup of the private sector — rather than to the public at large. This feature, in part, distinguishes them from the provision of free public services or public goods. For by its nature, a public good such as national defense cannot be provided solely to some special group in society; when it is provided to any one member of society, it is provided to all.

It was noted earlier that the subsidy device has been used to mitigate the normal workings of market demand and supply forces when it was deemed desirable. In other words, a subsidy is intended to directly influence the pattern of production and consumption in the private economy in a manner the Government may wish. More specifically, a subsidy involves a Government action that serves to modify, but not eliminate or take the place of, private market activities or prices. Thus, a fourth characteristic of a subsidy is that it seeks to change some particular private market behavior without doing away with the market.

This critierion of performance which distinguishes subsidy from welfare is of crucial importance in evaluating the extent to which a particular program is succeeding. Indeed, it is this expectation of a modification or alteration in some specific private sector performance which both the Government and the taxpaying public expect in return for the transfer of income through the subsidy. If there is no *quid pro quo* forthcoming from the recipient, such an income transfer should be more properly labeled welfare. This is not to imply that one category of public outlays is better than another, but rather that confusion between the two is often the fault of applying inappropriate standards for evaluation. The public has a right to expect performance in return for a subsidy; that is its justification, the benefit in return for the cost. In the absence of such performance, the subsidy program should be reevaluated to determine if the objects of the subsidy should instead be more appropriately objects of a welfare program.

From the preceding discussion, it should be clear that there is a wide variety of ways by which the Government can effect income transfers. It should be equally clear that not all such transfers should be regarded as subsidies, and that any meaningful definition of the term should encompass those characteristics which have some reasonable degree of economic merit. By these standards, the definition used by the OMB and cited earlier is far too restrictive. Given the preceding analysis dealing with the matter of definition, the proposal of the JEC appears to represent a far better alternative:

. . . a subsidy is defined as the provision of Federal economic assistance, at the expense of others in the economy, to the private sector producers or consumers of a particular good, service or factor of production. The Government receives no equivalent compensation in return, but conditions the assistance on a particular performance by the recipient — a quid pro quo — that has the effect of altering the price or costs of the particular good, service, or factor to the subsidy recipient, so as to encourage or discourage the output, supply, or use of these items and the related economic behavior.

ANOTHER LOOK AT SUBSIDY COSTS

The efforts of the JEC bore fruit in the form of estimates of Federal subsidy costs more in keeping with its expanded definition of the subsidy concept. These data are shown in Table 2 for the fiscal years 1970 and 1975.

Table 2 reveals the wide difference in estimates of subsidy costs by the JEC as compared to those cited earlier. In fiscal year 1970, the order of magnitude of subsidy costs shown in the budget was $4.4 billion, or $5.4 billion including Government enterprise deficits. As estimated by the JEC, those costs exceeded $64 billion. For the 1975 fiscal year, they were essentially unchanged in the budget. As seen in Table 2, however, they had increased nearly 50 per cent, to $95 billion, according to JEC estimates. While these aggregate change figures are notable in themselves, the varying trends among the different types of subsidy expenditures are of particular interest.

Direct cash subsidies represent cash payments from the Government to a firm or individual in the private sector engaged in a market activity as specified in the subsidy legislation. Among these activities are housing construction, school attendance, and production of certain crops, to name just a few. Overall, this type of subsidy showed very little change, rising from $11.6 billion in 1970 to $12.3 billion in 1975. Within this category, however, subsidies to agriculture fell dramatically, as did cash subsidies to the commerce category involving such programs as community action, model cities, and urban renewal and neighborhood development. The education category rose from less than $2 billion to $5 billion largely as a consequence of increased outlays for vererans' education and basic education opportunity grants. Other large gains occurred in manpower — through increased manpower revenue sharing outlays — and in housing, primarily as a result of increased cash subsidies for public housing assistance.

In contrast with stable to declining outlays for the direct cash and credit subsidies, benefit-in-kind subsidies increased during this same period nearly 130 per cent — from less than $9 billion in 1970 to

Table 2. *Summary of Federal Subsidy Costs (In Billions of Dollars)*

	Fiscal Year									
	Direct Cash Subsidies		Tax Subsidies		Credit Subsidies		Benefit-in-Kind Subsidies		Total Order of Magnitude	
	1970	1975	1970	1975	1970	1975	1970	1975	1970	1975
Agriculture	4.4	.6	.9	1.1	.4	.7	—	—	5.7	2.5
Food	—	—	—	—	—	—	1.5	5.9	1.5	5.9
Health	.8	.6	3.2	5.8	—	—	4.6	10.2	8.6	16.6
Manpower	2.0	3.3	.6	.7	—	—	.1	.1	2.6	4.1
Education	1.9	5.0	.8	1.0	.1	.1	.4	.4	3.2	6.5
International	.1	—	.3	1.5	.6	.9	—	—	1.0	2.4
Housing	.1	1.7	8.7	12.9	3.0	1.1	—	—	11.7	15.7
Natural resources	.1	.1	2.0	4.1	—	—	.1	.1	2.1	4.4
Transportation	.3	.6	—	.1	—	—	.2	1.7	.5	2.3
Commerce	2.0	.3	14.1	19.3	.1	—	1.8	1.9	18.0	21.5
Other	—	—	9.4	13.1	.1	.1	—	—	9.5	13.2
Total order of magnitude[1]	11.6	12.3	39.9	59.7	4.1	2.9	8.8	20.2	64.4	95.1

Source: Federal Subsidy Programs, Joint Economic Committee (Washington: U.S. Government Printing Office, 1974), p.5.
[1]Individual items may not add to totals due to rounding.

over $20 billion in 1975 — while tax subsidies rose $20 billion to nearly $60 billion. When the Government sells to the private sector a good or service at a price below the prevailing market price or below its actual cost in the case where a private market may not exist, a benefit-in-kind subsidy arises. One of the most notable examples is the food stamp program. Indeed, rising food stamp outlays, and to a lesser extent, increased expenditures for the school lunch program, were responsible for the nearly $4.5 billion increase from 1970 to 1975 in the food category. In the area of health, benefit-in-kind subsidies rose by about $5.5 billion in the same period as a consequence of sharp jumps in the medical assistance program (Medicaid) and in health insurance for the aged (Medicare). Quantitatively, one other item of significance was a more than $1 billion increase in urban mass transit capital improvement grants which accounted for most of the rise in the transportation category. Although commerce showed essentially no change over the period, benefit-in-kind subsidies to the postal service continued to account for the major share of expenditures in this category.

The type of subsidy showing the largest absolute increase in Table 2 is tax subsidies. A tax subsidy is generated when a special provision in the law allows an individual or a firm engaged in a specific market activity to make a smaller tax payment to the Government than would have otherwise been the case.

A CONCLUDING OBSERVATION

The foregoing analysis demonstrates that subsidies do exert a pervasive influence on our economy. Their scope of application, their diverse forms, and the significant sums of money involved are all persuasive reasons for ongoing public concern.

QUESTIONS

1. What has been the general trend in federal spending relative to GNP in recent years?
2. What are the characteristics of a government subsidy?
3. Why is national defense not a "subsidy" provided by the federal government?
4. What categories or types of subsidies have grown the most rapidly in recent years? Of what subsidies, if any, are you (or your family) the recipients?

PART ELEVEN

UNEMPLOYMENT AND INFLATION

41 INFLATION: WHO WINS AND WHO LOSES?
W. Lee Hoskins

Times of inflation are times of great concern — and not only for politicians then in power. There is an almost universal feeling that inflation is bad. Yet some people actually increase their wealth during an inflation — and some of these are the relatively poor. In this article, W. Lee Hoskins clarifies the issue of who is likely to win and who is likely to lose because of inflation, and indicates why, in spite of the gains and losses, society is generally the loser during inflation. Dr. Hoskins is vice president of research at the Philadelphia Federal Reserve Bank.

How much is inflation costing you? When the cash register rings, the Pavlovian response of most Americans is "plenty." This reaction, reinforced by news media, civic leaders, and streetcorner philosophers, may not be wholly warranted, for the burden of rising prices, like almost everything else, is not distributed equally among us. In fact, a sizeable number of Americans may actually gain from inflation.

EXPECTED VS. UNEXPECTED INFLATION

What people believe about the course of future events influences their present actions. Expectations about future inflation are no exception. If people, looking ahead, expect inflation, they may be able to adjust their *present* earning, purchasing, lending, and borrowing activities. By doing so, they may overcome the expected depreciation in the value of money. This process, recently dubbed "inflationary psychology," continues until people have reason to foresee or expect a stable price level.

One example of inflationary psychology in operation would be that of a lender who includes in his loan charges the expected or anticipated rate of

From W. Lee Hoskins, "Inflation: Gainers and Losers," Federal Reserve Bank of Philadelphia *Business Review* (February 1970), pp. 23–30. Reprinted by permission.

price inflation. His reason for doing so is obvious. Suppose you loan $1,000 to a friend for one year, and you expect the price level to rise by 10 percent during that period. What rate of interest would be appropriate if you wanted to earn a real return (in terms of constant purchasing power) of 5 percent? Answer: about 15 percent. This monetary return would allow you a *real return* of 5 percent, and you would avoid a loss of wealth, but perhaps not of a friend. If, however, in making the loan, you underestimated the rise in prices, the return you would receive would be insufficient to compensate fully for the reduced purchasing power of the repaid loan plus interest, and you would have joined ranks with inflation losers. Your failure to foresee accurately the rate of inflation would result in a redistribution of your wealth from you to your friend. Your friend would be an inflation gainer because he does not repay as much in terms of purchasing power as he borrowed.

Not all people are equally able to make the necessary adjustments in their earning, purchasing, lending, and borrowing activities to compensate for inflation they see on the horizon. Even if they were, that would not be the end of the story, for it is because inflation is incorrectly foreseen that gains and losses are often incurred. All people do not have equal ability or luck at predicting future events or doing something about it. Consequently, inflations in the United States have not been *fully* anticipated by all, and wealth redistribution has occurred. One key to this redistribution is the relationship between debtors and creditors.

THE ADVANTAGE OF DEBT

The reason wealth is taken from some and bestowed on others by unforeseen inflation stems from the fact that there are two kinds of assets, monetary and real, linking debtors and creditors. Monetary assets include bonds, certificates of deposit, promissory notes, accounts receivable, and other legal contracts that promise a *fixed number of dollars*. Of course, for every monetary asset there is a monetary liability. For instance, to the landlord a lease represents a monetary asset, while to the tenant it is a monetary liability — a promise to pay a fixed number of dollars. In return for this promise to pay, the tenant receives a real asset — living space. People may issue monetary liabilities in order to finance purchases of real assets (cars, houses, inventories, and factories) or for consumption.

The crucial difference between the two is that a real asset is a claim to a *fixed amount of goods or services* whose money value is tied to inflation, while a monetary asset represents a claim to a *fixed number of dollars* regardless of inflation. During an unexpected inflation, the dollar value of a real asset increases as prices rise, leaving its *real* value in terms of purchasing power unchanged; while the amount of dollars in a monetary asset (saving certificate) remains constant, and its real value falls. An investor holding a monetary asset loses purchasing power or wealth. (See Table 1.) The person who holds a monetary liability (in other words, who is in debt) during an unexpected inflation gains unexpectedly because he repays his debt in dollars that are worth less in terms of purchasing power.

Most families have real assets, monetary assets, and debts (monetary liabilities). The relative holdings of these items during periods of unanticipated increases in the price level determine whether or not a given family gains or loses from inflation. If a family holds more monetary liabilities than monetary assets, it gains. Conversely, if monetary assets exceed debts, the family loses. So, being in debt can have advantages during periods of unexpected inflation. This statement does *not* mean that saving makes no sense. Savings held in nonmonetary form do not lose value. Moreover, savings held in monetary form may lose value only when inflation is unanticipated. If inflation were accurately anticipated, adjustments could be made so that savings held in monetary asset form (except cash) would make sense as well.

TAKING ACCOUNT OF INCOME

A family's status as a net monetary debtor or creditor is not all that determines whether inflation robs it or blesses it. Income also fits into the picture. Let's focus first on income from certain pen-

Table 1. *The Change from 1958 to 1968 in Monetary Value of Selected Assets in Unadjusted Dollars and in Dollars of 1957–1959 Purchasing Power*

Asset	Percentage Change in Value	
	Unadjusted $	1957–59 $
Cash		−23.7
Bonds		
U.S. Treasury	−19.9	−35.3
N.Y. City	−21.4	−36.4
Preferred Stock Average	−23.2	−37.9
Common Stock Averages		
Industrials	+91.7	+55.0
Public utilities	+61.0	+30.2
New York City banks	+104.3	+65.2

sion plans, insurance policies, and other types of programs which promise to pay a *fixed number of dollars per year*. These promises to pay are monetary assets to the pensioner, and the *amount* they pay is unaffected by a rise in the price level.[1] People holding such assets are said to be on "fixed incomes"; hence, they suffer a loss from unanticipated inflation. However, the person on a "fixed income" may hold other monetary assets and liabilities as well. And it is the relative holdings of all of these that determine whether or not a person's wealth expands, shrinks, or is unaffected when the price level climbs unexpectedly.

Undoubtedly, the most important source of income for most families is wage and salary earnings. Unforeseen inflation can have an impact upon this type of income too. For example, a wage contract promising to deliver a specified number of hours of labor for a fixed number of dollars may cause the laborer to lose, for such a contract represents a monetary asset to him. Moreover, wages are bid up faster in some sectors than others because of the manner in which the inflation is introduced and transmitted through the economy. Consequently, some redistribution does occur. But generally, wages and salaries simply reflect what we receive in return for the sale of real assets (hours of labor), and as such are usually bid up during an inflation.

---

[1]Social Security payments do not appear to fall in this category. As prices climbed during the 1960s, Congress periodically raised the allowable monthly payments.

Table 2. *Estimated Net Debtor and Creditor Status (in Billions of Dollars) of Household, Corporate Business, and Government Sectors, 1945–1967* [1]

Sector	Year			
	1945	1952	1959	1967
Households	+213.8	+237.9	+306.4	+505.0
Corporate business (nonfinancial)	−4.2	−26.7	−42.0	−96.5
U.S. government	−221.8	−193.1	−208.1	−234.9

[1]Positive sign indicates net creditor and negative sign indicates net debtor.

For example, during the current period of rising prices, average hourly earnings increased at a faster pace than consumer prices. From 1965 through 1969, average hourly earnings soared 24 percent while the Consumer Price Index jumped only 16 percent. Of course, some of the increases in wage rates may have been caused by workers as they anticipated some but not all of the inflation. It is not clear, therefore, that even unanticipated inflation robs the average working man of his wage.

When income is taken into account, the problem of calculating gains and losses becomes more complicated, but the principle remains the same: The gainer is the guy who owes more money than is owed to him during an unforeseen inflation.

REDISTRIBUTION ON WHAT BASIS?

The household sector of the economy has been, by far, the leading net monetary creditor since World War II, while the federal government has been in the enviable position of the number one net monetary debtor. (See Table 2.) The nonfinancial corporate sector also has been a net monetary debtor but to a much smaller degree than the federal government. To the extent that the household sector holds monetary debts and liabilities of the federal government, unanticipated inflation results in a gain for the government and a loss to the household sector. This transfer of wealth is often called an inflation tax. But this does not end the process, because the government (which belongs to all of us) passes its gain along to someone. The gain in the corporate sector goes only to net debtor firms. And since people own business firms, they ultimately realize most of the fruits, be they bitter or sweet, that corporations receive from an unexpected rise in the price level.

More importantly, however, both the business and household sectors are composed of monetary creditor and debtor units, and it is the unexpected price level increases which cause redistribution of wealth and income within these groups that many people find objectionable about inflation. Redistribution of wealth and income on some criterion which is in accordance with our concept of fairness or equity is commonplace — witness the numerous subsidy and aid programs, not to mention that allegedly great equalizer, the progressive income tax. When inflation redistributes wealth, however, no consideration is given to individual circumstances, such as poverty, health, or number of dependents. Unanticipated inflation, unlike Robin Hood, takes from some and gives to others, be they poor, rich, young, or old. As a consequence, redistribution may not be on the basis of social goals or objectives.

Aside from its lack of social conscience, inflation has another trait which is reason for further concern. Use of money as a medium of exchange is an integral part of a high-output, specialized and complex economy. Money makes possible the efficient flow of goods and services by eliminationg the costly barter system. However, inflation makes the use of money more costly, and if severe enough, may cause a reduction in the real output of goods and services. People and business firms, in attempting to economize on the use of money, may resort to practices which tend to reduce specialization. They may spend time and effort searching out exchanges of goods and avoiding organized markets (for example, business firms integrating vertically to bypass supplier's and distributor's markets). Such actions would slash productivity in the economy. In a sense, society would be a loser.

ANTICIPATING INFLATION — HOW MUCH, FOR HOW LONG, AND AT WHAT COST

While there is little evidence that today's economy is coming apart at the seams, there are unmistakable signs that people, after experiencing four years of soaring prices, have come to expect future price increases. In order to protect themselves against the wealth-robbing effects of inflation, many people have acted upon their expectations. Consequently, we have high interest rates, built-in wage increases in some industries, reduced holdings of money balances by corporations and individuals, and wealth losses by those of us unfortunate enough to have had more money owed to us than we owed during these years.

Two considerable problems face the prospective anticipator of inflation. First, he must be able to estimate not only the amount or degree of inflation, but also its duration. That estimation is tough to make because the range of possible combinations of amounts and duration is infinite. For example, will prices rise 4 percent for the next 20 years and then stabilize, or will they rise 6 percent next year and then fall for several years? Even the best guru has trouble here. A correct answer would require an accurate forecast of future government monetary and fiscal decisions in addition to any major event or disaster that would affect the physical stock of goods and services available. Instead of making crystal-ball estimates, many people simply negotiate contracts with escalator clauses tied to the cost of living or acquire assets with an equity "kicker" (such as convertible bonds). Increased use of such clauses and kickers in recent years is a rough gauge of how uncertain people are about the degree of expected inflation.

But an accurate estimate of expected changes in the price level is only the first obstacle to be overcome in anticipating inflation. The second and perhaps even more difficult problem centers on the ability of an individual to alter his asset and liability holdings to avoid being hurt by the coming inflation. For example, a person may not be able to reduce his holdings of monetary assets if they are of the non-negotiable type, such as certain pension plans and insurance policies. Furthermore, he may not be able to contract enough debt to offset his holdings of monetary assets. In either case, even though the individual foresees the inflation, he is unable to forestall a loss in the purchasing power of his wealth when inflation occurs. Closely associated with this problem is that of the cost entailed in altering the form in which wealth is held. The cost of altering asset holdings depends upon the types of assets held; consequently, the cost of anticipating inflation differs among individuals holding different sets of assets.

Anticipating inflation for fun or profit is no easy matter. In addition, it is an expensive game to play because of the time and energy spent in calculating likely price level changes and attempting to alter the form in which wealth is held. If the costs and uncertainties entailed in anticipating inflation are added to those inefficiencies and inequities associated with inflation itself, it is easy to understand the merit of a stable price level. Price stability insures that gainers and losers will be determined on traditional values of thrift, hard work, and enterprise, rather than on the ability to anticipate and respond to price level changes.

QUESTIONS

1. What is the difference between expected and unexpected inflation? What groups are likely to have greater ability at predicting and adapting to inflation?
2. What is the advantage of holding debt during an inflation, if any? What is the advantage of holding debt during a deflation, if any?
3. What evidence is there that people in the United States are acting so as to anticipate and mitigate inflation? Has student behavior changed in any way due to an "inflationary psychology"?

42 WAGE-PRICE CONTROLS — THE CURE FOR INFLATION
John Kenneth Galbraith

John Kenneth Galbraith, now retired from Harvard University, is a prominent social critic who often directs his most withering remarks at his economist colleagues. A splendid writer, indeed a Fellow in Literature of the National Institute of Arts and Letters, Galbraith wrote The Affluent Society *and* The New Industrial State, *each of which spent weeks on the best seller lists. His influence on economic policy cannot be denied. It is exemplified by the following article in which he prescribes and predicts wage and price controls. This article should be read in conjunction with the one that follows it.*

THE BENIGN PHILLIPS CURVE

There was a doctrine that the United States economy could be regulated by general measures in such manner that prices would be approximately stable. A "trade-off," a new and popular word among economists, would exist between price stability and employment. The closer the approach to level prices, the more people who would be out of work; the lower the unemployment, the greater the rate of price increase. The relationship had been given quantitative expression by the so-called Phillips curve — the annual rate of price increase which, on the basis of historical data, could be expected to accompany any particular percentage of unemployment in the labor force. The choice between unemployment and inflation so shown seemed to be essentially benign — reasonable price stability could be combined with a tolerable level of unemployment. Also, an unspoken point, the unemployment would be among the unskilled, uneducated, mostly young black, who are also unorganized. These are assumed to accept unemployment philosophically,

The difference of opinion was not over the effi-

Abridged from John Kenneth Galbraith, *Economics, Peace and Laughter*, chap. 5; copyright © 1971 by John Kenneth Galbraith. Reprinted by permission of the publisher Houghton Mifflin Co., and Andre Deutsch Ltd., London.

cacy of the general measures but over technique. Since Keynes, most economists have placed major reliance on fiscal measures — on control of total spending in the economy by means of the Federal budget. Inflation being the problem, this policy consisted in making Federal taxes and spending sufficiently restraining on total demand in the economy. But in recent times there has been the so-called monetary revival. This makes control of spending from borrowed funds the key instrument in the control of prices. The difference between the exponents of fiscal and monetary management must not be exaggerated. Both believed in the efficacy of general measures. Both urged some combination of fiscal and monetary measures. The difference was in the mix.

The Nixon economists, when they came to office, were superlatively confident of such management. Under their guidance, the President promised never to interfere with wages and prices; in one of the more ecstatic examples of economic phrase-making, he said that inflation would be ended by "fine-tuning" the American economy — a figure of speech roughly comparable with one about fine-tuning a major Mississippi flood. The then current inflation was blamed on the previous bad management of the economy — on tuning that was too coarse. The reaction to anyone who suggested that wage and price restraint might be necessary was lofty.

Outside the Administration, the view was slightly less sanguine. But the economists who had served the Kennedy-Johnson Administration did not strongly question the reliance on general measures. In the early sixties, prices were fairly stable. Unemployment, though initially high, was falling — from an annual average of 6.7 percent of the labor force in 1961 to 4.5 in 1965. These were the years of the so-called guideposts, which meant that wage increases were held on the average to what industry generally could afford from productivity gains. And industry accordingly was persuaded to forego price increases. Enforcement was hortatory; it was a price increase by U.S. Steel in violation of this general understanding that provoked President Kennedy's eloquent denunciation of the corporation in April, 1962. The economics underlying the guideposts obviously accords a prime determining role in price-making to unions and corporations. That is why they must be restrained. But this power is not greatly stressed in standard, macroeconomic doctrine — roughly the economics of the textbooks — which holds that prices are set in markets and respond well to changes in demand. So even in the Kennedy-Johnson years, the guideposts were the poor relation to economic policy. When the guideposts later came under pressure from the Vietnam war, they were not strengthened but abandoned.

PRICE-WAGE REALITY

There was never any strong proof that high employment and stable prices could be combined. Much of the proof antedated modern corporate price-making and collective bargaining. Rather there were hope and faith. But in economics, hope and faith coexist with great scientific pretension and also a deep desire for respectability. Fiscal and monetary measures in whatever mix are impeccably respectable, and the question of the particular mix is the kind of thing that can be resolved between gentlemen. Control of wages and prices has no similar standing. Its advocates have been thought to lack subtlety of mind and manners — to go too abruptly to the point. The sociology of economics is not without interest and by no means unimportant.

The flaw in the respectable doctrine is the apalling obduracy of circumstance. Wages do now shove up prices. Prices do pull up wages. The bargaining that produces the wage and price increases continues even under conditions of severe fiscal and monetary restraint. It is almost as though those engaged in collective bargaining and corporate price-making were out to discredit the best economic scholarship. Circumstance can be unbelievably cruel.

The response of the Administration economists to their entrapment is a rewarding study — or would be were the matter not so serious. Economics, like foreign policy, allows for an escape from error through what may be called the Indochina effect. This generous device enables a man who has been wrong to denounce his previous position without admitting error and, by becoming right, thus greatly

to enhance his reputation. Arthur Burns, now Chairman of the Federal Reserve Board, has taken this route. He now demands the wage-price guideposts he previously condemned. His transmigration is still incomplete, for he proposes something less strong than the Kennedy-Johnson measures, which themselves proved too weak.

THE NEED FOR CONTROLS

For, in fact, the only answer is one that has for so long been dismissed as too disreputable. That is to act directly on the wage-price spiral — to have wage and price controls where the spiral contributes actively to inflation.

This must be real control. Dr. Burns and the economists of the Kennedy-Johnson period are ducking reality when they talk about a return to the voluntary guideposts. The guideposts will not do. They were not strong enough before; even stronger measures are now required. Also voluntary measures are highly discriminatory. They favor the individual or organization which refuses to comply and penalize those that are cooperative. This guarantees their eventual breakdown. And there is nothing to be said for billingsgate as an enforcement device. It is much better public practice to lay down fair firm rules after a careful consultation with all concerned and then, when someone violates the rules, have resort to law.

Given wage and price controls, interest rates can be reduced for they will not have to carry the present burden of inflation control, which they cannot carry anyway. With lower rates, home construction would increase, the pressure on small business would be reduced, employment would rise, and all without a new surge of inflation. Were this policy combined with prompt withdrawal from Indochina — which would ease the pressure of demand and, a more important matter, restore our reputation for elementary good sense — the immediate economic problem would be largely solved.

Such price and wage action, it is said, interferes with free markets. This is self-evident nonsense. The policy interferes with markets in which the interference of unions and corporations is already plenary. It fixes in the public interest prices that are already fixed.

Only prices that are so set by unions and strong corporations need to be (or should be) controlled. Prices of farm products, most services and products of small manufacturers need not and should not be touched. These are still subject to market influences. Where prices are still set by the market, general measures to restrict demand still work — or they do as much as can be done. As one needs to set prices that are already set, one does not need to interfere with the market where the market still governs.

Controls are not a temporary expedient. There must, alas, be a permanent system of restraint. That is because we will continue to have strong unions and strong corporations and a desire to minimize unemployment. The combination, in the absence of controls, is inflationary. It will not become otherwise in the future.

No one who has had experience with wartime price controls will be casual about the problems in managing it. Nor is it a formula for popularity; everyone unites in disliking the price-fixer. But if it is confined to the unions and to the corporations with market power, as here proposed, the administrative structure need not be vast. Dealings will be with only a few hundred unions and a few thousand firms, and for the latter it is sufficient to specify the limits within which average as distinct from individual prices may be moved. All price and wage control involves an arbitrary exercise of public power. But this is not an objection, for it replaces an arbitrary exercise of private power and one that has further and exceedingly arbitrary effects for those that suffer from the resulting inflation.

In the weeks and months ahead, more and more economists will come to accept the remedy here proposed — including, one suspects, those who advise the President. They are very decent men who have been substituting hope for reality, and hope unrequited does not sustain even an official economist forever. Promises of eventual price stability have become comic. Within the older framework of policy, the choice is between very severe inflation — worse than now — or severe unemployment, ex-

treme distortion within the economy, great turmoil among public employees, and serious strain in the financial markets — and along with all this, a good deal of inflation, too. Whoever made respectable economic policy a choice between such repellent alternatives had obviously a bad upbringing and is a very mean man. But so it is. So the less reputable course of controlling the wage-price bargain obtrudes itself. And, since there is no escape, it will continue to obtrude itself.

QUESTIONS

1. If only a small number of corporations and unions are responsible for the undesirable inflation, as Galbraith maintains, why is it seldom proposed (at least by Congress) that these corporations and unions be "broken up" so they can no longer dominate their respective markets? Would you support such action in place of wage—price controls? What advantages and disadvantages would you see in such an approach?
2. Assume the role of director of wage—price controls for the United States. The steel industry solicits a price increase of 8 percent and the steelworkers request a 9 percent annual pay raise. What methods would you use to decide the increases, if any, you would grant?
3. Ten days before this article was published, President Nixon in a television address to the nation said: "Wage and price controls only postpone a day of reckoning, and in so doing they rob every American of an important part of his freedom." Evaluate this statement on the basis of the American experience with the wage—price controls of August 1971.
4. "Wage and price controls can only 'hide' inflation — price increases will show up either in black markets, lower quality goods, or diversification by 'controlled' companies into uncontrolled sectors." Evaluate this claim.

43 WHAT WE SHOULD HAVE LEARNED ABOUT CONTROLS
Walter Guzzardi, Jr.

On August 16, 1971, President Nixon announced a wage–price freeze, followed by a period of various types of controls on wages and prices. Based on his evaluation of this experience, Walter Guzzardi concludes that controls are an ineffective and costly way of controlling inflation. Mr. Guzzardi is the author of The Young Executives *and a former vice-president of the brokerage firm of Merrill Lynch Pierce Fenner & Smith. Currently he is on the board of editors of* Fortune *magazine.*

In principle, just about everything is wrong with wage and price controls. They constitute a surrender of our basic beliefs in the efficiency of free and competitive markets, and in freedom of action for business and labor. By garbling the vital signals usually conveyed by the free pricing system, controls misallocate resources, create shortages, and deter capital investment. Delicate price relationships that have gained wide social acceptance are upset by controls; impossibly difficult moral judgments by men are substituted for the neutrality and anonymity of the marketplace. Regulations become ludicrously complex, and businessmen waste energy and ingenuity devising ways to circumvent them. Sometimes for brief periods, and especially when they are riding with deep currents in the economy, controls seem to be successful in reducing the inflation rate. This illusion may be their most damaging feature; it may encourage government officials to think that they can get away with inflationary monetary and fiscal policies — ensuring a price explosion later.

All these theoretical deficiencies of controls found practical expression during our recent dismal experience with them. This adventure began in exhilaration: on August 16, 1971, the day after President Nixon announced the wage–price freeze, the Dow Jones industrial average shot up thirty-three points on what was then an all-time record volume

Abridged from Walter Guzzardi, Jr., "What We Should Have Learned About Controls," *Fortune* (March 1975), 103 ff.

of 31.7 million shares traded. But the euphoria soon drained away. The elaborate structure of controls collapsed in confusion and defeat last year, when controls were mercifully ended.

THE BIGGEST FAILURE EVER

We now behold the aftermath of the great experiment. The economy [was] afflicted with the highest rate of inflation since a brief period following the end of World War II. The decline in real output of goods and services in 1974 was the sharpest since 1946. Surveying the ruins, George Schultz, former Secretary of the Treasury, whose usually influential voice was overruled when the decision for controls was made, describes the three years of controls as "the biggest failure in the history of economics."

The persistence of faith in controls, in the face of all the countervailing evidence, is in part explained by the dynamics of American politics. When Americans are outraged by inflation, and when elections are just around the corner — a particular coincidence occurring both in 1971 and 1975 — politicians are especially susceptible to the "do something" syndrome. So the air is blued with talk of controls.

But the demand for controls also has to be viewed as the triumph of an idea. For more than twenty-five years, that idea has been propounded by an eloquent and witty economist whose countless books and articles, promoted by a jet-set life-style, have made a wide public impression. John Kenneth Galbraith's arguments for controls have the attraction of simplicity. Galbraith concedes that controls would be useless or worse in a truly competitive economy. But he believes that our economy is shielded from competition by two great aggregates of power: big business and big labor, of which big business seems to be the greater sinner. These giants order prices upward, so that they can increase their profits and wages at public expense. The only preventive is to clamp controls on them.

Vital to Galbratih's thesis is the argument that wages and prices in "concentrated" industries — those in which large corporations with unionized labor have a major part of the market — set the level of prices for the economy at large. But this thesis presents several difficulties. Despite the high visibility of the auto, steel, and chemical industries, they represent only a corner of the total economy. Union labor represents only about 22 percent of the labor force. The industrialized sector, not all of which is "concentrated" anyway, comes to only about 28 percent of the economy at large. The service sector is much larger. It includes the services of lawyers and dentists and mechanics and repairmen — and, in view of the way their charges have gone up, it seems fair to conclude that their selflessness in fighting inflation has not been more notable than that of corporate or union executives.

Agriculture, so important to economic stability, is the property of neither big industrial operations nor big labor. And the biggest employer and the biggest consumer in the country is the government, whose power to print and spend money is the true engine of inflation. To control only corporations and labor unions, in short, is to stabilize a part of an immensity.

Furthermore, Galbraith's assumption that price increases come faster in concentrated industries is being rapidly destroyed by hard analysis. Detailed studies directed by J. Fred Weston, an economist at the Graduate School of Management at the University of California at Los Angeles, reveal that the concentrated industries show a "negative relationship between the degree of concentration and the percentage of price change."

WHAT DID YOU SAY A TRANSACTION WAS?

The thousand practical difficulties involved in controlling an economy as vast and dynamic as ours, with its wide dispersions and complex interactions, showed up from the first day of controls in 1971. The body of supreme controllers, the Cost of Living Council, was obliged to enforce a policy handed down from Camp David that prices during the August, 1971, freeze should be fixed at the level of "the substantial volume of actual transactions" occurring over the previous thirty days.

But Arnold Weber, the first executive director of the COLC, soon made a dismaying discovery:

"Transactions in the same category of goods or services often took place at different prices, and the term 'transaction' was itself imprecise."

CURIOUS BEHAVIOR OF CARS AND CABBAGES

Another source of frustration to the controllers arose from the undeniable but inconvenient truth that many products — cars and cabbages, to mention two — sell at different prices at different times of the year. The need for an adjustment for "seasonality" was easy to perceive, but hard to fill. Could resort hotels charge more over Labor Day than they charged over the Fourth of July? Was Halloween candy a seasonal product? Once quietly cared for by the free market, these problem children were now dumped bawling and squawking into the laps of mere men, who found them impossible to pacify.

From birth to death, the age of controls floundered hopelessly in agriculture's muddy fields. So many farms grow and sell so many different products on so many markets that to control them all would be expensive, complicated by "seasonality," and, even admitting the farmer's undying dedication to the national interest, probably unworkable. So raw farm products had to be exempted for the entire time that controls were in effect.

The result was administrative chaos. Was honey a "raw" food — or processed by the busy bees? What if the honey were strained or drained? What about fish and other seafood when "shelled, shucked, skinned, or sealed"? Since broilers were cut up and packaged before being sold, they were considered a processed food, and their price was frozen. When the price of feed went up, the farmer simply discontinued production; the nation was shocked at pictures of thousands of chicks being drowned.

Controls were also unable to cope with the complexities of the international economy:

At one juncture, the world price of zinc stood above the domestic price. To honor their commitments to their customers, domestic producers of zinc were selling at the lower price. But they had no incentive to expand the supply, and customers who didn't have commitments soon found themselves facing shortages.

Reinforcing bars, widely used in construction, are made from another internationally traded commodity, scrap steel. Controls on the bars were imposed at a time when the price was very low. But scrap was not controlled, out of fear that too much of it might be exported. Makers of the bars soon found the cost of their raw material shooting up and had no way to pass on the increases. Production was interrupted and construction hurt.

GUESSWORK BY GOVERNMENT

Phase II, which succeeded the freeze in mid-November, 1971, really amounted to an effort to substitute government judgments about prices for the sophisticated operation of the free pricing system. Phase II provided that a percentage of "allowable" cost increases could be "passed through" by corporations as price increases, but only after an application had been approved by the regulating authorities — a process that usually took several months. A ceiling was put on profit margins. Wage increases were limited to 5.5 percent, with "exceptions for gross inequalities." Hendrik Houthakker, a former member of the Council of Economic Advisers and a top economist at Harvard, points out that the ceiling on margins did indeed keep some efficient firms from raising their prices. But this had an unintended effect: it put the squeeze on smaller and less efficient companies. Some may have been driven into bankruptcy. Thus controls on profits may have increased concentration throughout the industrial sector.

AN UNKIND CUT FOR SERVICE

One hidden cost of controls was the time that managements spent in order to find ways to defeat them. In the lumber industry, some companies cut one-eighth of an inch off plywood sheets, described the cut as "a service," and then increased the price. Since domestic lumber was controlled but imported lumber was uncontrolled, lumber was "exported" and then "imported" — sometimes in fact, and

sometimes merely on paper while the lumber sat in the yards.

Corporate ingenuity also found other outlets. General Motors made some standard equipment into optional equipment on some models. Some companies introduced "superior" products at higher prices than the ones being replaced. Cheaper products were phased out, leaving only the more expensive available. Alternatively, many companies that kept their full line on the market achieved savings by allowing quality to deteriorate.

GRIEVANCES ON ALL SIDES

Looking back on their experience, large numbers of corporations say that they were hurt by price controls. Some 100 of 125 companies with annual revenues of over $50 million that responded to a questionnaire from the National Association of Manufacturers said they suffered "financial damage" because of controls. Virtually every one of them stated that it experienced "unusual difficulties" in getting important raw materials or supplies during controls.

Like business, labor also had means to fight controls, but also ended up claiming it was damaged. When Congress granted those retroactive wage increases and new provisions for fringe benefits in the Economic Stabilization Act Amendments of 1971, Congress was responding to labor's lobbying. In industry after industry — coal, railroads, and aerospace — settlements were made in excess of the 5.5 percent limit.

Claims of both business and labor about the unfairness of controls to each have to be appropriately discounted. The ultimate, hard question about controls is what they do to the inflation rate. And the short answer is that they make it worse.

In a free economy, the reasonable expectation of an adequate return is what attracts new capital. That capital is used for new and more efficient facilities that increase supply, meet growing demand, and provide an elemental anti-inflationary force. And to constrain prices discourages such investment.

A study by a leading New York bank shows that the gap between planned and actual cpaital spending was larger during the control years than at any other time since 1953. Alan Greenspan agrees strongly with the inference that controls were the principal deterrent to investment. Greespan believes that after the dollar was devalued in 1971, and the American steel industry became more competitive in world markets, a burst of badly needed capital investment would have gone into the domestic steel industry — had it not been for controls. Because of them, steel supplies in later years were less abundant and steel prices higher. Concludes Greenspan: "I argue that controls are not anti- but pro-inflationary."

Controls also keep prices high in other ways. When controls are on producers tend to keep their prices at the ceiling level. And when controls are anticipated, no business is likely to cut its list prices. In fact, when controls seemed imminent last fall, there was an immediate flurry of anticipatory price increases.

THE MARVEL DEMOLISHED

While the proof of what controls have done to inflation is all around us today, there were periods during the great experiment when things looked pretty good. At the end of the freeze, G.N.P. prices were increasing at only a 2.6 percent rate and the consumer price index at a rate of only 2.2 percent. But over the next three months, the post-freeze "bulge" wiped out the gains. The consumer price index's annual rate of increase doubled.

Toward the end of Phase II, controls once again seemed to be working pretty well. For all of 1972, the year of Phase II, both G.N.P. prices and the C.P.I. rose by only 3.4 percent. President Nixon's Economic Report to the Congress for that year hailed the controls program as "the marvel of the rest of the world."

But the marvel was scheduled for quick demolition. Some supporters of controls still insist that all would have gone well had Phase II been left in place. However, huge inflationary forces were building up in 1972, and no controls program could have contained them. In 1972 government policies provided for individual income-tax cuts, elimination of some

important excise taxes, and the effective devaluation of the dollar. Huge increases were made in the money supply; currency, demand deposits, and time deposits, which had grown at a rate of 7 percent for the second half of 1971, rose by 11 percent in 1972. The budget deficit was $23 billion for fiscal 1971 and another $23 billion for fiscal 1972. All this stimulus brought victories of a rather special sort: in the fall of 1972, Nixon won his election. The Dow broke 1,000.

In 1973, the bubble burst. The prices that deliver the message of excessive aggregate demand had been partly suppressed by controls, but [then,] controls or no, they made headlines. For the five months of Phase III, which first eased controls and then tried to tighten them, the C.P.I. rose at an annual rate of 8.3 percent. Food prices went up over 20 percent. Wholesale commodities went up 22.2 percent; wholesale farm produce jumped 48.9 percent. A frantically imposed freeze for sixty days beginning in mid-June, 1973, was halfhearted, ridiculed, and ineffective. Phase IV's effort to control areas in which price increases had been especially large — food, health care, insurance, petroleum — was futile. Every inflation indicator went through the roof in 1974. The great experiment was over.

THEY SHOULD HAVE TRIED HARDER

For the devout, all the aberrations born of controls, and the bad record they made, proved only the inadequacies of the controllers themselves. Galbraith has expressed the view that "any controls program run by Republicans is bound to be fouled up." Arthur Schlesinger Jr. remarked that "controls will work well only when administered by people who believe in them" — thus making it possible to explain every past failure, and every future one as well, by a shortfall of faith.

Controls never bring gains that are more than fleeting and illusory. And the price of these gains is added inflation.

QUESTIONS

1. "Price and wage controls intensify the forces of inflation." Comment.

2. What is the role of the labor union and the large corporation as contributors to inflation in the view of Messrs. Galbraith and Guzzardi?

3. What administrative complexities, if any, are involved in controlling prices?

44 INFLATION: AN ECLECTIC SOLUTION
Charles L. Schultze

If the causes of inflation are complex, there may be no single, simple solution to the problem of rising prices. Charles Schultze, formerly with the Brookings Institution and the economics faculty of the University of Maryland, is persuaded that inflation is a complicated phenomenon and requires a multi-pronged attack, including wage and price controls. Schultze was the director of the Bureau of the Budget in the Johnson administration and was President Jimmy Carter's choice to be chairman of his Council of Economic Advisers. The following is taken from testimony he gave to the Antitrust Subcommittee of the U.S. Senate.

In the announcement of these hearings, the subject of today's session was entitled, "Are there steps that make sense economically which would erase the need for wage and price controls?"

My short, and I hope, not unwelcome answer to this question is, "No." I am convinced that some sort of intervention by the Federal Government into the setting of wages and prices will for a long time to come be a necessary condition for simultaneously achieving full employment and reasonable price stability in our economy.

On the other hand, if the question were rephrased to ask whether there are economic measures which,

Abridged from Senate Committee on the Judiciary, *Controls or Competition,* Hearings before the Subcommittee on Antitrust and Monopoly, 92nd Congress, 2nd Session (Washington, D.C.: U.S. Government Printing Office, 1972), pp. 91–95.

while not erasing the need for controls, would reduce their rigor and severity and give them a better chance of success, then my answer would be, "Yes." I think there are economically sound measures which would moderate, even if they could not eliminate, the magnitude of the inflationary problem under high employment conditions.

In order to be more specific let me list and briefly discuss the major sets of economic conditions and industrial practices which either generate or perpetuate inflationary conditions.

Inflation can be generated and perpetuated by an excess demand for goods and services, a demand for goods and services larger than the economic capacity of the Nation to furnish them. When market demands are so high that the unemployment rate is pushed to very low levels; when the supply, particularly of experienced full-time workers in large sectors of the economy, becomes very tight so that employers are forced to bid up wages rapidly to get workers; when output presses hard on industrial capacity, inflation is bound to occur. Wages are bid up more rapidly than productivity gains, raw material prices soar, and on top of this, profit margins begin to widen, especially in competitive industries. But, paradoxically, inflation of this variety is not our major problem.

If inflation only occurred when, for one reason or another, the sum of consumer, business, and Government expenditures was excessive, the standard tools of monetary and fiscal policy could handle the situation by reducing this excessive overall level of demand. Mistakes might be made, and surely would be made, but there would be no reason for wage or price controls or for structural reforms introduced on grounds of inflation control alone. The only need [is] for better monetary and fiscal policies.

But the really intractable problem in our modern economy is that inflation occurs simultaneously with the existence of underutilized resources. In the current situation, an inflation which did indeed start with the overheated economy of the late 1960's has persisted for more than 2 years after the overheating disappeared, and persisted through a period of substantial unemployment. Earlier, in the mid-1950's we had significant inflation which began in the absence of economic overheating and continued for about 2 years, or slightly more.

There are, I think, five elements in the Nation's economic structure and habits which lead to the problem of inflation along with high unemployment:

First, there is the fact that in a large number of industries characterized by a high degree of economic concentration, prices tend to be rigid downward — they often do not fall when economic circumstances in a competitive environment would dictate that they should fall. This leads to two inflationary consequences:

1. Even under conditions of healthy and not excessive prosperity and economic growth, not all industries will experience the same rate of market expansion. Some markets will be expanding sharply, some moderately, and some will be falling. Costs and prices, we know, are likely to rise in industries whose markets are sharply advancing. If prices on the average are to remain stable, and that is what we mean by having no inflation, if prices on the average would remain stable, these price increases must be balanced by price cuts in industries whose markets are growing subnormally or are declining. This is what would happen in a competitive environment. But if prices in large concentrated industries are sticky, if they resist falling in periods of weak markets, then the price averages cannot fail to rise. In short, since some prices are always rising in a healthy economy, others must fall to preserve overall price stability. Paradoxically, therefore, unless some prices fall, the overall price index will assuredly rise, even when the economy as a whole is not overheated.

2. Productivity expands at widely differing rates among different industries. Bureau of Labor Statistics studies of productivity gains among individual industries confirm this fact. But the rise in wage rates among the different industries is much more uniform than the rise in productivity. As a consequence, if wages generally are to rise at a noninflationary rate — more or less in line with national productivity gains — then the unit labor costs of industries with greater than average productivity gains will fall. The above average productivity gains in these industries will be larger than the advance in

wages. As a consequence their prices should be reduced. If, however, prices are sticky downward in concentrated industries with higher than average productivity gains, then profit margins will widen. In turn, it is most unlikely that they will be allowed to go on unchallenged. Management will not let the margins rise too far above normal for fear of inviting unwanted new competition into the industry. Unions will seek to take the abnormal gains away and very often will succeed. Their success will be emulated by unions in other industries which do not have above-average productivity gains. And in turn, this will raise costs and prices in those other industries.

In summary, the failure of prices in concentrated industries to respond to downward economic pressures as they should can generate an inflationary bias in the economy; in part because some price cuts are always needed to balance the inevitable price increases, and in part because the failure to cut prices in response to large productivity gains invites excessive wage advances which tend to be emulated in other sectors of the economy.

The nature of wage bargaining is a second major factor producing inflationary bias. The so-called wage—wage spiral tends to perpetuate inflation once started. Union contracts typically cover periods of more than a year — 3-year contracts have become a common practice. A long-term contract signed during a period of economic overheating, say in 1968 or 1969, will usually contain a large wage increase, simply reflecting the inflationary conditions and tight labor market of the period. Subsequently, even when inflationary pressures subside and even if unemployment is rising, other unions signing new contracts will feel a necessity to win wage increases for their numbers equal to the wage won earlier by the first union. Settlements in such large industries as autos, steel, aluminum, aerospace, and can manufacturing influence each other. One large construction settlement, for a particular craft or in a particular locality, acts as a magnet for other crafts and other localities. Such mechanisms as the Davis—Bacon Act and the union contracts for public employees in many cities help spread these construction wage increases widely.

If inflation, once started, is ever to be brought under control the sheer arithmetic of the situation requires that contracts signed after an inflationary boom is over must contain lower wage advances than contracts signed earlier. But the wage—wage spiral and follow-the-leader union settlements substantially delay this period of adjustment and help perpetuate inflation long after labor markets have loosened up and excess capacity appears.

A third contributor to the current problem of inflation lies in the changing nature of the labor market; 15 years ago, when the overall unemployment rate was about 4 percent, about 30 percent of the unemployed were teenagers and young adults. In 1969, when the overall unemployment rate also averaged about 4 percent, half of the unemployed, 50 percent of them, were teenagers and young adults. Therefore, a smaller proportion of the unemployed are now skilled experienced adults than was true 15 years ago. To reach an average unemployment rate of 4 percent today would mean a much lower rate of unemployment among the core of the experienced labor force than was the case in earlier years. And it is the tightness of the labor market among such experienced adult workers which probably has the most sginificant impact on key wage bargains.

In short, 4 percent unemployment probably means tighter labor markets and larger wage increases than it did 10 or 15 years ago. Let me be very clear about it. This is not to say that we should abandon our attempts to reduce unemployment to 4 percent or less. But we do need to face the fact that at this overall unemployment level, 4-percent labor markets may be tighter and wage increases larger than they once were, and that specific manpower training and public employment programs may be needed to reduce the size of the inflationary problems which accompanies this fact.

A fourth set of factors which operates to produce inflationary bias in our economy relates to the price-fixing policies of the Federal Government itself. Transportation rate regulation which discourages rate reductions, expensive farm price supports, import quotas (both legal and voluntary), subsidies to an inefficient merchant marine, Davis—Bacon wage provisions in Government contracts, and many other similar cases, all operate in a generally inflationary direction, by reducing competition and putting relatively high floors under prices that contribute to the downward stickiness. Both Professor Weidenbaum and Professor Maltzer have covered this set of problems in their testimony. I need not repeat, but do wish to underscore, the importance of the point they make.

The fifth element of inflationary bias lies, I believe, in the ease with which highly concentrated industries pass on wage and other cost increases. Many observers have noted that these industries tend to follow target-rate-return pricing. During periods of economic overheating, they may raise prices by somewhat less than would be characteristic of competitive industries. But once monetary and fiscal policies succeed in throttling down the overheating in the economy, there is a tendency for inflationary price rises to be perpetuated by target-rates-of-return pricing. Despite weakening markets, firms with substantial market power continue to pass along cost increases fully. They do not absorb them very much or as much as they should. Their resistance to wage demands based on market conditions which no longer exist is weakened, because of their propensity to raise prices to cover the higher costs. Moreover, as sales level off while additional capacity continues to be installed, these industries sometimes attempt to recover their target return at a lower rate of capacity utilization. This occurred quite extensively during the 1956—57 inflation, 15 years ago. It is another factor which tends to perpetuate an inflation well past the period of economic overheating, and produce the paradox of general price increases during periods of less and sometimes substantially less than full employment.

All of these five features of our economic system interact with and reinforce each other. Follow-the-leader wage settlements help spread to other industries inflationary wage gains which arise when high productivity growth industries refuse to cut prices. The target-rate-of-return pricing helps perpetuate price increases long past the end of an economic boom and feeds back into wage increases through its effect on the cost of living. The total impact of these structural characteristics is greater than the sum of the individual parts.

An antitrust policy which concentrated explicitly on helping to reduce the inflationary bias in the economy would require important changes, I think, in traditional approaches. Anticompetitive behavior would have to be judged in terms of its departure from competitive pricing policy, particularly in terms of how prices in an industry behave in the face of softening markets or extra large productivity gains. Downward price rigidity would become a prima facie reason for viewing the industry structure with suspicion. The desirability of divestiture and the breaking up of large scale units would be judged in terms of its likely effect on price flexibility, not in terms of the particular practicies by which bigness had been attained or price rigidity maintained. I am not enough of an expert in antitrust matters to determine the extent to which this approach would require changes in the antitrust laws or could be carried out by a different execution of existing laws.

Let me close as I began. I believe that the current inflationary bias in the economy stems from a number of structural characteristics in our society. Not all of those structural characteristics can realistically be corrected by antitrust policy. If we are to have both full employment and reasonable price stability, some form of income policies will have to be around for the foreseeable future. But antitrust policy can attack some of the structural distortions in the economy; it can lessen, although not eradicate, the inflation which accompanies full employment; it can increase the likelihood that incomes policies will work. It can, therefore, help rescue economic policy from the cruel dilemma that it has been facing in recent years. A nation and its leaders should not be put in the terrible position of choosing between price stability and full employment. Both justice and economic efficiency require that we have both.

QUESTIONS

1. What factors does Schultze feel to be primarily responsible for inflationary price trends?
2. How might antitrust policy alleviate inflation in Schultze's view? How do his views of the role for antitrust contrast with those of Galbraith?
3. Why do differing productivity rates between industries contribute to the inflation problem?

45 THE ECONOMICS OF THE NEW UNEMPLOYMENT
Martin Feldstein

The economist's view of unemployment differs from the treatment usually given the problem by journalists and politicians. One of the most careful students of the nature of unemployment is Harvard University's Martin Feldstein; his research merits close attention. This paper is based on a study originally performed for the Joint Economic Committee of the U.S. Congress. Professor Feldstein is known for his ingenious techniques of analyzing and measuring such economic phenomena as unemployment, health care, social security, and fiscal policy.

A high level of unemployment is a persistent problem of the American economy. During the past 20 years, the average rate of unemployment exceeded 4.5 per cent. In only one post-War year (1953) did unemployment drop below three per cent. Although every segment of society is affected, some groups have unemployment rates that are several times as high as the national average. At the end of the first half of 1972, more than nine per cent of the non-white labor force was unemployed. Among men under 25, the unemployment rate was 11.5 per cent. These high unemployment rates imply substantial personal and aggregate losses. Moreover, as I shall emphasize below, the American pattern of unemployment is a symptom of a more serious failure in the development and use of our national manpower.

Reprinted with permission of Martin Feldstein from *The Public Interest*, No. 33. Fall 1973, pp. 3—42. Copyright © 1973 by National Affairs, Inc.

Unfortunately, there is no reason to expect that the next 20 years will be better than the last. Without substantial new policy initiatives, American unemployment rates will remain significantly higher than those that prevail in Western Europe and in most other industrial nations.

THE LIMITED EFFICACY OF INCREASING DEMAND

Most macroeconomic analyses of unemployment are based on ideas about the causes and structure of unemployment that are inappropriate and out of date. The basic framework of Keynesian economics, conditioned by the experience of the 1930's, has always emphasized the inadequacy of aggregate demand as the source of unemployment. The conventional view of post-War unemployment might be described as follows: "The growth of demand for goods and services does not always keep pace with the expansion of the labor force and the rise in output per man. Firms therefore lay off employees and fail to hire new members of the labor force at a sufficient rate. The result is a pool of potential workers who are unable to find jobs. Only policies to increase the growth of demand can create the jobs needed to absorb the unemployed."

This picture of a hard core of unemployed workers who are not able to find jobs is an inaccurate description of our economy and a misleading basis for policy. A more accurate description is an active labor market in which almost everyone who is out of work can find his usual type of job in a relatively short time. *The problem is not that these jobs are unavailable but that they are often unattractive.* Much of the unemployment and even more of the lost manpower occurs among individuals who find that the available jobs are neither appealing in themselves nor rewarding as pathways to better jobs in the future. For such individuals, job attachment is weak, quitting is common, and periods without work or active job seeking are frequent. *The major problem to be dealt with is not a chronic shortage of jobs but the instability of individual employment.* Decreasing the overall rate of unemployment requires not merely more jobs, but new incentives to encourage those who are out of work to seek employment more actively and those who are employed to remain at work. As I shall explain below, an important part of these incentives is a change in the kinds of jobs that are available.

It is difficult to replace our old notions about demand-determined unemployment by this new view. Let me therefore describe in more detail some of the characteristics of American unemployment during the past decade. I will begin with the experience of the total labor force and then consider differences among demographic groups.

First, the duration of unemployment is quite short. Even in a year like 1971 with a very high unemployment rate, 45 per cent of those unemployed had been out of work for less than five weeks. In 1969, this proportion was almost 58 per cent. Similarly, very few are without jobs for as long as 27 weeks; in 1969 this was 4.7 per cent and in 1971 it was 10.4 per cent of all the unemployed.

Second, loss of jobs accounts for less than half of total unemployment. In 1971, only 46 per cent of the unemployed had lost their previous jobs. In the more favorable market conditions of 1969, this proportion was only 36 percent. The remainder are those who voluntarily left their last jobs, are reentering the labor force, or never worked before. In 1969, with an overall unemployment rate of 3.5 per cent, losing one's job contributed only 1.2 per cent to this figure.

Third, the turnover of jobs is exremely high. Data collected from manufacturing establishments show that total hirings and separations have each exceeded four per cent of the labor force per month since 1960. Moreover, the number of quits has consistently exceeded layoffs during the past five years. Even with the high unemployment of 1971, more workers quit manufacturing jobs than were laid off.

A comparison of these figures with corresponding data for Great Britain indicates that the British achieve a generally lower unemployment rate partly by having a very different structure of unemployment. During the 1960's, Britain's average unemployment rate (as adjusted by the U.S. Department of Labor to the U.S. definition) was only 2.7 per

Table 1. *Differences in Unemployment Experience Among Demographic Groups*

Demographic Group	I Unemployment Rate, 1971	II Sensitivity To Rate of Mature Men	III Unemployment Rate When Mature Men[1] Unemployment Is 1.5 Per Cent
Males, 16—19	16.7	1.45	11.4
Females, 16—19	17.4	0.26	13.7
Whites, 16—19	15.2	1.03	10.8
Non-whites, 16—19	31.8	0.26	24.5
Males, white, 20+	4.0	0.92	1.7
Males, non-white, 20+	7.3	2.33	3.3
Females, white, 20+	5.3	0.59	3.2
Females, non-white, 20+	8.7	0.99	6.1

[1]The mature men unemployment rate refers to all men over age 24.

cent. The structure of British unemployment corresponds more closely to the traditional picture of cyclically inadequate demand, chronic structural unemployment in particular regions, and a very low level of "frictional" job search. Despite the lower overall unemployment rate, British durations of unemployment are much longer. While 13.6 per cent of unemployed men were out of work for 27 weeks or more in the United States in 1971, in Britain the corresponding figure was 23.8 per cent in a recent period of high unemployment (April 1969). Similarly, while only five eighths of American unemployed men were out more than five weeks, in Britain the same fraction of men was out more than eight weeks. This longer duration is compatible with a much lower overall unemployment rate only because many fewer men become unemployed in the first place. One indication of this is that British turnover rates are approximately half of U.S. levels. Britain achieves a low unemployment rate by completely avoiding much of the short-term unemployment that prevails in the United States. Some of the specific ways in which this [occurs] will be examined later in this article.

DEMOGRAPHIC DIFFERENCES

Perhaps the most important characteristic of our current unemployment problem is the differences in unemployment experience among demographic groups. The unemployment rates in certain groups are not only very high but are also quite unrespon-

sive to changes in the aggregate demand for labor. This implies that fiscal and monetary policies that drastically cut the unemployment rate of mature men would still leave a high overall unemployment rate.

To study these differences I have estimated the relation between the unemployment rate in each demographic group and the concurrent unemployment rate for men over 24 years of age. This rate for mature men provides one of the best measures of cyclical variation in labor market pressure. Table 1 presents the results of this analysis. Column I gives the 1971 unemployment rates in eight different demographic groups, ranging from four per cent for white men to 32 per cent for non-white teenagers. Column II shows the sensitivity of each unemployment rate to labor market pressure (i.e., the change in that specific unemployment rate that would occur when the rate for men over 24 years of age changes by one per cent). For example, a one per cent fall in the unemployment rate for mature men would lower the teenage male unemployment rate by about 1.5 per cent. A change in aggregate demand, therefore, has a greater absolute effect on the teenage unemployment rate than on the rate for mature men. Nevertheless, variations in aggregate demand account for a relatively small fraction of the high level of teenage male unemployment. Even if the rate for mature men were depressed to 1.5 per cent — below the level reached at any time in the post-War period — the analysis implies that the male teenage rate would be at about 11.4 per cent. This is shown in Column III. Although the absolute sensitivity of male teenage unemployment to changes in aggregate demand is a serious problem, it is the very high level of the cyclical troughs that prevents macroeconomic policy from reducing that unemployment to a level below five per cent.

The figures reported in Table 1 indicate that overall unemployment would remain high even in a very tight labor market, but they do not explain why individual unemployment rates behave so differently. Some understanding of this at a relatively crude empirical level can be obtained by examining the proportions of the unemployed in different demographic groups who are job leavers, job losers, new entrants, and reentrants.

Finally, non-white unemployment rates are higher in every category, but again job loss accounts for less than half of total unemployment. Even though non-whites have more difficulty in finding employment, unemployment due to voluntary separations and withdrawals from the labor force is approximately twice the level for whites.

The evidence presented in this section can be summarized briefly: *The current structure of unemployment in the American economy is not compatible with the traditional view of a hard core of unemployed who are unable to find jobs.* Even with the high unemployment rate of 1971, the durations of unemployment were short, job losers accounted for less than half of unemployment, and quit rates generally exceeded layoffs. An examination of the past experience of individual demographic groups indicates very substantial variation in the response of unemployment rates to aggregate demand and implies that even an extremely tight labor market would leave some groups with high unemployment rates. The next three sections examine why these unemployment rates are not more sensitive to aggregate demand and suggest possible policies to deal with these problems.

UNEMPLOYMENT AMONG YOUNG WORKERS

Unemployment rates for young persons seem outrageously high. In 1971, male teenagers had an unemployment rate of 16.6 per cent. Even among

those aged 20 through 24, the unemployment rate was 10.3 per cent. If unemployment in these groups could be reduced to the same rate as for mature men, the overall rate would fall by more than one third.

Youth unemployment is not primarily due to inadequate demand. The statistical analysis described above indicates that the unemployment rate of young persons would remain high even in a very tight labor market. There are two main sources of the chronic high unemployment in this age range: (1) unnecessarily slow absorption of new entrants and (2) low job attachment among those at work. Because of the slow absorption, a very significant part of the unemployment of young workers is among new entrants to the labor force and others who are seeking their first full-time job.

The single most effective way of reducing unemployment among new entrants as well as improving the quality of first jobs would probably be the establishment of a special Youth Employment Service. The British experience with such a program suggests its potential impact in America. In a recent year in which approximately 280,000 boys between 15 and 17 entered the labor force, the Youth Employment Service arranged 200,000 employment placements for boys in that age group. While some of these placements are not for new entrants, the magnitude of the British achievement is enormous. Part of their success is due to their direct contact with students: Nearly 80 per cent of school leavers who are not going to universities are interviewed in school by the Youth Employment Service.

THE INSTABILITY OF TEENAGE EMPLOYMENT

The second source of unemployment — the high rate at which young men and women lose jobs, quit jobs, and drop out of the labor force — is both a more serious problem and a more difficult one to solve. Much of the unemployment among experienced young workers occurs not because jobs are unavailable but because they are unattractive. For many young workers, the available entry-level jobs are also dead-end jobs. They offer neither valuable training nor opportunities for significant advancement within the firm. Since employers have made no investment in these workers, they do not hesitate to lay them off whenever demand falls. Since comparable jobs are easy to find, these young workers do not hesitate to quit. The growth of our economy during the past few decades now permits relatively high wages even for those with entry-level jobs. Among the young and single, these high wages encourage an increased demand for leisure. If the content of the job and the structure of the firm's employment policy do not outweigh this, job attachment will be weak and quit rates high.

All of the evidence points to this highly unstable character of employment, rather than to any long-term difficulty in finding jobs, as the primary source of unemployment among experienced young workers.

STUDENTS AND NON-STUDENTS

Why is employment so unstable and labor force attachment so weak in this age range? Why do young American workers experience unemployment rates so much higher than those of their British counterparts?

Part of the high quit rates and rates of leaving the labor force merely reflect the impact of our educational system and the seasonal character of the labor force activity of students. Those who have not stopped their formal education seek full-time employment when schools are closed and many also seek different part-time jobs during the school year. Since attending school is the major activity of more than 23 per cent of the labor force between 16 and 21 years of age, the peculiar labor market behavior of that group has a substantial impact on the statistical picture of youth unemployment. If those who are looking only for part-time work are not counted in the unemployed, the unemployment rate for 16–21 year olds in 1971 drops from 15.0 per cent to 10.2 per cent. Moreover, many of those who leave school and take jobs later return to being full-time students. High unemployment among young Americans is therefore in part a reflection of our commitment to providing many more years of

schooling than is common in other countries, and is a price we pay for a very fluid educational system which encourages people to move back and forth between full-time work and full-time education.

In considering the gap between the unemployment rates of young persons and of more mature workers, it is important not to lose sight of their differences in motivation and attitudes. Most young workers have no family responsibilities and many continue to live with their parents. It is significant that the 1971 unemployment rate for 16–24 year old males who were classified as "household heads" was only 6.4 per cent while all others in this age–sex group had an unemployment rate over 16 per cent. Although today's high wage rates provide a substantial reward for working, they also permit a comfortable standard of living with significantly less work or less responsible work than was required 20 years ago. Many young persons want more leisure than is consistent with full-time employment and a permanent attachment to a particular firm. They prefer to alternate between working and other activities rather than to seek and hold permanent employment. These remarks are not intended as criticism. The behavior of these young persons is seen in better perspective by comparison with our student population. The major activity of over 40 per cent of 16–21 year olds is attending school. The academic schedule provides frequent long vacations. For those in higher education, the daily routine is varied and the individual is generally free to choose his own activities and pace of work. Perhaps much of the high turnover and voluntary labor force withdrawal among young non-students reflects an attempt to enjoy the same freedom and occupational irresponsibility that we take for granted in our student population of the same age.

THE MINIMUM WAGE AND OPPORTUNITIES FOR TRAINING

At the root of this problem is the hard economic reality that firms cannot afford to offer useful on-the-job training to a broad class of young employees. A firm can generally provide the opportunity to acquire new marketable skills — by on-the-job training, detailed supervision, or even just learning by experience — only to a worker whose net product *during the period of training* is at least equal to his wage. Unfortunately, the current minimum wage law prevents many young people from accepting jobs with low pay but valuable experience. Those who come to the labor market with substantial skills and education need not be affected by the minimum wage. They are productive enough to permit employers to pay at least the minimum wage while also providing further training and opportunities for advancement. But for the disadvantaged young worker, with few skills and below-average eduaction, producing enough to earn the minimum wage is incompatible with the opportunity for adequate on-the-job learning. For this group, the minimum wage implies high short-run unemployment and the chronic poverty of a life of low-wage jobs.

The burden of this effect of the minimum wage law falls most heavily on the disadvantaged. Because they bring little to the labor market, they are able to obtain little in exchange. It is clear from the few successful programs in training the disadvantaged that for some time these workers produce little if any net revenue over the costs of training. A job at the minimum wage will not permit any significant amount of training. The disadvantaged youth for whom more formal education is unsuitable is therefore forced into dead-end jobs without training or opportunities for advancement. In the short run, this means high absenteeism, high quit rates, and high turnover. The long-run effects are even more serious. The lack of additional training for those who start with low skills makes them part of the permanent poor. For the disadvantaged, the minimum wage law may have the ironic effect of lowering lifetime incomes by a very large amount.

Some unemployment is, of course, the inevitable consequence of a healthy and dynamic economy. The changing mix of output and the process of technological advance displace workers who generally become temporarily unemployed. Families occasionally migrate to new areas in order to find better employment opportunities and then spend time searching for work. All of these sources of unemployment produce important gains for the economy and often for the unemployed themselves. It is clear that they should not be discouraged. In particular, it is important to avoid the temptation — to which other countries have sometimes succumbed — to prevent temporary unemployment by permanent subsidies for unwanted output and inefficient technology.

Although some unemployment among adults is appropriate, the actual unemployment rates among experienced men clearly represent an undesirable and unnecessary waste of resources.

FOUR SOURCES OF ADULT UNEMPLOYMENT

Unemployment among mature workers reflects several distinct problems. It is useful to distinguish and analyze the implications of four different sources of adult unemployment: (1) the cyclical and seasonal volatility of the demand for labor; (2) the weak labor force attachment of some groups of workers; (3) the particular difficulty in finding permanent employment for persons with very low skills or other employment disabilities; and (4) the average of several months of unemployment among job losers.

Cyclical and Seasonal Variation in Demand The American unemployment rate is not only higher than the rates observed in foreign countries but also much more cyclically volatile. During the 1960's, the total U.S. unemployment rate varied from 3.5 per cent to 6.7 per cent. The cyclical variation in unemployment — the gap between peak and trough — was 3.2 per cent. The unemployment rate was nearly twice as high in the worst year as in the best. During the same decade, the corresponding British unemployment rate (adjusted to U.S. definitions) varied from 2.1 to 3.4 per cent. The cyclical variation was only 1.3 per cent, substantially less than half of the U.S. gap.

A variety of special schemes might be developed in the United States to encourage firms to reduce the sensitivity of employment to changes in aggregate demand: required minimum notice before employees are laid off, large compulsory severance payments, a guaranteed annual wage, substantial tax penalties (or rewards) for volatile (or stable) employment, and the like. Similar policies have already been adopted by some European countries; however, such actions can only lower the volatility of unemployment by reducing the efficiency of the labor market and therefore lowering real wages. There is no reason for the government to impose a lower wage and correspondingly greater employment security than the employees themselves actually want.

Weak Labor Force Attachment Unemployment caused by weak labor force attachment is generally a smaller but more serious problem among adults than among young workers. While some of the unemployed adults who are not seeking permanent employment are still students or are mothers with young children, the social problems are associated with the group with low skills and little education. These adults suffer from the same limited opportunities as some of the young workers described in the last section. Because they have low skills, little education, and generally bad work habits, they never enter the mainstream of employment opportunities. The only jobs open to them are the dead-end jobs with low pay and no future.

High unemployment among the men and women in this "secondary labor market" reflects their rejection of the jobs that are available. Many of those with very limited job opportunities prefer to remain unemployed rather than accept what they consider undesirable jobs. Many others who take these jobs soon quit.

Boston's experience with trying to secure employment for a large group of such low-skill workers dramatically illustrates that the problem is not providing jobs but making these jobs acceptable to the unemployed. During the eight months beginning in September 1966, Boston's ABCD program referred some 15,000 disadvantaged workers to jobs. Seventy per cent were actually offered jobs. Nearly half of the job offers — 45 per cent — were rejected. Of those who did accept work, less than half remained on the job for one month. A very high proportion

of these separations were voluntary. Even among those over age 25 who were being paid more than $1.75 per hour in 1967, the separation rate in the first month was 33 per cent.

What can be done to reduce unemployment among low-skilled adult workers? It is clear that the problem cannot be solved by increasing aggregate demand in order to create more jobs. There is no evidence of a shortage of jobs for this group. The Boston experience shows that jobs can be found but that they will not be accepted. *Lowering the rate of unemployment requires steps to bring the characteristics of the actual jobs and the standards of the acceptable jobs closer together.*

Manpower Programs and Voluntary Non-Employment Recognition of these limits of expansionary macroeconomic policies has encouraged the creation of several major manpower programs during the past decade. All these programs share the common philosophy that the best way to reduce non-employment in the groups designated as disadvantaged is to provide training that can improve the quality of jobs open to them.

Despite 10 years of experience with these large programs, there has been no clear and definitive evaluation of their impact. We do not know whether unemployment rates are lower and participation rates higher for those who have enrolled in a manpower program than for those with the same characteristics of age, sex, education, etc., who have not.

Both macroeconomic policies and manpower programs seek to reduce non-employment by making the available work more attractive. It is important not to lose sight of the fact that the extent of voluntary non-employment also depends on the attractiveness of not working. Today's welfare rules are a notorious deterrent to work for those who are receiving welfare. Moreover, the rapid rise during the last decade in the value of public assistance available to a family with little or no earnings — including cash payments, Medicaid, food stamps, and housing subsidies — has substantially increased the attractiveness of non-employment or intermittent employment for those with low skills. The increased levels of unemployment compensation also encourage intermittent work, especially among the two-earner families.

The Current Unemployables In addition to those who are cyclically unemployed or voluntarily out of work, there is a substantial residue of unemployables who would be unable to find steady employment even in a very tight labor market. Permanent physical disability, subnormal intelligence, or psychological problems severely limit the productivity of these men and women. The problem is most serious among those with both a physical impairment and limited education. Law and custom prevent firms from lowering wages to the levels at which it would pay to hire handicapped individuals.

Although vocational rehabilitation could improve the prospects for some of them, in many cases — especially among those who are older and less educated — the costs of additional training would exceed the benefits. *Two forms of job creation for these permanently disadvantaged workers have been suggested: subsidies to firms and direct permanent public employment.*

Duration of Unemployment A worker who is laid off often does not accept the first job offer in his own line of work but investigates several job possibilities over a period of weeks before accepting new employment. Part of this process of searching is information gathering. The worker who has not recently been unemployed generally does not know what wage and working conditions his own skills and experience will command in the market. He spends time locating relevant jobs and learning about them. Part of the search also consists of delaying in the expectation that the next job offer may be better. The greater the individual's uncertainty and the greater the variance of wage rates and working conditions in his relevant market, the longer he will tend to search.

Not all unemployment can be interpreted as conscious or unconscious search. Some skilled workers and union members know just what the local market wage is in their occupation and prefer to wait until such work becomes available rather than accept alternative work at lower pay. Some workers are waiting to be rehired into the same job from which they were temporarily laid off because of a seasonal or cyclical fall in demand or because of scheduling problems. Some workers, especially those with severe handicaps, are not able to find any employment. At the other extreme, some of those who report themselves as unemployed and looking for work are actually temporarily out of the labor force and not interested in finding employment.

Any reduction in the mean duration of unemployment would lower the average unemployment rate. *A fall of one month in the average duration of unemployment would lower the unemployment rate from 4.5 per cent to less than 3.0 per cent. Even a two-week reduction would reduce the unemployment rate by 0.75 per cent.* Those who stress the importance of search activity suggest that the duration of unemployment could be reduced by improving the flow of job market information. The computerized "job banks" recently developed by the Department of Labor are a primary example of how this might be done.

The duration of unemployment also depends on the cost to the unemployed of remaining out of work. Our current system of unemployment compensation substantially reduces — indeed often almost completely eliminates — the cost of temporary unemployment.

THE EFFECTS OF UNEMPLOYMENT COMPENSATION

Consider a worker in Massachusetts in 1971 with a wife and two children. He earns $500 per month or $6000 per year if he experiences no unemployment. She earns $350 per month or $4200 per year if she experiences no unemployment. If he is unemployed for one month, he loses $500 in gross earnings but less than $100 in net income. How does this occur? A reduction of $500 in annual earnings reduces his federal income tax by $83, his Social Security payroll tax by $26, and his Massachusetts income tax by $25. The total reduction in taxes is $134. Unemployment compensation consists of 50 percent of his wage plus dependents' allowances of $6 per week for each child. Total unemployment compensation is therefore $302. This payment is not part of taxable income. His net income therefore falls from $366 for the month if he is employed (i.e., his $500 gross earnings less $134 in taxes) to the $302 paid as unemployment compensation. *The combination of taxes and unemployment compensation imposes an effective marginal tax rate of 87 per cent* — i.e., the man's net earnings fall by only 13 per cent of his gross pay ($64) when he is unemployed for a month. The same very high marginal rate continues for several more months. If he returns to work after one month, his annual net income is only $128 higher than if he returns after three months. Moreover, part of this increase in income would be offset by the cost of transportation to work and other expenses associated with employment.

If the man does not become unemployed but his wife loses her job, the implied marginal rate may be even higher. If she is unemployed for three months, her gross earnings fall by $1050 but the family's net income may fall by only $72. The fall in earnings reduces taxes by $297 while the unemployment compensation provides $525 in regular benefits and an additional $156 in dependents' benefits. *The effective marginal tax rate is over 93 per cent. If the family has three children instead of two, the family's net income is actually higher if the woman is unemployed for three months than if she works for that period.*

There is little room for doubt about the qualitative conclusion that our current system of unemployment compensation increases the rate and duration of unemployment. Although the magnitude of this effect is unknown, it should be emphasized that rather small changes in the duration of unemployment, the cyclical and seasonal fluctuation in labor demand, and the frequency of temporary jobs can have a very important impact on the overall rate of unemployment. A reduction of two weeks in the current average duration of three months would by itself lower the overall rate of unemployment by 0.75 per cent. If one third of the seasonal unemployment were avoided, the overall unemployment rate would fall by an additional 0.25 per cent. If

the cyclical variation in labor demand were also reduced by 20 per cent, this would reduce unemployment by another 0.25 per cent. A decrease in the number of casual temporary jobs would have a further impact. Although each of these changes is small, the total effect is a fall in the unemployment rate of more than 1.25 per cent. These numbers should not be interpreted as specific estimates of the extent to which our current system of unemployment compensation raises the unemployment rate. They should be viewed as illustrations of the powerful cumulative effect of small changes in the several sources of adult unemployment. It is quite possible, however, that the disincentive effects of our current system are responsible for at least this much increased unemployment.

Reducing the Rate of Unemployment All the analysis in the current study supports the conclusion that our permanent rate of unemployment can be lowered substantially without inducing an unacceptable rate of inflation. It is important to recognize, however, that macroeconomic policy is unlikely to lower the permanent rate of unemployment much below the 4.5 per cent that has prevailed during the post-War period. Nevertheless, a series of specific policies could reduce the unemployment rate for those seeking permanent full-time employment to a level significantly below three per cent and perhaps closer to two per cent.

Speeding the absorption of young workers into employment and stabilizing their employment through better on-the-job training could lower the overall unemployment rate by at least 0.5 per cent. The current minimum wage law prevents many young people from obtaining jobs with low pay but valuable experience. Reducing the minimum wage for young workers might be useful but it would not be sufficient. A more effective policy would emphasize Youth Employment Scholarships that temporarily supplement earnings and allow young workers to "buy" better on-the-job training.

Better management of aggregate demand has a more important role to play in lowering adult unemployment than in improving the teenage employment situation. Nevertheless, even here macroeconomic policy can only achieve a small part of the total possible reduction in unemployment. The current system of unemployment compensation encourages excessive delays in returning to work. It also provides both employers and employees with the incentive to organize production in a way that increases the level of unemployment by making the seasonal and cyclical variation in unemployment too large and by making temporary jobs too common. A restructuring of the unemployment compensation system could reduce the unemployment resulting from cyclical and seasonal instability and from unnecessarily long duration between jobs by an additional 1.25 per cent or more. Further desirable reductions in unemployment could be achieved by subsidizing wages or incomes for handicapped workers and others with very low skills. There is, in short, no reason to allow the high average rate of unemployment that has prevailed in the post-War period to continue in the future.

QUESTIONS

1. What is the distinction Professor Feldstein draws between the new unemployment and the old?
2. What distinctions are there in unemployment rates between different age, sex, and racial groups in the American economy? What accounts for these differences? In particular, what accounts for the unemployment rate among young people in the U.S. economy? What measures are suggested to reduce this rate?
3. What impact does unemployment insurance have upon unemployment in the United States?
4. What evidence does the author provide to support this statement that the American economy does not have a "hard core of unemployed who are unable to find jobs"?

46 A PERSPECTIVE ON STAGFLATION
John J. Seater

At one time it was popular to speak of a tradeoff between inflation and unemployment: Less of one was had at the expense of more of the other. But when Americans found both phenomena increasing concurrently, the term "stagflation" was utilized. John J. Seater of the Philadelphia Federal Reserve Bank has written a helpful analysis of the stagflation problem. This reading first appeared in the bank's Business Review.

Conventional economic wisdom holds that inflation and unemployment aren't supposed to increase at the same time. We're supposed to face a tradeoff — more of one and less of the other. Yet when both unemployment and inflation rise, there appears to be no tradeoff, only the worst of both worlds. This phenomenon — dubbed stagflation — is frustrating everyone. We're stuck with stagflation and economists have trouble explaining it, let alone knowing how to cure it.

An increasingly popular school of thought, however, holds that stagflation is neither inexplicable nor uncontrollable. This band of economists argues that stagflation is based on the old standbys of rational economic behavior — supply and demand, and monetary and fiscal policies. Hence, its cure must have the same foundations.

THE TYPES OF UNEMPLOYMENT

Getting to the whys and wherefores of stagflation requires an understanding of the three types of unemployment.

Even in the best of times, there are the voluntarily unemployed — people who have just entered the labor force or have quit their jobs to look for something better. These people, who choose to pass up low-paying or distasteful jobs in order to search for

Abridged from John J. Seater, "A Perspective on Stagflation," Federal Reserve Bank of Philadelphia *Business Review* (May 1975), 19—31.

higher-paying or more enjoyable jobs, are said to be *frictionally unemployed.*

Another group of unemployed consists of those who have been fired because of structural changes in the economy. For example, consumers may decide to buy fewer books and more TV sets. This means that some editors will be thrown out of work, and more electrical workers will be hired. Such structural changes occur continually, and it takes time for the newly unemployed to find jobs. These people are the *structurally unemployed.*

When the number of frictionally and structurally unemployed equals the number of job vacancies in the economy, unemployment can be said to be at its "natural rate," and the economy can be said to be at full employment. There are enough jobs around for the unemployed; the unemployed just don't fit the jobs. By this definition, full employment does not mean no unemployment; it means no unemployment *in excess of (or below!)* the natural rate.

A third type of unemployment, which we can call *excess unemployment,* arises when the total demand for the economy's goods and services (aggregate demand) falls below the sum of everything business wishes to produce (aggregate supply). For example, consumers decide to save more and spend less; in particular, suppose they decide to buy fewer automobiles. Then automobile producers, finding their cars unsold, will lay off workers. Unlike structural unemployment, excess unemployment is not matched by increases in vacancies because demand is not merely shifting from one market to another; it is decreasing in the total of all markets. So when aggregate demand falls below aggregate supply, the number of unemployed exceeds the number of vacancies.

Government can eliminate excess unemployment by applying monetary and fiscal policies that stimulate total demand — increasing the money supply, increasing Government spending, and reducing taxes. As demand increases, producers hire idle labor. However, once unemployment reaches its natural rate, the Federal Government cannot permanently reduce it further with just monetary and fiscal policies. When this is attempted, unemployment dips

temporarily, then bounces back to its natural rate. The rate of inflation, however, rises to a new level and stays there.

HISTORICAL PERSPECTIVE

In 1970, about when the current criticisms of economics and talk of stagflation began, the unemployment rate averaged 4.9 percent, almost equal to the assumed natural rate, but up from the low 3.5 percent rate of 1969. In 1974 the average unemployment rate was 5.6 percent. However, since 1913 there have been nine years outside the Great Depression which had unemployment rates higher than 1974's rate.

The extraordinary development of 1974 was not so much that the rates of unemployment and inflation were high, but rather that they rose simultaneously. Actually, this situation was not unprecedented; it has occurred six times before in this century.

AN EXPLANATION OF STAGFLATION

One explanation of stagflation that has gained favor among economists, though it is not universally accepted, holds that there are two parts to the stagflation story — unemployment and its relation to what business wants to produce (or, aggregate supply), and inflation expectations and their relation to what people want to buy (or, aggregate demand).

Unemployment Let's begin with unemployment. Unemployment rises above its natural rate when, because of some shock to the economy, aggregate supply exceeds aggregate demand. "Too much" is being produced or, as economists say, there is "excess aggregate supply." Whenever producers face excess aggregate supply, they lay off workers and curtail production, thereby tending to eliminate the oversupply of goods. However, the laid-off workers, suddenly finding their incomes reduced, curtail their spending. These cutbacks in turn reduce aggregate demand, so that producers still find they are producing "too much," which sets off another round of layoffs. Eventually, because of what economists call the multiplier, this process stops with the economy left in a state of lower output and higher unemployment. Recession has set in.

That prices may rise rather than fall during a recession — as in 1958, 1961, 1971, and 1974 — needs explanation. Indeed, these bouts of stagflation seem to contradict basic economic theory. Recessions are characterized by too much production relative to demand, and the textbook response to excess supply is a drop in prices. So, how can prices rise during a recession? The answer to this question seems to lie in people's *expectations* about future prices.

Expectations   People learn from experience. If they observe that prices have been rising at a constant rate for a long time they will come to believe that prices will continue to rise at that rate in the future — in other words, people will anticipate the inflation. Let's see how this relates to their economic behavior. Let's suppose that people change their expectations so that they suddenly anticipate higher inflation in the future. For example, suppose people were previously anticipating no inflation but now become convinced that a 10-percent price rise is more likely. They then figure their money will be worth less in the future than it is today. Since it will buy more today than it will tomorrow, they are better off spending their money now. If the economy is near full employment, this attempt to accelerate buying will jack up demand and drive up prices today. Changes in expectations about *future* prices therefore affect *today's* prices.

At the outset of inflation, however, people are unlikely to change their outlook for future price increases very rapidly. The reason is they cannot be sure at first that the price changes are permanent rather than temporary. If inflation persists, however, people will build more and more of it into their expectations, and in time they will completely adjust to it. At that point, when people fully anticipate inflation, the rate of inflation tends to level off.

A Theory of Stagflation   Stagflation gets underway as people revise their expectations about inflation and try to take additional steps to protect themselves from it. Once way they can protect themselves is to try to buy today what will cost more tomorrow. But with everybody playing the same game, more buying pressure is put on the economy and today's prices turn out to be higher than they otherwise would be.

Unemployment increases for a slightly different and more complicated reason, however. At first, people are "fooled" by increased inflation and take jobs they wouldn't ordinarily take in a less inflationary economy. But after a while, they catch on to their "errors" and revert to their old behavior.

Let's see how that can happen by taking a simple example of Sam Searcher, diligent job seeker. Sam lives in an environment where prices have been increasing at about 2 percent a year for sometime, so that everyone expects that this rate is likely to continue into the future. The unemployment rate is 4.8 percent (the presumed natural rate), and unfortunately Sam is one of the frictionally unemployed. Suppose that the Government pursues expansionary monetary and fiscal policies to bring unemployment to 3 percent — well below the natural rate. Since there is no "slack" in the economy, the effect of these stimulative policies must be a general rise in prices, say, on the order of 10 percent. Most of the increase in prices will be unanticipated, because people are expecting a 2-percent inflation based on past experience. What effect will this have on unemployment? Let's see what Sam Searcher is doing.

On April 1, Sam contacts the XYZ Corporation and learns of a vacancy at $10 an hour. He tells them he is unwilling to work for less than $11 an hour and goes back to searching. On April 2, inflation begins because of the Government's stimulative policies, and XYZ starts getting higher prices for its products. On April 3, XYZ decides to raise the wage associated with its vacancy to $11 an hour to attract more workers. They call Sam and tell him they are now willing to pay $11 an hour. Delighted, Searcher accepts and becomes employed. Multiply this situation across the country, and unemployment falls below its natural rate. Consequently, it seems that lower unemployment has been bought by higher inflation. However, by the time, say,

April Fools' Day 1976 has rolled around, Sam Searcher and others like him have learned that inflation has been galloping along at 10 percent and that as a result *all* wages and prices, not just their own, have risen. In fact, they discover that their current wages of $11 an hour are worth no more now than the $10-an-hour wage was worth on April 1, 1975. Because they were not willing to work at $10 an hour at the old prices, they are not willing to work at $11 an hour now at the new prices; for they recognize that relative wages and prices have not changed. They quit work and once again become unemployed. Unemployment returns to its natural rate. However, inflation continues at the rate of 10 percent.

Stagflation has set in. Inflation has increased from 2 to 10 percent as a result of overly stimulative policies, whereas after a temporary decline, unemployment has risen back to the natural rate. When people perceive that all prices have risen simultaneously and build this into their expectations, their behavior is no longer affected by inflation; so that even though inflation may be higher, unemplyment after a period of economic adjustment will end up back at its natural rate.

FROM THEORY TO REALITY

Economists who subscribe to the natural rate view say that it explains events in the U.S. economy since the middle '60s. In 1964, inflation was proceeding at the low rate of 1.2 percent, and unemployment was 5.2 percent. As the Vietnam War heated up, inflation rose to 6.1 percent in 1969, and unemployment fell below the natural rate to 3.5 percent. Subsequently, however, unemployment began to rise back toward the natural rate but inflation remained high, as the natural rate theory would predict. Unemployment continued to rise (except during 1973, when it fell somewhat following the highly stimulative monetary policy of 1972) above the assumed natural rate until in 1975 it reached the 8–9 percent range.

Why did unemployment rise far beyond the natural rate even though people were beginning to anticipate increased rates of inflation? The answer

seems to be that the Government believed that inflation was "too" high and had to be reduced. Consequently, restrictive monetary and fiscal policies were implemented. Total demand fell below the amount that businesses wanted to produce. As unwanted inventories began to pile up, firms cut back production and layoffs began, touching off a period of sharp contraction of economic activity. With the sharp slackening in demand the pace of inflation has slowed, but because double-digit inflation remains fresh in the minds of the people, inflationary expectations still plague the economy. As a result, prices are still rising at a fast clip by historical standards. But as people revise downward their inflation expectations and curtail further their attempt to "beat inflation," a further easing of price pressures is in the cards, according to the natural rate view.

In short, the process that brought the economy to a high rate of inflation is being reversed. Eventually both the actual and expected rates of inflation will fall to a more acceptable level, and unemployment will return to its natural rate. The economy will end up back in a state of full employment with little or no inflation. (See Box 1 for a graphical depiction of this whole process.) How rapidly the economy returns to this happy state depends on the policies pursued. The natural rate approach presents policymakers with a Hobson's choice — eliminating inflation *requires* some increase in unemployment. How much unemployment is chosen determines how quickly the inflation is eliminated.

POLICY CHOICES: HOW FAST TO GO AND WHO GETS HURT?

The natural rate approach suggests that the higher the unemployment rate now, the faster inflation will be eliminated, and the sooner the natural rate of unemployment can be restored. The more restrictive the Government makes its policies, the more demand declines. Hence, the rate of inflation subsides more rapidly, and people quickly revise down their expectations about inflation. However, more restricitve policies also mean more unemployment. Consequently, a clear tradeoff emerges. The faster the economy is forced to return to price stabi-

How the Natural Rate Process Works

The economy starts at point A, where inflation is 0 and unemployment is at the natural rate N. As inflation begins to rise, unemployment falls at first because people are fooled into thinking their wages have risen relative to prices and therefore accept employment more readily. Unemployment reaches its low point at B. As people begin to learn of inflation, unemployment begins to rise because people find that their wages in fact have not increased relative to prices by as much as they had thought, and they therefore leave employment more readily. Once everybody fully anticipates the inflation, the economy ends up at C. with inflation proceeding at 10 percent but employment back at its natural rate. If at this point inflation were to rise to 20 percent, the process would be repeated and the economy would move from C to D to E.

How can the economy be moved from C back to A? Suppose the economy is at C in Graph 2, which corresponds to C in Graph 1. The expected rate of inflation equals the actual rate. Suppose Uncle Sam ends the stimulative policies that brought the economy from A to C. Then aggregate demand falls below aggregate supply. This takes pressure off prices and reverses the process that brought the economy from point A to point C. The economy moves from C back to A via F. At point A, both the expected and actual rates of inflation are back down to 0 percent, and unemployment is at its natural rate. The economy is back in a state of full employment with no inflation.

Graph 3 shows the recent path of the U.S. economy.

Graph 1 How Increasing the Rate of Inflation Can Lower the Rate of Unemployment Remporarily But Not Permanently

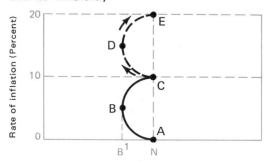

Rate of Unemployment (Percent)

Graph 2 How to Get Back to a Zero Rate of Inflation

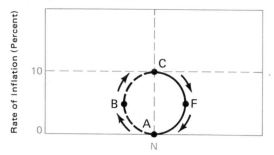

Rate of Unemployment (Percent)

Graph 3 The Recent Experience of the U.S. Economy

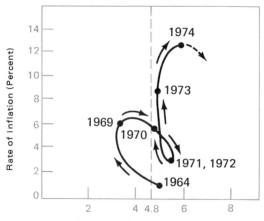

Rate of Unemployment (Percent)

lity and full employment, the higher is the unemployment that must be endured in the meantime. Conversely, the lower the rate of unemployment is kept, the longer the economy will take to return to price stability and full employment.

There are, then, two policy tradeoffs. First, there is a speed tradeoff. The faster society wants to reduce the rate of inflation, the greater the unemployment burden it must bear during the process of price reduction — but, the sooner it can return to normal conditions. Second, there is a distribution tradeoff. Whatever speed tradeoff society chooses, it must decide how to distribute the ensuing burden. It can adopt a "hands-off" policy, in which the unemployed bear a disproportionate share of the burden of reducing inflation, or it can attempt to alleviate unemployment through Government assistance, in which case some of the burden of reducing inflation is shifted to others.

QUESTIONS

1. What are the three types of unemployment, and how do they relate to the "natural rate" of unemployment?

2. What is the role of expectations in the inflationary process?

3. What is the "Hobson's choice" the author claims faces policy makers in attempting to solve the problem of stagflation?

PART TWELVE

FISCAL AND MONETARY POLICY

47 THE ECONOMICS OF DEMOCRATS AND REPUBLICANS
Donald J. Mullineaux

To what extent are the Republicans the party of big business? And the Democrats the party of labor? Do business firms or workers do better under one party than the other? In this paper Donald Mullineaux attempts to measure the economic folklore of party politics and in the process demonstrates some of the problems in measuring the accuracy of the "labels" often attached to the two major political parties. The author is a senior economist at the Philadelphia Federal Reserve Bank.

American political parties, unlike their European counterparts, differ but little on ideological questions such as the extent of individual freedom and the role of the state in the economy. Nevertheless, both major parties strive to differentiate their "product" from the competition's in an effort to attract new members.

One familiar tack adopted by party politicians involves the fostering of "labels" which identify their party with a particular social class or a favorable set of economic conditions. Thus, the Democratic Party proclaims itself champion of the workingman and vows to "put a tiger in the economy's tank" to accelerate spending and brake unemployment, the legacy of Republican "misrule." The GOP retorts that "spendthrift" Democratic policies have saddled the economy with excessive inflation, and that only Republican policies of "fiscal responsibility" and "orderly business conditions" will set the nation on the road to long-run prosperity.

Seldom are these claims elaborated or supported with any hard evidence. Thus, the sense in which Democrats represent the "party of labor" or Republicans the "party of business" remains unclear. His-

Abridged from Donald J. Mullineaux, "The Economic Folklore of Party Politics: Myths or Realities?" Federal Reserve Bank of Philadelphia *Business Review* (November 1973), 3–11.

torically, the Democrats have often authored and executed labor legislation of epic proportions, such as the Wagner Act. Similarly, in a number of instances, Republicans have reduced corporate taxes or softened business depreciation allowances. On many occasions, however, party politicians are not referring to these isolated events but rather are asserting that certain special interest groups are always better off when one or another political party is in power. Such a far-reaching proposition can be tested by examining changes in some broad economic gauges.

WHICH FACTS ARE IN FACT FACTS?

If political parties are continually more sensitive to the demands of some groups than others, the "favored" group should receive greater "benefits" *on average* when the patron party is in power than when it is out. For example, labor should in some sense "do better" under Democratic hegemony if the stereotype holds. Testing such a proposition involves deciding *how to measure benefits* as well as *defining what is meant by being "in power."*

For the purpose of drawing comparisons, Democrats were considered "in power" in years in which that party possessed the Presidency. The Executive is generally judged more responsible than the Congress for maintaining an "adequate" pace of economic activity. The Employment Act of 1946 directed the President to act very much like the economy's physician, performing an annual diagnosis with the aid of the Council of Economic Advisers and suggesting remedial legislation in an official report to Congress. There are constraints, however, on the amount of medication the President can pry from the pharmacies on Capitol Hill and the Federal Reserve Board. Since only Congress has the power to tax and appropriate funds for Federal expenditures, the President must employ a mix of logical and political persuasion in combination with the veto power to get his fiscal prescriptions filled. The Chief Executive has even more limited control over monetary-policy medication, however, where responsibility is vested in the independent Federal Reserve Board. Although members of the Board are appointed by the President subject to approval of Congress, their 14-year terms are staggered on a two-year basis to constrain a President's control over the composition of the Board. The president appoints the Chairman of the Board of Governors to a four-year term, but their terms are not coincidental. Thus, for obvious reasons, to be "in power" connotes too strong an image of the actual situation in which a President finds himself regarding economic affairs.

One way of measuring "benefits" during Democratic and Republican Presidential tenures is by examining the size of the *average annual percentage rates of change* in certain economic magnitudes over a specific period — in this case, from 1948 through 1972. Some variables were chosen to reflect the interest of special groups such as labor or business corporations. Others were selected to test hypothetical administrative characteristics of the parties, such as the Democrats' presumed proclivity for rapid changes in public spending. *Percentage changes* are examined because the levels of particular variables such as the unemployment rate will largely reflect policy actions taken in previous years when the "outs" may have been the "ins." Focusing on proportionate changes will remove some of the effect of *past* government policies on *current* observations, but because these policies often operate with a considerable time lag, this procedure cannot remove all the influence of the past. This problem becomes particularly acute in years when there is a switch from a Democratic to Republican adminstration, or vice versa, as in 1961 or 1969. The procedure adopted here is to include observed percentage changes in variables in such years in the sample observations of the competing party. For example, the percentage change in corporate profits in 1961 is included in the Republican sample. The justification is that the change in corporate profits in 1961 is influenced more by Republican actions in 1960 and preceding years than by Democratic actions in 1961. In addition, it should be recalled that the Federal budget for fiscal 1961 (July 1, 1960—June 30, 1961) was a Republican budget. This "rough-and-ready" adjustment should take sufficient ac-

Table 1. *Corporate Profits and Stock Prices Grow Faster During Republican Presidential Years, but the Difference is Not Significant*

Average Annual Percentage Rate of Change in:	Democrats	Republicans
Corporate profits	1.54%	2.39%
Standard & Poors stock index	7.14	11.39

Source: Business Conditions Digest.

count of the problem of time lags to make the following comparisons meaningful.

Republicans and Business   The view that the GOP tends to look favorably on business interests is a commonplace topic of parlor and taproom discussions of politics and economics. Cowboy-humorist Will Rogers once suggested that in order to find the place where the Republican party was formed you should find out where the first corporation was formed. But as Democrat Al Smith used to say, let's look at the record.

Examination of the course of corporate profits during different administrations (see Table 1) indicates that, on the average, growth rates of corporate profits have climbed faster under Republican Presidents. Similarly, the stock market as measured by Standard & Poor's index of 500 stocks has fared better under GOP rule. Statistics are not always infallible when prosecuting a point, however. Testing whether these observed differences are large enough to be judged "statistically significant" furnishes a cross-examination of sorts. Failure to confirm significance means that the findings can be attributed to chance as much as to the presence of systematic factors such as the party holding the Presidency. Neither of the differences in Table 1, it turns out, is statistically significant. In the final verdict, then, the common notion that the GOP is the patron of business gets little support from the behavior of corporate profits or stock market prices in post-war years.

Democrats and Labor   From the days of FDR until the 1960's, it was not unusual to find the national

Democratic Party running against Herbert Hoover and the Great Depression. References to the Democrats as the "party of prosperity" and the patron of the blue-collar voters dot their party platforms of the last 40 years. Recent evidence suggests that the Republicans have traditionally had very little success in swaying public opinion against this Democratic claim. For the last 20 years, the Gallup Poll has asked the following question: "Looking ahead for the next few years, which political party — Republican or Democratic — do you think will do better in keeping the country prosperous?" The GOP captured the brass ring just twice, in 1955 and 1972. One gauge of whether the public's perception is, on average, justified is a comparison of the behavior of the unemployment rate, labor's compensation (adjusted for inflation), labor's share of national income, and the rate of growth of the economy (adjusted for inflation) during Democratic and Republican administrations (see Table 2). These statistics tend to fortify the Democrats' claims as the champion of labor and the party of prosperity. Looking further, however, it turns out that only the difference between the real (inflation-adjusted) rate of growth of the economy during the Democratic and Republican administrations and the behavior of the unemployment rate can be classified as statistically significant. Neither the behavior of real wages nor labor's shares of income substantiates the claim that labor gains are larger under Democratic than Republican regimes.

WHY THE GROWTH RATE DIFFERENCES?

Voters' self-interest and the survival instinct in politicians both suggest that an explanation of the apparent differences in the economy's growth under Democratic and Republican Presidents would be more than welcome. In particular, does this difference reflect superior economic management skills on the part of one of our major parties or is it merely a phenomenon of chance, like the spin of a roulette wheel? Economists agree that differences in the amounts of stimulus applied to the economy through Government stabilization policies could

Table 2. *A Faster Growth Rate During Democratic Administrations Brings Significantly Better Performance of the Unemployment Rate, but Generates No Significant Differences in Labor's Compensation or Its Share of National Income*

Average Annual Percentage Rate of Change in:	Democrats	Republicans
Unemployment rate, all civilians	−5.02%[1]	16.90%[1]
Labor's compensation, adjusted for inflation	2.90	2.66
Labor's share of national income	1.01	0.48
Gross national product per capita, adjusted for inflation	3.46[1]	0.98[1]

Sources: Employment and Earnings, Business Conditions Digest, Economic Report of the President — 1973.
[1]The observed difference can be classified as statistically significant.

well be a primary causal factor. In fact, some have suggested that Republicans have been less vigorous in their attempts to reduce unemployment because the GOP places more weight on price stability than the Democrats. "To inflate or not to inflate, that is the Democratic question," goes another Will Rogers adage. A look at the data since 1948, however, shows average rates of increases in consumer prices have been virtually identical during Republican (2.26 percent) and Democratic (2.41 percent) administrations, and the same holds true for other prices. Of course, the fact that inflation rates are similar under both parties' administrations need not mean that Democrats and Republicans must be equally concerned about price level increases since the inflationary forces in the economy may have been greater on average under one or the other party.

Unfortunately, attempts to identify the administrations which pursued the most expansionary economic policies require (1) a measure of changes in policy actions and (2) a method of taking account of the long and shifting time lags before policy actions have their effect. Since considerable disagreement exists among economists concerning both of these factors, at present there is very little that can be said about the *causal* nature of the observed relations between economic events and the Presidential tenures of political parties. For example, one of the fundamental theorems of economic analysis is that increases in Government spending, other things equal, have an expansionary impact on real economic activity. However, some economists have contended that increases in spending by Government merely "replace" private spending that would otherwise have occurred, and thus have little net expansionary effect. Federal spending has increased significantly more rapidly under Democrats than Republicans. In fact, measured as a proportion of total spending, Government expenditures have declined on average under Republicans, while increasing about 9 percent when Democrats held the White House. Since real economic activity has shown more growth under Democratic Presidents, these figures make it difficult to accept the notion that Government expenditure policies have an insignificant effect on economic activity over the long run. Nevertheless, the pessimistic view of the potency of government spending cannot be ruled out by this simple argument, since some other factors may have been the determining elements of the observed differences in real growth rates.

Another factor which some economists focus on as the "prime mover" behind shifts in economic activity is the growth rate of the stock of money (currency plus checking-account deposits). Practically all economists agree that increases in the money-stock growth rate can have an expansionary impact on real economic activity in the short run. However, over the longer run increases in the growth rate of money are generally expected to bring on higher prices. Money has grown at a 3.68 percent rate on the average under Democrats and a 2.94 percent rate under Republicans since 1948 — a statistically insignificant difference. To the extent that the averaging process used here approximates the long run, the similar growth rates in money should have been reflected in similar price-level behavior across parties — a result confirmed above. Whether or not short-run changes in money-growth rates were the principal force accounting for differences in real growth is again a question that cannot be answered by this simple averaging process.

UNCONSTRUCTIVE LABELS OR CONSTRUCTIVE POLICIES: AN EMERGING CHOICE?

Summing up then, a simple examination of some broad economic gauges offers little support for a number of the "labels" that various party spokesmen often attempt to foster. For example, the figures do not reveal the Republicans as the "party of business" and Democrats may be viewed (with some caution) as the "party of labor" only in terms of the behavior of the unemployment rate, and not in terms of the behavior of wages (inflation-adjusted) or labor's share of income. The economy has grown more rapidly under Democratic Presidents, but no convincing evidence has emerged to relate this finding to that party's stabilization skills. Despite the rather limited evidence for their claims, party politicians continue to pursue the image-making strategy in search of both members and votes.

QUESTIONS

1. Summarize the measurement problems involved in measuring the economic impact of a political party. What complications are introduced by the existence of "lags"?

2. Summarize the findings of Mullineaux. Why do they seem to differ from the conventional wisdom regarding the economics of Democrats and Republicans?

3. What implications, if any, do the author's findings have for voting strategy for businessmen, workers, and consumers?

48 SLOWDOWNS AND RECESSIONS: WHAT'S BEEN GOVERNMENT'S ROLE?
Donald L. Raiff

To what extent can an economy's ups and downs be considered the result of government actions? This is one of the most difficult and most important issues in all of economic science. Donald L. Raiff attempts to assess the U.S. experience to determine if government policies have promoted economic growth or exacerbated downward economic trends. Dr. Raiff is on the economics staff of the Federal Reserve Bank of Philadelphia.

All industrialized countries have their economic ups and downs, and the United States has had its share. Between 1950 and 1970 we went through seven slowdowns. Are these fluctuations inherent in our economic system or has some outside force caused them? Some economists have suggested that changes in Government policy may be a cause of this instability or, at least, be aggravating the swings. Analyzing the severity of slowdowns and Government policy actions which accompanied them provides some insight into this question.

SLOWDOWNS AND RECESSIONS
SEVERITY IS THE ISSUE

In technical jargon, economic slowdowns are deviations *below* the trend of long-term growth. They include periods of *slow positive growth* as well as actual declines in economic activity. The severity of these slowdowns varies greatly. Some "slowdowns" are worse than others, and the business declines are tagged "recessions" (a really bad downturn, like in the 1930s, is labeled a depression). For example, of the seven slowdowns between 1950 and 1970 three weren't serious enough to qualify as recessions and four were.

Abridged from Donald L. Raiff, "Slowdowns and Recessions: What's Been Government's Role?" The Federal Reserve Bank of Philadelphia *Business Review* (October 1975), pp. 17–31. Reprinted by permission.

Causes of Slowdowns: Tough to Isolate One explanation of business cycles popular since the 1930s suggests that the economy is inherently unstable. This means that the economy, if left alone, will move along a path of positive growth on average but is likely to experience ups and downs along the way. This inherent instability of the economic system produces something like the following scenario. Consumers and businessmen *allegedly* spend rapidly for a period, then slow their purchasing for a while. Next, adjustments in inventories play a critical role. Optimistic businessmen overstock during prosperous times, but when spending slows, they're caught with too many goods on hand. So, to avoid mounting inventories businesses curtail production and lay off workers; current sales are met out of existing stocks of merchandise. The laid-off workers buy fewer goods, inventories rise still further, and another round of layoffs ensues. The process repeats itself and what starts off as a mild slowdown tailspins into a recession.

Government stabilization efforts are supposed to moderate the downward spiral by offsetting the downswing in private demand. Increasing Government spending and/or cutting taxes to spur consumer and business spending would be the standard fiscal policy response. Either of these actions would shrink a Federal budget surplus or would widen an existing deficit. Increasing the growth of the money stock would be an appropriate monetary policy response. This would stimulate spending by initially lowering interest rates and increasing wealth.

However, not all students of business cycles see the policy choices and their consequences in such a neat scenario. First, some argue that the economy is more inherently stable than implied in this scenario. Second, they believe Government actions in practice tend more often to aggravate rather than moderate slowdowns in economic activity.

Destabilizing changes in Government policy could occur, for example, because of ignorance about the timing and magnitude of the effects created by policy changes. For example, how much of a tax cut will people spend and when? Alternatively, destabilizing changes might result from Government responding to another problem, such as a high inflation rate. A tax cut may stimulate the economy, but it could also stimulate inflation, for instance. Thus, some business cycle scholars caution against using Government policy to "fine tune" the economy because they think too little is really known about how Government stabilization policies impact on the economy.

HAS STABILIZATION POLICY WORKED?

Applying statistical analysis to business fluctuations cannot *prove* the effectiveness (or lack of effectiveness) of Government stabilization policies in cushioning business slowdowns, but it can provide some clues. Clearly, stabilization policy has *not* prevented observed slowdowns. But have policy changes occurred (for whatever reason) which discouraged slowdowns from snowballing into recessions? Or, have restrictive policy moves aggravated slowdowns?

Congressional Decision-Making: Fiscal Policy   The simplest notion of fiscal policy is that the Federal deficit should be enlarged during slowdowns either by lowering taxes, raising expenditures, or a combination of both. Unfortunately, to look simply at changes in the size of the standard deficit as a measure of policymakers' response to a slowdown can be misleading. The reason is that the size of the budget deficit can change during a slowdown either *automatically* or because of conscious decisions by policymakers to increase spending programs or to lower tax rates. Revenues, for example, will automatically decline during slowdowns because among other reasons, corporate profits slip and thus corporate income taxes diminish. Similarly, there are automatic increases in expenditures — unemployment compensation payments, for example, which rise during slowdowns. These passive or automatic changes in spending and revenues have to be filtered out to isolate the conscious or active changes in policy, like a tax cut, that are made to cushion downturns.

The "high-employment" surplus or deficit attempts to isolate policy actions which are independent of the current state of the economy. To do this both spending and revenue are adjusted to the levels that would have resulted if the unemployment rate hovered around 4 percent — sometimes referred to as the high-employment level. To the extent this adjustment is successful, increases in the high-employment budget deficit or decreases in its surplus mean that fiscal policy is stimulating the economy with more than just the use of economic stabilizers. The Government is increasing overall demand for goods and services through a new spending program or making more income available for others to spend by way of tax-rate reductions. If such a policy is well-timed, it could offset a slowdown in economic activity. The opposite is also true. A high-employment budget deficit that has shrunk or a surplus that has increased means that Government fiscal policies are becoming more restrictive and reducing overall demand. During a slowdown, this would aggravate rather than alleviate the downturn.

Not all economists are convinced that fiscal policy changes affect the economy immediately, but many believe that the lags are quite short. It is estimated that a substantial part, say at a minimum 30 percent, or the total effect occurs within three months of the policy change. If so, then sorting out the influence of fiscal policy on slowdowns should be done with data from the same time periods as the slowdowns themselves. Such a comparison is shown in Table 1. The comparison suggests that Government policy, as reflected by changes in the high-employment budget, was on net injecting purchasing power into the spending stream during the three mild slowdowns. However, during the slowdowns which became recessions, changes in the high-employment budget indicate that fiscal policy was a drain on the economy.

The record in dealing with slowdowns is mixed and overall does not deserve high marks. Of the seven slowdowns observed, fiscal policy changed in the "right" direction only three times. During the other four slowdowns, fiscal policy changed either in the "wrong" direction or hardly at all. Of course, looking at slowdowns alone cannot tell us whether fiscal policy prevented some slowdowns which otherwise would have occurred. But, a reasonable conclusion from all of this is that fiscal policy has been largely "hit or miss" in mitigating economic slow-

Table 1. *During Recessions Fiscal Policy Has Not Changed to Stimulate Aggregate Demand*

Slowdowns (Ordered by Severity With Mildest Last)	Net Injection (+) or Drain (−) on the Economy by Changes in the Budget Position During the Slowdowns[1]	
	Standard Budget (Billions of Dollars)	High-Employment Budget (Billions of Dollars)
2/57–5/58	+6.6	− .1
2/60–2/61	−3.0	−5.1
3/53–9/54	+2.5	−1.1
6/69–12/70	+7.7	−5.2
5/51–7/52	+18.8	+13.9
4/62–4/63	− .8	+1.8
6/66–10/67	+8.7	+7.4

[1]Measured by subtracting the average budget position during the slowdown from the levels averaged over the two quarters before the slowdown. Because of the way the changes were computed, a positive number means that fiscal policy is moving in the right direction to offset a slowdown and vice versa. For example, during the 1951–52 slowdown, the average level of the high-employment budget surplus declined from $11.1 billion to an average deficit of $2.8 billion — a stimulative shift in the budget position of $13.9 billion.

downs — sometimes stabilizing, sometimes destabilizing, and sometimes "neutral."

Congressional Delegation: Monetary Policy Congress does not make the decisions involving discretionary monetary policy. Through the Federal Reserve Act and subsequent amendments Congress has delegated this power to the Federal Reserve System. The Fed's power to implement monetary policy is based on its ability to "control" the U.S. money stock (the public's currency and checking account balances). Changes in the rate of growth for money can be viewed as an indicator of discretionary monetary policy changes.

Theoretical and empirical studies have suggested that people get used to the growth rate in money over the long haul. To make a long story short, the past record of money growth gets built into current and future inflation rates, interest rates, and spending patterns. However, if there are substantial deviations (that is, lasting six months or so) from the recent experiences in terms of money growth, individuals and firms will be surprised and adjust accordingly. For example, if for six months the growth rate for money exceeds what people have become accustomed to, economic activity (either in terms of output, inflation, or both) would tend to speed up. This occurs as people and firms increase spending

and investment in financial assets as a response to their higher than previously anticipated balances of money. Thus, if monetary policy is to be used to offset slowdowns, the money growth rate should increase to offset a weakening economy. Conversely, downward movements in money growth would represent a policy which exacerbates a weakening of economic activity.

The actual time between monetary policy shifts, and the impact of those changes on economic activity is not known with certainty. If the time-lags were quite short, isolating the influence of monetary policy on slowdowns could be accomplished with data from the same periods as the slowdowns themselves. Then the time periods used in the analysis would be similar to those used for testing fiscal policy. However, economists have made a case for using longer time-lags in analyzing the effects of changing monetary policy. If monetary policy takes between two and three quarters to alter the course of economic activity substantially (for example, 30 percent of the total effect), it would be necessary to compare the growth rate of the money stock before the slowdown with its longer term average rate of growth.

Going into the milder slowdowns, money-stock growth increased relative to the long-term average rate of growth (see Table 2). However, this wasn't

Table 2. *The Monetary Growth Rate Has Typically Decelerated Prior To Recessions*

Growth Slowdowns (Ordered by Severity with the Mildest Last)	Net injection (+) or Drain (−) on the Economy by Changes in the Growth Rate of Money	
	During Slowdowns[1] (Percentage Points)	Before Slowdowns (Percentage Points)
2/57–5/28	−1.5	− .3
2/60–2/61	−1.3	−4.9
3/53–9/54	−3.4	−2.4
6/69–12/70	−2.7	−2.5
5/51–7/52	+3.4	+2.2
4/62–4/63	+ .5	+1.3
6/66–10/67	− .3	+ .1

[1]Measured by subtracting the growth rate (annual basis) over 24 months ending six months before the slowdown from the growth rate (annual basis) occurring during the slowdown period.

true prior to the recessions. A decline in the growth rate of money preceded each of these periods. Three of these four decelerations were substantial. Similar judgments about money growth also emerge from studying changes in the growth rate of money *during* the slowdowns.

Using the growth rate change just before the slowdowns as the main criterion, monetary policy, like fiscal policy, appears to have a mixed record between 1950 and 1970. Growth in the money stock rose substantially before only two of the seven slowdowns. Of the other five slowdowns of which four turned into recessions, money growth slowed appreciably in three and changed little in two.

From these observations alone, it would be difficult to blame every recession on monetary policy. Nonetheless, these data along with other more sophisticated forms of analysis provide the backdrop for concern that slowdowns in money-stock growth can happen at the wrong time with destabilizing effects on economic activity. Of course, monetary authorities may have been focusing on goals other than offsetting slowdowns, like fighting inflation. Also, monetary policymakers may have been looking at other policy targets such as interest rates rather than the money stock.

A RECAP

The thrust of stabilization policy which accompanied economic slowdowns between 1950 and 1970

can be analyzed with some simple tests. According to these tests, the record for monetary and fiscal policy, in terms of mitigating slowdowns in the economy, has been spotty at best. True, some slowdowns — those remaining mild — were aided by policy thrusts which provided "net injections" to economic activity. But, the slowdowns that became recessions were aggravated by policy thrusts which placed drains on the economy. Possibly these "drains" upon real growth resulted from policymakers pursuing goals other than maintaining high levels of steady economic growth. On balance, the Government's success in executing fiscal and monetary policies to smooth out business slowdowns appears to be a long way from fulfilling the dream of steady growth.

QUESTIONS

1. How are "business cycles" defined and measured?
2. To what extent, if any, are business cycles "natural" and to what extent, if any, are they a function of government economic policies?
3. What has been the record of both fiscal and monetary policy as a stabilizing influence on the U.S. economy?

49 THE EFFICACY OF FISCAL VERSUS MONETARY POLICY: THE GREAT DEBATE
Ira Kaminow

Few debates have engaged economic observers as that over monetary versus fiscal policy. And for good reason! The public policy implications of this issue are enormous. It would behoove the reader, qua citizen, to give some thought to these next two selections. Though parts may be rough going, considerable economics can be learned from them. Ira Kaminow, of the Philadelphia Federal Reserve Bank, presents the case for monetarism. (Discussion questions on this topic appear at the end of Reading 50.)

Times are changing. What is obvious today was obviously wrong yesterday; this is as true of questions involving economic issues as any others. Many of us, for example, believe in the efficacy of fiscal policy — in the Government's power to influence the level of national income by its own spending and taxing policies. Indeed, the expenditure-income chain explanation of the operation of fiscal policy is part of today's conventional wisdom. The Government spends more or spurs private spending by taxing less, and so creates more jobs and higher profits. The new income so created generates additional demand and private spending, creating even more income.

All this is Keynesian economics — the so-called New Economics. But it wasn't long ago that the Keynesian Revolution was rejected by most laymen, and not long before that, that it was rejected by most economists. Today, with victory in hand, the New Economics is facing a counterrevolution which may again change the economic thinking of the nation. There is a small but highly vocal group of economists who are suspicious of Keynesian economics in general and of fiscal policy in particular.

Abridged from Ira Kaminow, "The Myth of Fiscal Policy: The Monetarist View," *Federal Reserve Bank of Philadelphia Business Review* (December 1969), pp. 10—18. Reprinted by permission.

The members of the group are sometimes called Monetarists.[1]

Monetarists view the controversy over economic theories as being like a law suit. As judges, they rule that the New Economists have presented no acceptable historical evidence in support of the income-expenditure theory. As litigants, they present the following case: (1) Over the years, the major movements in national income have been associated with major movements in the money supply and *vice versa*; (2) no equally strong or systematic relation can be found to support the Keynesian view of the operation of fiscal policy; (3) therefore, monetary forces have played a much more important and/or more stable role in determining national income than fiscal forces. Monetarists do not claim that the income-expenditure chain is erroneous in principle — merely that history tells us it is too weak or unpredictable to be of much use for economic policy.

A SIMPLE EXPLANATION OF THE MONETARIST VIEW

How do the Monetarists reconcile their view of history with the apparently powerful logic of the income-expenditure chain?[2] The heart of the Monetarist view is the supply of and demand for money — a dramatic shift from the usual emphasis. Because of the near total victory of the New Economics (at least in introductory textbooks on economics) in the fifties and sixties, the spotlight of popular pol-

---

[1] Strictly speaking, the Monetarist view involves more than mere suspicion of the efficacy of fiscal policy. Indeed, one can be a Monetarist and still agree that fiscal policy has a powerful and systematic influence on the economy. Nevertheless, the popular press identifies Monetarist with those who believe that monetary policy is much more important than fiscal policy, and this usage of the term is adopted here.

[2] A completely accurate answer to this question is extremely complex. There is no reason, however, why the complexities and nuances should keep us from the essence of the Monetarist argument. A look at the simplest version of the theory (a version not seriously proposed by anyone) will reveal more than an investigation of one which requires endless digressions and footnotes and which reflects the particular views of only one or two Monetarists.

icy discussions has been firmly set on the pivot point of Keynesian economics — the demand for goods.

A look at the economy from the perspective of the money side of things (or the goods side, for that matter) will reveal only a partial and perhaps slightly distorted picture of the economy. Nevertheless, anyone who has been to the circus knows how difficult it is to look at all three rings at once and that there is something to be gained from looking at only one at a time.

Although not all economists agree on the definition of money, we will not break too much with tradition if we use the term to mean all assets that are generally accepted as a means of payment. More concretely, we can define money as the sum of coins, paper currency, and checking account deposits.

An easy way to illustrate the Monetarist view is to suppose that a certain quantity of money is required to support any particular level of income. When national economic activity (as measured by income) rises, more money is required to carry on conveniently day-to-day transactions; when economic activity declines, households and businesses find that they engage in fewer transactions, and hence, need less money. More specifically, we can assume that the demand for money balances *relative* to the level of income (what economists call desired *relative* money balances) is fixed. By way of illustration, we can imagine that institutional arrangements — like the availability of credit cards and the length of the average pay period — lead the public to desire money balances equal in value to 10 percent of national income. If annual national income is $800 billion, then desired balances would be $80 billion.

What happens if the economy has more money than it requires? Say, for the sake of argument, that the actual stock of money in the previous example is $90 billion, or $10 billion more than is required. Since money yields no pecuniary return, households and businesses will attempt to exchange money for other assets — assets that yield satisfaction directly (like television sets) and assets that yield a pecuniary return (like stocks and bonds). The increased demand for goods and services will stimulate greater output and perhaps will boost

prices as markets respond to the new demand. At the same time, the increased demand for financial assets like stocks and bonds will drive interest rates down. The decline in interest rates will further encourage the demand for goods by making credit cheaper. This will induce still higher prices and output. The pace of economic activity will quicken. Economic activity will continue to increase until income is pushed up to a level consistent with the $90 billion money stock — that is, to $900 billion.

The rigid relationship between the demand for money and national income makes this environment inhospitable to fiscal policy. If the national goal is to raise income, it can be achieved only by raising the money stock. An increase in Government expenditures won't work except for a very short time. As soon as income rises a bit, the money stock will be inadequate. There will be a general scramble for money, and the private demand for goods will decline as businesses and households try to increase their holdings of money. Consequently, income and output will be pulled back down by the limited money stock.

Stated somewhat differently, any increase in Government expenditures (not accompanied by an appropriate increase in the money stock) will be matched by an equal decline in private expenditures; any decrease in Government expenditures (not accompanied by an appropriate decline in the money stock) will be matched by an equal increase in private expenditures.

The key that allowed monetary policy to work in the simple world just described is the constancy of desired *relative* money balances. In order to achieve an equilibrium, annual national income will always adjust so that it is ten times the stock of money. If we can control the money supply we can control national income. The key that locked fiscal policy out is that Government taxing and spending policies have no effect on desired relative money balances. No matter what fiscal policies are followed, annual national income will always tend to be ten times higher than the stock of money. In these two keys are the germs of the Monetarist position: (1) Although demand for relative money balances is not fixed, it is the most stable and predictable variable on which we can count for economic policy. (2) Although fiscal policies may have some influence on desired relative money balances, they do not have a strong predictable influence; therefore, fiscal policies are of relatively little or no use.

A LOOK AT THE NEW ECONOMICS FROM THE MONEY SIDE

Advocates of the New Economics do not agree that income is the only variable that exerts a strong, predictable influence on the demand for money. They argue that a typical family might find it very convenient at some given level of income to go about its daily business with an average checking account balance of $100. But convenience must be balanced against cost. One hundred dollars in the checking account is not earning interest. When the interest rate on savings accounts is very low, the household may indeed hold a $100 checking account balance. But let the interest rate rise substantially and the household may decide that it can get by with only $75 or $50 worth of money. The lower money balance might mean more bother — more accurate balancing of the checkbook, more trips to the bank — but the bother is compensated by the greater interest income. In short, the New Economists argue that both the level of income and the interest rate determine the desired stock of money. By adding this additional ingredient — interest rates — the New Economist can salvage the argument for the expenditure-income chain.

Keynesians expect roughly the same kind of initial response to fiscal policy as do the Monetarists. An increase in Government expenditures drives income up, and the existing stock of money becomes inadequate to handle the additional income. In an effort to acquire more money, people try to sell nonmonetary financial assets such as bonds. As the supply of these assets rises relative to demand, interest rates begin to rise to make them more attractive to buyers. This hike in interest rates is the key that is supposed to let fiscal policy back in. Higher interest rates mean that the economy will be able to support a higher level of income with the given stock of money. With higher interest rates, house-

holds and businesses find it advantageous to economize on the use of money — to make the existing stock "go farther." The economy will, after the initial shock of added Government expenditures, come to rest at a higher level of national income — and higher interest rates. The higher interest rates are necessary; otherwise, the public could not be induced to hold the same quantity of money at the higher level of activity. Put in slightly different terms, the ratio of desired money balances to income will decline because interest rates have risen.

An extreme version of the Keynesian view gives rise to the so-called liquidity trap. Imagine what would happen if the public were willing to hold whatever money balances were offered at the prevailing interest rate. The public would make no attempt to convert new money balances into other assets, regardless of how much money the authorities pumped into the economy. Any new money that was placed in the economy would be willingly held at the existing interest rate and income. Monetary policy is completely frustrated if and when we get into the trap because then the public's actions are unaffected by changes in the money supply.

In contrast, recall that in the simple Monetarist case the demand for *relative* money balances doesn't change. Individual members of the public never will be willing to hold unlimited quantities of money. If new money is added to the economy, the public will have "too much" money and will try to get rid of the excess. This process will drive income up to a new equilibrium.

The single most revealing element in the encounter between Monetarists and New Economists is that they cannot agree on the relevance of the interest rate. The Monetarist Milton Friedman wrote:

. . . in my opinion no "fundamental issues" in either monetary theory or monetary policy hinge on whether [the demand for money depends on interest rates].

The Keynesian Paul Samuelson wrote:

. . . the minute you believe that [the demand for money depends on interest rates] you have moved to . . . the post-Keynesian position.

Keynesians insist that the interest rate is the added gear in the mechanism that allows fiscal policy to work. For them, fiscal policy (viewed from the money side of the economy) gives authorities control over the interest rate and, through the interest rate, control over desired *relative* money balances. The Monetarists insist that this control must be inconsequential because they see no evidence that it has worked in the past (New Economists, of course, dispute the charge of lack of evidence). For the Monetarists there are two possibilities: (1) Fiscal policy has had an erratic, unsystematic effect on the interest rate and, hence, an unobservable effect on national income, or (2) fiscal policies have been so mild as to have only a small effect on interest rates.

The issue (regarding the demand for money) that is of primary importance to the Monetarist is the stability and predictability of desired relative money balances. Evidence of a highly unstable and unpredictable ratio of money balances to national income would directly contradict the efficacy of monetary policy. In terms of the Keynesian theory, the instability would arise if we fell into a liquidity trap. The Monetarists are therefore considerably more interested in whether a trap exists than in whether the demand for money is sensitive to the interest rate.

It is time to fish or cut bait. A number of issues have been raised and questions asked about the demand for money. What kinds of answers does history provide? To make things manageable, we can concentrate on three key questions: (1) Does the demand for money depend on income? (2) Is the demand for money sensitive to interest rates? (3) Have we ever been caught in a liquidity trap?

Question One: What Role for Income? Virtually every empirical study undertaken has shown that the demand for money depends on the level of income. Sometimes the relationship is based on a linkage between current income and money demand through the level of transactions of the sort we discussed earlier. Sometimes the relationship is based on more subtle arguments.

These more subtle discussions generally presume that economic well-being is a more important determinant of the demand for money than is the volume of transactions. The discussions take as their point of departure the notion that improved economic status for a nation (or an individual) means a greater demand for most assets, including money. In fact, at least one economist believes that money is a luxury in the sense that the demand for it rises very rapidly as a nation (or individual) moves up the economic ladder.

The two measures of economic well-being that have been used to explain the demand for money are wealth and permanent income. Everyone is familiar with the notion of wealth, and there should be no dispute that it is one measure of economic well-being. The meaning of permanent income, however, is not widely known.

Permanent income is most simply described as expected average lifetime income. It is a good measure of economic well-being because it is adjusted for temporary ups and downs. A day laborer who happens to be working his way through medical school has a higher *permanent* income than his co-worker whose actual or *measured* income is the same but whose ambitions and income expectations are more modest.

Economists who take the permanent income approach do not deny the importance of measured income. They argue that current and past levels of measured income are the most important influences on permanent income. They claim that expectations are largely formulated on the basis of past experience.

Question Two: How Important Is the Interest Rate?
Historically, the interest rate has influenced the demand for money.[3] This much we know with virtual certainty of knowledge. There is some disagreement, however, on just how important the interest rate has been. Some economists, like Milton Fried-

[3] There are, of course, many interest rates. We shall ignore here the important question of selecting the appropriate one.

man and Maurice Allais, take the view that the interest rate is so unimportant in determining the demand for money that little is lost if it is ignored. Other investigators, however, have presented evidence that the demand for money is highly sensitive to changes in the rate of interest. Perhaps the most sensitive relationship was found by Allan Meltzer who estimated on one occasion that any given percentage change in long-term interest rates would be matched by an equal percentage change (in the opposite direction) in the demand for money.

The disagreement over the importance of the interest does not follow "party lines." As it turns out, all three of the economists mentioned in the last paragraph are Monetarists. Estimates of the interest sensitivity by Keynesians are greater than zero but less than Meltzer's.

A major reason for all this disagreement about the importance of the interest rate is that it is often difficult to untangle the influence of interest rates from other influences on the demand for money. Interest rates vary in a more or less systematic way over the business cycle — they generally go up during economic contractions.

Other variables that are likely to influence the demand for money also behave more or less predictably over the cycle. This raises the possibility that an investigator will wrongly attribute the influence of some other variable to interest rates, or the influence of interest rates to other variables.

Milton Friedman and Anna J. Schwartz, in particular, argue that an uncritical reading of history has led to an overemphasis on the role of the interest rate in determining the demand for money.

It is well known that relative money balances (the ratio of money balances to income) fall during expansions and rise during contractions. Generally speaking, therefore, relative money balances are high when interest rates are low (during slumps), and are low when interest rates are high (during booms). The interest rate seems to do a good job in explaining movements in the demand for relative money balances.

Friedman and Schwartz argue that there is another factor to explain movements in relative money balances over the cycle. It is based on the idea of permanent income (expected average lifetime income) mentioned earlier. During economic downturns, people anticipate that things will get better; so permanent income is higher than measured income. During periods of prosperity, people guess that incomes are unusually high; so permanent income is lower than measured income. Over the cycle, permanent income fluctuates much less than measured income because people recognize that a good deal of income fluctuations are transitory. If the demand for money depends on permanent income, it will fluctuate relatively little over the business cycle because permanent income is relatively stable over the cycle. Therefore, during periods of recovery, the demand for money will rise more slowly than measured income, so relative money balances (the ratio of money balances to measured national income) will fall. During periods of contraction, the demand for money will fall more slowly than measured income, and relative money balances will rise.

Friedman and Schwartz offer some evidence in support of their views in their famous study *A Monetary History of the United States.* For example, they point to the period, 1932–1937, during which both interest rates and relative money balances fell. This pattern is clearly inconsistent with the interest-rate explanation of movements in the demand for money. The 1932–1937 experience is very easily explained by the permanent income concept. In the mid-1930s, the economy started to climb out of the depths of the Great Depression. Income was rising. Nevertheless, vivid memories of 1929, 1930, and 1931 lingered. People were not so sure that the recovery was going to be sustained. Permanent income rose, but not so fast as measured income. Desired money balances, which respond to permanent income, grew more slowly than measured income. So, the ratio of money balances to measured income fell.

Not all economists agree that the Friedman and Schwartz evidence is convincing. A number of studies have shown that the interest rate has had a strong influence even if one accepts the permanent income hypothesis. In fact, Friedman and Schwartz seem to have retreated slightly on this point. In 1966, Friedman wrote "most estimates [of the interest rate sensitivity], including some we have obtained in our own subsequent work, are higher . . . than the estimate Anna J. Schwartz and I used in *A Monetary History.*"

Question Three: Have We Ever Been Trapped? The answer to this question can be stated very succinctly: The great weight of historical evidence indicates that we have never been in a liquidity trap. A number of studies have attempted to find periods in American history when the public was willing to hold whatever quantity of money balances made available. Over the periods investigated, the public has always made attempts to unload excess money balances in exchange for other assets.

Studies of the demand for money can be thought of as the first round in the debate over the efficacy of monetary and fiscal policy. The nice thing about the first round is that each side can go back to its corner confident that it took the round on points. Monetarists smell victory because of the absence of any evidence of the existence of a trap. To them this is the crucial issue. Keynesians are delighted with the outcome because of the overwhelming evidence of the interest sensitivity of the demand for money.

HISTORICAL EVIDENCE II: THE MONETARISTS' GRAND EXPERIMENTS

The second round in the debate brings us back to the beginning — to the Monetarist claim that (1) the major movements in national income have been associated with major movements in the money supply and *vice versa*, and (2) no equally strong or systematic relationship can be found to support the Keynesian theories. For the Monetarist, none of the evidence on interest rates and the demand for money can change these facts. For Keynesians, these "facts" are highly debatable.

Without getting involved in the technical arguments, we can briefly indicate the debate on this evidence.

Keynesian Objection 1   Mere association does not imply causation. The close relationship between money and national income could reflect a causal influence running from money to income; from income to money (if, for example, the monetary authorities tried to provide enough money to meet the needs of trade); a dependence of both money and income on some third variable; or, as is most likely, a little bit of all three. There is, in short, no way to determine the strength or predictability of the causal link from money to national income using the Monetarist's tools.

Monetarist Response   We agree that mere association does not imply causation. Indeed, we even agree that there has been some influence running from income to money. Our point is that a major cause of the observed coincidence of movement is the effect of monetary forces on national income. There is no need to debate this on a conjectural level, however, because history is not totally silent on this point. There is some opportunity to examine situations in which it is unlikely that the direction of causation went from income to money. One illustration includes those times in history when the money supply has increased because of gold inflows or for other reasons unrelated to income. During these periods, income has risen after the rise in the money supply.

Keynesian Objection 2   The Monetarist's tools may be too crude to pick up the strong influences of fiscal policies. It is a mistake to presume such influences do not exist simply because the impact of fiscal policies cannot be measured by the somewhat naive techniques of the Monetarist. The workings of fiscal and monetary policies on the economy are very complex. There is no shortcut to the very hard work of learning about complex and subtle interrelations in the economy.

Monetarist Response   We could not agree more. The economy is certainly complex, and we know very little about it. In fact, this is what we have been saying right along. We conclude that on the grounds of our ignorance, we ought to go with what we've got, and what we've got is this relationship between the supply of money and national income. If more complicated tests show how fiscal policy works then it will be time to use them. Right now we cannot unlock the code.

Keynesian Objection 3 Your tests are not as conclusive as you think. The definition of monetary and fiscal variables is open to question. We have come up with definitions different from yours that show a strong correlation between fiscal policy and national income.

Monetarist Response We believe that our measures of fiscal and monetary forces are superior to the Keynesians' measures. We frequently get the impression that the Keynesians choose their measures more because they give good results than because they seem reasonable from an economic standpoint.

A SUMMING UP

It is easy to be pessimistic over the state of the art of economic policy. One can find competent economists at every point on the spectrum between "only money matters" and "money doesn't matter at all." To be sure, the great majority take more moderate positions, but even the moderate range is wide and offers rather diverse policy prescriptions. It would be safe to say that the economics profession could under no conceivable set of circumstances offer anything like a "standard" policy prescription. The point is frequently made that the only thing on which most economists will agree is that policy was wrong. But there is rarely any agreement on what correct policy would have been or even what the actual policy was.

The gloominess of the state of affairs, however, is broken by occasional rays of hope. We are currently devoting more resources than ever before toward finding out how the economy works. Millions of dollars have been spent on large-scale econometric models of the United States. Builders of these models claim that they have made long strides in the past decades. It is in these models and in other attempts to interpret economic history that the real hope lies.

There has been a marked shift in the great economic debate since the initial victories of the New Economics. In the late 1940s and early 1950s, it was generally believed by Keynesians that money didn't matter at all. By the early and mid-1960s, the Monetarists had made sufficient headway to shift the question from "does money matter?" to "does fiscal policy matter?" The New Economists have largely recognized the importance of money, but not its dominance. The Monetarists, however, continue to question the empirical relevance of fiscal policy.

 **MONETARISM OBJECTIVELY EVALUATED**
Paul A. Samuelson

M.I.T.'s Paul A. Samuelson is one of the world's most illustrious economists and America's first winner of a Nobel Prize in economics. His academic reputation is in the field of economic theory, but he is also known as a textbook writer and columnist. Here in reply to the case for monetarism, he argues that fiscal policy must retain an important role in economic analysis and policy.

There are fashions within science. Nowhere is the oscillating pendulum of opinion more marked in the field of economics than in the area of money. By the end of the 1930s, after the so-called Keynesian revolution, courses and textbooks continued to be devoted to money. But in fact money had almost completely dropped out of them and the emphasis had shifted to analysis of income determination in terms of such Keynesian concepts as the multiplier and the propensity to consume.

Abridged from Paul A. Samuelson, "Monetarism Objectively Evaluated," in Samuelson, ed., *Readings in Economics,* 6th ed. (New York: McGraw-Hill, 1970), pp. 145—154. Reprinted by permission. This selection as it appears in Samuelson is from the article "Monetarism No," copyright Paul A. Samuelson. All rights reserved.

COMEBACK OF MONEY

If the market quotation for monetary theory sagged in the decade after 1936, by the early 1950s there were unmistakable signs of a comeback. It was Professor Howard S. Ellis of the University of California who coined in those years the expression, "the rediscovery of money." And the famous Accord of 1951, which gave back to the Federal Reserve its freedom to pursue an autonomous monetary policy independently of the needs and desires of President Truman's Treasury, was the objective counterpart of the reappearance of money in the theoretical models of academic scholars.

Of course, we cannot expect recovery to take place at the same time in all markets. Within Britain, the historic home of central banking, the news of the revival of money was late in coming; and even later in being believed. As recently as 1959 the prestigious Radcliffe Report, technically known as the Committee on the Working of the Monetary System, devoted upwards of 3½ million words to the subject. Yet the unanimous conclusion of this distinguished group of British academics and men of finance was, in the end, that money as such did not matter.

Often, if a stock goes down too far in *price,* in reaction it may subsequently go up too far. There is danger of this in the case of monetary theory. A crude monetarism is now stalking the land. In the present article I wish to provide a scientifically objective evaluation of the issues and a balanced history of the oscillations in monetary doctrines.

FRIEDMAN AND THE CHICAGO SCHOOL

Undoubtedly the popularity of monetarism can be traced in large part to one man, namely Professor Milton Friedman of the University of Chicago. His monumental *Monetary History of the United States, 1867–1960,* written with Mrs. Anna Schwartz, is the bible of the movement; and let me say as an infidel that it is a classic source of data and analysis to which all scholars will turn for years to come. In addition to this scholarly work, Professor Friedman has published numerous statistical studies in learned economic journals. He has testified before Congress and lectured before lay groups. His influential columns in *Newsweek* and writings for the financial press have hammered away at one simple message:

It is the rate of growth of the money supply that is the prime determinant of the state of aggregate dollar demand. If the Federal Reserve will keep the money supply growing at a steady rate — say, 4 to 5 percent by one or another definition of the money supply, but the fact of steadiness being more important than the rate agreed upon — then it will be doing all a central bank can usefully do to cope with the problems of inflation, unemployment, and business instability.

Fiscal policy as such has no independent, systematic effect upon aggregate dollar demand. Increasing tax rates, *but with the understanding that money growth remains unchanged,* will have no effect *in lessening the degree of inflation; it will have no* independent *effect in increasing the level of unemployment in a period of deflation; changes in public expenditure out of the budget (it being understood that the rate of growth of the money supply is held unchanged) will also have* no lasting effects on inflationary or deflationary gaps.

In the past, budgetary deficits and budgetary surpluses have often been accompanied by central bank creation of new money or deceleration of growth of new money. Therefore, many people have wrongly inferred that fiscal deficits and surpluses have predictable *expansionary and contracting effects upon the total of aggregate spending. But this is a complete confusion.* It is the changes in the rate of growth of the money supply which alone have substantive effects. *After we have controlled or allowed for monetary changes, fiscal policy has negligible independent potency.*[1]

---

[1] Professor Friedman is careful to specify that fiscal policy does have important effects upon the *composition* of any given total of gross national product. Thus increases in government expenditures will pull resources out of the private sector into the public. John Kenneth Galbraith might like this but Milton Friedman does not. Also, increasing taxation relative to public expenditure, although having no independent effect on aggregate demand, will tend to lower consumption and reduce interest rates. This

This is my summary of the Friedman-type monetarism. No doubt he would word things somewhat differently. And I should like to emphasize that there are many qualifications in his scientific writing which do not logically entail the *simpliste* version of monetarism outlined above.

Moreover, Professor Friedman does not stand alone. His mountains of data, cogency of reasoning and formidable powers of patient persuasion have raised unto him a host of followers. Graduates of the Chicago workshops in monetary theory carry to new universities the message. A number of other scholars, such as Professors Allan Meltzer at Carnegie-Mellon University in Pittsburgh and Karl Brunner of the University of Rochester have also produced research in support of monetarism. Professor Harry Johnson leads the campaign to export monetarism to the British Isles. One of our twelve regional Federal Reserve Banks, that of St. Louis, has carried the torch for monetarism, providing up-to-date numerical information on the vagaries of the money supply, and promoting quantitative research on the lagged potency of money. Distinguished graduates of the University of Chicago, such as Dr. Beryl Sprinkel of the Harris Trust Company Bank in Chicago, and Dr. James Meigs of the First National City Bank of New York, profess to be monetarists who improve the accuracy of their business forecasts by concentrating primarily on money. At one time or another the editorial pages of the influential *Washington Post* and *New York Times* have become permeated by monetarism. Finally, the Joint Economic Committee of Congress, when it was under the chairmanship of Senator William Proxmire, reacted strongly against the use of fiscal policy as a stabilization device, and recommended to the Federal Reserve Board that it never permit the money supply to grow at rates widely different from some agreed-upon constant.

contrived increase in thriftiness will move the mix of full-employment output in the direction of more rapid capital formation; it will speed up the rate of growth of productivity and real output, and will increase the rate of growth of real wages. If the trend of the money supply remains unchanged, this will tend toward a lower price level in the future or a less rapidly rising one.

KEYNES AND KEYNESIANS

Thus monetarism is a movement to reckon with. I believe monetarism could be deemed fruitful, to the degree that it has pushed economists away from a *simpliste* Keynesian model, popular in the United States during the Great Depression and still lingering on in Britain, and made economists more willing to recognize that monetary policy is an important stabilization weapon, fully coordinate with fiscal policy as a macroeconomic control instrument. However, my reading of the development of modern economic doctrine does not suggest to me that the post-Keynesian position that I myself hold, and of which Professor James Tobin of Yale and Franco Modigliani of M.I.T. are leading exponents, has been materially influenced by monetarism. Indeed, speaking for myself, the excessive claims for money as an exclusive determinant of aggregate demand would, if anything, have slowed down and delayed my appreciation of money's true quantitative and qualitative role.[2]

KEYNES VS. KEYNESIANS

Although the neglect of money is often said to be a characteristic of Keynesian economists and a heritage of the analysis in Keynes' 1936 classic *General Theory of Employment, Interest and Money*, it is doubtful that Keynes himself can be properly described as ever having believed that "money does not matter." If one writes down in the form of equations or graphs the boney structure of the *General Theory*, he sees that money enters into the liquidity-preference function in such a way that an increase in the money supply lowers interest rates,

[2] To clarify my point, let me state my belief that Professor Friedman has been a force of the first magnitude in getting economists generally to realize the desirability of flexible exchange rates. He, and Professors Frank Knight and Henry Simons at Chicago before him, deserve an honored place in the history of economic thought in influencing economists to appreciate the merits of market pricing as against direct government interventions. But I do not believe that the positions today of the Tobins and Modiglianis of the modern scene would be very different if a Chicago school had never existed.

thereby inducing an increase in investment, and through multiplier mechanism causes a rise in employment and production, or, if employment is already full and output at capacity levels, causes upward pressure on the price level.

For a quarter of a century before 1936, Keynes was the principal exponent of monetary theory and the inheritor of the Cambridge tradition of Marshall and Pigou. Although the *General Theory* did represent the repudiation of some of the doctrines Keynes espoused in his 1930 *Treatise on Money,* it represented a continuation and culmination of many of those monetary doctrines. At frequent intervals in the last decade before Keynes' death in 1946, he affirmed and reaffirmed in print and private correspondence his faith that, if the long-term interest rate could be brought down low enough, monetary policy could play an effective role in curing depression and stagnation.

How is it that some Keynesians should ever have become identified with the doctrine that money does not matter? Most converts to Keynesianism became converts during the slump years of the late 1930s. Then the deep-depression polar case did seem to be the realistic case. It is a sad fact about many scholars that they learn and unlearn nothing after the age of 29, so that there exist in chairs of economics around the world many economists who still live mentally in the year 1938. For 1938, when the interest rate on Treasury Bills was often a fraction of a fraction of a fraction of a percent, even a monetarist might despair of the potency of central bank monetary policy.

As one who lived through those times, I can testify by recall how money got lost so that it could later be rediscovered. First, multiple correlation studies by people like Jan Tinbergen, of the Netherlands, who pioneered for the League of Nations macrodynamic models of the business cycle, invariably found that such variables as interest rates turned up with *zero or perversely-signed weights in their estimating equations.* Second, case studies at the Harvard Business School and elsewhere invariably registered the result that *the cost and availability of credit was not a significant determinant of business behavior and investment.* Third, large-scale

questionnaire surveys, like those emanating from Oxford and associated with the names of Sir Robert Hall, Sir Hubert Henderson, Sir Roy Harrod, Charles Hitch, and Phillip Andrews, uniformly recorded answers denying the importance of interest rates and monetary conditions. Fourth, as Professor Alvin Hansen and other contemporary writers noted, the inflow to the States of billions of dollars of gold resulting from distrust of Hitler's Europe, produced almost a controlled experiment in which the reserves of the banking system were vastly expanded and yet no commensurate expansion in business activity or even in the total money supply was achieved. Finally, it was fashionable in those days for theorists to argue that interest was a negligible cost where short-term investment projects were involved, the irreducible uncertainties of expectations served to dwarf the importance of the interest rate as a controlling variable.

However realistic it may have been in the 1930s to denigrate the importance of money, and with hindsight I do believe that even this may have been overdone, still in the high-employment epoch that is characteristic of the post-World-War-II years there was little excuse to remain frozen in an archaic denial of money.

HOW IT WORKS

By the 1950s and 1960s a body of analysis and data had been accumulated which led to a positive, strong belief that open-market and discount operations by the central bank could have *pronounced macroeconomic effects upon investment and consumption spending in the succeeding several months and quarters.* One of the principal preoccupations of the post-Keynesian economists, which is to say of the ruling orthodoxy of American establishment economics, has been to trace out the *causal* mechanisms whereby monetary and fiscal variables produce their effects upon the total of spending and its composition.

Thus, an open-market purchase of Treasury bills by the Fed first bids up bond prices and lowers their yield; this spreads to *a reduction* in *yields* on competing securities, such as longer-term government bonds or corporate bonds or home mortgages. The lowering of interest costs will typically be accompanied by *a relaxation in the degree of credit rationing,* and this can be expected *to stimulate investment spending* that would otherwise not have taken place. The lowering of interest rates generally also brings about an *upward capitalization of the value of exising assets,* and this increase in the money value of wealth can be expected to have a certain *expansionary influence on consumer spending,* and in a degree on business spending for investment. As a limit upon the stimulus stemming from money creation by orthodox open-market operations, must be reckoned the fact that as the central bank pumps new money into the system, it is in return taking from the system *an almost equal quantum of money substitutes* in the form of government securities. In a sense the Federal Reserve of the Bank of England is merely a dealer in second-hand assets, contriving transfer exchanges of one type of asset for another, and in the process affecting the interest rate structure that constitutes the terms of trade among them.

What needs to be stressed is the fact that one cannot expect money created by this process of central-bank open-market operations *alone,* with say the fiscal budget held always in balance, to have at all the same functional relationship to the level of the GNP and of the price index that could be the case for money created by gold mining or money created by the printing press of national governments or the Fed and used to finance public expenditures in excess of tax receipts. Not only would the creation of these last kinds of money involve a flow of production and spendable income in their very *act of being born,* but in addition the community would be *left permanently richer* in its ownership of monetary wealth. In money terms the community *feels* richer, in money terms the community *is* richer. And this can be expected to reflect itself in a higher price level or a lower rate of unemployment or both.

By contrast, money created through conventional central-bank operations quite divorced from the financing of fiscal deficits or the production of mining output does not entail an equivalent permanent increase in net wealth as viewed by people in the community. Post-Keynesians emphasize that extinguishing the outstanding interest-bearing public debt, whether by a capital levy or by open-market purchase of it, does rationally make the community *feel poorer* than would be the case if the same amount of money existed and the public debt had been unreduced. All men are mortal. Most men do not concern themselves with the well-being of their remote posterity. Hence, government bonds as an asset are not completely offset in their minds by the recognition of the liability of paying in perpetuity taxes to carry the interest on those bonds. Only if people live forever, foreseeing correctly the tax payments they (or the posterity as dear to them in the most remote future as is their own lifetime well-being) must make on account of the perpetual future interest payments on government bonds — only then would it be true to say that retirement of public debt would have no substantive effects upon the reckoning of wealth, the levels of spending, and the level of prices generally. Rejecting such a perpetual-life model as extreme and unrealistic, we must debit against an increase in money through open-market operations a parital offset in the form of retirement of some of the outstanding public debt.

Finally, to clarify the significant difference between the post-Keynesian analysis which most modern economists believe to be plausible as against the tenets of monetarism, I must point out that even when the money supply is held constant:

1. Any significant changes in thriftiness and the propensity to consume can be expected to have systematic independent effects on the money value of current output, affecting average prices or aggregate production or both.

2. Likewise an exogenous burst of investment opportunities or animal spirits on the part of business can be expected to have systematic effects on total GNP.

3. Increases in public expenditure, or reductions in tax rates — and even increases in public expenditure balanced by increases in taxation — can be expected to have systematic effects upon aggregate GNP.

All these tenets of the modern eclectic position are quite incompatible with monetarism. (Indeed that is the differentiating definition by which we distinguish the Chicago School monetarism from the post-Keynesian positions with which it has so much overlap.) The eclectic position is incompatible with monetarism, but it is not incompatible with a *sophisticated* version of the Quantity Theory of Money. For as soon as one follows the logic of neo-classical analysis (expecting that less of any kind of inventory will be held if, other things equal, the cost of holding it has gone up) and postulates that the *velocity of circulation of money is a rising function of the interest rate,* the post-Keynesian (and even the simple Keynesian) model becomes compatible with the Quantity Theory. One way of looking at Keynesian liquidity preference is as *a theory of the velocity of circulation.*

FAULTY LOGIC

When post-Keynesians study recent economic history, they find that interest rates and money do enter into their estimating equations and with the theoretically expected algebraic signs. Case studies bear out the importance for investment decisions of the cost and availability of credit. Properly phrased questionnaires to business elicit answers that point in the same direction. And plausible theories to explain how businessmen make their investment decisions and how they ought to also bear out the fact that monetary policy does matter. So there is simply no excuse for living in a 1938 dream world in which money does not matter.

The bearing of all this on monetarism is well illustrated by an incident a few years ago at an American Bankers Association symposium where leading academic economists were commenting upon Professor Friedman's writings. Professor James Tobin went to the blackboard and wrote down three sentences:

1. Money does not matter.
2. Money matters.
3. Money alone matters.

He went on to say: Professor Friedman produces evidence to prove that the first proposition, Money doesn't matter, is false: he purports to have demonstrated from this that the third proposition, Money

alone matters, is true; whereas the correct logical conclusion is that the second propostion, Money does matter, is all that follows. And on that there is no quarrel among leading modern macroeconomic economists.

I think there is much wisdom in this. When Professor Friedman defends monetarism, as for example in a late-1968 debate at New York University with new economist Walter Heller, he refers to a mountain of evidence that supports monetarism. But how many members of the thousands in the overflow crowd attending that debate were able to appraise that evidence to see whether it supports proposition 2, that money matters, rather than the central tenet of monetarism, that (when it comes to predictable systematic effects on aggregate demand and on inflationary or deflationary gaps) money alone matters? Sir Ronald Fisher, the greatest statistician of our age, pointed out that replication a thousandfold of an inconclusive experiment does nothing to add to its value. In terms of the language of statistics, most of the evidence compiled about money has little or no power to differentiate between propositions 2 and 3. Let me illustrate.

A typical bit of historical evidence put forth to support monetarism goes like the following. "In 1919, after World War I, the U.S. Treasury wished to stabilize the interest rate. Keeping the Discount Rate constant resulted in a great increase in the money supply and in strong inflation. Then, early in 1920 on an identifiable date, the Treasury changed its policy; there followed a sharp reduction in the growth of the money supply; there followed a collapse of prices and the Recession of 1920–21. Ergo monetarism is true." But surely, for our purpose, this is a complete *non sequitur.* If we accept the chronology as given, it should indeed give pause to some witness before the Radcliffe Committee who argues that money never matters. But a whole range of mountains of evidence of this type does not tell us whether other factors — such as fiscal policy — may not also have an independent influence on the pace of inflation. Replicating a refutation does not add commensurately to its weight, so I shall forebear from giving other examples of similar reasoning.

Let me mention one last kind of evidence that

allegedly bears out the position of monetarism. Dr. Friedman, with the collaboration of Dr. David Meiselman, prepared for our Commission on Money and Credit a comparison of which does better for prediction: a simple correlation of money with GNP, or a simple correlation of some kind of Keynesian multiplicand with GNP or a related measure. They end up with a somewhat larger correlation coefficient for money. Ergo, monetarism is correct; Keynesianism has been defeated in a trial of honor. In my view this is simply silly. I waive the fact that the choice of variables and periods selected for the study has been subject to much criticism and debate. The post-Keynesian position which I adhere to does not believe in either of the simple theories set up as straw men, and is not particularly interested in which has the higher simple correlation coefficient. Even the St. Louis Federal Reserve Bank, a bastion of monetarism, when it came to compare either simple theory with an eclectic combination of both — which was still, in my eyes, an overly simple model and not one optimally formulated at that — they found that there was a statistically significant reduction in unexplained variance from a combination of the two simple theories. I do not wish to conclude with the impression that there is no possible evidence that would convert me to monetarism. Its tenets are clear cut and are operationally refutable in principle. Personally, as a scientist, I would cheerfully accept *any hypothesis that would deliver the goods and explain the facts.* As a fallible human being, I do not relish having to change my mind but if economists had to hang from the ceiling in order to do their job, then there would be nothing for it than to do so. But monetarism does not deliver the goods. I could make a fortune giving good predictions to large corporations and banks based on monetarism if it would work. But I have tried every version of it. And none do.

To this there are two standard answers. The first is that nothing works well. Fine tuning is an illusion. There is much "noise" in the data. No one can claim that monetarism would enable the Federal Reserve to iron out all the variation in the economy. All we can say for it is that stabilizing the growth rate of money is the best policy that the ingenuity of man can ever arrive at. All this involves what I call the chipmunk syndrome. The nimble monetarist sticks his neck out in an occasional prediction: that prediction is not always free of ambiguity, but it does seem to point qualitatively in one direction, often a direction counter to the conventional wisdom of the moment: then if subsequent events do seem to go in the indicated direction, the prediction is trumpeted to be a feather in the cap of monetarism. If, as is happening all the time, events do not particularly go in that direction — or if as happens often, events go somewhat in a direction that neither competing theory has been subjected to a test of any resolving power — the chipmunk pulls in his head, saying that there is no way of fine tuning the economy or making completely accurate predictions.

The other argument against the view that monetarism simply does not work is the assertion, "Monetarism does work. So and so at the Black bank uses it and he beats the crowd in batting average." I believe this to be a serious and important subject for investigation. Let me therefore, because of space limitations, confine myself to a few observations based upon preliminary investigations of the matter.

1. Those analysts who use their monetarism *neat* really do *not* perform well.

2. A number of bank economists, who give great weight to the money factor but who *also* pay attention to what is happening to defense spending and inventories and a host of other factors, seem to me to have compiled an excellent record at forecasting. Not a perfect record. Who has a perfect record? And not, as far as quantitative studies known to me suggest, a better record than the best macroeconomic forecasters who do not consciously put special stress on the money factor (but who do not neglect it either!). In short, it is impossible to separate "flair" in forecasting from success attributable primarily to use of money-supply variables.

3. The years 1966–67 are often referred to as years of a crucial test in which monetarism defeated Keynesianism. I have gone over all the main forecasts used by both schools during that period and I must report that this is a misapprehension. There

was a *wide range* of forecasts by practitioners of both schools: there was a *wide overlap* between these two ranges. On the whole, the monetarists averaged better and *earlier* in their perception of the slowdown beginning to be seen in late 1966 in consequence of the money crunch of 1966. And one would expect this to be the case from an eclectic viewpoint since the independent variable of money received the biggest alteration in *that* period. But many of the monetarists went overboard in predicting a recession in 1967 of the National Bureau type: indeed some of the more astute monetarists warned their brethren against following the logic of the method, lest it discredit the method! And some of the largest squared errors of estimate for 1967 that I have in my files came from dogmatic monetarists who did not heed the warning from inside their own camp.

4. Again, the year 1969 is thought by some to provide a test of some power between the two theories. Yet I, who am an eclectic, have my own GNP forecast for the year nicely bracketed by the two banks that heve been most successful in the past in using monetarism in their projections. And though I must admit that the last part of 1968 was stronger than those who believe in the potency of fiscal policy and the mid-1969 tax surcharge to be, I do not interpret that extra strength as being a negation of any such potency or as due solely or primarily to the behavior of money during the last 12 months. Without the tax surcharge, I believe the GNP would have surprised us by soaring even faster above predictions. Since history cannot be rerun to perform controlled experiments, I cannot prove this. But the weight of all the evidence known to me does point in this direction. In a soft science like economics, that is all even the best practitioner can say.

CONCLUSION

The bulk of my remarks have been critical of an overly simple doctrine of monetarism. But they must not be interpreted as supporting the view that money does not matter. There are parts of the world, particularly in Britain and the Commonwealth, where it might be better to believe in overly simple

monetarism than in overly simple denial of the role of money.

In the *Sunday Telegraph* (London, December 15, 1968) I was able to invert the Tobin syllogisms to isolate the fatal flaw in the reasoning of the Radcliffe Report. The Radcliffe Committee heard much convincing testimony to show that there existed no invariable velocity of circulation of money to enable one to predict GNP accurately from the money supply alone. In effect then, Radcliffe established the falsity of Tobin's third proposition, Money alone matters. And, in a *non sequitur,* they concluded the truth of his first propostion, that Money does not matter. For all their talking around the subject of liquidity as a substitute concept for money alone, they and the fossil-Keynesians who hailed their report should have recognized the fact that both theory and experience give to money (along with fiscal and other variables) an important role in the macroeconomic scenario of modern times.

QUESTIONS

1. What is monetarism? In what sense does it differ from Keynesianism and the New Economics?
2. What evidence do the monetarists rely upon to support their position? What evidence does Samuelson summarize in rebuttal? How do you evaluate the evidence?
3. What character of the demand for money is crucial to the monetarist position? Why? From the standpoint of the New Economics, what is the role of the interest rate on the demand for money and on the income—expenditure process?

51 THE BURDEN OF THE NATIONAL DEBT
Abba P. Lerner

Perhaps one measure of the increasing economic so-
phistication of the general populace is the gradual
diminishing of concern with the size of the national
debt. Still, to many people this issue is of substan-
tial importance and the debt is a cause of consterna-
tion and impending doom. As will be apparent, Pro-
fessor Abba Lerner of the City University of New
York loses little sleep over the size of the national
debt. Lerner, one of Lord Keynes' most famous
students, is a Distinguished Professor at Queens Col-
lege of the City University of New York.

When an editor of a newspaper or a cartoonist runs
out of ideas, he can always call attention to the "national debt." The cartoonist can show the citizen
being crushed by an enormous burden. The editorial writer will express himself arithmetically. Since
nobody knows what is meant by a million dollars,
let alone two hundred and ninety billions of dollars,
the arithmetic can be very impressive. For example,
he might ask how long you thought it would take
you to pay off the national debt if you were given a
full-time job of repaying it at the rate of one dollar
a second. Years? Maybe hundreds of years? Not so
easy. To pay out two hundred and ninety billion
dollars at one dollar per second for seven hours a
day working three hundred days a year would take
about 40,000 years. And at the end of the 40,000
years would the national debt have disappeared?
On the contrary, all this repayment would not even
have begun to make a dent on the compounding of
the debt into really astronomic trillions of trillions
of dollars. It would take a *thousand* people each
paying out a dollar a second just to pay off the interest so as to stop the debt from growing any bigger than the accumulated unpaid interest.

On Mondays, Wednesdays and Fridays the edito-

rials frighten us with these unimaginably large numbers and tell us that the country is being destroyed
by the tremendous national debt. But on Tuesdays,
Thursdays and Saturdays the same editorial page
will remind us that we are enjoying a higher standard of living and greater prosperity than ever before.
If we remembered Monday's editorial on Tuesday
we might wonder how we are able to manage so well
in spite of the national debt and whether this could
possibly be because we owe it only to ourselves.

THE COLLECTIVE DEBT

Editorials dismiss the notion that we owe the national debt to ourselves as too ridiculous to deserve
further analysis, and continue their arithmetical exercises. But when the scoffing and the arithmetic
are over, the question still remains, "If we do not
owe the national debt to ourselves, to whom *do* we
owe it?" To this there is no answer. There *is no-*
body else to whom we owe the debt. The national
debt is a debt which the people in the United States
owe, through the government, to the holders of the
government bonds who, with some insignificant exceptions, happen to be the people in the U.S. No
matter how funny it may seem to some, we don't
owe it to Germany or Japan or Russia or any other
country. We do, as a nation, owe the national debt
to ourselves.

Our owing it to ourselves has important consequences. First, there is no analogy between the national debt and a private, personal, or business debt.
If I have a personal debt, I am that much poorer.
The man to whom I owe this debt can ask me to
pay it at some time. If I pay him, it is a sacrifice on
my part, and it may come at an extremely inconvenient time. The payment of my private debt means,
for a time, consuming and enjoying less than I
would otherwise be able to. I may have to tighten
my belt.

But if part of the national debt is repaid, it is not
true that the nation has to tighten its belt. The productive resources of the country are no less; the
amount of goods produced is not diminished. What
happens when a part of the national debt is repaid is
that some money is taken from some of the inhabi-

From Abba P. Lerner, *Everybody's Business* (East Lansing:
Michigan State University Press, 1962), chap. 13, pp. 104—
114. Reprinted by permission.

tants of the country and is given to others. The nation as a whole does not have to consume any less than before.

The analogy between personal debt and national debt is false because a personal debt is really an *interpersonal* debt — a debt of one person to another. The proper analogy to a personal debt is an *international* debt — a debt of one nation to another. The paying nation then does have to tighten its belt. But, it must be impressed upon the reader, a national debt is completely different, and repaying it does not involve any tightening of the national belt.

This would not sound so surprising if we remembered that there is the same difference when national and personal debts are *incurred*. When I incur a *personal* debt, the borrowed money enables me to consume more than I produce and earn myself. This is not true of *national* debt. Since the lenders are also inhabitants of the country, the borrowing of national debt only means a transfer among consumers and investors within the country (including the government as a consumer or investor on behalf of the public). The borrowing does not enable the nation to consume more than it produces. It does not allow the nation to loosen its belt in the first place and that is why it does not force it to tighten it again when the debt is repaid.

THE IMAGINARY EFFECTS

Yet it would be false to give the impression that the national debt doesn't matter at all. It is important to distinguish between the imaginary effects and the real effects of the national debt and to deny only the imaginary effects. But to many people the denial of imaginary effects looks like a denial of *all* the effects. This is sometimes the fault of those who deny the imaginary effects in using unnecessarily strong language. They tend to speak rather like a person whose twisted ankle has been exaggerated by rumor into a near fatality. He is tempted to say "Why it's nothing at all!" He doesn't really mean it is nothing at all; a twisted ankle can be extremely painful. He merely means to say that the other story is quite false. In the same way, to deny the imaginary effects of national debt is not to imply that there are no real effects to be concerned about.

The first imaginary effect I want to deal with is the notion that national debt is a national impoverishment. People speak as if the United States is poorer by two hundred and ninety billion dollars, the size of its national debt, just as any individual is poorer by the amount of his personal debt. To show his "net worth" in his balance sheet, the individual must subtract his debts from his assets. The mistake in applying this procedure to the nation is in forgetting that every debit has a credit.

If anybody owes money, there is somebody to whom the money is owed. This is always the case; there are no exceptions. The wealth of the nation includes the net worth of all the individuals in it, yet the nation is never poorer on account of a private debt by one individual in the country to another. This is because although the debt must be subtracted to get the figure for the net worth of the debtor, it must be added to get the figure for the net worth of the creditor, and the two items cancel when they are added in to show the wealth of the nation. And when the debt is paid, again the nation is not impoverished because the creditor receives all the money that the debtor pays, and the two opposite aspects of the transfer are equally part of the account of the nation.

All this seems to be very well understood by almost everybody, *but only for private debt.* Yet it applies in exactly the same way to public debt. For every dollar which you and I as residents of the United States owe, through our government, to the owners of the national debt, there is a corresponding creditor who owns a United Sates debt certificate of one kind or another. When we total the debt, it is our duty, if we do not want to mislead, to total the credit too. And if we count both, they cancel out.

While it is common for only the debit side of the national debt to be counted, I don't know of anybody who has counted only the credit side. But it could be said with equal logic, or rather illogic, that the United States is *richer* because among the things which Americans own are two hundred and ninety billions of national debt — in the form of first-class, gilt-edged securities guaranteed by the United States government. You can repeat the arithmetical exercises of the editorialist and see how long it would take to count this part of our *wealth*. This, of course, would be just as silly as doing the opposite. The United States is not any richer on account of the national debt than it is poorer because of it. Against the credit there is a debit, just as against the debit there is a credit.

It is commonly stated that the national debt will lead the United States to bankruptcy. What does this mean? A person is bankrupt if he cannot meet the demands of his creditors, is brought into court and declared bankrupt by a judge. He then knows that if he were to borrow any more money without warning the lender that he has been declared bankrupt, he could be sent to jail. It is perfectly clear that this couldn't be done by any judge to the United States. In the first place, the United States government can always legally meet its obligations by creating legal-tender money — and it is not illegal for the government to do that, even though it is illegal for anybody else. And in the second place, if for any reason the United States should refuse to meet any of its obligations, nobody has the power to do anything about it.

At this point the argument is generally changed and bankruptcy is declared to mean not bankruptcy, but a decline of the purchasing power of the dollar, which is quite a different and very serious thing. The national debt can contribute to a rise in prices, which means a fall in the value of the dollar. It may do this to a large or to a small degree, or not at all, depending upon many other factors, but we can only deal with this problem if we are clear that we are talking about changes in prices, and not about bankruptcy. I shall discuss such effects on prices later in dealing with the possible *real* effects of the national debt.

Another bogey is the question of what will happen when the national debt has to be repaid. One answer to this we have already given. If and when the repayment is made, the repayment will be received by the people in this country and there will be no net deprivation involved for the country as a whole. The other and perhaps more important answer is that there is no date when the national debt

has to be repaid. It is, of course, true that government bonds fall due at certain dates, but this does not mean that new bonds cannot then be issued — often even to the very same people. Many owners of national debt would be very unhappy if they could not re-invest the money all over again in the same way and for the same reasons as before.

There is a possibility of a sudden loss of confidence in the government and people may then want to cash in their government securities. It would be a very serious matter for any individual or corporation if it were suddenly called on to pay off its creditors in cash; but not for the government. This is because the government can create the money people want to hold instead of government bonds, and everybody can be happy. People who want cash can have cash, and as long as they only want to hold on to the cash no harm is done; the government may also feel happier because it now does not have to pay so much interest. On the other hand, people may not want to hold the money, but may decide to spend it. This could cause some real troubles which will soon be considered.

Another argument — and this one is quite a tear-jerker — is that the national debt will be a burden on our grandchildren, and that it is immoral and heartless of us to allow posterity to pay for our profligacy. This is nothing but an echo of the original confusion. If the debt should be repaid by our grandchildren, it is hard to see who would be receiving the repayment except our grandchildren. There is, besides, the other question as to whether or not the debt would in fact ever need to be paid off, and this applies just as much in our grandchildren's time as in the present.

At this point in the argument, there usually comes a bothersome snag phrased something like this: "Well, the mere existence of the national debt may not be so dangerous, nor is it likely to be called on to be repaid, and if it is we can probably handle that all right, but what about the *interest* on the national debt?" This is perhaps the most curious of all the objections. The man who brings it up is like a woodsman miraculously still sitting up in the air on a tree branch which he has sawed off. If the mere existence of the national debt doesn't do any harm, then there is no need for one to worry about the interest. One way of dealing with the interest is to borrow more money with which to pay it. All that would happen then is an increase in the national debt — which, it has been demonstrated, itself does no harm.

The apparent danger, or wickedness, or the profligacy of a person's spending more than his income — from which we get the false analogy to national debt — seems to apply doubly in the case of interest. I am not only failing to repay my debt, but I am actually getting deeper into debt meeting the interest. This is so doubly dangerous a course of behavior for any individual that it is twice as hard to remember that it is different for the nation. But the logic applied previously cannot be avoided here. The interest payments, just like national debt repayments, are paid by Americans to Americans. The nation as a whole is not impoverished by the interest payments any more than it is enriched by them.

Another objection we have to meet is that of the person who points to the physical destruction during the wars when most of our debt was incurred, and our failure to build houses or factories during these times. This lack is pointed to as constituting the real burden of the national debt on our children and grandchildren. The answer to this is that the destruction and failure to reconstruct will undoubtedly be a very real burden on our children and grandchildren. Many people in Europe and other parts of the world have suffered cruelly because of it. But the destruction would have been just as bad if no debt whatever had been contracted in connection with it. If all the money spent by governments during the wars had been raised by taxes, but there had been the same destruction and failure to replace factories, houses, and other useful things, there would be exactly the same real burden on our children and grandchildren. It is on the wars that we must blame the destruction, not on the debt.

A more respectable argument is made by certain accountants who say that we have a false picture of how rich we are. They have suggested that every person, in order to get an accurate picture of how well off he is, ought to subtract from his visible wealth his share of the national debt. This would be a sound corrective for people who are prone to underestimate the burden of that part of his taxes, present and future, which is due to the existence of the national debt. But taxpayers are more prone to exaggerate than to underestimate these burdens, and even for those who underestimate this burden, counting their share of the national debt as an *additional* burden (however they may compute what is their share) would constitute a preposterous overcorrecting unless (a) they had counted the expected taxes as zero and (b) it was in fact decided to impose enough in taxes to pay off the whole national debt. Such calculations would not however make many people believe that the wealth at their disposal is really curtailed, so that not much harm could be done apart from the political effects of exaggerating the debit side of the national debt. This would hamper the development of rational policies in the incurring and repayment of national debt.

After all this, it may seem as though we should just forget about the national debt, and simply write it off. If we owe it to ourselves, why bother to keep an account? The reason why the national debt cannot be simply repudiated is that the "we" does not indicate exactly the same people as the "ourselves." Although, *as a nation*, we owe the national debt to ourselves, some people owe more than they are owed; other people are owed more than they owe. Those who have a larger part of their wealth in the form of government securities than others would be hurt by a cancellation or repudiation of the national debt. We have persuaded them in the name of patriotism (often with dubious arguments) to buy government securities. It would be bad faith not to honor the national obligations to those who responded to the appeal.

Certain left-wingers maintain that the existence of national debt makes the rich richer and the poor poorer. They point out that most of the national debt belongs to rich people. (This of course is not surprising; after all, that is one reason why they are rich.) But everybody, including the poor, is taxed to provide the interest payments to the rich. On the other hand, right-wingers and rich people point out that rich people are taxed much more heavily than the poor, and that government bonds are owned by very large numbers of people most of whom are by no means rich.

Actually these two arguments more or less negate each other. The rich as a class would lose more than the poor from a repudiation of the bonds, but they would also gain more than the poor from the reduction in taxes that would accompany it. Just as a rich man gets much more in interest he also pays much more in taxes than a poor man. All in all it is doubtful whether the existence of the national debt has any appreciable effect on the relationhip between the rich and poor.

THE REAL EFFECTS

Now let us discuss the *real* effects of the national debt. The mere *existence* of the national debt has an effect on total spending. The people who own the national debt feel richer because of it and therefore they spend more money. Whether the extra spending is good or bad in its effect depends upon what the economy needs. If the economy is in a state of depression because there is not enough spending, then the extra spending brought about by the national debt is a good thing. It results in better business, more employment and a higher national income. But if there is enough spending to begin with, so that there is no depression, or if there is already too much spending so that the economy is suffering from inflationary pressures, the extra spending brought about by the national debt is a bad thing. It creates inflationary pressures or it increases them.

One way to stop people from spending too much is to increase taxes so that they have less money left to spend. This would not *really* impoverish them, whatever the individual taxpayer may feel about it, because all that the extra taxes would do would be to take away the extra money with which people were bidding up prices in trying to buy more than was available. After they pay the taxes, although they would be *spending* less, they would still be *buying* just as much as before but at lower prices. Only the *inflation* would be reduced by the extra taxation, not the quantities of goods and services that the public could actually obtain.

Nowadays governments for various reasons have to undertake large expenditures. There is at the same time so much expenditure for private consumption and private investment that if it were not for heavy taxes there would be too much spending and inflation. Since the existence of the national debt causes extra consumption, there must be more taxation to avoid inflation. Such additional taxation, although it does not constitute a subtraction from real income, does have harmful indirect effects. . . .

Even though it would be immoral to repudiate the national debt now that we have it, would it not have been better if we had not incurred it in the first place and so avoided these harmful indirect effects? What if the government had not spent the money or if it had raised the money by taxing instead of borrowing?

The answer is that our national income would have been less all throughout history, and not only by the amount of the national debt but by a multiple of that amount. Whenever the government (or any business or anybody else for that matter) spends money, income is created for the producers of what is bought. The income thus created results in more spending by those who have received it and this in turn creates extra income for still others so that the total income is increased by several times the initial increase in spending. The two hundred and ninety billion dollars of government spending (which was financed by the borrowing that built up the national debt to its present size) has thus resulted in contributing several times that amount to our total national income up to date — perhaps a thousand billion dollars. Without this two hundred and ninety billion dollars of government spending, and if no other spending had taken its place, we would have been in a really bad way. Some of the spending we could very well have done without, because there was at certain periods too much spending, which resulted in inflation. But without the income created directly and indirectly by the $290 billion of government expenditure we would have suffered from much longer and much deeper depressions throughout our history. Not only would we have consumed less over the period, but there would have been less investment too. We would today have fewer and poorer factories and roads and houses than we have. In real terms we would be much poorer not richer.

Let us now suppose that the national income had been maintained all through history *without* creating any national debt — that private companies and corporations had spent money instead of the government with the same effect in maintaining income, consumption and investment; so that the real wealth of the country — its productive equipment — would be the same. We would then have no national debt. Would we be any better off?

Not at all. The expenditures by corporations and business and individuals would have built up private claims to wealth in exactly the same way that they have been built up by the national debt. American citizens would now own an extra two hundred and ninety billion dollars in shares of General Motors and other corporations. These shares would make them feel just as rich as government securities do (or perhaps richer inasmuch as dividend payments are generally higher than interest payments on the national debt). We would therefore have the same extra spending or more. There would be exactly the same inflationary pressures and it would be just as necessary for the government to levy heavy taxes to prevent the inflation.

Our heavy taxes are made necessary by our great accumulation of private claims to wealth. These have the same effects whether they are in the form of national debt or whether they are in the form of ownership of property in business and corporations and houses. It is the ownership of claims to wealth which makes people spend more, and if this would otherwise lead to too much spending, there has to be more taxation to protect us from inflation. The blame lies not with the existence of national debt as such but with the existence of *any* claims to wealth.

This is, of course, no argument against increasing our national wealth. The benefits from an increase in wealth are certainly very much greater than the difficulties that accompany the increase.

Our conclusion is that we *do* owe the national debt to ourselves, that it is not a terrible danger to our society as imagined by those who think it is the same kind of thing as personal or interpersonal debt, and that there are some real problems, but that these problems are due to the existence and growth of *any* private claims to national wealth rather than of that part of private claims to wealth that are the counterpart of the national debt.

QUESTIONS

1. Distinguish between a national debt and a private personal or business debt. Is this a distinction of form or substance?

2. Nation A has a national debt of $1 billion, the debt being held in the form of bonds by that nation's citizens. Nation B also owes $1 billion to bondholders — in this case, the governments of nations C and D. Both A and B pay off their national debts. What is the impact, if any, on the collective wealth of the people in A and B?

3. "The real burden of the national debt will be upon future generations." Comment.

4. What are the real effects of the government's incurring a deficit?

PART THIRTEEN

INTERNATIONAL ECONOMICS

WORLD TRADE —
LAMPOON STYLE
The Harvard *Lampoon*

Humor and economics do not frequently mix. Recall that Carlyle described economics as the dismal science. However, the Harvard Lampoon *parody of* Time *magazine provides this satirical account of world trade and the ideas of Yale University's Arthur Gringo.*

The steaming jungles of Equador spawn a cornucopia of vegetation, but none so vital to the life and breath of the country as the towering banana trees, which each year yield a crop of millions of bunches of the golden-skinned fruit. The seering tundras and barren matàs of Colombia, where tumbleweed may roll for miles unimpeded by obstructions, allows only one organism to survive: the coffee-bean tree, which at maturity may reach as high as five hundred feet.

As a result of these geographical quirks, Equador has a surplus of bananas but no coffee beans, while Colombia has a superabundance of coffee beans but no bananas.

THE NOSE ON YOUR FACE

For centuries the two South American countries have been grappling with this difficult but important issue without success. Last week in Buenos Aires, both countries heard a solution to their problems aired at a conference on economic planning, hosting leading economists from the United States.

To Professor Arthur Gringo of Yale University, the problem looked like a case of the "two-country, two-product phenomenon" which he and his fellow department members have been struggling with for a decade at the historic institution in Tunafish, Connecticut. "We finally discovered that the answer was simple," remarked Gringo modestly. "It's hard to believe now that it took us so many painful years of trial and error, hit and miss."

From "Time," Harvard *Lampoon* Parody, p. 78. ©1970 Harvard Lampoon, Inc., Cambridge, Mass. Reprinted by permission.

In layman's terms, the "Gringo Plan" involves the establishment of "trade relations" between the two countries. Once these lines of communication have been set up, the two countries may begin to "exchange" the product they have an excess of for the product they have a deficit of. In that way "maximum utility" is achieved, because each country receives what it would like to have yet doesn't have but the other country has and is willing to give the other country for what it has because they would like to have it.

GRINGO PLAN IN ACTION

And trade they did. At week's end, a full mobilization of the "Gringo Plan" was ordered into effect by the governments of both participating countries. Jointly, the two parties authorized the purchase of a small armada of American-made flying cranes of the type used to lift heavy I-beams in the construction of skyscrapers. Along with the cranes, tractors and small twin-engined airplanes were bought, and thousands of wheelbarrows and shovels were acquired.

As curious Colombians and Equadorians began to ask questions about the investments being made, the heads of state of the two governments issued a joint statement concerning the new intercountry agreement. "We hab a new idea how we gonna feex dees banana-beans problem. We gonna gib de udder guy soma our trees, he gonna gib us soma hees trees. We gonna 'trade.' "

The next day, before an incredulous audience of banana workers, the giant cranes began flying through the rain forests, stopping precisely at every hundredth tree, attaching heavy cables to their upper branches, and plucking them from the earth, roots and all. The cranes then sped to Colombia, where they inserted the trees in the thousands of holes in the tundra which had been left when a second battalion of cranes had extirpated the giant coffee-bean trees.

Almost immediately after the air-lift operation had been termed a success, though, problems developed. In Colombia the banana trees responded to their new environment by dropping all their leaves onto the parched earth. Efforts to restore the leaves to the trees by various means were of no avail. It was then decided that airplanes should be deployed to seed the sky to produce rain. In minutes the sky blackened and torrents of rain issued from the man-made clouds, and the rain having begun, seemed to refuse to stop. Government officials beamed as the listless banana trees began to regain their turgor, and to sprout new leaves, but frowned when they realized that virtually the entire coffee-bean tree population had suddenly died of moisture poisoning.

Simultaneously, in Equador, the coffee-bean trees were reacting violently to the wetness of the rain forests. With the rigidity in the trunks impaired, the large trees reclined and lolled on the ground. Worried government officials knuckled their brows for a solution to the problem, when suddenly it dawned on them that the way to save the trees was to dry out the portion of the forest which they inhabited with the use of controlled forest fires. Banana trees contiguous with the coffee-bean trees would be set ablaze, thereby drying the coffee-bean trees with the heat emitted. The ingenious plan proved a success, particularly because coffee-bean trees are not flammable, but the old Equadorian saying, "Nothing burns like a banana tree," was born out with tragic realism as virtually the entire banana-tree population literally went up in smoke.

At the beginning of this week Equador had coffee beans but no bananas, and Colombia had bananas but no coffee beans. Puzzled, bewildered, and angry, Equadorians and Colombians turned to Gringo to account for the disastrous consequences of the "Gringo Plan." As flames consumed his effigy in hundreds of village outposts on the pampas and in the forests, Gringo, from a hideout in Rio, observed caustically, "Somehow, I believe they missed the point." Nevertheless the two governments signed separate resolutions in which they vowed never to trade anything with anybody again.

53 PROTECTIONISM: PRO
George Meany

Should the United States protect its domestic industry from foreign competition through such devices as tariffs and quotas? Yes, replies George Meany, for many years president of the AFL—CIO. As head of the nation's largest affiliation of labor unions, Meany could serve as the chief spokesman for organized labor. The following article is based on a speech given before the Aluminum Association of America and should be compared with the next article by Ilse Mintz. Discussion questions follow the second article.

The problem of the rapid deterioration of our country's position in the world economy is a problem of mutual concern to business management and organized labor. It is a problem that affects workers directly and immediately, because it involves the loss of jobs and incomes. I believe it is a problem that also affects American business — in the long run, if not in the short run — because a continuing erosion of industrial payrolls will weaken the consumer markets that are the basis for business prosperity.

At stake are the American standard of living and America's prospects for remaining an industrial nation with a wide range of industries, products and employment.

It was reasonable to expect some decline in America's economic position in the world after World War II. That was a time when the war-torn economies of the other industrial countries were reviving with the help of American economic aid. But this decline did not halt at the end of the 1950's, when those industrial nations were back on their feet. Instead America's share in the world's exports of manufactured goods continued to move down rapidly.

In the past dozen years imports have shot up sharply. The rise of exports has lagged. Within a

Abridged from *A Modern Trade Policy for the Seventies* (Washington, D.C.: American Federation of Labor and Congress of Industrial Organizations, 1973), pp. 3—15.

period of only a few years, the U.S. has become a net importer of an increasingly wide variety of products. These include goods for which America was world-famous only five or ten years earlier, such as autos, typewriters, steel and electrical consumer goods. Even in products of which the U.S. has thus far remained a net exporter, such as machinery for construction and mining, the American share of world exports has moved down in the 1960's.

The problem is concentrated in manufactured products and components. Back in 1960, American exports of manufactured goods were close to twice as great as manufactured imports. By 1972 imports of manufactured goods are running some $3 billion greater than manufactured exports. I think it is a fair guess that about three-quarters of imports today are competing with American-produced goods.

In this process of rapid and drastic change, large parts of entire industries are being wiped out. It is not one industry or two industries, and it is not merely the older industries. Some people talk as if this problem is a textile problem alone, or a garment problem or a glass problem. That is not true at all.

THE SCOPE OF THE PROBLEM

As president of the AFL-CIO, I get reports on conditions in all kinds of industries. I can assure you that the problem is pretty much across the board — in new and sophisticated products, as well as in older industries.

In addition, there is a ripple effect — or a compounding effect — from one industry to another. When the shipbuilding industry was hit, steel production was affected. When the shoe industry was hit, the shoe-machinery industry was also hit. The displacement of American auto production has an impact on tires and parts. If the American aircraft industry goes down, the aluminum industry cannot escape the effects. It is like a fast-creeping disease.

According to *Fortune,* imports now account for about half of the sales in the U.S. of black and white television sets, 96 percent of portable tape recorders, 100 percent of 35mm still cameras and 80 percent of electronic microscopes.

Estimates are about 15 percent of steel sold in the U.S. is imported; about 20 percent of autos; nearly 60 percent of sewing machines and calculating machines and 35 percent or more of shoes.

Baseball is an American game, but about 90 percent of baseball mitts sold in the U.S. are imports. Similarly, a large percentage of other goods sold in the U.S. are imported, including typewriters and shirts, color TV sets and textiles, pianos and tires, work clothes and glass.

Imports now also account for many of the components of products that are assembled in the U.S. Look at an American-made TV set and you will find that much of it is composed of imported parts.

This toll of American products and components is depressing.

These factors that displace American production also displace American employment. The AFL-CIO staff estimates that the decline of America's position in the world economy resulted in a net loss of about 900,000 job opportunities from 1966 to 1971. The worsening situation in 1972 means the further loss of tens of thousands of job opportunities.

According to the Electronic Industries Association, there was a direct displacement of 122,500 American jobs in radio, TV and electronic component production between 1965 and 1970. Scores of thousands of additional jobs have been wiped out with the shutdown of entire plants and departments in a spreading number of industries. They include skilled and technical jobs, as well as unskilled and semi-skilled.

Communities throughout the country are adversely affected. The loss of industrial payrolls means the erosion of the tax base of many communities and the loss of retail sales for local merchants.

THE CAUSES

There are many causes of this situation. One is that foreign nations have direct and indirect subsidies for their exports, combined with various types of barriers to imports. The result is that foreign products flood American markets and the expansion of American exports is blocked or held down.

Another factor is the export of American technology by American companies to their own foreign subsidiaries or to foreign companies with whom they have license and patent agreements. Connected with the export of technology is the sharp increase of investments of American companies in foreign operations and the rapid spread of multinational companies, most of them based in the U.S.

The result of this combination of developments has been the export of American production facilities, the export of American technology and know-how, the export of American jobs.

In talking of the auto industry, Mr. Stuart Perkins, president of Volkswagen of America Inc., stated: "The Americans exported their industry where other countries exported their products." The same can be said of one industry after another.

A *New York Times* report last April 2 indicated the complex and confusing nature of the realities of America's position in the world economy. It said: "The Chrysler Corporation now imports an English car and calls it a Plymouth Cricket, and a Japanese car and calls it a Dodge Colt. General Motors and Ford import Japanese-made trucks and give them American names. And that American Pinto may carry a German engine and be assembled in Canada."

The sales of American-owned foreign manufacturing subsidiaries in recent years have been more than twice as great as the exports of manufactured goods from the U.S. Some of these products of the foreign subsidiaries of American companies are shipped back to the U.S., in direct competition with U.S.-made goods. Another portion of these sales is in foreign markets, frequently in competition with American exports.

There undoubtedly is a fast buck to be made in foreign-plant operations — or at least there is the hope of a fast buck. With American technology and know-how, such a foreign plant is as efficient or nearly as efficient as a similar plant in the U.S. With wages of 12 cents, 25 cents, or even 50 cents an hour, the labor-cost advantage is clear. There are tax advantages, as well.

How can an American worker possibly compete under such conditions? The American factory worker, with an average wage of about $3.80 an hour, can't possibly compete with foreign workers, using the same machinery and know-how and with wages that are 50 percent to 90 percent less.

But workers making 12 cents, 25 cents, or even 50 cents an hour cannot possibly provide much of a market for the sale of TV sets or most other consumer goods that are not immediate necessities.

Where does this leave the company? Its main market — and this is true of almost every American company, even most of the big multinationals — is here at home, in the United States. And that market is based on the American standard of living, on American wages, on the buying power of American consumers.

But the American worker who loses his job is a lost customer for the products of American business. He is also a lost taxpayer. He can't buy much on unemployment insurance payments. When they run out, he may be forced to go on welfare. That adds to the burden of the community.

However, we are not talking of one worker or one plant. We are talking of entire industries and entire communities that are being hit. We are talking of scores of thousands of jobs that are being exported each year.

Here's the way one businessman has described these events of recent years. In an article in the *Chemical and Engineering News,* Mr. Nathaniel Brenner, the director of marketing of Coates and Weller Corp., stated:

"For many years our advanced products enabled us to compete in international markets despite high prices (and high wage rates).

"What has happened in the 1960's and continues is that American corporations, via licensing agreements, foreign plant construction and other multinational arrangements, have given away for a very small portion of real cost and value this advanced technology and, with it, the jobs it created. Where a multinational corporation licenses a product abroad, it gives away the technology created by Americans educated at public expense, and the American jobs which produce that product, for the 5 or 10 percent represented by the license fee or return on invested capital. Result — the American worker loses a job, the U.S. loses an export product and becomes an importer of that product, but the corporation still nets 5 or 10 percent. Result — unemployment plus balance of payments problems. Naturally, the foreign producer can sell for less — he hasn't had to invest in the education, the R & D, or the wages which support the American system." This quotation, I emphasize, is from an American businessman.

The basic source of American economic strength is here in the United States — in our people, in our free institutions, in our schools and skills, in our research and development. Yet part of that basic strength is being given away.

We in the AFL-CIO are concerned about the deterioration of America's position in the world economy — about the export of American jobs and technology. We do not believe that either business or workers can possibly prosper, in the long-run, if America becomes a nation of hamburger stands, hotels, importers and international banks, without the broad base of various types of industries and production. We do not believe that American business, any more than American workers, can prosper over a period of years, if one industry after another goes down the drain.

THE CURE

That is why the AFL-CIO is strongly supporting the Burke-Hartke bill, which is aimed at dealing with the causes of America's deteriorating position in international economic relationships.

As we see it, this bill represents a practical and moderate response to the realities of the world economy. If these realities are not met by practical remedies in the next year or so, there may well be the spread of extremist proposals that none of us would like to see.

The bill would provide government regulation of the export of American technology and capital: regulation not elimination.

It would also set up a "sliding-door" limitation on most imports, except on those goods that are not produced here or that are in short supply: a "sliding-door" limitation, not a high wall to block out imports.

Quotas would be related to the level of American production. In fact, imports would be guaranteed a share of the American market and would be permitted to increase as American production increases. But imports would not be permitted to flood American markets and quickly wipe out American industries.

In addition, the bill would remove the tax subsidies and other special incentives that encourage American companies to establish foreign subsidiaries.

We of the AFL-CIO seek a strong and growing American economy that is an integral part of the world economy. We are not isolationists and have no intention of becoming isolationists. We are convinced that the practical alternative to senseless isolationism is the adoption of realistic government policies to meet America's needs in the world economy.

54 PROTECTIONISM: CON
Ilse Mintz

Should American business receive protection from import competition through tariffs and quotas? Ilse Mintz, former professor of economics at Columbia University and now a senior staff member of the National Bureau of Economic Research, warns against the current protectionist sentiment and presents estimates of the costs consumers must bear because of existing quotas on certain products. Her essay should be read along with the preceding one.

THE RISING IMPORTANCE OF IMPORT QUOTAS

United States foreign trade policy, like that of most other countries, faces in opposite directions. On the one hand, it stands for trade liberalization and in fact, under the Trade Agreements Act and its extensions, tariffs have been reduced substantially. On the other hand, policy is guided by a "no injury philosophy." As soon as the lowering of tariffs or oth-

Abridged from Ilse Mintz, *U.S. Import Quotas: Costs and Consequences* (Washington, D.C.: American Enterprise Institute. 1973), pp. 1–10.

er circumstances lead to a more than negligible rise in imports and thus could begin to have the beneficial effect of pushing resources from inefficient to efficient uses, the policy is reversed and measures are taken to prevent such "disruption."

This posture is reflected in the U.S. trade policy of the fifties and sixties. While tariffs have been reduced in successive steps culminating in the Kennedy Round, the use of nontariff barriers has increased and continues to increase rapidly. How is this possible since such controls not only have been prohibited specifically by the General Agreement on Tariffs and Trade (GATT), but also have been consistently opposed by the United States? It is possible because a new protectionist device has been invented, a device which gets around all international prohibitions and domestic inhibitions and which is combatible with an official posture of unalterable opposition to quotas.

This new tool is the "voluntary" quota, imposed by exporters or an exporting nation on its sales of certain commodities. Since it is the exporter who "wishes" to limit his exports, such quotas are regarded as an entirely different species of control than the ones proscribed by GATT and rejected by the U.S. government. After all, so the reasoning goes, international regulation cannot prescribe to an exporter how much he is to sell and the fact that he informs the importing country of his intentions does not make this country guilty of trade restrictions. Thus liberal consciences are assuaged while a particularly harmful form of restriction is spreading. That the exporter's restrictions are imposed under the threat that the importer will otherwise use compulsion and that the "voluntary" character is a myth does not seem to matter.

The shift in the U.S. attitude toward trade restriction is part of a worldwide trend. In the early years after World War II it was the basic philosophy of the Bretton Woods system that quotas should not be used as a means of regulating international trade, and this principle underlies some of the fundamental rules of GATT. Although these rules allow for many exceptions they helped in the step-by-step reduction of the use of direct controls which had been built up, first in the depression of the 1930s, then

during the war and the so-called dollar shortage thereafter.

The GATT rules were an attempt to prevent repetition of the disastrous effects on economic activity and international goodwill that had resulted from the trade barriers of the 1930's. GATT became so successful in its fight for abolition of controls that it published, in 1959 and 1960, "liberalization communiques" which announced proudly that one or another country had removed restrictions on imports. The greater freedom helped to bring about a record expansion of international trade which enriched the world.

The present, changed attitude is reflected in the proposed Foreign Trade and Investment Act, widely known as the Burke-Hartke bill. If enacted, this bill would place virtually all U.S. imports under quotas, excepting only imports of goods not produced domestically. All covered imports would be limited to the average import level of 1965–69. The result would be a very large cutback in imports. The bill has considerable support in Congress, in the general public, and particularly in sectors of organized labor.

It is not surprising that those who stand to gain directly from protection will fight for it. But it is also understandable that many other well-meaning people join them in the belief that most imports are harmful to the national economy.

PROTECTIONISM: FOR AND AGAINST

The most important protectionist argument is the cheap-labor or low-wage argument. The question is always asked: How can U.S. industry compete with the industry of countries where wages are only a fraction of U.S. wages? To many people and organizations the obvious answer is a call for protection to overcome the wage differential. However, high U.S. wages clearly reflect high U.S. productivity. This fact can best be demonstrated by recalling that the United States, where wages since colonial days have been generally higher than in the rest of the world, nevertheless has sold more abroad than it bought in 92 of the last 96 years (from 1876 through 1971).

But in certain industries, it will be replied, the

difference in productivity is not sufficient to offset the difference in wages. While this is true it merely points to the fact that the productivity of certain industries is substantially *below average*. If average wages in the U.S. are, say, three times as high as those abroad, average U.S. productivity must be about three times as high as foreign productivity. But of course this average ratio does not prevail in every industry and with respect to every product.

Industries suffering from import competition are typically those whose productivity is below average and which pay the lowest wages, whereas the opposite is typically true of export industries. What the protectionist argument in fact suggests is that as much labor and capital as possible be kept in industries with low wages and productivity instead of letting such industries contract in favor of those where both factors are high even by U.S. standards. But just as the production of wheat on the eastern seaboard had to give way to production in the midwestern plains, so production of certain goods should be reduced or discontinued when acquiring them abroad in exchange for exports is more economical.

This argument should not be construed to imply criticism of any import-competing industry. Just as the New England farmer was not any less efficient than the farmer in the Dakotas, so the weak industry may be perfectly modern and efficient in using available resources. The "inefficiency" lies in the nature of an industry that requires relatively large amounts of relatively expensive resources to turn out a product procured more cheaply elsewhere.

Another protectionist argument is — for good reasons — rarely stated explicitly, but may be more influential than any other. Its gist is that changes in relative international costs should not be permitted to cause shifts from one industry to another because such shifts are too painful for those involved. This argument disregards the continuous rapid changes which characterize the American economy. How incredibly mobile this economy is can be seen, for instance, from the fact that in manufacturing alone almost 11 million job changes and new hires occurred in a recent year. The vast majority of shifts is not due to imports, of course, but to changes in

technology, in consumers' tastes, and — mainly — in government policies (such as the recent decline in the aerospace industry). These shifts are accepted because it is generally understood that a dynamic economy must adapt to change and that inability to transform means economic stagnation. Why should an exception be made for industries hurt by imports?

A third protectionist argument, particularly impressive in a time of high unemployment, is that rising imports reduce the number of jobs available to American workers. The effect of imports on employment seems too obvious to be questioned. And yet, a quick look at the data should raise doubts, since it is by no means usual for falling imports to be accompanied by rising employment. The argument is, indeed, fallacious because it ignores the fact that the government would create sufficient demand for a reduction of unemployment were it not for the fear of increasing inflation. But when domestic purchasing power is absorbed by rising imports it can be replaced without danger of inflationary effects. The total demand for domestic goods thus should not be reduced by the growth of imports. Put another way, reduction of imports requires reduction of total domestic demand if it is not to be inflationary.

Also, this protectionist argument overlooks the connection between exports and imports. After a while, a rise in imports will cause an approximately equal rise in exports, for the number of workers required to produce an extra dollar's worth of exports is only negligibly smaller than the number set free by an extra dollar's worth of imports. Temporary unemployment will, of course, arise here as with any other change in the economy, but its volume and duration can be lessened by the adjustment assistance that is discussed below.

Nor are the interests of labor served by freezing jobs in the industries competing with imports. These jobs typically pay less well than do jobs in export industries, even if wages in the former were high compared to foreign ones.

A fourth protectionist argument, which appears especially appealing in 1972, claims that the U.S. balance of payments deficit could be reduced by import controls. Again the argument overlooks the repercussions of import restrictions. These are likely to appear in several ways. Less developed countries whose sales in the U.S. are cut will simply have fewer dollars to spend on U.S. goods. These and other foreign countries may also retaliate by taking similar measures against U.S. goods.

Domestically, the money not spent by Americans on imports will, for the most part, be diverted to other goods, thereby driving up their prices and encouraging imports while curtailing exports. Due to these repercussions, attempts to improve the balance of payments for more than a few months through increased protection have usually failed.

Moreover, exports suffer from import reduction even without retaliation. Many imported goods are used in producing export goods so that when prices of imports are raised through protection exports too become more expensive and less competitive.

PROTECTIVE IMPORT QUOTAS

Among protective devices import quotas are by far the most effective. One of their particularly harmful aspects is the unpredictability of the price rises they set in motion. When raising tariff rates the government knows the upper limit to which the price of the protected good may rise, but with quantitative restrictions there is no such limit.

The allocation of quotas is another troublesome aspect. The profitable rights to import must somehow be assigned either through a government agency or an industrial cartel. The dangers of having public or private officials decide who is to get what share of a valuable privilege is obvious. In addition, the machinery and red tape needed to assign and control the quotas are costly for government and business alike.

A further disadvantage of quotas as compared with tariffs is their effect on income distribution. The revenue from a tariff is received by the government and thus by the public at large. Quota profits, on the other hand, go to those who hold the rights to import under the quotas. The windfall may go to the foreign exporters or the domestic importers. (It is possible to auction off the quotas in order to

channel this profit to the government, but this method has never been applied in the U.S.)

ADJUSTMENT ASSISTANCE

Import restriction is not the only possible policy for aiding an industry which suffers from growing foreign competition. A much less expensive and more efficient approach is to facilitate the adjustments that injured firms and workers must make.

Since all citizens share the benefits of a liberal trade policy, its costs should not be a burden for a few. This principle is recognized by the adjustment assistance provisions of the Trade Expansion Act of 1962. These provisions enable the government to assist through grants and loans the transfer of resources into more productive and competitive branches of industry. The assistance takes the form of programs for relocating and retraining workers and extending financial help to business firms so that they can shift into more competitive production lines. The aim is to shift resources *out* of the industry instead of *into* it.

It would be desirable to broaden the program even more so that assistance could be offered to entire communities injured by import competition to help them diversify their industrial base. One important point in favor of this policy is financial. The costs of adjustment assistance are by their very nature transitory. They must decline and finally vanish as the transfer of labor and other resources is effected.

Needless to say, adjustment assistance is not costless. It is the price paid to an injured minority by a majority which benefits from the greater efficiency of the economy. Some argue, nevertheless, that in the case of large industries this price would be too high. Thus Stanley Nehmer, deputy assistant secretary of commerce, believes that such assistance to the textile industry "would bring us to the threshold of a major financial undertaking that staggers the imagination." However, this argument disregards the fact that the cost of *not* adjusting is as much a function of the size of the industry as is the cost of adjusting. What matters is how many dollars of future costs can be saved by each dollar invested in adjustment assistance. "Invested" is the correct term here because, to repeat, the cost of transition is a one-time outlay in contrast to the long-term or even indefinite cost of protection by import quotas.

QUOTA COSTS SUMMARIZED

[I have made] a rough estimate of the costs of import quotas. These costs are from $1,500 million to $2,000 million a year. The costs of sugar quotas come to around $400 million a year, or as much as 20 to 25 percent of the retail value of U.S. sugar consumption. If these percentages are at all typical, they show that the nation's loss from quotas equals a very sizable part of the value of the products concerned.

The total annual cost of textile quotas (all fibers) amounts to $2,500 million to $4,800 million. This estimate is based on the cautious assumption that import quotas raise textile prices by a mere 5 to 10 percent. Regarding meat quotas, the total user cost has been estimated at $600 million annually.

No matter how rough these figures are, they indicate clearly that quotas impose a heavy burden on consumers. Moreover, the burden weighs most heavily on those with low incomes because the prohibited imports consist, in many instances, of inexpensive goods, such as the cheaper cuts of meat and low-price textiles. A sales tax on such goods, of equal impact on income, would be considered intolerable — and so would import quotas if the public understood their effect.

QUESTIONS

1. What is a volunatry quota? Distinguish between a tariff and a quota as an import restriction.
2. Without import restrictions how can American industry compete with foreign producers who have access to cheap labor?
3. If the government is going to levy some form of import restriction, should this be done through tariffs or through quotas? Why? What explanation exists for the present tendency to use the quota device?
4. Can a case be made for giving adjustment assistance to workers and businesses displaced by foreign competition? Is there any distinction between giving assistance to a worker unemployed because of imports and a worker unemployed because of changes in technology or changes in consumer preferences within the domestic economy?
5. What are the estimates Mintz makes of the cost of selected quotas? Given the magnitude of these estimates, why are consumer protection groups not adamantly opposed to import restrictions?
6. What is the relationship, if any, between import restrictions and the nation's balance of payments?

55 THE MULTINATIONAL CORPORATION
Lawrence B. Krause

To what extent is the multinational corporation a threat to free competition? And what are the implications of this form of enterprise for national sovereignty and an individual country's domestic economic policies? Lawrence B. Krause answers these and other questions about the rapidly growing phenomenon of multinational corporations. Krause is a senior fellow at the Brookings Institution, Washington, D.C., and his specialty is international trade and international finance.

The multinational corporation is now having a revolutionary effect upon the international economic system, but ironically, it is neither a very new development in itself, nor an unknown phenomenon in economic history. The consequences can properly be described as revolutionary because the growth of international transactions of multinational corporations has already overwhelmed the more traditional forms of international trade and capital flows for

Reprinted from "The International Economic System and the Multinational Corporation" by Lawrence B. Krause in Volume No. 403 of *The Annals* of The American Academy of Political and Social Science. Copyright © 1972 by The American Academy of Political and Social Science.

some countries, and has become much more important to the world economy in general. But multinational corporations are not new. Some currently operating companies were already in existence and conducting international business in the early 1900s.

THE ESSENCE OF A MULTINATIONAL CORPORATION

A number of characteristics are used to identify the multinational corporation, but the essential element of such a firm is that it makes direct investments in other countries and thereby extends the organic operations of the firm across national borders.

The multinational corporation may have a profound effect upon the economy of the country in which it operates and to a lesser extent on the parent and third countries as well. It works to break down the isolation of individual economies and to integrate them into a world system. In this respect the phenomenon of the multinational corporation is analogous to the development of national corporations in the United States in the 1880s and 1890s. Despite the fact that the Constitution guaranteed an absence of trade barriers, before 1880 product markets were not unified within the United States, and labor and capital markets were even more fragmented. Essentially the United States consisted of a series of interconnected regional markets with quite distinctive characteristics.

The rise of national corporations reduced the distortions arising from separation of regional markets and thus increased economic efficiency within the United States. With improvements in communications via railroads, the telegraph, and telephone, firms could expand the area within which they could effectively manage their operations. Since wages were higher in the New England, Middle Atlantic, and Western states than in the South or Midwest, firms moved facilities or directed their expansion to these areas to take advantage of cheaper labor. Capital could be borrowed more efficiently and at lower interest rates in financial centers such as New York, Philadelphia, Boston, and Chicago; so firms borrowed in those centers, but utilized the money elsewhere in the country. Firms increased

their own efficiency and improved factor markets by bringing capital and technology to labor because labor was the more difficult factor of production to move. By producing near regional centers of population, firms often reduced the costs of shipping products to markets. Striving to develop brand-name consciousness across the entire country, firms utilized nationwide advertising and thereby created truly national markets.

The rise of national corporations in the United States, however, was a mixed blessing. Some purely local or regional firms found that they could no longer compete successfully and either died or were absorbed by larger firms. Local banks found they could no longer completely control the economic life of their locale and had to settle for a much smaller role. Many observers began to worry about the future of market competition in the country both because of the power of a few firms and because of the business tactics being utilized by them. What resulted was the development of institutions to regulate the activities of firms based on antitrust laws.

THE MULTINATIONAL CORPORATION AND THE WORLD ECONOMY

What the national corporation did for the U.S. economy, the multinational corporation is doing for the world economy. Some quantitative dimensions are helpful in coming to a qualitative judgment regarding the importance of multinational firms. The United States is the largest parent of multinational companies, and U.S. data provide the best available evidence concerning their operations. First, between 1950 and 1970, the book value of U.S. direct investment abroad increased from $11.8 billion to $78.1 billion — close to a sevenfold increase. A comparable concept for corporate investment in the United States increased by less than fivefold over this same period (net value of corporate structures, plant, and equipment calculated at historical costs). Second, there is some evidence that the value of exports of multinational firms to their affiliates is expanding at a faster rate than total U.S. exports.

These magnitudes relate to the United States, but Americans are by no means alone in forming and operating multinational companies. While the data are not available to prove the point, obtainable evidence indicates that foreign-owned multinational companies are growing as fast or faster than their American counterparts. For instance, Japanese direct investment abroad has recently been increasing by more than 30 percent per year and reached a book value of more than $3 billion by March 1971 — fiscal year 1970.

WORLD PRODUCT MARKETS

The most visible consequence of multinational corporations is the integration of product markets; indeed, a product like Coca-Cola is bottled and consumed almost everywhere. The major welfare gains from unifying product markets come from making goods that were not previously offered for sale not only available to consumers, but at prices not much different from their point of origin. To a degree this can be accomplished through international trade, and, as noted above, multinational corporations are active traders. But often foreign production is required, and it is the foreign production of multinational corporations that gives them their distinctive character.

Multinational companies have overcome both natural and man-made barriers that have separated product markets in the past. They have almost destroyed the natural barriers of distance and ignorance and have surmounted man-made tariff walls through local production. In so doing they have improved economic efficiency, but like the national corporation, the multinational corporation has raised the fear of possible excessive market power.

TRANSFER OF TECHNOLOGY

It would not be completely unfair to say that one of the major consequences of multinational corporations is the greater diffusion of new industrial technology around the world. It is true that even before multinational corporations became important, new technology did spread from country to country, but now this occurs more widely and with greater speed. One important consequence is the increase in payoff

to research and development (R & D) within the multinational firm through higher earnings from successful innovations. Higher earnings stimulate even more R & D expenditures, and thus the process is reinforcing.

Another consequence is that it substantially raises the level of technology in the country in which it is transplanted through direct and indirect effects. In order to utilize new technology, the multinational firm must train workers and managers who are primarily local citizens. This training invariably seeps beyond the enterprise because non-affiliated firms that provide local services to the enterprise have to be made technologically competent. Also, local competitors may lure the trained workers and managers who will carry much industrial knowledge with them. Some technology is patentable and cannot legally be copied, but much cannot be protected and is fair game for competitors. Furthermore, local firms will be stimulated to increase their own R & D expenditures to maintain their competitive position. Thus an indirect consequence of the multinational corporation is a spurring of R & D effort generally throughout the host's economy. The aggregative effect of this spread is to reduce the technological gap among nations and thereby reduce income differentials. Countries obtain newest technology much faster, and it becomes more widely adopted throughout the industry.

The technological aspect of multinational companies has caused a dilemma for some governments. In countries where economic self-sufficiency is an important goal, officials may prefer domestic industry to be locally owned in order to maintain independence, but they are hesitant to restrict multinational companies for fear of becoming technologically backward. However, they also fear that once multinational firms obtain a foothold within the economy, locally owned firms will never catch up. Can an electronics firm compete in third- or fourth-generation computers if it has not learned the lessons from producing the first two generations? Furthermore, multinational firms may do their research at home, and thus local citizens are not encouraged to become scientists or engineers, or even worse, they may emigrate to other countries after local training. A simple-minded solution of insisting that multinationals undertake some research locally may make the situation worse, since the multinationals would then absorb the often scarce scientific talent, making it even more difficult for local firms to compete. Clearly, the supply of locally available scientific talent must be increased faster than the demand for it by multinational firms in order to promote R & D in locally owned firms, and this requires more complex policies.

INTEGRATION OF CAPITAL MARKETS

One of the most far-reaching effects of multinational companies is on world capital markets. Governments have often desired to keep domestic capital markets separated, but multinational companies have made this all but impossible. The linkages of capital markets go far beyond the original equity investment, although this transnational flow of funds by multinational corporations is important in itself. Actually, every transaction between a parent firm and its affiliate either contains elements of a capital flow or can easily be made to encompass such effects.

In the absence of major distortions in both capital markets and foreign exchange markets, economic welfare is improved by multinational firms transferring capital from countries in which rates of return are low to countries where the return is higher.

Since multinational firms enter equity, debt, and short-term capital markets, they almost fully integrate world capital markets. This has profound effects upon the economies of most countries, the effectiveness of national monetary policies, and the workings of the international monetary system. By joining capital markets, firms help spread economic impulses from one country to another. Furthermore, the independence of national monetary authorities is undermined. If the central bank tries to enforce tight money to fight inflation, firms borrow abroad and avoid the restraint. If the authorities try to stimulate the economy through easy money policies, they may have their efforts frustrated as firms utilize their liquidity to invest abroad for higher rates of return. Attempts by central banks to

achieve domestic monetary objectives by exchange controls are also frustrated by multinational firms, which can transfer capital in different ways to avoid controls. Since these flows also affect the balance of payments to which governments respond, all governments have lost some of their sovereignty in economic policy making to the private sector, although the United States, because of its large size, has lost less than others.

STRESS ON THE INTERNATIONAL SYSTEM

As noted above, multinational firms cause certain problems for countries, and taken together, they cause considerable stress upon the international economy. Most immediate concern is about international monetary arrangements. The old Bretton Woods system, based on fixed exchange rates with narrow bands of fluctuations in which parities were adjusted only through large, discrete changes, cannot function well when national money markets are closely integrated and governments try to follow independent monetary policies — and multinational firms have insured that money markets are closely integrated. Furthermore, these firms keep capital controls from being very effective. Thus designs for a new monetary system will have to take into account the existence of these firms. Basically, to achieve national stability, the new system will have to utilize market forces to which firms respond, and this means wider permissible fluctuations of market exchange rates plus smaller and possibly more frequent changes in parities.

Another major fear of many governments is that multinational companies will become so powerful that they will destroy the desirable degree of competition in world markets, that they will be more powerful than the governments trying to control or regulate them, and that individual firm decisions may not correspond to the needs or desires of countries. These fears are fed by some naive extrapolations that suggest a handful of companies could control most of the world's industrial output within this generation. While such forecasts no doubt greatly exaggerate both the present and likely future role of multinational firms, the point that a great deal of power will be held in private hands, albeit still subject to national laws, deserves attention.

At present there is no administrative or legal authority that is charged with protecting competition from a worldwide point of view. Some countries have domestic antitrust laws, and the European Economic Community has a code for the whole Common Market, but these laws do not apply to international competition — and often through specific exclusions. United States laws theoretically include extraterritorial applications, but attempts by American courts to extend their jurisdiction abroad is generally resisted by other countries as an infringement upon their sovereignty. Clearly a new approach is required to deal with the threat by multinational corporations to effective world competition.

CONCLUSION

There is little question that multinational corporations have benefited the international economy, but they have been a mixed blessing for many countries. By integrating the economies of different countries into a worldwide system, they have reduced the distortions erected by man and nature. New products have been introduced to consumers, and prices on existing products have been reduced. Methods of production have been improved through the spread of technology and industrial knowledge. Capital markets of most countries have been linked, improving the world distribution of financial resources. An international market has been created for labor skills, which has benefits for relatively backward areas. The totality of these effects improves economic welfare by stimulating growth and efficiency. The stimulus comes directly from the activities of multinational corporations and also indirectly from local business firms striving to compete with them.

In the wake of the changes brought by multinational corporations, new problems have been created for the international system, and some existing difficulties have been exacerbated. Out-of-date international monetary arrangements were made almost inoperative as multinational firms learned to move massive amounts of short-term capital from country to country in response to interest rate incentives and prospects for speculative windfalls.

Thus, it will take much ingenuity to meet the myriad of challenges posed by the multinational corporation. Solutions to problems must be found which meet the needs of national interest without constraining the process or destroying the benefits of multinational firms, as in the case of confiscatory taxation. Because of the benefits of multinational firms, the search for appropriate solutions to these problems should be well worthwhile.

QUESTIONS

1. What are the parallels between the expansion of the corporate enterprise into a national operation in the U.S. and the corporation's expansion to international scope?

2. Discuss the effects of the multinational corporation on a country's fiscal and monetary policy. What impact might multinational corporations have on attempts to peg currency exchange rates?

3. What are the anticompetitive implications of the multinational corporation? What policies can you suggest that would deter them from securing undue monopoly power?

PART FOURTEEN

ECONOMIC GROWTH
AND POPULATION

56 ECONOMIC GROWTH: UNDESIRABLE
E. J. Mishan

E. J. Mishan, of the London School of Economics and Political Science, is accomplished in the worlds of both positive and normative economics. He is known for his persuasive articulation of an antieconomic growth view. This reading is taken from his book The Costs of Economic Growth. *It and other writings of this genre illustrate the changing nature and fashions of economics. In the early 1960s, much of economic thinking was devoted to stimulating economic growth. In the 1970s, writers like Mishan question the value of pursuing economic growth.*

We have already indicated that the concept of expanding choices has little application to the range of opportunities that face working men. The loss of esthetic and instinctual gratification suffered by ordinary working men over two centuries of technological innovation that changed them from artisans and craftsmen into machine-minders and dial-readers must remain a matter of speculation. It need not, however, be supposed that every phase of this historical transformation produced a change for the worse: It may well be that, beginning from some period in the first half of the nineteenth century, the conditions of work have been steadily improving. Yet the conditions of work, including the social facilities provided, may not be the chief factors contributing to the satisfaction derived by men from their daily tasks. It is more than just possible that the chief source of men's satisfaction resides in the kind of work they are called upon to perform and on the regard in which the product of their work is held by their fellows. Two centuries ago, before the "industrial revolution" was properly launched, a skilled workman in this country was a

From E. J. Mishan, "The Cult of Efficiency," in his *The Costs of Economic Growth* (London: MacGibbon & Kee, 1967), pp. 206–213. Copyright © 1967 by E. J. Mishan. Published in the United States by Praeger Publishers, Inc., New York, 1967. Reprinted by permission.

craftsman. Whether he worked in wood, clay, leather, stone, metal or glass, he was the master of his material, and the thing he produced grew in his hands from the substance of the earth to the finished article. He was ever-mindful that he was a member of an honoured craft; that he had reached his position after long apprenticeship; and he took legitimate pride in the excellence of his work.

We are far removed today from that state of society in which craftsmen worked with their own tools in transforming the material into the finished product. And though few workmen alive will have known a situation when it was otherwise, it does not follow that no loss is experienced. Certainly those who have lived through the transitional phases have borne eloquent testimony to their misgivings. Leaving aside such episodes of open resistance to technological improvements, there is no lack of expressions of sadness and regret in the English literature at the passing of the skilled handworker. One that comes to hand is the touching lament reproduced from George Sturt's *The Wheelwright's Shop:*

Of course wages are higher — many a workman today receives a larger income than I was ever able to get as 'profit' when I was an employer. But no higher wage, no income, will buy for men that satisfaction which of old — until machinery made drudges of them — streamed into their muscles all day long from close contact with iron, timber, clay, wind and wave, horse-strength. It tingled up in the niceties of touch, sight, scent. The very ears unawares received it, as when the plane went ringing over the wood, or the exact chisel went tapping in (under the mallet) to the hard ash with gentle sound. But these intimacies are over. Although they have so much more leisure men can now take little solace in life, of the sort the skilled handwork used to yield them. Just as the seaman today has to face the stokehole rather than the gale and knows more of heatwaves than of seawaves, so throughout. In what was once the wheelwright's shop, where Englishmen grew friendly with the grain of timber and with sharp tools, nowadays untrained youths wait upon machines, hardly knowing oak from ash or caring for the qualities of either.

The growing popularity of do-it-yourself kits and craft hobbies is evidence surely of a search to recapture something of the deep satisfaction enjoyed by the craftsmen of old that comes of mastering the material and creating with the hands. The pity of it is that such hobbies can be enjoyed only briefly after the day's work, or at weekends, instead of being the daily work itself. Of course, we are assured by the technocrats that once we reach the promised land of Newfanglia the opportunities for leisurely enjoyments — at least in the "long run" after all the initial economic disturbances have been overcome — will be immense. To the engineering cast of mind, work, any kind of work, is input only; it is the effort expended in producing output. Since *all* input is regarded as a "disutility," and *all* output as a "utility," efficieny consists of reducing the ratio of input to output. If the engineer is able to "lighten men's toil" to such a degree that the "curse of Adam" is effectively removed, then surely man is forever freed from the daily grind. He need only do the sort of work that interests him, and then only when he feels the inclination. Surely a dazzling prospect for man!

But what of the innate needs of ordinary men? It is not just a question of the limits to leisure that can be enjoyed: Few of the rich, in fact, devote themselves full time to the hectic pursuit of pleasure. Many of them adopt causes, or continue to engage in empire-building of sorts: For most men need to feel that their work matters to society — a need that is harder to fulfil as society becomes increasingly more impersonal. The creative satisfaction enjoyed by the craftsman of old, critical though it was in the pattern of his well-being, did not of itself suffice. Social recognition of his work must be added thereto before his contentment was assured. If a master-baker, displaced by the invention of completely automatic ovens, were so fortunate as to be compensated with a sum of money enabling him to buy a set of his old-fashioned ovens and withal to live comfortably, though he could now continue to bake his five hundred loaves a day, he would be unlikely to continue it as a hobby. What he creates as a hobby may well be an excellent thing, or it may not

be. His friends may admire it or they may just be polite about it. But whatever their response, it is plain enough that it does not matter very much to others whether he continues or discontinues with the work. And this is a fact that makes all the difference to the basic self-respect of our displaced baker. Even a great artist will not escape a feeling of bitterness if society pays no heed to his work. And the ordinary worker stands in need of more reassurance than the great artist. For the craftsman who produces directly for a community that both appreciates and needs the product of his hand and brain, and evinces that need by a readiness to pay for his skill, there is that blessed feeling of belonging and of being an indispensable part of the daily life of his community. Whatever else may have been lacking in that smaller scale of society in which the yeoman tilled the soil and masters and apprentices worked with patient skill at their craft, there was always this unassailable self-respect and, therefore, that abiding sense of security which is no common thing in the feverish jostling world of today.

And not only a sense of our own worth but a sense of the worth of others is being lost in pursuit of efficiency. The more we become fascinated with the measurable aspects of human achievement the easier it is to slip into a frame of mind that judges people according to numerical systems and that ranks their worth on some scale of efficiency. In time we lose sight both of the subtle and engaging facets of the character of each individual and of the intrinsic value of each human life. In continually directing our calculations to the uses of other men, regarded as means to the attainment of material ends, the modern world's preoccupation with efficiency tends to blunt our moral sensibilities.

EFFICIENCY AND WELFARE

There are other vital sources of gratification, equally unmeasurable by the engineer's yardstick, that are being lost in the obsessive scramble of the rich countries to exploit technological opportunities. For many of the incidental consequences of the mode of production which technocrats, in their overriding task of spreading innovation and increasing efficiency, would regard as irrelevant happen to be the essential factors in human welfare. An open, easy and full-hearted relationship with one's fellows, for instance, is not something that can be bought, or contrived, or willed into being. The indispensable ingredient of such a relationship is mutual trust, a quality nurtured in the small agrarian society based on mutual dependence, and one of the first casualties in any society whose energies are drawn into the competitive scramble for material ends.

It is undeniably more efficient that infants should imbibe amusement from the television screen rather than that a parent's time and energy be diverted to the telling of bedtime stories. It is incomparably more efficient to turn a knob of a panel in order to capture the music of a celebrated symphony orchestra than to depend upon a solo or duet performance by members of the family or by family friends. The reproduction on a modern record player of the voice of some great singer is, on an esthetic plane, likely to be far superior to the sound produced by a man's daughter playing the piano, or the harpsichord. Yet with the passing of these once-common domestic occasions, victims of technological progress, some essential sweetness in the lives of men has also passed away. And it must be said yet again that, although these options are not necessarily closed to us merely because we now have, in addition, gramophones, radios and television sets, their reality is effectively destroyed. Just as in the passing of the independent craftsman, what matters is the altered social significance of these activities in the modern world. The old-time family evening, entertaining each other with song, music or reading, is a pretty thing yet, and in defying the high-powered entertainment world of today, brave even to poignancy. But when the sound of music can flood a room at a flick of a finger, nobody depends any longer for his comfort or cheer upon the affection of his family, the alacrity of his neighbors, or the heartiness of the assembled company. It must be owned that efficiency has triumphed, and the pleasure that once flowed between player and listener in the home, and the singing in which the family

would join and warm to each other — these things, in the West, belong to the world we have lost.

Passing on to the teaching machines that are currently being developed, it is readily granted that the high hopes placed on them by our most spirited pace-setters will be fulfilled, and that their gradual improvement will enable future generations to be taught more efficiently than students are taught today. As for the university-of-the-air project mooted by our go-ahead politicans, it is all too plausible a vision of the morrow. As surely as efficiency remains the touchstone, it will be realized in the not-too-distant future. After all, it does not require a particularly bright technocrat to pose the question: Why pay several score lecturers to teach the same subject in different universities in Britain when the growing army of undergraduates, hungry for the "meal-ticket" and increasingly fearful of not getting the very best, could all simultaneously tune in to some silver-tongued superlecturer? Televised lectures would be supplemented by autoinstructional programs in the homes as an efficient and highly economical substitute for conventional tutorials and seminars. Indeed, in view of the existing technological possibilities, it is legitimate to doubt whether the universities as we know them today, as seats of both teaching and learning, will survive the turn of the century.

Yet if people are to be taught more effectively in the future while employing but a fraction of the teaching resources required today, there will also be a loss, the unmeasurable loss of human contact. Just as television has already succeeded in fragmenting the family, and in impoverishing the common fund of mutual experience through which the sense of family is nourished, so also must television apparatus and teaching machines that are being installed in our universities and our schools serve in time to isolate people further. The youngster of today, seen from the future, is a victim of the wastes of conventional teaching methods and is, consequently, less proficient than the youngster of tomorrow. But today, at least, he is held together in companionship with his classmates — together with them to exult and despair, to groan and to laugh — sharing with them the vital interchanges of sympathy that accompany their learning through a teacher with, and through whom, whether they mostly love him or hate him, they explore the resources of human feeling.

With this crucial factor in mind one may appreciate the acknowledged difficulty of giving impetus in the newly built suburbs and towns to something resembling a community spirit — something that was common enough in yesterday's slums which, for all the dirt and distress, had much in them that was warmly human. A strong sense of community is not a synthetic product to be created *ab initio* by skillful plugging at common interests. The sense of community requires the fact of community, an environment of direct human interdependence. And though scientists and scholars may still be able to share intellectual experiences at some point along the extending frontiers of knowledge, for the common man this prospect does not exist. For him, the doors of communication with his fellows, indeed with his family, are gradually closing as his overt need of them disappears before the relentless advance of an all-embracing technology.

In the older forms of social organization which began to disappear in the early nineteenth century it was just this inescapable fact of close interdependence that held the family and the community together. In the historical circumstances the interdependence was inevitable, yet there was unabashed satisfaction in affirming it. The centripetal forces of modern transport and communications had yet to emerge. In the meantime, in village or town, the lives of the inhabitants were dominated by local events. Narrow though their lives might appear by our megalopolitan standards they had, rich and poor, young and old, their place in the natural order of things, a settled relationship to one another guided by a network of custom and mutual obligation. Inevitably, then, they were, all of them, at the centre of the gossip and the interest, all of them part of the prior and absorbing concern of the community they dwelt in.

LACK OF A REFUGE

Generations have passed, and, like the woods and hedges that sheltered it, the rich local life centered on township, parish and village has been uprooted and blown away by the winds of change. Today no refuge remains from the desperate universal clamour for more efficiency, more excitement, and more novelty that goads us furiously onward, competing, accumulating, innovating — and inevitably destroying. Every step forward in technological progress, and particularly in the things most eagerly anticipated — swifter travel, depersonalized services, all the pushbutton comforts and round-the-clock synthetic entertainment that are promised us — effectively transfers our dependence upon other human beings to dependence upon machines[1] and, therefore, unavoidably constricts yet further the direct flow of understanding and sympathy between people. Thus in the unending pursuit of progress men are driven ever farther apart and come to depend instead, for all their services and experiences, directly upon the creations of technology.

[1]Neighborhoods have degenerated into geographical locations — "dormitory areas" in which people of like circumstances occupy the houses or blocks of flats along several streets. Each family, nay, each member of each family, has, or soon hopes to have, his own television set and private automobile, the elegant instruments of his estrangement from others. Is it even conceivable for a community to take root in a neighborhood teeming with cars, transistors and television sets, in which people do not know, or care to know, the names of their neighbors, in which the character of ordinary people, their eccentricities, their spontaneity their convictions, their once-intimate gossip have all been dried up by the ever-flickering screen? Already we hesitate to call upon friends lest we disturb their television viewings. And, in case we should have nothing better to do than strike up an acquaintance with the adjacent airline-passenger, individual motion-picture entertainment is being installed in order to distract our attention during the whole of the flight.

The era is dawning in which film, television and programmed material will substitute for human teachers; in which the duties of hospital nurses will be taken over by patient-monitoring devices, and medical diagnoses performed by computers. While office staff and skilled workers are being automated into obsolescence, and executives replaced by decision-making machines, game-playing machines are rendering human partners unnecessary. As for sex, for procreative purposes, it is already something of an anachronism. Advances in genetics are about to make fathers expendable; and with the perfection of the mechanical womb, mothers also will become superfluous. We cannot be far from the day of the conversation-machine that will relieve us of the obligation to greet politely the occasional recognizable human that strays across our path.

QUESTIONS

1. "The vital advantage of efficiency and economic growth is that it provides *both* more goods and more leisure time. It is in this leisure time that men can fulfill their innate needs to be craftsmen and artists. The affluence provided by a highly extended division of labor provides the time for the individual to express himself in projects of his own choosing." Evaluate.

2. Can one be sympathetic to the normative thrust of Mishan's essay and still support foreign aid to economically underdeveloped countries? How?

3. Ask a student from an underdeveloped country how he views the cult of efficiency.

ECONOMIC GROWTH: DESIRABLE
W. Arthur Lewis

Sir W. Arthur Lewis, the James Madison Professor of Political Economy at Princeton University, is noted for his scholarly writings on economic development and his personal involvement in decision making in less developed countries. Recently honored as a Distinguished Fellow of the American Economic Association, Professor Lewis seems to anticipate the current critics of economic growth in this selection from his The Theory of Economic Growth.

Like everything else, economic growth has its costs. If economic growth could be achieved without any disadvantages, everybody would be wholly in its favor. But since growth has real disadvantages, people differ in their attitude to growth according to the different assessment which they give to its advantages and disadvantages. They may dislike the kind of society which is associated with economic

Abridged from W. Arthur Lewis, "Is Economic Growth Desirable?" appendix to his *The Theory of Economic Growth* (Homewood, Ill.: R. D. Irwin, 1955), pp. 420–430. Reprinted by permission.

growth, preferring the attitudes and institutions which prevail in stable societies. Or, even if they are reconciled to the institutions of growing societies, they may dislike the transitional processes in the course of which stable societies are converted into growing societies; they may therefore conclude either that the benefits of growth are not worth the cost of the disturbance it involves, or also that growth should be introduced slowly, so that the society may have as long as possible to adjust itself to the changes which economic growth requires. We shall begin with the advantages of growth, and then consider the costs of growth in terms of the attitudes it requires, and in terms of the disturbances involved in the process of transition.

THE BENEFITS OF ECONOMIC GROWTH

The advantage of economic growth is not that wealth increases happiness, but that it increases the range of human choice. It is very hard to correlate wealth and happiness. Happiness results from the way one looks at life, taking it as it comes, dwelling on the pleasant rather than the unpleasant, and living without fear of what the future may bring. Wealth would increase happiness if it increased resources more than it increased wants, but it does not necessarily do this, and there is no evidence that the rich are happier than the poor, or that individuals grow happier as their incomes increase. Wealth decreases happiness if in the acquisition of wealth one ceases to take life as it comes, and worries more about resources and the future. There is, indeed, some evidence that this is the case; insofar as economic growth results from alertness in seeking out and seizing economic opportunites, it is only to be expected that it should be associated with less happiness than we find in societies where people are not so concerned with growth. There is evidence of much greater mental disturbances in the United States of America than there is in other countries, and, even when allowance is made for differences in statistical reporting, it is at least plausible that the higher suicide rate is causally connected with the drive for greater success in an already rich community. We certainly cannot say that an increase in wealth makes people happier. We cannot say, either that an increase in wealth makes people less happy, and even if we could say this, it would not be a decisive argument against economic growth, since happiness is not the only good thing in life. We do not know what the purpose of life is, but if it were happiness, then evolution could just as well have stopped a long time ago, since there is no reason to believe that men are happier than pigs, or than fishes. What distinguishes men from pigs is that men have greater control over their environment; not that they are more happy. And on this test, economic growth is greatly to be desired.

The case for economic growth is that it gives man greater control over his environment, and thereby increases his freedom.

We can see this first in man's relations with nature. At primitive levels, man has to struggle for subsistence. With great drudgery he succeeds in wresting from the soil barely enough to keep himself alive. Every year he passes through a starvation period for several months, because the year's crop barely lasts out until the next harvest. Regularly he is visited by famine, plague or pestilence. Half his children die before reaching the age of ten, and at forty his wife is wrinkled and old. Economic growth enables him to escape from this servitude. Improved techniques yield more abundant and more varied food for less labour. Famine is banished, the infant mortality rate falls from 300 to 30 per thousand; the death rate from 40 to 10 per thousand. Cholera, smallpox, malaria, hookworm, yellow fever, plague, leprosy and tuberculosis disappear altogether. Thus life itself is freed from some of nature's menaces. Not everybody considers this a gain. If you think that it is better to die than to live, and best not to be born, you are not impressed by the fact that economic growth permits a reduction of death rates. but most of us are still primitive enough to take it as axiomatic that life is better than death.

Economic growth also gives us freedom to choose greater leisure. In the primitive state we have to work extremely hard merely to keep alive. With economic growth we can choose to have more leisure or more goods, and we do indeed choose to have more of both. The opposite impression is created if a comparison is made between impoverished agricultural countries and rich industrial countries, since in the former labor is idle through much of the year, when the weather is unfavorable to agriculture, whereas in the latter men work regularly throughout the year; but this is a false comparison. If we compare not industry with agriculture, but the industrial sector in rich with the industrial sector in poor countries, and similarly the agricultural sector in both countries, we shall find almost invariably shorter hours of work in each sector, as income grows; and also less drudgery, with increased use of mechanical power.

Also, it is economic growth which permits us to have more services, as well as more goods or leisure. In the poorest communities 60 or 70 percent of the people are needed in agriculture to procure food; whereas in the richest countries 12 to 15 percent suffice to give a standard of nutrition twice as good, the richer countries can therefore spare more people for other activities — to be doctors, nurses and dentists; to be teachers; to be actors and entertainers; to be artists or musicians. Many of the "higher" activities which philosophers value — art, music, the study of philosophy itself — are in a sense a luxury which society can afford to develop only as economic growth permits it to spare increasing numbers from the basic task of growing food. It is true that only a relatively small surplus is needed to support the arts, and that some of the highest artistic achievements date back to societies where the masses of the people were very poor. The raising of living standards over the past century has widened the opportunity to appreciate and practice the arts, without necessarily affecting the quality or quantity of the best art one way or the other. However, leaving aside the highest art, there has without doubt been an enormous increase in popular leisure and the popular opportunities for enjoying what were previously the luxuries open to very few. Relatively far more people hear the work of the best composers today than heard the work of Mozart or of Bach in their own times, or saw the work of Rembrandt or of El Greco.

Women benefit from these changes even more

than men. In most underdeveloped countries woman is a drudge, doing in the household tasks which in more advanced societies are done by mechanical power — grinding grain for hours, walking miles to fetch pails of water, and so on. Economic growth transfers these and many other tasks — spinning and weaving, teaching children, minding the sick — to external establishments, where they are done with greater specialization and greater capital, and with all the advantages of large-scale production. In the process woman gains freedom from drudgery, is emancipated from the seclusion of the household, and gains at last the chance to be a full human being, exercising her mind and her talents in the same way as men. It is open to men to debate whether economic progress is good for men or not, but for women to debate the desirability to economic growth is to debate whether women should have the chance to cease to be beasts of burden, and to join the human race.

Economic growth also permits mankind to indulge in the luxury of greater humanitarianism. For instance, at the lowest levels of subsistence there is little to spare for those who cannot help themselves, and the weakest must go to the wall. It is only as the surplus increases that men take increasing care of the leper, the mentally deranged, the crippled, the blind, and other victims of chance. The desire to care for the sick, the incompetent, the unlucky, the widow and the orphan is not necessarily greater in civilized than in primitive societies, but the former have more means to spare for the purpose, and therefore do in fact display greater humanitarianism. Some people are disturbed by this; they think that it is against the eugenic interest of society to maintain persons who are not able to keep up in a competitive struggle, and they consider that the long run effect will be to reduce biological vigour unless such persons are sterilized. But these are as yet in a minority.

THE ACQUISITIVE SOCIETY

If the benefits listed above were available without cost, nearly everyone would favor them. Many people, however, consider that the attitudes and institutions which are necessary for economic growth are undesirable in themselves; they prefer the attitudes and institutions which belong to stable societies.

In the first place, they dislike the economizing spirit, which is one of the conditions of economic growth. If other things are equal, growth is most rapid in those societies where people give their minds to seeking out and seizing opportunities of economic gain, whether by means of increasing earnings, or by means of reducing costs. And this propensity to economize, though it might equally well spring solely from a desire to reduce drudgery and increase the leisure available for enjoyment or for spiritual pursuits, seems in practice not to be well developed except when it is associated with a desire for wealth, either for its own sake, or for the social prestige or the power over people which it brings. It is arguable that economy is a virtue, in the sense that there is the same sacred duty imposed upon man to abhor waste and to make the best use of his resources as there is to abhor murder and to look after the widows and orphans — in fact the parable of the talents says that this is so. Not everyone agrees that we have a sacred duty to fuss and bother about resources, or about fleeting time; these would say that economy costs too much in nervous energy and human happiness, and is rather a vice than a virtue. They might admit a duty to economize or work enough to reach some minimum standard of living, necessary for health and comfort (a dubious concept), but would argue that economy beyond this level is not worth the effort. Moreover, even those who accept economy to be a virtue may nevertheless deplore the fact (if it is a fact) that this virtue is found only in association with the vice (if it is a vice) of materialism. It is possible to desire that children should be taught to make the best use of the resources and opportunities available to them (the virtue of economy), and at the same time not to want more than they already have (to avoid the vice of cupidity). If this were done, and if the teaching were effective, there would still be economic growth; only, instead of its showing itself in ever rising material standards of living it would show itself in ever increasing leisure at constant material standards; and if this leisure were not to result also in the ever-increasing vice of idleness (if this is a vice), children would have also to be taught to use their leisure in ways which resulted neither in idleness, nor in the production of economic goods and services. We cannot, in practice, get very far by pursuing lines of enquiry which depend on assuming human nature to be other than it is. Man likes to have more wealth, likes to economize, and likes to be idle. None of these desires seems to be intrinsically either virtuous or vicious, but any one of them pursued to its extremes, in disregard of other duties, obligations or rights results in unbalanced personalities and also in harm to other persons. It is just as much possible for a society to be "not materialistic enough," as it is for it to be "too materialistic." Or, to put the matter the other way round, economic growth is desirable, but we can certainly have too much of it (more than is good for spiritual or social health) just as well as we may have too little of it.

Exactly the same comment can be made in relation to individualism, which is the second score on which economic growth is attacked. It seems to be the case that economic growth is more likely if individuals attend primarily to their own interests and those of their more immediate relations than if they are bound by a much wider net of social obligations. This is why economic growth is associated, both as cause and as effect, with the disappearance of extended family and joint family systems; with the erosion of social systems based on status (slavery, serfdom, caste, age, family, race) and their substitution by systems based upon contract and upon equality of opportunity; with a high level of vertical social mobility; and with the decline of tribal bonds, and the reduced recognition generally of the claims of social groups. This is another problem which cannot be solved by making a virtue of one side of the argument and a vice of the other. There are some rights which all individuals ought to have, and which should be protected against all social claims; and at the same time every individual belongs to a group, or whole series of groups, whose existence is necessary to his own social health, and whose continuance depends upon his recognizing the claims of the group and loyally accepting its au-

thority. The growth of individualism in the past five hundred years has had its evil side, but it has also been a valuable and liberating influence. Economic growth cannot therefore be attacked for being associated with individualism as if the only good things in human relations were tribalism, social status, extended family relations, and political authoritarianism.

A third line of attack upon economic growth derives from its association with reliance on reason. Economic growth depends upon improving technology, and this in turn is greatest where men have a reasoning attitude both toward nature and also toward social relations. Now the reasoning mind is suspect, either because it is believed to result in religious agnosticism or in atheism, or also because it is considered incompatible with the acceptance of authority. As for religious belief, it is an open question whether decline of belief in God or gods is to be blamed for the evils of our time, or even whether the evils of our time are greater than those of previous ages in which religious belief was commoner. But, in any case, it is not true that belief in the importance of reason is inconsistent with belief in God. The existence of God cannot be proved or disproved by rational means, so there is no reason whatsoever why the most rational of men should not also believe in the existence of God. Reason erodes not religion but authority, and it is only insofar as religion is based upon authority that the reasoning mind is hostile to religion.

A fourth line of attack is pursued by those who do not like the growth of scale which is associated with economic growth. The economics of scale show themselves, in the first instance, in the division of labor, and in the use of machinery. This is disliked by some who dislike machine made goods, and who prefer the products of the skilled handicraftsman. Economic growth destroys old handcraft skills, and though it creates even more new skills, machine skills and others (for specialization greatly increases the range of skills) there are many people who regret the passing of the old skills and the old craft products, and who find no consolation either in the growth of the new skills or in the multiplication and cheapening of output which mass-production makes possible. The principle of specialization is itself attacked, for specialization results in people having to do the same thing over and over again and this, whether it be turning nuts on bolts, or packing chocolates into boxes, or repeating the same university lecture, or practising musical scales, or taking out appendixes, is necessarily boring, until one gets so used to one's job that one can do it without giving the whole of one's mind to it.

Large-scale organizations are also disliked because of the discipline they impose; day after day men must rise at the same hour, arrive at their place of work at the same hour, do much the same things, and return home at the same time. Some think that this makes life drab and monotonous, and reduces human beings to the mechanical role of cogs in some vast wheel. They would prefer that men should not be tied to the clock, and should have greater freedom of choice from day to day, though it is by no means clear either that the man who works in the one-man business is less a slave of the clock or that having regular habits is something to be deplored.

The economics of large-scale organization also result in the growth of towns, especially when this is associated with growing real income per head, which increases the demand for manufactured products and for services relatively to the demand for agricultural products. Insofar as the revolt against large towns is associated with a preference for agricultural occupations, it is really a revolt against technological progress. For it is technological progress which enables a country to produce with 15 percent of its population enough food to feed the whole, and if we are to return to the days when 70 percent of the people were needed upon the land either we must abandon all that agricultural science has taught us, or else we must reduce hours of work to about ten a week. It is technological progress in agriculture which results in the growth of urban occupations, but it is the economies of large-scale organization which result in these urban occupations being concentrated in ever larger towns. That this is undesirable is by no means clear. The majority of people, when given the chance of working in the town or in

the village, choose the town — this is why towns grow at the expense of villages; only a minority prefer the village to the town, and many of those who denounce the town are in fact careful to avoid living in villages. If towns are thrown up in a great hurry, without proper planning or control, they can indeed be slummy, drab, ugly and unhealthy; but in these days there is no reason why new towns (or even old ones for that matter) should not be as beautiful, gracious, healthy and inspiring as any village, as well as providing far wider opportunities for exercising body, mind and soul than any village could ever hope to offer.

Three conclusions follow from this analysis. First, some of the alleged costs of economic growth are not necessary consequences of growth at all — the ugliness of towns or the impoverishment of the working classes, for instance. Secondly, some of the alleged evils are not in fact intrinsically evil — the growth of individualism, or of reasoning, or of towns, for example. As in all human life, such things can be taken to excess, but they are not intrinsically any less desirable than their opposites. From this it follows, however, thirdly, that the rate of economic growth can be too high for the health of society. Economic growth is only one good thing among many, and we can take it to excess. Excessive growth may result in, or be the result of, excessive materialism, excessive individualism, exessive mobility of population, excessive inequality of income, or the like. Societies are not necessarily wise to choose to speed up their rate of growth above its current level; if they do, they will enjoy substantial benefits, but they may also incur substantial costs, in social or in spiritual terms, and whether the potential gains exceed the potential losses must be assessed separately in each situation as best we may. It is because economic growth has both its gains and its losses that we are all almost without exception ambivalent in our attitudes toward economic growth. We demand the abolition of poverty, illiteracy and disease, but we cling desperately to the beliefs, habits and social arrangements which we like, even when these are the very cause of the poverty which we deplore.

QUESTIONS

1. "The advantage of economic growth is not that wealth increases happiness, but that it increases the range of human choice." Describe the conditions under which this statement is true. Is this statement ever false?

2. What individuals or groups with whom you are familiar express the greatest distaste for increasing wealth? What factors account for their displeasure with economic growth? What is their general economic status?

3. What impact does economic growth have on the arts? On women? On humanitarianism?

4. Comparing this essay by Lewis with the earlier piece by Mishan, articulate the views of each. Where do they disagree?

58 POPULATION GROWTH AND ECONOMIC GROWTH: THE CASE FOR ZPG
Stephen Enke

Does economic growth require an increasing population? Stephen Enke argues that it does not. After surveying recent fertility trends in the United States, he concludes that zero population growth is a sensible public policy. A Canadian by birth, Dr. Enke's career included faculty appointments at Yale University, the University of California at Los Angeles, and Duke University, and positions with a number of the nation's leading think tanks. Until his death, he was associated with TEMPO, a research organization in Washington, D.C.

The old issue of whether population growth is necessary for useful economic growth is now being reconsidered because of a recent U.S. Census Bureau publication predicting reduced fertility. The current "best guess" is that the fertility level of women in the United States has fallen during the past few years to the point where it is now at a replacement rate of 2.1 children per woman during her childbearing life (ages 14 through 49). Many demographers were estimating only a few years ago that declining fertility would not fall to this replacement level until the 1990's. Because of net immigration, a replacement level fertility of 2.1 children does not mean that Zero Population Growth (ZPG) is anticipated by this projection. But fertility does seem to be declining, and this has predictable economic and social consequences, more of them good than bad.

The main reasons why the Census has published its new Report are (a) the sharp drop in experienced fertility since 1970 and (b) the marked decline in the expected fertility of young wives aged 18 to 24 years during the past five years. For *experienced* fertility, the rate has declined 10 percent in a year. And as to *expected* fertility, young wives surveyed in 1967 expected to have about 2.9 children, but in

The Public Interest, No. 32 (Summer 1973), pp. 86—96.
Copyright © by National Affairs, Inc., 1973.

1971 and 1972 they expected typically to have 2.3 children. If allowance is made for women who never marry, these expectations are compatible respectively with completed family sizes of about 2.6 and 2.1 children for all women aged 18 to 24 today — a decline of almost 20 percent within five years. Such reductions are dramatic news indeed.

If U.S. women were indefinitely to maintain a replacement fertility rate of 2.1 children, and *if net immigration were zero*, population would continue to grow until it attained 277 million around the middle of the 21st century. Zero population growth is hence about 70 million people and 70 years away, even under these circumstances. This is because the age distribution of our population will shift only slowly, until it becomes older and compatible with reduced fertility. Meanwhile, with comparatively too many younger wives in the population, births will continue to exceed deaths. Also, net immigration is not expected to fall to zero, so the new Census information does not mean ZPG even in the lifetimes of our children.

THE UNCERTAINTY OF FERTILITY PREDICTIONS

Predictions about fertility are always dangerous — which is why no one population projection should ever be taken too seriously. During the last 25 years, there have been marked changes in the average ages of women at first childbirth. The post-World War II pattern of having children early has now reversed itself for the time being. In part, this may be attributed to the greater difficulty young men and women have in finding jobs during the past few years. Also, in 1970 paternity ceased to give automatic deferment from the draft. And abortion has become more available in several states during the past few years. But some of the change may be due simply to changing "fashion." In the United States, where it is estimated that four fifths of young couples know a good deal about contraception, relatively ephemeral changes in values can affect fertility to an extent impossible in more backward countries.

Some of these speculations are clearly fanciful. But they illustrate the point that fertility rates over the next 30 to 50 years cannot be predicted with any confidence. Hence, "if-then" projections of population, each based on a single postulated fertility rate, are essentially arbitrary. If a single rate of future fertility for the next 50 years had to be picked, 2.1 children now appears more reasonable than any higher rate, and a consideration of possible future developments suggests that 1.8 might be still closer to the mark. If ultimate fertility rates were slowly to decline from 2.1 today to 1.8 by the year 2000, even though net immigration continued at 400,000 a year, ZPG would be attainable during the latter half of the next century.

FUTURE IMMIGRATION POLICY

If a slower rate of population growth is preferable, on balance, for economic and social reasons, future U.S. governments may wish to reduce immigration so that attainment of ZPG does not require U.S. parents to reduce their completed family sizes to less than two children.

Reducing the absolute number of immigrants could become a controversial political issue if early attainment of ZPG ever became national policy. During the balance of this century, deaths will average around 2.5 million a year. Thus, an early attainment of ZPG arithmetically requires that net immigration plus births not exceed approximately 2.5 million annually. With a net immigration of 400,000, this in turn means 2.1 million births a year, which is hardly conceivable given current births of 3.2 million. Even if an annual surplus of 500,000 were permitted, as long as net immigration remained at 400,000, U.S. women would have to limit themselves to 2.6 million births. This would mean an annual prevention of about 600,000 otherwise expected births. If most of these prevented births were also *wanted* births, and the government were deliberately making it more costly to have and rear children, political pressures to reduce gross immigration would seem likely.

The U.S. government would then have to decide not only the number of immigrants to accept, but the basis of their eligibility. One criterion would probably be consanguinity to existing residents.

Another might be the possession of useful scientific, professional, and technical skills. Congressmen may be pressured to favor immigration on the basis of family ties; the national interest, however, should probably favor immigrants who are highly educated and have been trained at the expense of other national economies.

ECONOMIC CONSEQUENCES OF REDUCED FERTILITY

Analyses of possible ZPG attainment often seem to imply that this would be desirable on environmental grounds. But reduced fertility may also be desirable on economic grounds. As this is contrary to a popular view that population growth is "good for business," it needs some explaining. What mostly makes for higher living standards (i.e., higher GNP per capita) is advances in technology (which increase productivity) and increases in stocks of capital per worker (which permit each employee to increase "his" output). U.S. history tends to confirm this assertion. It is true that GNP grew with population, but what counts is improvement in GNP per head, which has risen so spectacularly since the Civil War. Perhaps two thirds of this improvement has been due to compounded technological advances. The other one third is probably due to the rapid increase in investment per head. Initially, some of this investment was financed from Europe, but that flow reversed itself during World War I. Anything that contributes to increased saving and investment within the United States also contributes to a rising national output per capita.

THE IMPACT OF DECLINING FERTILITY ON BUSINESS

The belief that population growth is "good for business" may be based on too simple an analogy. For a single business in a particular city, more population may mean more dollar sales for a while, and this may "spread the overhead" and bring in more profits. But over a longer period, a larger city population may mean more competing businesses (among restaurants, cleaners, and beauty parlors, for ex-

ample), as well as more customers. For local service industries, extra population does not necessarily mean more customers per firm in the long run.

Obviously, the impact of declining fertility differs among industries, because of family-income effects. Sales of some industries are more income elastic than those of others: Larger family incomes mean more sales for television manufacturers but perhaps smaller sales for potato growers. The sales of some industries are sensitive to age-distribution shifts: A declining fertility rate means relatively fewer children and adolescents, and relatively more senior citizens, with all that this implies for sales of school books, pop records, and medical diagnostic equipment.

Superficially, one might suppose that all industries would tend to have slower increases in dollar sales with declining fertility, because there would be fewer extra buyers. But this in not the case. The quantity of almost every product and service sold varies with buyers' incomes. Fewer people with more money to spend individually may buy as many units of a product as would more people with less money to spend. They may also pay a higher price for better quality. Footwear is a good example. A smaller population certainly means fewer pairs of feet to be shod. But each person may buy more and better shoes if there is a higher income per capita.

DO WE NEED A POLICY ON FERTILITY?

If ZPG would be good for the economy, should not its attainment, sooner rather than later, become a national objective? The United States — unlike France, for example — has never had an explicit fertility policy. However, it has always had an implicit pro-natalist policy, including laws against abortion and contraception in some states, free public education, income tax exemptions for dependents, and so on. The effect of such provisions is to encourage fertility by making birth control difficult and children less expensive. Perhaps the time has come, not to eliminate free education, but to counter various pro-natalist consequences with explicit *anti*-natalist taxes and subsidies.

An immediate question is whether this will be

necessary. If parents reduce their fertility sufficiently below the replacement rate, so that the deficit of births below deaths in time compensates for net immigration, federal and state action may be quite unnecessary. Some demographers feel that something approaching ZPG will eventually result if there are no longer any unwanted births. Current federal programs to assist indigent women in practicing contraception are contributing to this outcome. Legal abortion may have a greater impact on fertility than is yet realized.

Yet even though there may be fewer unwanted children in the future (and hence fewer babies for adoption), some observers wonder whether there may not also be more *wanted* children. Medical techniques, including artificial insemination, are being used more frequently to assist sterile couples to have children. But more important, over the next 50 years increasing leisure and consumption levels may cause more couples to want and to have additional children as consumption goods. Along with the third TV and third car, as a deliberate consumer decision may come the third child. If this ever threatened to become a typical behavior pattern, an explicit national policy favoring "replacement" fertility and reduced immigration would become an urgent necessity.

The possibilities for government action are obviously limited in a free society. The most that federal and state governments can practically do is financially to reward parents that have fewer children and penalize parents that have more children. This could be done through the income tax, for instance. Exemptions, increasing with the age of the taxpayer, could be given for not having children instead of for having them. In this way, at each taxable income level, less fertile parents would not be subsidizing more fertile couples to the extent that they do today. (The children of really poor parents would not suffer because the latter do not pay income taxes.)

The time is coming when having "large" families, i.e., above the replacement level, will be considered anti-social. With abortion and contraception available, "excess" children will be considered *wanted children*, and parents may have to suffer the usual penalties of antisocial behavior. Large families are today subsidized by small families — but this may not be true by A.D. 2000.

QUESTIONS

1. Summarize current trends in fertility in the United States. What impact does immigration have on population growth in this country? Given these fertility trends and present immigration policy, what is the earliest date at which ZPG might be expected?

2. What factors in your opinion have contributed to the recent decline in fertility rate in the United States?

3. Should the business sector support ZPG for economic reasons? What businesses, if any, should be more enthusiastic than others?

59 IS THE END OF THE WORLD AT HAND?
Robert M. Solow

Does economic growth contribute to human extinction? Will resources soon be exhausted? Robert M. Solow, a distinguished economic theorist at M.I.T., provides an assessment of the doomsayer's warnings. This paper originally was presented at a symposium on this subject at Lehigh University. It dovetails with the earlier articles by Nathan Rosenberg and Stephen Enke. Professor Solow, a recipient of the John Bates Clark medal in economics, has authored books on economic growth theory and capital theory.

There is, as you know, a school of thought that claims that continued economic growth is in fact not possible anymore, or at least not for very long. This judgment has been expressed more or less casually by several observers in recent years. What distinguishes the "Doomsday Models" from their predecessors is that they claim to much more than a casual judgment: they deduce their beliefs about future prospects from mathematical models or systems analysis. They don't merely say that the end of the world is at hand — they can show you computer output that says the same thing.

Characteristically, the Doomsday Models do more than just say that continued economic growth is impossible. They tell us why: in brief, because (*a*) the earth's natural resources will soon be used up; (*b*) increased industrial production will soon strangle us in pollution. and (*c*) increasing population will eventually outrun the world's capacity to grow food, so that famine must eventually result. And, finally, the models tell us one more thing: the world will end with a bang, not a whimper. The natural evolution of the world economy is not at all toward some kind of smooth approach to its natural limits, wherever they are. Instead, it is inevitable — unless we make drastic changes in the way we live

Abridged from Robert M. Solow, "Is the End of the World at Hand?" *Challenge* (March/April 1973) 39—50. Reprinted by permission.

and organize ourselves — that the world will overshoot any level of population and production it can possibly sustain and will then collapse, probably by the middle of the next century.

I would like to say why I think that the Doomsday Models are bad science and therefore bad guides to public policy. I hope nobody will conclude that I believe the problems of population control, environmental degradation, and resource exhaustion to be unimportant, or that I am one of those people who believe that an adequate response to such problems is a vague confidence that some technological solution will turn up. On the contrary, it is precisely because these are important problems that public policy had better be based on sound and careful analysis. I want to explain some of my reasons for believing that the global models don't provide even the beginnings of a foundation of that kind.

The first thing to realize is that the characteristic conclusion of the Doomsday Models is very near the surface. It is, in fact, more nearly an assumption than a conclusion, in the sense that the chain of logic from the assumptions to the conclusion is very short and rather obvious.

The basic assumption is that stocks of things like the world's natural resources and the waste-disposal capacity of the environment are finite, that the world economy tends to consume the stock at an increasing rate (through the mining of minerals and the production of goods), and that there are no built-in mechanisms by which approaching exhaustion tends to turn off consumption gradually and in advance. You hardly need a giant computer to tell you that a system with those behavior rules is going to bounce off its ceiling and collapse to a low level. Then, in case anyone is inclined to relax into the optimistic belief that maybe things aren't that bad, we are told: Imagine that the stock of natural resources were actually twice as big as the best current evidence suggests, or imagine that the annual amount of pollution could be halved all at once and then set to growing again. All that would happen is that the date of collapse would be postponed by T years, where T is not a large number. But once you grasp the quite simple essence of the models, this should come as no surprise. It is important to realize where these powerful conclusions come from, because, if you ask yourself "Why didn't I realize earlier that the end of the world was at hand?" the answer is not that you weren't clever enough to figure it out for yourself. The answer is that the imminent end of the world is an immediate deduction from certain assumptions, and one must really ask if the assumptions are any good.

It is a commonplace that if you calculate the annual output of any production process, large or small, and divide it by the annual employment of labor, you get a ratio that is called the productivity of labor. At the most aggregative level, for example, we can say that the GNP in 1971 was $1,050 billion and that about 82 million people were employed in producing it, so that GNP per worker or the productivity of a year of labor was about $12,800. Symmetrically, though the usage is less common, one could just as well calculate the GNP per unit of some particular natural resource and call that the productivity of coal, or GNP per pound of vanadium. We usually think of the productivity of labor as rising more or less exponentially, say at 2 or 3 percent a year, because that is the way it has in fact behaved over the past century or so since the statistics began to be collected. The rate of increase in the productivity of labor is not a constant of nature. Sometimes it is faster, sometimes slower. For example, we know that labor productivity must have increased more slowly a long time ago, because if we extrapolate backward at 2 percent a year, we come to a much lower labor productivity in 1492 than can possibly have been the case. And the productivity of labor has risen faster in the past 25 years than in the 50 years before that. It also varies from place to place, being faster in Japan and Germany and slower in Great Britain, for reasons that are not at all certain. But it rises, and we expect it to keep rising.

Now, how about the productivity of natural resources? All the Doomsday Models will allow is a one-time hypothetical increase in the world supply of natural resources, which is the equivalent of a one-time increase in the productivity of natural resources. Why shouldn't the productivity of most natural resources rise more or less steadily through time, like the productivity of labor?

Of course it does for some resources, but not for others. Real GNP roughly doubled between 1950 and 1970. But the consumption of primary and scrap iron increased by about 20 percent, so the productivity of iron, GNP per ton of iron, increased by about 2.5 percent a year on the average during those 20 years. The U.S. consumption of manganese went up by some 70 percent in 20 years, a bit under 2.25 percent a year. Aggregate consumption of nickel just about doubled, like GNP, so the productivity of nickel didn't change. U.S. consumption of copper, both primary and secondary, went up by a third between 1951 and 1970, so GNP per pound of copper rose at 2 percent a year on the average. The story on lead and zinc is very similar, so their productivity increased at some 2 percent a year. The productivity of bituminous coal rose at 3 percent a year.

Naturally, there are important exceptions, and unimportant exceptions. GNP per barrel of oil was about the same in 1970 as in 1951: no productivity increase there. The consumption of natural gas tripled in the same period, so GNP per cubic foot of natural gas fell at about 2.5 percent a year. Our industrial demand for aluminum quadrupled in two decades, so the productivity of aluminum fell at a good 3.5 percent a year. And industrial demand for columbium was multiplied by a factor of 25: in 1951 we managed $2.25 million of GNP (in 1967 prices) per pound of columbium, whereas in 1970 we were down to $170 thousand of GNP per pound of columbium. On the other hand, it is a little hard to imagine civilization toppling because of a shortage of columbium.

SCARCITY — AND HIGH PRICES

There is at least one reason for believing that the Doomsday story is almost certainly wrong. The most glaring defect of these models is the absence of any sort of functioning price system. I am no believer that the market is always right, and I am certainly no advocate of laissez-faire where the environment is concerned. But the price system is, after all, the main social institution evolved by capitalist economies (and, to an increasing extent, socialist economies too) for registering and reacting to relative scarcity. There are several ways that the working of the price system will push our society into faster and more systematic increases in the productivity of natural resources.

First of all, let me go back to the analogy between natural resources and labor. We are not surprised to learn that industry quite consciously tries to make inventions that save labor, i.e., permit the same product to be made with fewer man-hours of work. After all, on the average, labor costs amount to almost three-fourths of all costs in our economy. An invention that reduces labor requirements per unit of GNP by 1 percent reduces all costs by about 0.75 percent. Natural resource costs are a much smaller proportion of total GNP, something nearer 5 percent. So industry and engineering have a much stronger motive to reduce labor requirements by 1 percent than to reduce resource requirements by 1 percent, assuming — which may or not be true — that it is about as hard to do one as to do the other. But then, as the earth's supply of particular natural resources nears exhaustion, and as natural resources become more and more valuable, the motive to economize those natural resources should become as strong as the motive to economize labor. The productivity of resources should rise faster than now — it is hard to imagine otherwise.

There are other ways in which the market mechanism can be expected to push us all to economize on natural resources as they become scarcer. Higher and rising prices of exhaustible resources lead competing producers to substitute other materials that are more plentiful and therefore cheaper. To the extent that it is impossible to design around or find substitutes for expensive natural resources, the prices of commodities that contain a lot of them will rise relative to the prices of other goods and services that don't use up a lot of resources. Consumers will be driven to buy fewer resource-intensive goods and more of other things. All these effects work automatically to increase the productivity of natural resources, i.e., to reduce resource requirements per unit of GNP.

The historical steadiness of resource prices suggests that buyers and sellers in the market have not been acting as if they foresaw exhaustion in the absence of substitutes, and therefore sharply higher future prices. They may turn out to be wrong; but the Doomsday Models give us absolutely no reason to expect that — in fact, they claim to get whatever meager empirical basis they have from such experts.

Why is it true that if the market saw higher prices in the future, prices would already be rising? It is a rather technical point, but I want to explain it because, in a way, it summarizes the important thing about natural resources: conserving a mineral deposit is just as much of an investment as building a factory, and it has to be analyzed that way. Any owner of a mineral deposit owns a valuable asset, whether the owner is a private capitalist or the government of an underdeveloped country. The asset is worth keeping only if at the margin it earns a return equal to that earned on other kinds of assets. A factory produces things each year of its life, but a mineral deposit just lies there: its owner can realize a return only if he either mines the deposit or if it *increases in value*. So if you are sitting on your little pile of X and confidently expect to be able to sell it for a very high price in the year 2000 because it will be very scarce by then, you must be earning your 5 percent a year, or 10 percent a year, or whatever the going rate of return is, each year between now and 2000. The only way this can happen is for the value of X to go up by 5 percent a year or 10 percent a year. And that means that anyone who wants to use any X any time between now and 2000 will have to pay a price for it that is rising at that same 5 percent or 10 percent a year. Well, it's not happening.

CROWDING ON PLANET EARTH

I have less to say about the question of population growth, because it doesn't seem to involve any difficult conceptual problems. At any time, in any place, there is presumably an optimal size of population — with the property that the average person would be somewhat worse off if the population were a bit larger, and also worse off if the population were a bit smaller. In any real case it must be very difficult to know what the optimum population is, especially because it will change over time as technology changes, and also becasue it is probably more like a band or zone than a sharply defined number. I mean that if you could somehow plot a graph of economic welfare per person against population size, there would be a very gentle dome or plateau at the top, rather than a sharp peak.

I don't intend to guess what the optimal population for the United States may be. But I am prepared to hazard the guess that there is no point in opting for a perceptibly larger population than we now have, and we might well be content with a slightly smaller one. (I want to emphasize the likelihood that a 15 percent larger or 15 percent smaller population would make very little difference in our standard of well-being. I also want to emphasize that I am talking only about our own country. The underdeveloped world offers very special problems.) My general reason for believing that we should not want a substantially larger population is this. We all know the bad consequences of too large a population: crowding, congestion, excessive pollution, the disappearance of open space — that is why the curve of average well-being eventually turns down at large population sizes. Why does the curve ever climb to a peak in the first place? The generic reason is because of what economists call economies of scale, because it takes a population of a certain size and density to support an efficient chemical industry, or publishing industry, or symphony orchestra, or engineering university, or airline, or computer hardware and software industry, especially if you would like several firms in each, so that they can be partially regulated by their own competition. But after all, it only takes a population of a *certain* size or density to get the benefit of these economies of scale. And I'm prepared to guess that the U.S. economy is already big enough to do so; I find it hard to believe that sheer efficiency would be much served in the United States by having a larger market.

As it happens, recent figures seem to show that the United States is heading for a stationary population: that is to say, the current generation of parents seem to be establishing fertility patterns that will, if continued, cause the population to stabilize some time during the next century. Even so, the absolute size of the population will increase for a while, and level off higher than it is now, because decades of population growth have left us with a bulge of population in the childbearing ages. But I have already argued that a few million more or less hardly make a difference; and a population that has once stabilized might actually decrease, if that came to seem desirable.

PAYING FOR POLLUTION

Resource exhaustion and overpopulation: that leaves pollution as the last of the Doomsday Devils. The subject is worth a whole lecture in itself, because it is one of those problems about which economists actually have something important to say to the world, not just to each other. But I must be brief. The annual cost that would be necessary to meet decent pollution-abatement standards by the end of the century is large, but not staggering. One estimate says that in 1970 we spent about $8.5 billion (in 1967 prices), or 1 percent of GNP, for pollution abatement. An active pollution abatement policy would cost perhaps $50 billion a year by 2000, which would be about 2 percent of GNP by then. That is a small investment of resources: you can see how small it is when you consider that GNP grows by 4 percent or so every year, on the average. Cleaning up air and water would entail a cost that would be a bit like losing one-half of one year's growth, between now and the year 2000. What stands between us and a decent environment is not the curse of industrialization, not an unbearable burden of cost, but just the need to organize ourselves consciously to do some simple and knowable things. Compared with the possibility of an active abatement policy, the policy of stopping economic growth in order to stop pollution would be incredibly inefficient. It would not actually accomplish much, because one really wants to reduce the amount of, say, hydrocarbon emmission to a third or a half of *what it is now*. And what no-growth would accomplish, it would do by cutting off your face to spite your nose.

QUESTIONS

1. What is total output divided by total labor hours? What has been the trend of this figure for the U.S. economy? What has been the trend of output in relation to raw material use? What conclusion does Professor Solow draw from figures such as these?

2. How does the price mechanism serve to conserve exhaustible stocks of natural resources? What implication does the author see from a relatively constant price for a given raw material?

3. In what sense is there an optimum population size? How could an economy's population be too small?

PART FIFTEEN

COMPARATIVE ECONOMIC SYSTEMS

60 THE ECONOMY OF CHINA
James Tobin

The operation and dimensions of the economy of the People's Republic of China remain rather inscrutable to the Western observer. But three American professors of economics were recently invited to China for a two-week tour hosted by the government. One, James Tobin, offers these reflections on the organization of this Marxist economy. Tobin is Sterling Professor of Economics at Yale, a former president of the American Economic Association, and one of this country's leading economic theorists.

I visited the People's Republic of China for two weeks, September 8–22, 1972, together with Professors John Kenneth Galbraith and Wassily Leontief, in the first of a series of visits by U.S. academicians and scientists arranged by the Federation of American Scientists and the Chinese Academy of Sciences.

In this report I have tried to summarize my impressions. They are personal ones, which my traveling companions may not share. Moreover, I am fully aware of the extraordinary margins of uncertainty which surround them. To write about so large and complex a subject on such short and fragmentary acquaintance is certainly presumptuous. It is justified only by the tremendous interest and ignorance in the West concerning a country with which we have had so little contact for a quarter of a century.

CHINA'S GNP

There really is no information on Chinese national accounts. Indeed, as orthodox Marxists, the Chinese do not recognize bourgeois national accounting concepts. They subscribe to a materialist definition of national output and regard the provision of services as "unproductive" activity. Figures are scanty even for their definition.

Abridged from James Tobin, "The Economy of China: A Tourist's View," *Challenge* (March/April 1973), 20–31.

Nevertheless, I have thought it a worthwhile exercise of imagination to try to construct some plausible, consistent, primitive national accounts from the hints and scraps of data we were able to pick up. Needless to say, the standard errors of these guesses are vast, but the numbers may be indicative of orders of magnitude.

THE DUAL ECONOMY OF CHINA

For most countries, a principal feature of economic development is the transfer of population from countryside to city, from agriculture to industry and commerce. This is an important source of growth, because labor productivity is much higher in industry than in agriculture. Moreover, the process raises labor productivity in agriculture as well. Industry provides tractors, combines, fertilizers, electricity. With the help of capital and new technology, crop yields per acre rise while direct human labor per acre declines. During the process of transfer, growth rates are very high. Once the shift is largely completed, as in a mature economy like that of the United States, growth depends solely on the slower processes of capital accumulation and technological advance *within* the two sectors.

Industrialization brings growth; but as we know all too well, it brings social disruption and misery as well. This was true of England's Industrial Revolution, and even in the United States we are experiencing the social convulsions incident to the last wave of migration from Southern agriculture to cities. In many developing countries, high wages and glittering city lights attract hordes from the countryside to take their chances on a scarce supply of urban jobs. In these countries the cities are crowded with people unemployed or unproductively occupied in nuisance jobs on the fringes of urban society. Their housing is squalid, and they overwhelm the capacities of municipal services, as the incidence of begging and crime attests.

China is not undergoing economic development in this sense, and by the same token is not suffering from the social problems that accompany it. There is no unemployment in China. The Chinese proudly make this claim, and I find it easy to credit. Individual Chinese do not have free choice of occupation, job, and place of residence. Neither adults nor young people just completing school can leave the countryside of their own volition. On reaching adulthood, a young man or woman simply becomes a full working member of the commune in which he has grown up, gone to school, and worked right along. A rural resident could get nowhere in the city even if he were permitted to travel there, because no factory or other employer would have the right to hire him.

As a result of this policy, the relative distribution of population between countryside and city has remained stable, roughly 80 percent of the population being rural. Since the rate of natural increase is higher for the rural population, stability implies some industrial and urban recruitment of rural youth. But the classic process of development by shift of labor force has yet to begin. China has not succeeded in expanding the number of urban jobs much faster than the natural increase of urban population itself.

The happy consequence of strict central control of the labor market is that Chinese cities do not exhibit the distressing urban pathologies from which so many cities elsewhere suffer, and for which some Chinese cities were notorious before the revolution. There are no beggars on the streets, no idlers on the corners, no derelicts without beds or roofs, no sidewalk clamor of peddlers and vendors. Litter goes into litter cans with a regularity that would astound and delight [the mayor] of New York. Streets, parks, and public lavatories are clean and well kept. In all these public places, as well as in your home or hotel, your person and property are secure day and night. The careless foreign traveler can count on speedy recovery of the full Hongkong shopping bag left behind in the railway coach.

But China is still a miserably backward and poor country, especially rural China. One can travel two days on the train through fields of rice, cotton, jute, maize, wheat, and sorghum and see no tractors and surprisingly few draft animals. Water pumps are fairly frequent, but the main sources of power in agricultural work are the peasants themselves. Even

human-powered farm implements, beyond the simplest tools, are rarely in evidence.

THE PEOPLE'S COMMUNES

The Chinese countryside is organized into people's communes, which are geographical and administrative subdivisions of government as well as economic units for agricultural, and some nonagricultural, production. The communes vary in size from 5,000 to 40,000 persons. They are in turn divided into production brigades of roughly 1,000 members, and these in turn into production teams of 150–200 members. The team is the basic unit of production, responsible for cultivating its assigned land and for allocating and organizing the work of its members. A part of the proceeds of each team is appropriated by the brigade and the communes for local public services, administrative costs, welfare benefits, and investments. These levies are of the order of 10–15 percent. In addition, there is the 6 percent state tax previously referred to. The brigades and communes own certain equipment — tractors, threshers, transplanters. Teams are charged rent for their use.

After all these charges are met, the remainder is available for distribution to the members of the team, although the team itself may decide to appropriate some for collective purposes. Distribution among team members follows what the Chinese describe as the socialist principle of remuneration: "to each according to his work." Specifically, each member accumulates work points each day he works, up to a maximum of 13 per day. Distributions are in proportion to accumulated points. These are meant to reflect strength, skill, diligence, and "attitude." The scores are publicly determined at meetings once a month. Each peasant suggests his own score, and his suggestion usually prevails without dissent. Sometimes his colleagues argue that his score should be higher. Less frequently, we were told, they try to persuade him it should be lower. It was hard to pin down how decisions are made in these cases, but we were told that it was done by "democratic centralism." In the commune we visited near Shanghai, the average daily score was said to be about 11.

Prices are set by the state and are extremely stable. The notion that prices fluctuate with supply and demand is regarded as a bourgeois doctrine inappropriate to a planned economy. Worse still, it is regarded as a revisionist heresy, associated with Eastern European experiments with market socialism and the hated Khrushchev's gestures in the same direction. The ideological heroes in China, one may judge from the portraits that adorn every meeting room in every institution, are Marx, Engels, Lenin, Stalin, and of course Mao.

INCOME DIFFERENCES

One of the aims of the anti-elitist, anti-intellectual Cultural Revolution was to narrow income differentials, especially those that gave educated people superior status to workers and peasants. We were given to understand that the high wages paid to older engineers, doctors, craftsmen, and professors are obsolete vestiges of the past, maintained for present incumbents out of humanity and charity but certainly not anticipated for their successors.

China really is at the beginning of an experiment to see if nonpecuniary incentives can be substituted for substantial income differences as inducements for high-quality professional, scientific, and administrative performance. Of course the chances of success are facilitated by the state's control of job allocations and the denial of free choice of jobs and occupations. Once a university student, for example, chooses his field of study, he has in effect lost control of his career. The engineering student will go where he is assigned, just like an officer newly graduated from a military academy. In conversation with our Chinese companions, I was surprised at how easily and cheerfully they accepted this fact of their lives, and how little value they placed on the freedom of choice they lack. One after another simply said, "I go where the state needs me most."

QUESTIONS

1. Tobin recounts that China has no unemployment problem. Does the Chinese economy offer or suggest any policy prescriptions which might solve the unemployment problem in the United States?

2. What measures have been taken to reduce the problems of urban blight and congestion so often associated with economic development?

3. Describe the operation of a Chinese commune. How does it differ from an American commune or an Israeli kibbutz?

 ## MARX AS AN ECONOMIST
Maurice Dobb

Few American economists would tag themselves as Marxists but fewer still would doubt Marx's importance in the history of economics. The essay below, while no substitute for reading Marx himself, offers a concise introduction to Marxian analysis and an interesting look at the man himself. Maurice Dobb is a Fellow in Economics at Trinity College, Cambridge University.

In 1842 Marx had emerged from his university period into a brief career of political journalism, as editor of the newly formed organ of radical thought in Western Germany called the *Rheinische Zeitung*. At this time he had reached an intellectual position which was to be expressed in his own words a few years later as follows: "ruthless criticism of everything that exists, ruthless in the sense that this criticism will not shrink either from its own conclusions or from conflict with the powers that be." Marx had been sent by his father, first in 1835 for a year to the University of Berlin, with the primary intention of studying law. But from law his interest had very soon shifted to history and then to philosophy, no doubt driven thereto by an impulse to find a philosophy of law and and a philosophy of his-

Abridged from Maurice Dobb, *Marx as an Economist* (New York: International Publishers, 1945), pp. 3—21. Reprinted by permission of International Publishers Co., Inc. Copyright © 1945.

tory; and it was to philosophy that the intellectual passion of his university years was to be chiefly directed. Within a few months of his arrival in Berlin he had become an active member of a club of "young Hegelians" (or "left Hegelians" as they were sometimes called); and when he took his doctorate in 1841 at the University of Jena, this was on the basis of a dissertation on philosophy (an essay in the philosophies of Democritus and Epicurus).

"Ruthless criticism" was at this time still confined within the realm of abstract ideas. But his brief occupation of the editorial chair of the *Rheinische Zeitung* was to bring him into touch with economic and social questions. His paper, for example, had occasion to take up the question of the conditions of the Moselle peasantry; and when on one occasion a rival journal accused him of flirting with communism, he started to make the acquaintance of contemporary socialist writings. By the time he left Germany for Paris in 1843, he was to complete the above-quoted phrase about criticism with the statement that the task of critical philosophy was to give society a consciousness of itself, which it had previously lacked — to "show it why it struggles" — and that criticism must begin by "taking part in politics, that is to say in real struggles." This statement summed up an attitude that was exceedingly rare among contemporary thinkers: an attitude which, as it matured, was to cause his way increasingly to diverge from that of most of the friends of his student years. The years he spent in Paris in the middle 1840s brought him into contact, not only with the ideas of the French socialists, but also with the writings of the English economists. It was here that he made his first serious study of the writings of Adam Smith and Ricardo, of McCulloch and James Mill and the French economist Jean Baptiste Say. In 1846 he paid his first visit to England, traveling there from Brussels in the company of Engels, and had his first introduction to the English labor movement in the shape of the Chartists and the early trade unionists. In the winter of 1847 he traveled again to London, this time to attend a meeting of a body known as the Fraternal Democrats, and to be present at the second Congress of the recently formed Communist League. Finally, in 1849, having been expelled successively from Germany and from Paris for his activities during the revolutionary year 1848, he made the move to London that was to prove permanent. From the continent of Europe, where the bourgeois-democratic revolution was only partially completed, he had arrived in the country where capitalism had been earliest born and had appeared in its classic form: a country where (he was quick to realize) the popular movement had reached a quite new stage of historical development and the issue was (as he afterwards wrote) "not of republic *versus* monarchy, but of the rule of the working class and the rule of the bourgeoisie." From thenceforth the focus of his interest was shifted toward the criticism of capitalist society itself — toward a critical analysis of the social and economic roots of contemporary society, as a key to understanding "the law of motion" of that society and how man could change it. "The philosophers have *interpreted* the world in various ways: the point, however, is to change it."

For the remainder of Marx's life, such time as was not occupied in political work was very largely devoted to this task of economic criticism. This involved a comprehensive study both of capitalist society itself and of the ideas which economic writers had held about it. Throughout the 1850s a large part of each day was spent in the Reading Room of the British Museum exploring "the confounded ramifications of Political Economy." Here he would work from 9 o'clock till 7, returning to his Soho lodgings (or later to Grafton Terrace or Maitland Park Road, near Chalk Farm) to read and write into the small hours, smoking inordinately (mostly cheap cigars) as he worked — long spells of concentration that were broken only by an occasional game of chess with a visitor, by the reading of Aeschylus in the Greek or family recitations of Shakespeare or Goethe. At the British Museum works on history, government blue books and obscure economic pamphlets were all grist to his mill. In fact, of the literature of economic thought and discussion Marx had an unusually wide knowledge; and an example of his thoroughness is that, while he was writing his chapters on machinery, he attended a practical course in technology at the Geological Institute in

Jermyn St. (even though, as he wrote to Engels, "the simplest technical reality demanding perception is harder to me than to the biggest blockheads"). At the same time he taught classes for workers (chiefly political refugees from the Continent) in political economy, devoting to his explanations, as Liebknecht tells us, the most painstaking care.

In 1859 was published an introductory essay entitled *Towards a Critique of Political Economy*. By 1865 the manuscript of the first volume of his great work on economic theory was completed: the volume which was published two years later in German under the title of *Das Kapital: Der Produktionsprozess des Kapitals.* Work on the later two volumes was, however, to be interrupted and delayed by pressure of renewed political activity and later by illness. In 1864 the inaugural meeting of the First International took place in London; and Marx was to become secretary of its very important German section. Round 1870 he was closely implicated in the struggle within the International between the General Council and the Anarchists led by Bakunin; and in 1871 he wrote on behalf of the General Council his famous pamphlet in defense of the Paris Commune, *Civil War in France* — a document which made him (in his own words) "the best calumniated man in London." In the later 1870s failing health accentuated, no doubt, by the struggles and the poverty of his early years, forced him to take prolonged periods of rest from work, and on his doctors' advice to visit successively Harrogate and Malverne, the Channel Islands, Karlsbad, Algiers, Geneva and the South of France. Volume 1 went into a second German edition within five years of its first publication. In 1875 an authorized translation appeared in France; and in Russia in particular his work quickly won for him extensive recognition. But the material for the second and third volumes was not to be completed during his lifetime; and on his death in 1883 these volumes remained as unfinished drafts and notes, which Engels was faithfully to piece together and to publish later — Volume 2 in 1885 and Volume 3 in 1894.

MARX AND CAPITALISM

For any complete understanding, Marx's work needs to be appreciated against the background both of his general theory of social development, of which this was a particular application, and of contemporary economic thought and discussion. In contrast to the Idealist interpretation of Hegel, Marx had developed the view that the general shape of any given historical epoch was determined by the prevailing mode of production. By "mode of production" he was not referring simply to technique (which was included among what he termed the "forces of production"), but also to the "relations of production" — the relations into which men entered with one another by reason of the various positions which they occupied in the productive process. In medieval society the dominant relationship had been that between feudal lords and serfs. In the classical world it had been that between master and slave, the relationship of servitude between them depending on the fact that the master-class possessed, not only the instruments with which work was done and the product of labor, but also the producer himself as a personal chattel. In capitalist society the legal bonds which tied the producer to a lord or master no longer existed. The laborer had been emancipated, and before the law he was a free agent, entering into a contractual relationship with an employer which was in form akin to any other market contract. In other words, labor for a master was no longer obligatory; employment was by virtue of an act of sale of labor power on the market by free exchange. This marked the essential difference between the social relationship that was typical of capitalist society and those which characterized earlier forms of class society. On the face of the market it appeared that free and equal contractual relationships had been substituted for a relationship of exploitation: that freedom and equality had been realized and that resemblance to the older class societies no longer remained. The point at which Marx as an economist differed from other economists was in his preoccupation with the relations of production which lay *behind* the market, and gave substance to the contractual relationships into which men entered in the act of exchange. It was the secret of capitalism as a mode of production that he was concerned to probe; and thereby to reveal the specific character of the conflicts within this mode of production which would determine its place in history, its growth and movement and the future society that was destined to supplant it. With prices and exchange values he was also concerned, as were other economists; but he held that they were only capable of final explanation in terms of the class relations which underlay them, since it was of the essence of the capitalist mode of production that in this system class relations veiled themselves in a value-form.

The classical economists of the school of Adam Smith and Ricardo had made a signal contribution to the development of human thought in recognizing that the economic affairs of men were ruled by law as was the realm of organic nature: moreover, by laws which operated despite the wills and intentions of individuals and even in defiance of their wills. This was the significance of Adam Smith's "invisible hand" of natural law which operated behind the backs of producers. It was the point of his famous remark that "it is not from the benevolence of the butcher, the brewer or the baker that we expect our dinner, but from their regard to their own interest" and of his reference to the individual as being "led by an invisible hand to promote an end which was no part of his intention"; as many years earlier it was of Mandeville's paradox of "private vices, public virtues." By reason of market competition it came about that the behavior of all those who operated on the market was shaped to a certain pattern. Although each individual looked only to promote his own advantage, he was only one unit among a multitude, and his intentions were powerless to control the total situation; with the result that the net outcome of the actions of the individuals composing the market was such as to fulfil the behests of a "natural law" — to fulfil ends which no individual had ever designed or intended.

Marx must have been struck by the similarity between this central theme of the economists and a leading doctrine of Hegel's philosophy of history (a doctrine which constituted the objective element in that philosophy): "out of the actions of men comes something quite different from what they intend and directly know and will."

The economists had found the kernel of this law which ruled exchange-relationships in the law of value. The normal value of a commodity was not dependent on the dictate of some individual seller; it was not the product of chance or custom; nor was it dependent on the valuation which the user placed upon it — its utility. Commodities exchanged for one another (in the "normal" case and as a long-run tendency) in proportion to the amount of labor that their production cost. If temporarily the market price of a thing were high relatively to the labor required to produce it (whether because the demand for it was keen or the supply abnormally short), producers would be attracted to the manufacture of it, and by dint of competition its exchange value, in the fulness of time, would fall; and vice versa where the market price was low relatively to the labor required to produce it. Exchange value, in other words, was the market expression of the manner in which, under the rule of competition, labor was distributed between various lines of production and of the productivity of that labor in each case. As the productivity of labor changed — for example, as it increased with improved technique or greater division of labor — so accordingly would the supply of commodities yielded by a day's labor alter, and accordingly their value.

[H]aving enunciated their law of value as governing exchange, the economists had looked no further into the matter. In particular, they had not explained how and why it was that, while value was determined by quantity of embodied labor, part of the value produced should accrue to the capitalist who contributed no labor to the productive process. Although Ricardo had declared that "the principal problem in Political Economy" was distribution ("the laws which determine the division of the produce of industry among the classes which concur in its formation"), and although he had clearly shown land-rent to be a surplus, which bore no relation to any productive contribution on the landowners' part, and had depicted capitalists' profit as simply the difference between the value of the product and the wages paid to the laborers who created that product, he had said nothing further about the character and origin of profit. On this crucial qualitative question he was silent. Yet without an answer to it even the quantitative question as to how the amount of profit was determined could not be satisfactorily answered. Moreover, the successors of Ricardo — the "vulgar economists" as Marx termed them — increasingly turned to a justification of profit as the reward for some productive activity, and increasingly depicted the "invisible hand" of natural law which ruled the market as beneficent in character — as bringing harmony out of chaos and causing individual self-interest unconsciously to promote the common good. This was the notorious glorification of laisser faire, which still, even in the monopolistic age of today, does rusty service in defending private enterprise against any limitation or encroachment.

MARX ON VALUE

Here, where the classical economists left off, Marx's analysis of capitalist production began. In the first place, he accepted the labor theory of value and enunciated it in an unambiguous form. All commodities (i.e., things produced for a market) had the double property of being utilities (serving some human want) and of being the product of human activity. But, while the former was a necessary condition for anything to have value, value as a social relation between the producers of commodities was dependent on the amount of "socially necessary human labor" that the production of the thing in question (on the average and under "normal" conditions) entailed.

The crucial problem for Marx was this: How, then, if all things exchange in proportion to the labor embodied in them and all exchange is of equivalents against equivalents, comes it about that

one class apparently gets something for nothing — acquires part of the produced value as profit for itself without contributing any labor (or its equivalent) in return? It was clear enough to Marx that capitalism had this similarity with previous forms of society: that the ruling class lived by exploiting the laboring class, or by appropriating the surplus labor of the workers, in the same sense in which this was true of a feudal or a slave society. If this was the case, how was it to be made consistent with the "freedom" of the worker in modern society — with the fact that the relation between him and his employer took the form of a contract on a freely competitive market? This riddle was not to be explained as some of his predecessors had tried to do (e.g., Sismondi and Thompson and Bray) by the fact that the capitalist, through cheating or *force majeure,* purchased something *below* its value or sold something else *above* its value. Such explanations were open to an easy answer from the orthodox economists: namely, that, if such exploitation of either workpeople or consumers occurred, this could only be due to the imperfect operation of competition (otherwise the pressure of the market would cause things to exchange at their values), and the cure for such a situation was more perfect competition, which was precisely what the bourgeois free traders were advocating. Marx somewhere says: "Surplus value must be explained on the assumption that commodities exchange at their values, or it cannot be explained at all."

The answer that Marx gave is simple enough once it is stated: so simple that it might seem surprising that so much ink has been spilled to disprove it and to propound alternative explanations in terms of the "services" rendered by the capitalist in the shape of the "abstinence" they suffer in saving money, or in terms of the "specific productivity" of capital. The answer amounted to an explanation in terms of the historical circumstances out of which capitalism had grown — the social conditions or productive relations which underlay exchange. Capitalist production implied, at one and the same time, both a concentration of property in the hands of a section of society and the *dis*possession of the larger section of society. This latter class, divorced from the means of production and lacking alternative means of livelihood, were forced by the situation in which they found themselves to sell themselves to a master — to a propertied master, possessed of the means of production with which labor could be set to work. In other words, labor power — the working activity or physical energy of a human being for a given period of time — itself became a commodity, offered on the market and trafficked in like any other commodity, such as wheat or iron or cloth. Like any other commodity, its value was determined by the labor time that its production normally cost.

What, then, was this labor power, and in what sense could one speak of its production? Labor power, said Marx, is essentially "energy transferred to a human organism by means of nourishing matter." Its production and periodic reproduction, therefore, consisted in the input of "nourishing matter" into the human organism to replace the energy used up in work — in other words, the subsistence of the worker. Hence the value of labor power of, say, a week's duration was governed by the labor time required to produce the subsistence of a worker for a week. But under the conditions of modern industry, with modern technique and modern division of labor, labor power had this property, peculiar among all commodities: Its consumption, or utilization, occasioned a value *greater than its own value*. In other words, no more than a part of the worker's working day needed to be spent in replacing the equivalent in value of the worker's subsistence for a day. Let us suppose the latter represented 4 hours of labor. This Marx called "necessary labor time" — necessary in the sense that without it production would stop because the workers would fail to replace the energy expended in work and eventually they would die. If the working day was 8 hours, the remaining 4 hours represented the "surplus labor time" available to produce value for the capitalist; and since the capitalist had bought labor power at a price equivalent to 4 hours and had the disposal of the product of 8 hours' labor, his gain from the transaction, or his "surplus value," consisted in the difference between these two quantities. Under these conditions the ratio of capitalists' income to wages would be as 4 : 4, or 100 percent: a

ratio which Marx termed the "rate of surplus value,"[1] or alternatively the "rate of exploitation." This exploitation-ratio was a crucial and fundamental factor on which the distribution of the product between labor and capital depended. It was uniquely dependent on two factors: on the cost (in labor time) required to produce what in the circumstances of the time and place was regarded as necessary subsistence for a worker with his family and on the length of the working day.

What, then, did this explanation of the source of capitalists' income amount to, and wherein did it essentially differ from rival explanations? Firstly, as we have seen, it threw into relief the character of profit, or surplus value, as a historical category, product of a particular set of historical conditions, of which the crucial one was the existence of a propertyless class. These historical conditions it was in the interest of one class to perpetuate at all costs and of the other class to destroy; whence arose an antagonism between them which was irreconcilable within the confines of that system. This was a qualitative statement about the contrasted character of the two classes of income, wages and profits: the one a return to a human productive activity of the equivalent of what that activity "cost" or used up; the other a payment which was as independent of any productive activity on the recipient's part as the income of a feudal lord or a slaveowner had been. But joined with this was a quantitative statement: namely, that, given the size of the employed labor force, total surplus value, or capitalist income, depended uniquely on the proportion of that labor force which was needed to produce subsistence for the workers; or, as Marx put it more graphically, on the portion of the working day during which (on the average) the worker was merely reproducing his own value (i.e., his own wages). This was the basic

---

[1]This is what Marx called the "simple rate of surplus value." Later, in Vol. 2, he is careful to point out that when one comes to deal with the rate of profit (the ratio that surplus value bears, not to the wage-bill, but to total capital) it is the "annual rate of surplus value" that is relevant, the latter being related to the former according to the number of times that a given variable capital is turned over in the course of a year.

exploitation-ratio on which the distribution of income between the classes essentially depended, and on which the constellation of exchange relationships turned.

In addition to the chapters of analysis, Volume 1 of Marx's best-known work is rich in historical material. This ranges from an examination of the various transitional stages between handicraft and modern machinery to quotations from the reports of factory inspectors on the wretched conditions of factory labor, and back again from contemporary blue-books to an account of the historical process — the process of "primitive accumulation" by which a proletariat was formed. The uncompleted Volumes 2 and 3, in addition to much penetrating analysis, are also interspersed with historical illustrations and some acute historical comment.

THE PROBLEM OF PARTICULAR PRICES

Volume 3, which has "Capitalist Production as a Whole" as its subtitle, comes closer to the problem of particular prices, and is concerned in the first place with the rate of profit on capital, and subsequently with the division of the *genus* surplus value into the sub-species of profit, interest and rent. This involves a closer approximation to the complex detail of reality, and a discarding of some of the assumptions made for the purpose of analysis in Volume 1. The preoccupation of Volume 1 was with the *rate of surplus value,* defined as the ratio of surplus value to that part of the capital (called variable capital) which is laid out in the purchase of labor power.

It is also in Volume 3, together with the third part of Volume 2 and a section in the *Theorien,* that the torso of Marx's theory of economic crises is to be found. The classical economists had tended to identify the rule of economic law with the postulation of an underlying stability and harmony in the economic system. There had been a famous controversy between Malthus and Ricardo as to the cause of periodic "gluts" of commodities and as to whether it was possible for general overproduction of commodities to occur. But the view which was to become the orthodox doctrine of Ricardo's suc-

cessors was that, given free trade and the removal of all obstacles to capital accumulation and the growth of industry, there was no reason for general "gluts" to occur and no reason for the rate of profit on capital to fall.[2]

To this optimistic view Marx opposed the notion that capitalism was not a stable but an unstable system. While he accepted (even emphasized) the view that its movements were ruled by objective law, he was at the same time concerned to show that, as a mode of production, it rested on certain contradictions, and that the very forces which operated to yield an equilibrium of its elements generated counter-forces which periodically disrupted that equilibrium. In fact, any smooth mechanistic model, shaped in terms of equilibrium situations and smooth vectors of movement, was inappropriate. Conflict and interaction were of the essence of the system; and it was only by an appreciation of this fact that one could acquire any vision of its "law of motion" and its historical destiny.

THE IMPACT OF CAPITAL

Within 10 to 15 years after the appearance of the first volume of *Capital,* official Political Economy, as it reigned in the seats of learning, was fast beating a retreat from the position of the classical school. The labor theory of value was being discarded as a primitive and discredited solution; and in its place the new Utility Theories, preached by Menger and Wieser in Vienna and by Jevons in this country, were being enthroned. It can hardly be a coincidence that these new doctrines found such rapid acceptance so soon after Marx had turned Ricardo's reasoning to dangerous conclusions. A novel doctrine is more often than not slow to find acceptance in the face of established tradition. But with this new fashion it was the reverse: it was welcomed with unprecedented quickness. With its acceptance

---

[2] For Ricardo the only sufficient reason for a fall in the profit rate was a rise of wages due to a rise in the value of subsistence through the operation of the law of diminishing returns on land. Given free trade and the possibility of food imports from overseas there was no need for diminishing returns on land to operate.

went a crucial shift both of emphasis and of scope. In place of the broad sweep and larger vision of the classical school, with its interest in questions of the distribution of the product between classes, there came a concentration on the microscopic problems of particular prices. Explanation of the phenomena of the market was no longer sought in conditions of production, but instead in the relationship between commodities and the subjective attitudes of individual consumers. The inconvenient problem of surplus value, and questions as to whether profit was the fruit of exploitation, were skillfully dropped by the device of inventing an apparatus of thought in which such questions could have no meaning.

This price economics proceeded to claim that it was dealing with exchange relationships which were common to any economic system, and that the "laws" and "necessities" which it enunciated had a wide range of generality. The result was subtly to shift attention away from the specific characteristics and results of capitalist society to an abstract economic society and an "economic problem" which would remain the same whatever the system of property relations. This tendency has increased rather than decreased in recent years, in the degree in which the analysis of price-interdependence has become more mathematically refined and more formal; with the result that even certain economists who are critics of capitalism have claimed to deduce from their price equations laws which would govern a socialist economy and the type of mechanism which these "necessities" of the economic problem would force such an economy to observe. By contrast, it was the view of Marx and Engels (as expressed in Engels' words) that political economy was a "historical science," which "must first investigate the special laws of each separate stage in the evolution of production and exchange, and only when it has completed this investigation will it be able to establish the few quite general laws which hold good for production and exchange considered as a whole." To this he added: "Anyone who wishes to bring under the same law the political economy of Tierra del Fuego and that of modern England can produce nothing but the most vulgar commonplaces."

It is hardly surprising that, when he was not be-

ing "refuted," Marx should have been treated with contemptuous silence by most of the official economists of the past half century. Those who have deigned to assign him a place in the history of economic thought have generally treated him as a propagandist, who turned economic learning to his own purposes, but who as an economist contributed little or nothing of permanent value. The author of a much-used textbook of the history of economic thought expresses a judgment that is not untypical of the lack of understanding, if not actual hostility, that Marx has generally met with in such circles. The economic works of Marx are here dismissed with the judgment that "nowhere is there in print such a miracle of confusion, such a supreme example of how not to reason," and with references to "pedantic parade of learning, the display of rather puerile mathematical formulae, the dexterous skating on thin ice, the subtlety approaching at times perilously near to sophistry." To this is added the curious remark: "despite Marx's affected omniscience, *Capital* reveals very little real knowledge of the world. . . . He was too much in the British Museum and too little on the Epsom Downs on Derby Day" [Alexander Gray, *The Development of Economic Doctrine,* 1931].

It has sometimes been said that what economists create is tools for the handling of particular problems, and that it is as general purpose toolmakers that they must be judged. This analogy seems clearly insufficient. An economic theory such as Marx created must be judged as being a *model* of actual capitalist society — an abstract picture which is to be judged according as it throws into relief before our eyes what are the most significant features and the dominant tendencies in the world of complex detail which we have first to understand before we can effectively act upon it. Viewed in this light, can any reasonable doubt remain today as to which system of thought affords the most illuminating model of actual capitalist society — that of Marx or of his opponents? To a growing number of those who have acquired any full appreciation of the nature of modern capitalism (not only from sitting on Epsom Downs!) it must appear that there is no comparison between the two pictures, and that while the one has shown a prophetic insight of genius, the other has been characterized by obscurantism and false prognosis. That Marx's method at least posed the questions which have been proved by events to be the right ones is today conceded by an increasing number even of his opponents. Indeed, it seems clear that it is only in Marxist terms that any satisfactory definition of capitalism as an economic system, differentiated from alternative systems, is possible; and as witness to this the great majority of economists have eschewed the notion of capitalism altogether and even denied it the right to exist at all.

Thought has been led towards a new recognition of the importance of Marx's economic doctrines by two features especially of the modern world: recent developments in monopolistic organization and practices and the appearance of chronic economic crisis and mass unemployment in the leading capitalist countries in the two decades between wars. These events have prompted important developments in traditional economic theory (I refer particularly to modern theories of monopoly and imperfect competition and to the now fashionable critique of the traditional theory of employment), which themselves sap the foundations of traditional theories about "economic harmonies" and of a self-regulating system of consumers' sovereignty. There are still those who, echoing the German Revisionists (Bernstein and others) of half a century ago, claim that Marx's prophecies about the future of capitalism have been refuted by events. A recent example of this type of attack on Marxism appeared in a volume in the Labor Book Service, and rested its case chiefly on the alledged "embourgeoisement" of the proletariat in countries like Britain and America and on a growth instead of a decline in the numerical importance of the "middle class" [E.F.M.Durbin, *The Politics of Democratic Socialism,* 1940]. The details of such criticisms we have not space to examine here. One can only remark, as an example of how superficial such criticism can be, that in the instance just quoted the alleged growth of the "middle class," was supported by statistics which lumped all clerical workers and shop assistants with the "middle class," and ignored the fact that over three-quarters of clerical workers have (in a normal peacetime year) incomes of under £5 a week and about a third of them under 50/- a weak. It ignored likewise the fact that both clerical workers and important strata of technical and professional workers have recently grown increasingly akin, both in status and in the problems confronting them (for example, in their tendency to form trade unions), to the wage-earning proletariat, and that they bear little resemblance to that middle class of independent producers and small property-owners of which Marx spoke.

It would indeed be surprising if any social forecast of this type were to turn out true in every detail; and there were many developments in latter-day capitalism which Marx and Engels, writing in the mid-nineteenth century, were not in a position to foresee. An example of these is the concrete detail of modern Imperialism as it was analyzed in Lenin's famous study, written 30 years after the death of Marx. But when we view the matter in full perspective, the impressive and remarkable fact, surely, is how right, in all essential points, Marx's forecasts have proved to be. Growing instability of the capitalist mode of production, torn by a class struggle between the interests of capital and labor; an accentuating, not a mollification, of periodic crises, with a growing industrial reserve army as their consequence; a growing concentration and centralization of capitals, with a consequent subordination of economic life to a narrowing circle of large capitalists, whose rule would increasingly become, both in essence and in appearance, a "fetter of production."

Finally, one may ask what better witness could one have of Marx's contention that capitalism was a transitory historical stage, destined itself to undergo revolution and to be replaced by socialism, than events in the U.S.S.R. since 1917, especially the economic might and the social cohesion shown by that formerly backward country whose achievements over the years have amazed the world?

QUESTIONS

1. Articulate Marx's explanation of how a worker, who voluntarily contracts with an employer to work

and who is free to resign, is exploited under capitalism. Define the "rate of surplus value" or the "rate of exploitation."

2. Having read this essay, in what ways (if at all) do the manners and ideas of Marx differ from those you have known who claim to be Marxists?

3. What is the "labor theory of value"? The classical economists and Marx both held a labor theory of value. Most American economists reject this theory. On the basis of your economics textbook (which most likely does not hold a labor theory of value) defend the rejection of the labor theory of value.

4. What are the contradictions Marx saw in capitalism that would, he predicted, lead to its demise?

5. Some of the broad predictions of the future of capitalism are recounted at the end of this essay. Some observers have examined contemporary economic events in the view of Marx's predictions and declared them on the whole accurate. Others point to contemporary economic events as a rebuttal of Marx. How can this be? What is your evaluation?

62 WHAT THE RADICAL ECONOMISTS ARE SAYING
Martin Bronfenbrenner

Radical economists frequently use a different paradigm or method of analysis than expounded in the most popular economics textbooks. Yet their views should not remain foreign to students of economics. As this article proves, radical economics itself is fractured into different perspectives. Martin Bronfenbrenner, Kenan Professor of Economics at Duke University, describes radical economics and classifies its positions. Professor Bronfenbrenner is one of the most widely published of American economists. In addition to his economics research and prolific writings, he is also an authority on Japan and teaches a course in Japanese studies at Duke.

My late mother-in-law thought that *all* economists were radicals. "Why study the system," she asked, "instead of just letting it alone, unless they want to overthrow it?"

A mild recession and the scaling down of the Indochina war have given us a respite from radicalism, including radical economics. While some observers see this development as the inglorious end of the whole "New Left" episode, the more usual view, which I share, sees it as only an intermission. In any case, it is a time for taking stock.

Taking stock should start with what radical economics and economists are not. Not every economist with long hair and deep "concern" is a radical. Nor is radical economics a monolithic organized movement, let alone a conspiracy. And, perhaps most important, radical economics has never been solely North American; what we say about radical economics in the United States is more or less true for the economics of French *Gauchisme* or of Japanese *Zengakuren*.

Let me propose four characteristics that most

Abridged from Martin Bronfenbrenner, "What the Radical Economists Are Saying," *Harvard Business Review* (September/October 1973), pp. 26ff. Copyright ©1973 by the President and Fellows of Harvard College; all rights reserved. Reprinted by permission.

radical economists seem to have in common with each other (and also with the Radical Right, which we are not discussing here). Taken together — no one alone will do — these characteristics constitute a kind of *differentia specifica* for radical economists, as distinguished from liberals:

1. Radical economists believe not only that economics has concentrated on the wrong set of problems — neglecting income distribution, for example, or the "quality of life" — but also that the economy needs some kind of "radical restructuring." If the economy is not restructured, the result will be chaos, or 1984, or a drastic decline in living standards, or perhaps the destruction of the human race. Radical economists are relatively unconcerned about the danger that matters will be made worse instead of better, if it is restuctured. There are no blueprints in advance; what is to be done will become clear in the course of doing it.

The definition of radical restructuring differs among the radical sects. But it always transcends such marginal adjustments or "gimmicks" as monetary rules, income floors, restoration of competition, free trade, land-value taxation, or even incomes policies. And, as a corollary, radical economists are sure that conventional economic analysis is irrelevant, because it recommends no more than marginal adjustments to make the system work better and stave off the evil day of its collapse.

2. Radical economists believe that the restructuring of the economy must be done in this generation, because the world may otherwise be blown up in World War III or become uninhabitable for the human race.

3. Radical economists distrust free elections and parliamentary democracy as methods of economic change — they want revolution, preferably brief and bloodless. At best, free elections and parliamentary democracy are too slow, given the preceding requirement of speed. At worst, they can be corrupted by the holders of economic power who supply campaign funds, control mass media, and hire lawyers to vitiate liberal reforms.

4. New Leftists generally, but radical economists to a lesser degree than their coreligionists from other specialities, accept intuition, emotion, and other "nonrational ways of knowing." Even the lyrics of popular songs become supplements, and occasionally alternatives, to further deduction and accumulation of *empirical* evidence in support of "The Movement."

I should note that radical economists themselves dispute the importance of this anti-intellectualist aspect. Individual radicals have contributed research on the impact of education on income distribution by amount, sex, and race. They have tried to measure the effectiveness or noneffectiveness, of job training and other methods of alleviating ghetto poverty. They have devised and supported theories of labor-market fragmentation with a permanent "under-class," and theories of personal saving as primarily a "disequilibrium" response to increased income.

RADICALS IN PERSPECTIVE

I have said, and repeat, that radical economics as a whole is not an organized and coordinated movement. I have found a fivefold classification scheme helpful for my own observations. My scheme consists of:

Two consciously or subconsciously anarchist camps, which I call Anarchism I and II.

Two quite consciously socialist (or communist) camps, which I call Socialism I and II.

A single nascent syndicalist camp, which I call Syndicalism I/II, but which may well increase in relative importance in the next upsurge of radicalism.

THE ANARCHIST GROUPS

My analysis begins with the two anarchist groups with no order of importance attached to the numbering system.

Anarchism I is composed of the variations on the hippie counterculture. Its common feature is the withdrawal of its adherents from organized society into quasi-independent communes. These groups may eventually demonstrate to the larger society the error of its ways. The result of such a demonstration may be either a vast proliferation of individual communes or the reorganization of society as a kind of large commune. The first outcome would be strictly anarchistic; the second would be socialistic in the pre-Marxian (Utopian) sense of the almost-forgotten Fourier and Saint Simon. Few of today's commune dwellers bother to look that far ahead.

More than any other radical sect, Anarchism I tends to dismisss even "radical" economic issues as irrelevant, and few economists are included among its adherents. Thus, while most radicals demand, or at least accept, massive redistribution of income and wealth in favor of the poor, Anarchism I devotees take the opposite view. As Jan Pen put it:

"Distribution is irrelevant because income is irrelevant. There is already too much consumption of the wrong kind: soulless, artificial 'satisfaction' encouraged by advertising, which robs people of their freedom, makes them empty and unhappy. Property is theft, and 'income distribution' is the sort of expression that fits in with it. We ought to abandon the whole rotten production and consumption structure of industrialism, we ought to live in communes, be directly supplied with simple, natural goods, and arrange distribution in direct consultation with one another."

Unlike the proponents of Anarchism I, those people who adhere to Anarchism II work within society, but only for the purpose of destroying it.

Anarchism II harbors the larger share of the ideological playboys of the Western, or at least the U.S., world. It is seldom easy to guess when these playboys mean what they say and when they are merely out to shock "the little old lady from Dubuque." They are the Yippies, and now the Zippies, in the great tradition of Till Eulenspiegel, Voltaire, and Bernard Shaw. They are the apostles of "revolution for the hell of it," who propose to wreck anything and everything in a long afternoon of merry pranks — fraternity initiations on a Superman scale — and then (perhaps) to worry about replacing it.

In his heyday as Yippie high priest, Abbie Hoffman circulated at the 1968 Democratic Convention in Chicago a Yippie manifesto in which the economic content is confined to planks 7 and 8. I quote these planks in full, as being fairly representative of Anarchism II:

"7. The Abolition of Money. The abolition of pay housing, pay media, pay transportation, pay food, pay education, pay clothing, pay medical help, and pay toilets.

"8. A society which works toward and actively promotes the concept of full unemployment. A society in which people are free from the drudgery of work. Adoption of the concept, 'Let the machines do it.'"

"The machines" are expected to produce everything people need (and repair each other in their spare time), regardless of what may be done to them in the course of the anarchist revolution. Meanwhile, the people sing, dance, write poetry, make love, and heighten their awarenesses through "body" chemistry.

THE SOCIALIST GROUPS

The socialists are more rationalistic, if not more rational, than their anarchist rivals. Marx, Engels, and Lenin rank higher on the scale of social-science giants than Bukharin, Kropotkin, or any of the other anarchist luminaries. It is therefore no surprise to find radical economists of socialist persuasion awakening rapidly from a generation or two of theological subservence to sacred formulas, a subservience for which it is customary to blame Stalin.

Socialism I embodies this "me-for-dictator," neo-Stalinist approach. The economy is to be planned or regimented on allegedly scientific principles. As Stalin said, "A plan is a command." Plans are accordingly to be enforced, meaning that any shortcomings are likely to be traced to the individuals responsible, who are in turn liable to be punished — by death in extreme cases. I like to characterize this sort of planning as "a set of materials balances (or an input-output table) plus a machine gun (or a firing squad)," which is more of an exaggeration in some countries than in others.

Economic dissent, as well as other types, is to be tolerated only "repressively," if at all (through a set of devices whereby dissenters may "let off steam" harmlessly, short of effective action). Monopoly of the formal means of propaganda is not only to be imposed but reinforced, if necessary, by study, mutual criticism, and what some might consider group-therapy sessions. In these sessions, Marxian orthodoxy is inculcated unopposed and applied to practical problems; moreover, one is not permitted to remain silent or to conceal dissent under the mask of ignorance.

"Liberty," Lenin is reported to have said, "is a commodity so precious that it must be rationed." So, for economic reasons, conventional civil rights will be attenuated in a regime of Socialism I.

All in all, Socialism I seems less like a "workers' paradise" than a hybrid between a large-scale concentration camp and a well-run military base. But holders of the faith insist that revolutionary harshness can be dispensed with in a generation or two (in an economically advanced society like the United States), and that some compromise can be permitted in the direction of what Chairman Mao refers to as "rotten liberalism."

The camp which I call Socialism II is usually termed "Marxist Humanism" by its adherents. Its inspiration comes from the early Marx of the *Economic-Philosophical Manuscripts* — a philosopher first and an economist second — rather than from the mature Marx of *Das Kapital.* (The former was more concerned with "human values" and less with "class struggles" than the latter. The *Communist Manifesto* of 1848 can be seen as a watershed between the two.)

In theory, Socialism II is less authoritarian than Socialism I and less concerned with allegiance to Marxian orthodoxy in matters economic and political. In practice, it may lead to the substitution of mob rule for bureaucracy, as in the Chinese Cultural Revolution, or serve as an intermission between two bouts of Socialism I.

Four leading doctrines of Socialism II are:

1. Equality of income and wealth.

2. Availability of a widening range of goods and services completely free of charge.

3. Replacement of "material incentives" by "moral incentives."

4. Release for all from the hierarchical and psychologically alienating aspects of modern industrial society.

The *first* doctrine is crucial, if one is to avoid the contradictions of having white-collar and blue-collar workers, or having the managerial elite and the "toiling masses." (Stalin, by contrast, rejected egalitarianism as a petit-bourgeois heresy.)

The *second* doctrine is often combined with the first in the proposition that consumer goods and services should either be available to all free of charge (at least in adequate rations), or owned publicly if there are not enough to go around. Services would be parcelled out on some basis such as need or "first come, first served"; one's ration would not be a function of his income or status.

The *third* doctrine implies an effective monopoly of education and propaganda, so that "New Socialist Man" will neither demand more than he needs nor shirk in supplying the community with the highest quantity and quality of skills at his command. There would then be no need for forced labor, stringent rationing or other abuses of civil rights. This means, of course, that no one would stoop to increasing his own income by restricting output to raise prices, or restricting membership in his trade to raise its wages. It also means that people would resrict their consumption and make their savings available for public investment without the payment of interest.

The *fourth* doctrine follows from the belief of many radicals that the present hierarchical organization of factories and offices — foremen, supervisors, managers, and the like — should be replaced by teams of workers of equal rank. These work teams could allocate and alternate tasks among their own members, so that nobody would be stuck with the dirty work all the time and everybody would have a share in decision making. There would then be great gains in psychological satisfaction, to compensate for possible losses in efficiency or productivity (as conventionally measured), while the engineering genius was taking his turn at sweeping the floor or the moronic janitor was taking his turn at designing the machinery.

THE SYNDICALIST GROUP

Unlike anarchism and socialism, syndicalism is an almost-forgotten word. A syndicate is another name for a guild or a trade union. Syndicalism is a system of economic and political rule by syndicates, which are themselves more or less above the law. For some syndicalists, the so-called Guild Socialists, this means reconstitution of Congress or Parliament as a national confederation of syndicates, a bigger and better AFL/CIO, or, if you will, a Corporate State. For other syndicalists, called Anarcho-Syndicalists, it means the withering away of the State as such, with each syndicate running its own plant, firm or industry on an autonomous basis.

For the purposes of this article, however, the most interesting feature of syndicalism is its strategy of using the strike rather than the political revolution as the weapon of social change. Syndicalists propose to operate by winning strikes, which means not only securing improvements in wages and working conditions but also forcing the payment for such improvements out of profits.

This process, repeated over and over again, is expected to reduce the value of the owners' equity to zero, so that the workers can buy out their employers for little or nothing. Starting with individual plants and companies, it would spread to the entire economy as local and partial strikes expanded to general strikes, and as the issues expanded from the purely economic to the openly political. It goes without saying that the union would be above capitalist law, and that legal restrictions on the conduct of strikes and the use of the strike weapon would be ignored.

CONCLUSION

Such conclusions as I can present here do not follow with any rigor from the material which has preceded them, and they are not in some cases even related to that material. However, for better or worse:

Most, if not quite all, of the radical economists are as sincere as their opponents, although they may not necessarily remain radical economists all their lives.

Radical economics is a viable worldwide movement. It will not fade away of its own accord, even in the United States.

Attempts at purging and repressing radical econo-

mists are mistaken and ill conceived. They will serve mainly to drive the movement underground and lower its quality, since forbidden fruit is always sweeter. If one feels strongly opposed to one or another sect of radical economics, or to the movement as a whole, the place to combat it is in the free, if imperfectly competitive, marketplace of ideas.

QUESTIONS

1. Critique the assertion that radical economics is a monolithic paradigm.

2. Professor Bronfenbrenner delineates five categories of radical economics. How does Anarchism I differ from Anarchism II? What differences exist between Anarchism I and the communal experiments in the United States, such as Robert Owen's New Harmony and Brook Farm in Massachusetts?

3. What are the goals or ideals of Socialism II? To what extent are these goals attainable under another variant of the radical economics or through the operations of a market economy?

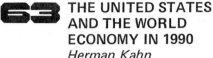

THE UNITED STATES AND THE WORLD ECONOMY IN 1990
Herman Kahn

What will the American economy be like as the year 2000 approaches? Herman Kahn recently offered the following predictions. Kahn, who has made a reputation as a mathematician, military analyst, physicist, and political scientist, is the director of the Hudson Institute think tank and is one of America's foremost prognosticators.

The United States in 1990 will still be the world's greatest economy. But, instead of being the overwhelmingly dominant economy it was in the immediate post-World War II years, it will simply be the largest among many large economies. It will have only about one-quarter of the Gross World Product (GWP), or but one-half of that in the immediate post-war years. The comparative GNPs of principal areas of the world will, in 1980, be about as shown in Table 1. We are a big economy and will remain a big economy, although we are smaller relative to the remainder of the world than we used to be.

By 1980 the Japanese economy should be about one-third the size of the U.S. economy (up from one-fifth today). By 1990 the Japanese economy should be about one-half our size. It is likely to be more highly internationalized than the U.S. economy. Thus even by 1980 it begins to have an effect on the remainder of the world about equal to that of the United States. From the viewpoint of Asia and most of the remainder of the world, Japan's economy might seem equal to or larger than that of the United States over the whole decade of 1980—1990.

In other words, an economy about the size of the present European Economic Community (EEC) will suddenly have been created off the coast of Asia by

Abridged from Herman Kahn, "A View of the Economic World of 1990," from *A Look at Business in 1990,* Proceedings of the White House Conference on the Industrial World Ahead (Washington, D.C.: U.S. Government Printing Office, 1972), pp. 13—27.

Table 1. *Likely GNP of Major World Areas in 1980 (in trillions of 1970 dollars)*

Area	GNP
United States	1.5
USSR	0.9
Japan	0.5
France and West Germany	0.25
China, United Kingdom, Italy, Canada India	0.1—0.2
Brazil, Australia, East Germany, Mexico, Sweden, Poland, Argentina, Indonesia	0.05—0.1

1980. Further, this economy will tend to grow during the ensuing ten years at almost twice the rate of EEC. This will have all kinds of consequences for the world in general and for American business in particular.

I believe that the rapid growth of Japan will contribute enormously to the creation of dynamic and prosperous economies everywhere, particularly in Asia and in North and South America. Despite the recent criticism of Japan, I believe that, in fact, even in the past, its huge growth rate has contributed helpfully to the U.S. growth rate and is likely to do so even more in the future.

Incidentally, although Mainland China and India have about one-half of the world's population, neither is likely to play a major role in the world economy in the 1990 period, but it will be greater than at present.

CHARACTER OF THE WORK FORCE CHANGES

The character of the U.S. work force has changed enormously over the last 20 years, and will continue to change. In 1950 the United States had almost 60 million workers, about equally divided between goods-producing industries and service industries. About another 20 million has been added since — almost all in the service sector. Between 1947 and 1980 the workers in service-producing industries (transportation, public utilities, finance, insurance, real estate, government, services, and trade) will have risen from about 24 million to some 60 million, while those in goods-producing industries will be showing a rise from about 27 million to only a little over 30 million. In some ways these numbers underestimate the rate of change, because even in the goods-producing industries, people increasingly, are white-collar workers. While the service industries have large numbers of blue-collar workers, their percentage is decreasing. And, the white-collar workers are less likely to be relatively unskilled women workers than highly trained professional and technical workers. This, in the most literal terms, is what we mean by the postindustrial culture: the relative number of blue-collar workers declines; the construction and manufacturing industries become a smaller and smaller part of the nation's activity, and relative to the total national effort, become easier and easier to do; and the technical and professional labor force increases enormously (an increase by a factor of 1.5 in the decade of the '60s).

The situation in agriculture is similar. In 1850, half of all Americans worked in agriculture. Today, less than three percent of the American work force produces more than 95 percent of the foods and fibers we need. It could probably increase production by half or more without particularly increasing the number of people engaged in agriculture. Thus, we in the United States live in a "post-agricultural culture." It is not that the product is unimportant; it is that the national effort in producing the product is small relative to other efforts in the economy. Most of the growth of the U.S. economy today is in the service sector — at least in terms of additions to the work force.

One of the present problems of the United States is that we may not be making these additions to the work force wisely. In New York City in the last five years 100,000 city government employees have been added while the population of the city was declining by about the same number. The cost of city services has increased by about 50 percent, yet it is difficult to find service much improved as a result of these additional city employees and city costs.

In general, service industries have the unfortunate characteristic that output is difficult to measure quantitatively — and quality even more so. As a result of this, both governments and companies have a tendency to add service personnel who do not increase productivity significantly. They may pro-

duce something measured by the institution itself, but this may be a part of the process of "institutionalizing" — when the institution starts to serve its own interests instead of those of the general community. In any case, one of the standard characteristics of an institution in the process of institutionalizing is a large increase in service personnel and a relative decrease in the number of people who directly turn out useful products.

Service industries are, of course, important and valuable. One characteristic of a successful large company or a successfully developed nation is an emphasis on the service sector — on managers, engineers, designers, marketers, financial experts, the people who deal with other kinds of knowledge, administration, etc. The wave of the future is service, not production. It is easier to be incompetent in service industries than in any other; sometimes the very concept of competence does not have any clearcut application.

TWO MAJOR CHANGES IN HISTORY — A THIRD IS IMMINENT

What I am suggesting is that whereas today we no longer have an agricultural state, but a postagricultural state, we will, in the future, have a postindustrial state — not a new industrial state. All manner of changes and innovations will ensue from this. I shall first emphasize the changes; later the continuities.

In a review of the history of man, two incidents of first-order magnitude stand out.

The first incident was the agricultural revolution about 10,000 years ago, which laid the foundation of civilization. Civilization means civic culture or living in cities. But not many lived in cities. Roughly only about one in twenty did so. Rather surprisingly the average per capita income did not change much during this prolonged agricultural era. This era survived until about 200 years ago, as basically characterized by an income in the range of $50–250 per capita, or roughly $100 per capita average. China, India, and Indonesia are still in this category.

The next big change was initiated about 200

years ago in England. It was the so-called Industrial Revolution. For the first time man achieved sustained growth rates. Medium-term British growth rates have been remarkably constant — averaging between 2–2½ percent per year for the last 200 years or so. This is impressive. An average of 2.3 percent per year means that every 100 years change is by a factor of 10, or an increase of 900 percent. From a historical point of view, that is a big change. In fact, a change of this magnitude, particularly if it is in GNP per capita rather than total GNP, changes the character of a culture enormously. Just as the pre-industrial culture is a factor of 10 higher, or $500–$2500 per capita.

Many people, including myself, believe that in the next 10, 20, or 30 years we will see another factor-of-10 change: the attainment in many countries of GNP per capita will be in the range $5000 to $20,000 (in 1970 dollars). This will induce as great a transition in society — or at least initiate the early phase of such a transition — as these first two great historical transitions did some 200 and some 10,000 years ago.

THE SKYROCKET RISE OF TRANSNATIONAL COMPANIES

Another phenomenon on the industrial scene is the recent rapid rise and even greater future growth of multinational companies, or transnational companies as I prefer to call them. By this I mean any corporation doing significant business, other than simple import/export operations, in many sovereignties. Already, for the United States, such corporations sell about $5 for every dollar we export. The dynamism of the transnational companies (TNC) is suggested by the following. Basically, Gross World Product — or the total amount of goods and services produced around the world — grows by about 5 percent per year.

The United States grows at a slightly lower rate than the world as a whole and hence we have a declining portion of GWP. World trade, including that of the United States grows about 50 percent faster than GWP. Business has developed an increasingly internationalized world economy. Rather interes-

tingly — and most overlooked by economists heretofore — the true internationalization of the world economy is now beginning to derive less from the movement of the products of industry from one country to another than from the movement of actual resources and national ownership and management. The transnational corporation now grows at a rate almost double that of GWP.

Despite many difficulties it is likely to continue — for a while — to grow at that rate. Thus the world is being increasingly internationalized, but less by world trade than by the operations of transnational corporations. These themselves are increasingly becoming multinational in the simple sense of multinational operation, multinational decision making, and multinational ownership. The transnational company is becoming the major engine of rapid economic development in both the Third World and in the rapidly developing world.

PROTECTIONISM OR FREE TRADE?

The United States will not, in my view, go protectionist despite recent changes. While the attitude in the United States will change — it will probably not change as much as many now believe. From 1934 to 1967 every major initiative for free trade came from the United States. This will not happen in the future — that is my guess. To have free trade, somebody else will be needed to fight for it. Who will take the initiative in the future? Rather interestingly, the Council of Ministers of the European Economic Commission issued a statement in late 1971 that went completely unnoticed in the world press. It said that it was willing to discuss, with the United States and others, all issues of free trade, including things like agriculture policy. Previously the Commission had absolutely refused to consider this kind of issue. If this is a straw in the wind, it indicates that the Commission may be willing to take the initiative in free trade. My own reading of the European mind is that this is unlikely. It is hard for me to believe that even an expanded EEC will take any serious new initiatives on lowering external tariff barriers. Let us hope I am wrong.

RISE OF PACIFIC BASIN TRADE

Another important trend in world trade is the movement of trade from the Atlantic to the Pacific in much the same way that it once moved from the Mediterranean to the Atlantic. We are accustomed to the idea that the great volume of world trade is conducted among the nations bordering the North Atlantic. Several developments of the last few years suggest that the next decade will see the development of a new trading and investment area, the business and economic reality of which may in turn underlie important political and eventually perhaps military possibilities.

Consider some likely magnitudes. By 1980 each of the major nations of the Pacific hemisphere will probably be conducting more than half of their trade and making (or receiving) more than half of their investments with other countries in the Pacific hemisphere. The principle components of this Pacific hemisphere trading and investment community (PAHTIA) are Japan, the Sinic culture areas on the border of Asia (South Korea, Taiwan, Hong Kong, Singapore, Thailand, South Vietnam), Indonesia, Philippines, Australia, New Zealand, Brazil, Colombia, Venezuela, Mexico, the United States, Canada, and perhaps Argentina and Chile.

The principal economic forces operating today which we expect will continue to operate strongly through the '70s that will create this PAHTIA are these:

The continued economic growth of Japan at a much greater than world rate and the growth of Japanese international trade at at least the rate of world trade in general.

The continued rapid growth of the Sinic culture areas and their increased share of world trade.

The expanding need of the developed countries, particularly the United States and Japan, to export manufacturing operations to areas of low labor cost, such as the Sinic Culture areas of Asia, and increasingly by the end of the decade to such areas as Malaysia, the Philippines, and Indonesia as well.

A shifting orientation of Australia and New Zealand away from Europe and toward Japan, the Pacific, and the United States. This will come in part

from England's move into the Common Market and in part from the increased availability of Japanese capital and Japanese markets, and other factors as well.

Increased Japanese investment and marketing interest in South America, and especially in Brazil, the only other major country in addition to the United States where Japanese have gone in large numbers to settle as immigrants. (There are now about 750,000 Brazilians of Japanese descent, and, on the whole, they have tended — unlike the United States — to back up ties with Japan.)

Inasmuch as the Americas face both across the Atlantic and across the Pacific, it is possible for an Atlantic hemisphere trading and investment area and a Pacific trading and investment area to exist simultaneously, and for the members of both to trade at least 50 percent with each other. The Pacific hemisphere trading area deserves special attention of the two because it is the newer development in economic and business life and during the '70s (and quite possibly the '80s) the more dynamic. Important business events are often generated by changes in the underlying economic factors, so it is important to focus on that which is most rapidly changing — particularly as those new constellations of trade and investment may require changing business orientations elsewhere as well.

PAHTIA can be thought of as the merger of the area that has been dominated by the United States with the area that Japan seems to be in a position potentially to dominate in a similar way. (Japanese dominance is not likely to be like that of the United States for several reasons: it comes a century later; Japan has a smaller percent of the total population of the area; distances are larger; and other countries in the area were developed before Japan.) The merger of these two areas means that in the natural struggle between small countries and large ones, small countries will have two large countries to play off against each other. Both the struggle and the playing off of one country against the other can be, and well may be a relatively benign process.

It is better for a small country to be in an area containing two large countries than one. To some extent the United States (and Japan) also benefits from being part of an area of two large powers. The other large power, in effect, will rake off some of the heat. Today, in much of the world, modernization tends to be synonymous in people's minds with Americanization. While almost everybody in the world wants to be modern, this is a painful process with many ugly and evil by-products. If Japan catches up with the United States as the most advanced nation, and the one most present in a particular country, then it may become true that modernization is as much identified with Japanization as it is with Americanization. To the extent that this becomes true — and it isn't clear whether this is a possibility for the '80s, for the '90s, or for the next century — many of the political, psychological overtones of international affairs can be expected to change, partly to our detriment, but perhaps even more to the benefit of the United States.

One of the real advantages of having a double leadership of some group over a single leadership is not just that it dilutes the hostility toward the single leader, but that it really changes the relationship almost completely. The smaller members of the group can find a considerable self-assertion and self-actualization and independence in the fact that the leadership is divided, and that the whole relationship then changes extensively. Power that is divided is simply much smaller than power that is unified. This can make for a much more wholesome relationship for all concerned.

QUESTIONS

1. In Kahn's opinion, will the United States still be the largest economy (in terms of output) in the world? What changes does he see in its relative position?

2. What roles does Kahn forecast for China, India, and Japan in the world economy?

3. Kahn predicts an increasing internationalization of the world economy. What phenomenon does he see as the cutting edge of this growing interdependence?

79 80 9 8 7 6 5 4 3